Letters of Mary, Queen of Scots, Volume II

Agnes Strickland

BIBLIOLIFE

LETTERS

OF

MARY, QUEEN OF SCOTS.

—

VOL. II.

LETTERS

OF

MARY,

QUEEN OF SCOTS.

QUEEN SCROLL

II TS OF THE QUEENS OF I CLA.

VOL. II.

LONDON

HENRY COLBURN, GREAT MARLBOROUGH STREET

LETTERS

OF

MARY, QUEEN OF SCOTS.

NOW

FIRST PUBLISHED FROM THE ORIGINALS,

COLLECTED FROM VARIOUS SOURCES,

PRIVATE AS WELL AS PUBLIC,

WITH

AN HISTORICAL INTRODUCTION AND NOTES,

BY AGNES STRICKLAND,

AUTHOR OF "THE LIVES OF THE QUEENS OF ENGLAND."

"Whoever corrects the relations of history by the private letters of those who were the actors of the times will learn at every step, as he advances, to distrust the prejudices of others and his own."

Sir John Dalrymple.

𝔄 𝔑𝔢𝔴 𝔈𝔡𝔦𝔱𝔦𝔬𝔫.

IN TWO VOLUMES.

VOL. II.

LONDON:

HENRY COLBURN, PUBLISHER,

GREAT MARLBOROUGH STREET.

MDCCCXLV.

1 2

LONDON :

PRINTED BY G. J. PALMER, SAVOY STREET, STRAND.

CONTENTS

OF

THE SECOND VOLUME.

viii CONTENTS.

LETTERS

MARY, QUEEN OF SCOTS.

The Queen of Scots to the Archbishop of Glasgow.

Sheffield, the 12th of January, 1577.

Monsieur de Glascow,—According to the promise I made you in the last letters from my hand, I have spoken three times to our adopted daughter, who, after several remonstrances and objections, founded on the respect and observance due to the honour of her house, according to the customs of my country, but especially as regards her alleged vow, which she said she could not, in her opinion, conscientiously and honourably break, has at length, on my remonstrances and urgent persuasions by her considered, according to her duty, as the orders of a good mistress, one who stands her in stead of a mother, made up her mind to submit to my commands, in the assurance that I shall respect her confidence and reputation. Being desirous of gratifying you, I have taken the charge upon myself, and in the first place, to get her released from her said alleged vow, which I consider as null and void; and if, in the opinion of the divines, it proves to be so, I shall take charge of the rest, or have another in her place; for, having resigned herself to me, instead of appealing to your opinion, I must take hers. Now, as to the first point, our man, whom I had to see her, has undertaken very readily, considering the difficulties attending it, to take the journey himself, to obtain and bring back the absolution from the vow, and at the same time the decision that you will be able to come in three months. I shall solicit a passport for him here; do for him all you can over there, for there will be urgent occasion for it, seeing that time flies with me. For the rest, it will be necessary to write again, by the first opportunity, to her brother, to inquire what he thinks I can do to give the requisite colouring to the observance of the customs of the country, where there may be some difference in respect to qualities or titles. Your brother will inform you of all I have done in this affair; about which he has expressed himself perfectly satisfied; he endeavours, if possible, more than ever, to do all in his power to serve me diligently and agreeably, which I take in very good part. In the hope of some opportunity which may enable me to prove my good-will towards you both, I conclude, referring, about my affairs, to what I have heretofore written to you, in order to rest myself, and pray God to have you, M. de Glascow, in his holy keeping.

Your good mistress and best friend,

M. R.

I have communicated the above to the girl, who accuses me of too great partiality, seeing that I had omitted (for brevity's sake) giving all the particulars of her submission made to me according to her duty; but, in the hope of finding some favour for the

8

observance of her vow, which is null, she wishes that her inclination for a long time, particularly in our prison, should be considered, which has always been more in favour of continuing in her present state, than entering into that of matrimony. I promised to represent all this to you, and to pay regard to it, as the confidence which she places in me deserves; and I shall continue to act in all things as my conscience dictates to be for the best; taking care, however, not to expose myself to the danger of being blamed afterwards for anything she may do by my advice and admonition, in case I find greater reason to induce me to persuade her to enter into that state which is least agreeable to her. Great stress is laid on difference of titles and qualities, and she alleges, for example, the fault which is found with the marriage of the two sisters Levingston, merely because they married the younger brothers of their equals; and she fears that the relations, living in a country where such formalities are kept up, may not have so good an opinion of her as she says they had before. But, as the queen of both, I have offered to take upon myself to set this matter to rights by all the means in my power, in the state in which I am ; so that you will have no need to make any demonstration or remonstrance, unless to desire her brother to write frankly what he thinks about it.

The Queen of Scots to the Duchesse de Nevers.

Sheffield, Feb. 28, 1577.

My cousin,—My ambassador, the Bishop of Glasgow,[1] having informed me of the remembrance you still cherish of our ancient friendship, and the care with which you always inquire news of me, I would not fail, by these few

[1] The Archbishop of Glasgow had, it would seem, mentioned the kind inquiries of an early friend whom Mary had known in her

words, to thank you for it, and to testify the great satisfaction it has given me. I pray you, then, that our early intercourse be renewed, and occasionally impart to me news of yourself, and love me as I promise to love you.

At this time, not having much leisure, I will not tire you with a longer letter, but entreat you to give my affectionate remembrances to my cousin your husband, M. de Nevers, and, while taking your due share, I pray God to keep you, my cousin, in health and long and happy life.

From Sheffield, this last of February.

Your very affectionate cousin and ancient friend,

MARIE.

The Queen of Scots to the Duchesse de Nemours,
(late Duchesse de Guise.)[1]

Sheffield, May 26, 1577.

My aunt,—I am much concerned to hear, by my chancellor, present bearer, that you are ill, otherwise I had hoped you would have imparted your good news, and those of my uncle, Monsieur de Nemours; I entreat that you will do so the first convenient opportunity that you may have. Meantime, let me always continue in your good graces, as one who desires to obey you, and who respects you like a good niece.

childhood. A chord was touched which responded pleasantly in her bosom, and she wrote this pretty affectionate billet on the spur of the moment. The duchess of Nevers was wife to Louis de Gonzague duke of Nevers, a nobleman much devoted to the catholic interest and much condemned by the duke of Sully in his memoirs. This letter is in the Bibliothèque du Roi. Bethune Col. MS. No. 8702. The date of the year ranges between 1577 and 1584, but it is too cheerful for the latter epoch.

[1] Bethune MS., No. 9126. Bibliothèque du Roi, Paris. Autograph.

In all things, I pray you give credence to this bearer, who will give you a full account of our news here, and especially of my health, which, for a year or more, has been very bad, but now begins a little to amend ; and, not to tire you without a better subject, I will pray God to give you, my aunt, in health, a very happy and long life.

From Sheffield, this 26th of May.

Your very obedient and affectionate good niece,

MARIE.

[Endorsed, To my aunt, Madame la Duchesse de Nemours.]

The Queen of Scots to the Duc de Nemours.[1]

Chatsworth, July 22, 1577.

My cousin,—Well do I know that my letters can only serve to tire those who receive them, so little good here have I to write of; yet having so favourable an opportunity as by the Sieur de Poigni, present bearer, I will not fail to send you these few words, to recall myself to your good grace and all my affairs, the state of which you have rendered better and more secure, witness my handwriting, the which I would draw to a close; but first I must thank you for your great favour and courtesy to a poor afflicted widow,[2] who has the honour of being your ally, and one whom I have always loved as much as one friend can love another; not but what I know that the relations of the late M. de Martigues have no need of any one to bespeak your kindness; but I received so much good from him, that I cannot do less than write to you, praying you to continue to be favour-

[1] Bethune MS. No. 9126. Bibliothèque du Roi, Paris. Autograph.

[2] The widow of M. de Martigues

able to his daughter, who is my god-daughter. And in recompence, after having recommended myself, with a very good heart, to you, I will pray to God to give you, my cousin, in health a long 'and happy life. From Chatsworth, this 22nd of July.

Your very affectionate and good cousin,

MARIE.

The Queen of Scots to the Duc de Nemours.[1]

Sheffield, July 31, 1577.

My cousin,—I have received your kind and courteous letter with great satisfaction, for the testimony it affords me that my long adversity has not had the power of bereaving me of your goodwill, which has always been manifested towards me, as one of my best friends and relatives, whenever an opportunity presented itself; therefore I will not neglect an offer from you of like aid, and supplicate you to stand my friend at present in the affair of my duchy of Tourraine, which they[2] are taking from me, and that you will give me and my people favour and counsel as to the acceptance of the exchange they will offer me ; so that I may not suffer by it any very great loss. You know enough of the state in which I am here, to suppose I have no need of hard treatment there [i. e. in France].

I will say no more on this head, except to pray you to perform the office of my good friend ; my ambassador[3] will tell you all about the business.

As to my health, this bearer will inform you regarding it, which will prevent me from further wearying

[1] MS. Béthune, No. 8702. Bibliothèque du Roi, Paris.
[2] The French government ; it was part of her dower, as widow of Francis II.
[3] Beaton, Archbishop of Glasgow, resident in France.

you; therefore, after commending myself, with a very warm heart, to your good graces, and praying God that he will give you, my cousin, in health a long and happy life. From Sheffield, this last day of July.

Your very affectionate good cousin,

MARIE.

1577. Mary Stuart goes to the baths at Buxton, and so does Burleigh, during the sojourn of Elizabeth at Kenilworth.

1578. *January* —. James VI, now in his thirteenth year, is placed at the head of the government, and Morton is obliged to resign his functions as regent.

March 12. Morton forces his way into Stirling Castle, seizes the young prince and the royal authority.

The Queen of Scots to her Ambassador in France, the Archbishop of Glasgow.[1]

Sheffield, May 2, 1578.

The countess of Lenox, my mother-in-law, died about a month ago; and the queen of England has taken into her care her ladyship's grand-daughter. [This, no doubt, is the Lady Arabella Stuart, only child to Charles Earl of Lenox, who died anno 1576.] I would desire those who are about my son to make instances in his name for this succession; not for any desire I have that he should actually succeed unto it, but rather to testify, that neither he, nor I, ought to be reputed or treated as foreigners in England, who are born within the same isle. This good lady was, thanks to God, in very good correspondence with me these five or six years bygone, and has confessed to me, by sundry letters under her hand, which I carefully preserve, the injury she did me by the unjust pursuits which she allowed to go out against me in her name, through bad information, but principally, she

[1] Keith's History of Scotland, Appendix, p. 145.

said, through the express orders of the Queen of England and the persuasion of her council, who also took much solicitude that she and I might never come to good un-derstanding together. But as soon as she came to know of my innocence, she desisted from any further pursuit against me; nay, went so far as to refuse her consent to anything they should set against me in her name.

The Queen of Scots to the Duc de Guise.

From Sheffield, the last day of May [1578].

My cousin,—In a matter in which you take so warm an interest as you have shown me that you do in behalf of the request of the Sieur de Saint Luc, you had good reason to make sure that you would not be re-fused, especially as I understand that he has the means and inclination to serve you, which cannot be without his having the like devotion, when occasion shall occur, towards every one connected with you; I have there-fore commanded my secretary to do all that is necessary on this occasion; and should I at any time require your interest for any of my friends, I shall, from the convic-tion of your good-will towards me, claim your favour for them, as you have now done mine, in which I shall never be wanting, seeing the many obligations which I acknowledge I owe you.

I have neither seen Gondi, nor received any better treatment; and, from not being permitted to take exer-cise, I have been obliged to use purgatives for the whole of this month of May; which is all that I can tell you at present, being still rather weak, and annoyed at having no convenience, excepting for the service of my person.

I beg you will do all you can for Lord Farnehest and other friends and servants of mine, whenever they may have need of your favour; and apologise for me to

my cousin your wife, for my not having written to her
this time, nor to any of our relatives; but I will acquit
myself of this on the first opportunity. After affectionately recommending myself to your good graces, as
also to those of my cousin your wife, I pray God to
grant you, my good cousin, good health and a long
life.

Your very affectionate cousin and best friend,

MARY.

The Queen of Scots to Monsieur d'Humières.

Sheffield, June 20, 1578

Monsr de Humières,—I am so mindful of the old servants of the late king my lord and husband, that, for
the honour and respect which I bear, and shall bear as
long as I live, for his memory, I shall always esteem
myself happy in being able to gratify them in anything
that lies in my power. Besides this, the particular
obligation which I owe to you and yours, for the many
demonstrations of their good-will towards me, renders
still more agreeable the request you lately made of
some seignorial rights, the grant of which I have commanded my secretary to despatch to you; at the same
time assuring you that, if ever a better occasion presents
itself, you will always find me ready to serve you and
yours as heartily as I now pray God to have you, Monsr
de Humières, in his holy and worthy keeping.

Written at the manor of Sheffield, this xxth day of
June, 1578.

Your very sincere and old friend,

MARY R.

[Endorsed Monsieur d'Humières, Chevalier of the
Order of the Most Christian King Monsieur my good
Brother, and Gentleman of the Bedchamber.]

B 5

1578. *June* —. Mary Stuart goes to Chatsworth.

The Queen of Scots to Monsieur Rambouillet.

Chatsworth, August 31, 1578.

Monsieur de Rambouillet,—Besides the important and continual obligations which I owe to his Most Christian Majesty monsieur my good brother, for the regard which he is pleased to pay to my condition and treatment in this captivity, I feel particularly grateful for the express charge which you inform me he has given you to intercede in his name in my behalf with the Queen of England, my good sister and cousin. For, besides your good qualities and merit, which are worthy of every respect, I hope you will not show less good-will in my cause than I formerly experienced from your two brothers on a similar occasion. I, therefore, beg you affectionately, that, before your departure from this kingdom, I may, through your kind means, feel the good effects of the intercession and favourable recommendation of the king my said lord and brother ; having as much need of it as ever, from the cruel treatment which I have for some time so unworthily received, in consequence of the false impressions made by my enemies on the queen my said good sister, with whom (in my opinion) nothing tends more to injure me than my near relationship. Leaving the Sieur de Mauvissière to communicate to you the particulars wherein it will be needful to employ you, as he has for a long time been well acquainted with them, I will not make this longer than to thank you for the good offices which you have already done me, assuring you of my desire and readiness to return them to you and yours whenever occasion may present itself. I pray God to have you, Monsieur de Rambouillet, in His holy and worthy keeping.

Written at Chattesworth, this last day of August, 1578.

Your very good friend,
MARY.

[Endorsed to Monsieur Rambouillet, Knight of the Order of His Most Christian Majesty, my good Brother, and Captain of his guards.]

1578. *October* —. Stuart, Lord d'Aubigny, becomes the favourite of James VI., who creates him Duke of Lenox.

The Queen of Scots to the Cardinal of Guise.[1]

From Sheffield, the 2nd of January [1578].

My good uncle,—I kiss your hands on the news of the peace. But as I do not see what will come of it, I shall be afraid that they have only left off to take breath. This is only supposition on my part, for in reality I know nothing, as I have not received news from any one in France for a long time, excepting requests, not even about my own affairs, till now by Arnault, and he has not been able to obtain permission to see me. It will be very annoying if I am not allowed to let you know at least once a year by some one of my servants how I am, and to inquire in the same way about you and about my affairs. The time draws very

[1] The Cardinal of Guise, Louis de Lorraine, Bishop of Metz, having died in 1578, the above letter, with the two following, must necessarily have been written in the year 1578, and not in 1579, which is the date given in the manuscript. The last of them was evidently written before Mary was aware of her uncle's decease, which occurred a little more than a month previously. The peace alluded to at the commencement of this letter must be the Treaty of Bergerac, concluded on the 7th September, 1577, between Henry III. and the Protestants. It cannot be the second Cardinal of Guise, who was killed at Blois in 1588, to whom Mary addressed these letters, as he was only cousin-german to the queen.

near when my attendants will expect to be paid, and I
to have money; for it is not a trifle I require to keep
me here, though they do talk so much about what I cost
them. But, as my wants are not immediate, I will wait
patiently until I can be honestly and faithfully served,
and give answer concerning my affairs in your country.

I beg you will afford me your assistance in this
matter, as you will see necessary by the directions which
I give on the subject to my ambassador, to be guided by
your advice, and likewise respecting my affairs, especially my dowry, so that I may not be a loser by any
partialities or delays. Trusting that, as you promised,
you will be a good uncle to me, I will say no more
about this at present, but only make one request, which
you must not refuse if you love me; this is, the gift of
the first vacant priory in your abbey of Bourgueil for
one of the nephews of *Raleigh*.[1] His services you are
acquainted with, and how the late M. the Cardinal
wished him to be about me, and how fond the late king
my lord was of him; and then this last journey in his
old age compels me to have recourse to you, because I
have no other means of gratifying him. I shall not
only feel myself under great obligation to you, but,
whenever occasion occurs for serving some one of your
friends by any means in my power, you have only to
claim the return, and I shall most willingly make it.
Not to trouble you too much, I will conclude by affectionately recommending myself to your favour.

I want to beg something else of you: it is, now I can
no longer see you, that you would send me your portrait, and that of M. the Cardinal, and if you can obtain
my late grandfather's,[2] it would afford me great plea-

[1] This person is probably Rallay, one of her suite often mentioned in her correspondence.
[2] The first Duc de Guise.

sure to see, at least in my cabinet, the likenesses of relations from whom I am so far distant.

Your very obedient and affectionate
good niece,

MARY.

The Queen of Scots to the Same.

At Sheffield, the last day of January, 1579 [1578.]

My good uncle,—I find, by your last letters, that all
our relations are in good health, for which I praise
God; and, as for the ill treatment which I receive, you
and they may be assured that it is without having deserved it from my good sister the Queen of England,
whom I have never offended in word, deed, or thought,
except that I think it wrong to be so hardly used;
for which I blame some of her ministers, who, as I
have had proofs, are continually seeking my ruin, either
by instilling into the mind of the queen unjust suspicions of me, or by underhand dealings, which you,
who are at liberty, have an opportunity of becoming
better acquainted with than I, who am a prisoner. Yet
these ministers have neither the qualities, nor the fidelity
towards her, which she deserves by the confidence which
she places in them out of her good-nature, but are full
of craft and dissimulation. This is said to be a monster
but too common near persons of our rank, when, misled
by far-fetched appearances, we are not on our guard
against it. But, as I am sure of the rectitude of my
conduct, I trust that the evil they strive to do me will
turn to their own ruin; and, therefore, it is my intention
to entreat the said lady, my good sister, to let me know
what is laid to my charge, so that I may justify myself:
for, as to letters, all that I have written have passed
through the hands of Walsingham, and I have written
no others, and there is nothing in them which I am not

ready to avow as being in no respect offensive either to
the queen or to her state. The king, monsieur my good
brother, the queen, madame my mother-in-law, you and
my cousin of Guise, can bear witness to this, as I write
to nobody else, excepting now and then, which letters
you see too, and which contain only kind recommendations to my ambassador, to my friends and relatives,
and to the prayers of madame my grandmother,[1] who
does not make much disturbance in the world. There
can be no other ground to find the least fault with me,
seeing the care that is taken to confine me closely.
This is all I can do, and offer to answer anything that
may be requisite for the satisfaction of my said good
sister. On this point, therefore, be under no apprehension that I have done anything that can be prejudicial
to me; but as for any uneasiness you may feel at not
hearing from me, if I am but permitted, I will soon
relieve you from that; but, if I am not permitted, I
leave it to your discretion and good-will to solicit in
my behalf, when you are in doubt, or await a future
opportunity, if it is to my prejudice: and meanwhile
I beg leave to commend to you all my affairs in France.

I have granted the request which you recommended
to my notice, and shall be very glad, according to my
means, of obliging all those whom you may recommend
to me, and you, I trust, will do the same for those who
may be recommended by me to you. If some person
be not permitted to come over here to render an account of my affairs and to bring me money, I and my
servants shall be badly off this Lent, for we have none
left, and all that we want here is not to be had for
nothing. For my own part, if I could but have attendance, I would not care much; but very often I

---

[1] Antoinette de Bourbon, the old Duchess of Guise.

suffer in every way. This is the worst letter I have ever written; if it reach you, it will give you a hint in a similar case in future. When you return, kiss for me the hands of the king, monsieur my brother-in-law, and mesdames the queens, my mother-in-law and my sister, and monsieur my brother-in-law, and commend me to their good offices; beg them to command their ambassador, M. de Mauvissière, to defend me to the Queen of England, my good sister; and if they would be pleased to add a favourable recommendation to some of the principal persons, such as the Earl of Leicester, and others of the like quality, who, in order that my enemies may be compelled to inform me what they accuse me of, so that they may be answered, might without . . . . . . I think it would be of great service to me, and I shall feel the more obliged to them. And in this place, after commending myself most affectionately to your good grace, I pray God to grant you, my good uncle, health and a long and happy life.

Your most affectionate and obedient niece,

MARY.

The Queen of Scots to the Same.

From Sheffield, the 6th of May, 1579 [1578.]

My uncle,—Since the arrival of my secretary, I have been so indisposed, that, having taken up my pen once or twice to write to the king monsieur my good brother, the queen madam my good mother, and the queen madam my good sister, I was forced to lay it down again, hoping that, before the return of my tailor, whom I shall send off in ten or twelve days, I shall be better able to write, and to return my most humble thanks for the honour they have done me in writing in so kind a manner, and so much to my consolation, at a time when I was so dejected by the great losses which we have recently sustained; and for this reason I wish very much that I were able to write you a longer letter than I can at present, to beg you to attend to my affairs; about which at this time I shall not trouble you further, because I have not leisure or convenience, any more than to answer you and all our relatives who have been pleased to write to me. Of one thing I will assure you, which is, that the advice you have given me, to endeavour by all means to conciliate the Queen of England, madam my good sister, is so much in unison with my inclination, that, had you, who have always the power of commanding me, not advised it, I should have followed that course of myself, as I hope to let you know more at length by M. de la Mothe on his return, who is better able than any other person to give you an account of all my actions. And, awaiting his convenience, I shall make you a very affectionate request, on the same conditions that I did to the late Cardinal my uncle, and which is that you must grant it, or I will never ask another from you. It is for the priory of Carennac, which M. de la Mothe informs me is only in the hands of a person whom you can dispose of: he wishes to have it for his brother, instead of that which I requested for him of monsieur the late cardinal. This priory, I am told, is in litigation, and consequently of no great importance, so that you cannot refuse it to your niece; for it is to me that you will give it, my good uncle. Do not let me have the same difficulty about it as I had with the other, and let me have your answer by the first opportunity; for I am under such obligations to the said Sieur de la Mothe, that I should be extremely grieved to see him kept in suspense, by those so related to me, particularly in regard to a matter of such little consequence. I promise myself so much from your friendship, that I shall have a speedy reply to the above, and therefore shall conclude, begging you to present my most humble respects to the king, monsieur my good brother, and to the queens my good mother and sister; and my apologies for not having written either to them or to our other relations, particularly to my cousin of Guise and his wife, and the Duke of Maine: I shall deem it my duty to do so on the first opportunity. After kissing your hands, my good uncle, I shall pray God to keep you in good health, and to grant you a long and happy life.

Your very obedient, affectionate niece,

MARY.

The Queen of Scots to the most Christian King, Henry 3d.

Sheffield, the last day of May, 1579

Monsieur my brother-in-law,—Foreseeing that, for the accomplishment of what has passed between my son and me, it will be necessary for my ambassador, the Archbishop of Glascow, to go to Scotland to my son, I beseech you, by these presents, when occasion shall require, and whenever he may demand your permission, to be pleased to grant it for a period : in the which my son and myself will be the more obliged to you, inasmuch as the beginning was designed by you, and the affair has thus far been authorised and favoured by you. In return for which, he and I shall remain kindly affected toward you, and ready to serve you in whatever you may please to command us.

After humbly commending myself to your good grace, I pray God to give you, monsieur my good brother-in-law, health and a long and happy life.

Your very affectionate and humble sister
and cousin,

MARY.

1579. Gregory XII. founds a College at Rome for the English and Scotch Catholic refugees. Allen establishes similar Colleges at Douay, Rheims, and St Omer.

Mary Stuart sends Nau, her secretary, with letters and presents for James VI., but they are refused, because he is not addressed as King of Scotland

The Queen of Scots to the Archbishop of Glasgow.
From Schastuinn, June 24, 1579.

Monsr de Glascow,—Owing to the absence of Nau, who set out a fortnight ago for Scotland, on a visit to my son,[1] and to my having been rather indisposed—many thanks to Du Val, whom I expected here to physic [*purger*] me for this whole summer—I could not give an earlier answer to your last letters. I shall therefore begin by requesting you to put the irons in the fire again, and try to find me another physician who is not a deceiver, and make Lusgeri do the same; and, meanwhile, give me your opinion of any who may offer themselves. I have ordered Duvergier, my chancellor, if he knows of any person, to send him to you; so that you may speak to him, and be able to give me your opinion. I fear he will find work cut out for him, as I begin to be unwell, and am suffering from what I have not had for a long time—a very bad, dry cough. I am glad that you have gone to the baths for the benefit of your health, but am sorry that you could not be present, according to my desire, at the rendering of the accounts of Dolu, my treasurer. I hope soon to be able to inform you whom I intend to appoint in his place. As to the affair of Madame de Humières, you will do well to make inquiry

[1] " About this time, Mary sent by Naue, her secretary, a letter to her son, together with some jewels of value, and a vest, embroidered with her own hand. But, as she gave him only the title of Prince of Scotland, the messenger was dismissed without being admitted into his presence."—ROBERTSON'S *Hist. of Scotl.* b. vi.

about it, for I think it a sad thing that the fief should be so much diminished, since she herself wrote to me, at her leisure, respecting it. Touching the request of your secretary, I cannot for several reasons comply with it at present. I beg you, on your return, to give me a full account of the state of my affairs, and to look well after them ; and, in return, I hope to be able, on the arrival of Nau, to inform you of that of your old mistress and your young master. So the latter be but satisfactory the former cannot be otherwise. And, in this place, after heartily commending myself to you, I pray God to give you, M. de Glascow, a long and happy life.

Your very good mistress and best friend,

MARY R.

1579. July —. The Queen goes to Buxton again.

The Queen of Scots to the Most Christian King.

From Buxton, the 27th of July [1579].

Monsieur my good brother,—I have despatched this gentleman for a purpose which my ambassador will tell you. I therefore beg you will give him an audience, and a brief answer, such as you may judge that the case requires ; and I will not trouble you at present with a longer letter; but merely present my humble commendations to your good grace, praying God to give you, monsieur my good brother, health and a long and happy life.

Your very kind sister,

MARY.

The Queen of Scots to the Archbishop of Glasgow.

Buxton, August 10, 1579.

Monsieur de Glascow,—As the indisposition of Nau

prevents me from giving you a detailed answer to your preceding letters, I write in the mean time to inform you of my arrival at the Baths, and of the benefit I have derived from them in relieving the inveterate pain in my side. As ill luck would have it, at Sheffield, those who were assisting me to mount my horse, let me fall backwards on the steps of the door, from which I received so violent a blow on the spine of the back, that, for some days past, I have not been able to hold myself upright. I hope, however, with the good remedies which I have employed, to be quite well before I leave this place. We have not been wholly free from the epidemic disorder: but it has been much more violent among the people of the country than those of my household, not one of which is now, thank God, affected by it.

Do not fail to send me all the things which I directed you, notwithstanding the danger that you tell me you apprehend on your side of the water, and which is not less here, and write to me on all occasions, according to the opportunity you have. Whereupon, I pray God to have you, M. de Glascow, in his holy keeping.

Your very good mistress and best friend,

MARY R.

1579. *September* —. The Duke of Anjou makes a short visit to England; Elizabeth is much pleased with him.

The Queen of Scots to the same.

From Sheffield, 12th October [1579].

Monsieur de Glascow,—We certify to you our having received from M. de Schrewsbury the sum of five hundred crowns, by you delivered to his man, to whom you will return his promise for so much, which we have sent you, with an order for its reimbursement and discharge.

The said Sieur de Schrewsbury has since furnished us, upon our receipt, with the sum of a thousand crowns, which sum you must not fail to return forthwith to his said man, the bearer of this, taking his receipt for the same. It is our intention that the said sum of a thousand crowns shall be entered in the account of our treasurer. Given at the manor of Sheffield.

Your good mistress and best friend,

MARY R.

1579. *December* 21. Morton is apprehended on the information of Stuart, son of Lord Ochiltree, who accuses him of the murder of Darnley.

The Queen of Scots to M. de Mauvissière.

Sheffield, Sept. 3, 1580.

Monsieur de Mauvissière,—Having purchased two beautiful and rare nags[1] for my cousin, Monsieur de Guise, it was my intention to have immediately sent them both in charge of the bearer, who is obliged to return to France with his wife, for the cure of a disorder with which she has been afflicted ever since last winter. But one of the said horses having been foundered for the last seven or eight days, I thought it advisable not to miss this opportunity, nor the season, for sending the other, which I have given in charge to the groom, who has for some time past had it under his particular care, and I have given him strict orders to take it to your house; and you will oblige me to let it be led by one of your grooms to my ambassador, in order that he may present it, in my name, to my said cousin, and to pay any expences incurred. I think you will have no difficulty about his journey, with the passport

[1] The French word used by the queen is *guilledins*, which is derived from our *gelding*.

which it will be necessary to obtain for the purpose, any more than for that of any of my said officers; I shall, therefore, not give you any more particular directions on the subject, praying God, Monsieur de Mauvissière, to have you in his holy and worthy care. Written at the manor of Sheffield, the iii day of September, 1580.

Your very obliged and best friend,

MARY R.

The Queen of Scots to the Marshal de Cossé.[1]

Sheffield, Oct. 3, 1580.

Monsieur le Maréschal,—The honour that I had of being brought up with and closely allied to your king, seems sufficiently to authorise me to recommend my present estate to you, and all others his good and faithful councillors, in a cause both just and reasonable, being no other than the preservation of my dower. I pray you then, on this consideration, to aid me by your credit and favour against Monsieur le Duc, my brother-in-law, [The Duke of Anjou.] The remonstrances that I have given charge to my council to make to you about my wood of Espernay, and the trouble I have received in the peaceable enjoyment of it, from the Sieur de Rosni,[2] under the name of the said duke. I never was proceeded with in this fashion till I was deprived of my duchy of Tourraine.

Nevertheless I will hope, that, being better informed by you of this affair, he will redress the wrong he has there done to me.

[1] MS. Bethune, No. 9126. Bibliothèque du Roi, Paris.

[2] This was no doubt the renowned Maximilian de Bethune, Sieur de Rosni, and afterwards prime minister of Henry the Great, by the title of Duc de Sully; for it may be seen in the first volume of his Memoirs, that he had entered into the service of the Duke of Alençon (Anjou), though he hated him heartily. Perhaps he was not loth to annoy the Queen of Scots, who was a warm ally of the house of Guise.

Offering you, in recompense, all the good I can do for you and yours in this place, with the same earnestness with which I pray God, Monsieur le Maréschal, to have you in his holy and worthy keeping.

From the Castle of Sheffield this 3rd of October, (supposed 1580).

Your entirely good friend,

MARIE R.

Instructions of the Queen of Scots to the Bishop of Ross.

Sheffield, December 24, 1580.

Instructions given to our reverend father in God Iohn, Bishop of Ross, our trusty counsellor and ambassador towards the queen of England our good sister, to be used by him with the advice and concurrence of the reverend father in God, also, Alexander, Bishop of Galloway, and William Lord Livingston, who are sent in commission by our lieutenants and nobility, our good subjects to be joined with our said ambassador in the treaty to be made with the said good sister, or her commissioners, as well for appeasing of all controversies, and contracting of further amity between us, our realm and subjects, as also for her pleasure tending to the assurance of our subjects in Scotland.

First, he shall consider diligently the articles and . . . . . . which was proposed to us by Sir William Cecil, Knt., the queen our good sister's principal secretary, and Sir Walter Mildmay, chancellor of her exchequer, her counsellers and commissioners, at Chatsworth, in the month of October last, together with our answer unto iii cases : if the same be now proposed to you again, ye shall answer to the same, in manner following.

As to the first of the said articles, you shall condescend

to the same with the provision made in our answers
thereto at Chatsworth.

Then, as to the second article, bearing the confirmation of the last treaty made at Edinburgh in the month
of July, 1560, you shall condescend to the confirmation
thereof. Providing always that the same be not hurtful
nor prejudicial to my title in succession to the crown of
England, failure of the queen my good sister and her
lawful issue, and to that effect, you shall require my
said good sister in 'most friendly loving manner to make
allowances by her provisions as may be sufficient in law
for preservation of my said title in succession. And because the same depends upon the subtilties and quid-
dities of the laws of this realm, therefore you shall require that you may have counsel of the best learnt of
the laws, for the better consideration of this point, by
what advice he may the better resolve thereupon to the
queen our good sister's contentment and for our good
assurance.

Then, as to the third article, you shall assure the
queen our good sister of constant amitie and good friendship in times ending, so that no prince and country shall
be able to persuade me to do any thing that may be
offensive to her estate or country, trusting assuredly to
receive the like at her hands. And therefore you shall
desire⸴her to consider and weigh our case, and great loss
which may follow to us, our country, subiects and people of Scotland, in case we would agree to these articles
as it is demanded ; for thereby we shall be in danger to
lose our dowry in France, the privileges which our subjects has enjoyed many hundred years by the old league
of the intwinement of my arms,archers of the guard,
and xxiiii archers of the corps keepers of the king's
body ; with all other privileges that merchants, students,
and others, who has heritages, benefices, and pensions of

that realme, with many other commodities and honourable promotions; besides that we and our country shall
be need of the assistance that our predecessors and we
was wont to have for a defence in case England or any
other nation under whatsoever colours should invade
Scotland . . . being foreseen, and provisions being made
therefore that we may save sufficient recompense for our
losses to the like privileges, commodities, and immu-
nities, to be assured to us and our subjects. We will
rather contract friendship with the queen our good sister
nor any prince in Christendom. Otherwise you will be
hard our subjects to agree unto. At any rate we will
not refuse to contract with the queen our good sister
and in her defence, in case any prince or country
shall invade her without just cause first given by England to that prince or country   And so being also that
in case England give the first occasion of war to them,
it shall be lawful to us to join with our old friends and
allies for their defence without break of the present
treaty. Providing always that the like bond of friendship . . . . to us reciprocity of the queen our good
sister's part.

Then, as to the fourth article. You shall agree unto,
with provision that as well English as French men of war
shall be removed forth from Scotland if any be within a
month after our returning within our said realme, so
that only Scottish men of war shall remain within the
same country : if it shall happen some rebellion shall be
attempted against us, as be the forces of the country can
not suppress it, and in that case it shall be . . . . . .
to us to require and receive aid of strangers as well
of the queen our good sister, as of other princes our
allies and confederates, without prejudice or violating
of this present treaty. Providing that our said good
sister shall be warned thereof by us and made privy

thereunto. And that these strangers shall not be suffered to remain within the realme after the peace-offering
of the rebellion.

Then to the fifth article. That it be plainly declared
what is meant by intelligences mentioned in the same.
For we are content to forbeare all intelligences that may
be prejudiciall either to the queen our good sister, her
estate or country. And you shall require the said
article be reciprocitly made for the queen of England's
part.

Then for the sixth article. You shall condescend as
my former answer, assuring always that there is no
Englishman presently within the realme of Scotland and
of those who sought refuge saving those that are in
keeping of our rebelles, for all the rest have been released conformably to the promises made by the Bishop
of Ross, our ambassador at the beginning of this treaty.

Then to the seventh article. You shall accord, as in
my former answers.

As to the ninth article, concerning the prince our son.
You shall consider the advice which the nobility our
good subjects send to us thereuppon. And inform our
good sister upon the same, assuring her . . . . for our
part that we shall leave nothing undone that consists in
our power to her satisfaction in that point, trusting
always that she will not press us and our good subjects
further now for our consent, in respect that the delivering of the prince our son stands not in our hands,
he being kept by our rebels, and being made one also
of their pretended rebellion, to our great hurt and prejudice. And therefore the delivery of his person should
not hinder our liberty, as being a thing impossible to
us, unless the queen our good sister will make us to be
freely restored within our realme. In the mean time
receive other pledges of our nobility. And in that case

we shall cause that part of the treaty be fulfilled by the special assistance and concurrence of our said good sister. And besides, that those conditions proposed by us in our former answer at Chatsworth be agreed unto.

The tenth article seems not honourable to be put in any treaty, because it is contrary to all laws and good reason to put a bridle to marriage[1] not . . . . we refer to our former answer given thereto.

The eleventh article should be well considered of, conforming to the instructions sent by our nobility thereanent.

Touching the twelfth article, we refer to our former answers.

The manner of the assurance.

The first article is agreed.

As to the second article, we refer to our former answers given thereto.

The third article seems to be the most perilous of all, for that it bears so many captious and general terms, whereupon occasion may be taken to our great hurt and prejudice, or rather to the . . . of our title, as well in succession of the crown of England as to the present title of our own realme—principally in these terms to aid or any ways comfort any notorious traytor or rebel of England, and which would be interpreted as is contained in the articles sent by our nobility. And therefore it is necessary that you require the queen our good sister to make it lawful to you to have the counsel and advice of the best learned in the laws of this realme upon this article, being so prejudicial as it is to our whole estate, which being so reasonable, we are assured you will not be refused, by whose advice and your own wisdom you shall agree to that thing

---

[1] By this observation, it would seem that Queen Elizabeth had chosen to put a restraining clause on any wedlock Mary might contract.

most convenient for the queen our good sister's surety
and ours also.

To the fourth article it appears very necessary that
the like order be kept, in making assurance to us by the
queen our good sister, and the estate of the realme of
England, for keeping of the points of this treaty, as she
has required us and our estates to do conform to the
advice sent to us by our nobility.

As to the fifth article, concerning the Castle of Hume,
we refer as to our former answer.

And . . . . of the sixth article, for we cannot agree
that any strangers possess any strength within our realm.

Also for as . . . . as the assurance taken at the queen
our good sister's desire, betwixt the Earl of Sussex, her
lieutenant, and our lieutenants in Scotland, and the Earl
of Lenox and his assisters, which has been truly and
inviolable kept by all our good subjects, and nevertheless
the same is violated and broken by the adversary party,
in such sort that there is great spoilies . . . and op-
pressions exerted by them against our said good subjects, contrary to their promises, which besides . . . our
said good sister of her honour to cause redress ! . . . .
you shall desire her most affectionately to cause the said
wrongs and injuries be repaired. And that order be
taken during this treaty, no parliament be holden in
their pretended manner ; nor none of our good subjects
be molested or troubled in their bodies, lands, possessions, goods, or living gear ; but that they be suffered
peaceably to enjoy their livings and possessions without
any further trouble. The particular declaration hereof
we refer to the information to be given by the Lords of
Galloway and Livingstone ; and as you shall get further
knowledge thereof from tyme to tyme, fail not to make
most earnest instance, according to all reason, equity,
and good conscience.

And, finally, our pleasure is, that you consider diligently the articles and instructions sent by our nobility
at this present, which we find very good in all respects.
And because they have reserved to our judgment and
pleasure to agree to whatsoever conditions may serve for
the advancement of our liberty and restoration, we likewise do commit the same to your wisdom and discretion,
to be used of the said Bishop of Galloway and Lord
Livingston, as well in this matter, which are to be treated
betwixt the queen our good sister and us, as in any
others which shall happen to be proposed for the assurance of our unnatural subjects, in case, for the pleasure of our said good sister, we shall be persuaded to
show our clemency towards them. Whereof for particular advize we refer to the information which we have
given you, conforming to the answer which we made to
our said good sister's commissioners at Chatsworth. Promising faithfully to ratify, approve, and affirm whatsoever you shall do in this behalf, and observe and keep
the same inviolably in all points. In witness of which
we have subscribed the same with our own hand, and
affix our signet thereto. At Sheffield, the xxvith day
of December, 1580.

MARY R.

---

*James VI., King of Scotland, to his mother, the
Queen.*[1]

January 29, 1580-1.

Madame,—I entreat you, very humbly, to believe
that it was not according to my goodwill that your
secretary returned without giving me your letter, or
letting me hear what it was you had commanded him

[1] State Paper MS., edited in the original French, Retrospective
Review, New Series. The postscript regarding the little ape is in
James's own hand; he was fourteen years of age.

to tell me, having felt much regret at what has happened about him, for I should be infinitely vexed, if it could be believed that I did not bear towards you the honour and duty which I owe to you, having hope that, with time, God will give me grace to offer you my good and loving services, knowing well enough, that all the honour I have in this world I hold from you.

I received the ring it pleased you to send me, which I will take great care of in honour to you ; and I send you another, which I very humbly entreat you to receive from me with as good a heart as I took yours. You have made it appear very plainly, by your last letter, how good a mother you are. If you should learn any more of that which I have just begun, you are entreated very humbly, to apprise me of it, that I may take order to do the best that will be possible for me to effect ; let us hear this by the Earl of Lenox. We also supplicate you to be aiding, and to give me your good counsel and advice, the which I will entirely follow. Deem it most certain, that in all things on which it will please you to command me, you will find me your very obedient son. Kissing your hands most humbly, and praying God to preserve you, I am your obedient son for ever,

JACQUES R.

Madame, I commend to you the fidelity of my little ape,[1] who never stirs from near me. I will often send you news of us, (*i. e.* of him and his ape.)

To the queen of Scotland, my very honoured dame.

---

[1] It is supposed Mary had sent this creature to her son, yet the extreme jealousy, with which all communication between the mother and son was regarded by Elizabeth on her side, and the Scotch Calvinists on his, and which rendered even the conveyance of a ring and a letter difficult, is rather against such a supposition. It is apparent by this letter, that Mary's secretary, Nau, could

The Queen of Scots to M. de la Mauvissière.

Sheffield, February, 1581.

Monsieur de Mauvissière,—I beg that you carefully forward the enclosed packet to Monsieur de Glasgow, and procure a passport for my tailor, whom he is shortly to send with some trunks full of clothes for me. I am exceedingly displeased on account of the disappointment you have met with from the members of my council respecting your treasurership of Victry, directly contrary to my order and intention. My ambassador has informed me that it had been conferred on a doctor of divinity, who was long in possession of it, and who

not obtain access to the young king to deliver the letter and token, to which this is an answer, and it is very certain that this very letter found its way into Elizabeth's State Paper Office, where it is now, instead of into the hands of the poor mother, who was longing for it. It is probable that James, when told to add some words in his own hand to his mother, like any other schoolboy, wrote what was nearest to his heart, being the demeanour of his favourite animal. If the generalizing histories of Scotland written in the last century are opened, who can refrain from derision, when, at a date parallel to this letter, grave reprobation of the young king is found for the political mischief he did by the preference he bestowed on his favourites!! meaning, by the poor boy's favourites, fierce grown-up men, chiefs of struggling factions, earnestly employed in the laudable endeavour of cutting each other's throat. No doubt the friendless boy shrunk from the vicinity of his imputed favourites, expecting each in turn would prove his murderer, and consoled himself by caressing his real favourite, the faithful little ape :" who would not leave him." Dates and documents overturn many a pompous falsehood, and, however simple the truth may be, it is far more consistent with common sense to find a kind-hearted boy of fourteen petting a little animal than troubling a state; no doubt the cunning politicians, who were contending for power, told the demi-barbarians, who bolstered their authority by force of arms, a great deal regarding their favour with the poor child, but that historians in a civilized century should lay any stress on the opinions of a boy of fourteen is too absurd.

had incurred various expenses, for which he ought to be re-imbursed. I have, nevertheless, again ordered most expressly, in the enclosed letters, that the said doctor shall resign to your almoner the said benefice, till the first vacancy; for I will not suffer my orders to be disobeyed, as they have heretofore been but too much, even in many things for myself, otherwise I shall be compelled to put my affairs into the hands of my chancellor, du Verger. I feel too much obliged to you to prefer any one to you when a better occasion shall occur, and still less to break my promise to you, which I never will do. I beg you to hasten as much as possible the remittance of my money, and of the wages of my officers, of which I assure you every one is in great need, and myself in particular. My illness increased much during the last five or six days; and though I have been, I may say, at extremity, I could not obtain what was requisite and necessary for my health. At present I am a little better, though very weak and reduced. I should feel obliged, if the Queen of England, my good sister, would pay a little attention to the things necessary for the complete recovery and preservation of my health, such as exercise on horseback round about here, when I shall get well. Be so good as to represent this, and do not fail to write me an answer by the first opportunity; till when, I pray God, Monsieur de Mauvissière, to have you in his holy keeping.

Written at the manor of Sheffield, the   day of February, 1581.

1581. *April* 18—. A French ambassador arrives to treat with England, relative to the marriage of the queen with the Duke of Anjou.

May —. Morton is condemned to death and executed, in spite of the entreaties and threats of Elizabeth.

June 11. The English and French commissioners sign the contract of marriage between Elizabeth and the Duke of Anjou.

July —. Parsons, the Jesuit, sends Waytes to the court at Holyrood to implore the protection of Lenox for Mary Stuart and the Catholics; he receives the most flattering promises.

The United Provinces renounce their allegiance to the King of Spain, and acknowledge the Duke of Anjou as their sovereign. This prince assents, and enters Flanders with sixteen thousand men.

September 10. The Council of England deliberates, by order of the queen, upon bringing Mary Stuart to trial; and breaks up at the end of three days, without concurring in the views of Elizabeth.

November —. The Duke of Anjou visits London a second time, and is received by Elizabeth with the warmest interest.

November 19. She signs a promise of marriage, but the ceremony is postponed for some months.

November —. Beale, Elizabeth's secretary, and brother-in-law to Walsingham, goes to Sheffield upon pretext of treating with Mary Stuart concerning her liberation, but, in reality, to discover what were her hopes in regard to Scotland.

1582. *February* 8. The Duke of Anjou sets out for Flanders; Elizabeth accompanies him as far as Canterbury.

March —. Parsons sends Creighton, the Jesuit, to Scotland, to ascertain the intentions of the Duke of Lenox.

The Queen of Scots to her Cousins.

This 18th of March [1582.]

My cousins,—The great interest I feel assured you take in all that concerns the welfare, grandeur, and preservation of my son, together with the duty of good and faithful subjects towards me, as things joined and united together, has particularly induced me to despatch this gentleman to communicate some matters to you, and, if you think proper, to my son, and which greatly concern the prosperity and advancement of our

c 5

affairs, affectionately begging you to pay assiduous and careful attention to what he will communicate to you on my behalf, or on that of M. de Guise, my cousin, to whom you may, in all things, give the same credit as to myself. And, trusting that God will give me grace to acknowledge your duty and fidelity, I pray God to have you in his holy keeping.

                    Your very good cousin and friend,
                                        MARY R.

1582. *May* —. Parsons and Creighton return to Paris, and propose, with the Duke of Guise, Castelli, the Pope's nuncio, and Taxis, the Spanish ambassador, that Mary and James possess conjointly the throne of Scotland.

June —. They obtain the consent of Mary Stuart and the Scotch Cabinet. The King of Spain and the Pope promise succours in money

August 23. The Earl of Gowry, the head of the English faction in Scotland, seizes the person of King James in the castle of Ruthven; the Duke of Lenox flies to France.

The Queen of Scots to M. de Mauvissière.

                              Sheffield, September 2nd, 1582.

Monsieur de Mauvissière,—In addition to the information which the bearer, the S^r. du Ruisseau, will give you on my situation and the state of my health, I shall say that I never had such need of the favour and indulgence of the queen of England, madam my good sister, in respect to my liberty and ordinary treatment, having, eight days ago, fallen very ill, that if it does not please her to meliorate my situation in this captivity, according to the remonstrances I charged the said du Ruisseau to make her in my name, I see but little hopes of surviving the next winter. The said du Ruisseau will inform you of every thing, that you may have the goodness to make the like representations to the said queen and the principal persons of her council, so that I may obtain the reply.

I think that monsieur the duke, my brother-in-law, cannot be aware of the proceedings which his officers have commenced against me for the payment of a part of the woods of Espernay, notwithstanding the payment which, according to his gift and power of attorney, has already been made to the S^r. de Rosni, who is very far from the good-will which you have told me the duke has of holding me entirely quit, for the said part. I beg you will write to him and to the S^r. de Quinsey, his secretary, by the first opportunity you have, to procure for me letters to the said officers, ordering them to stay the said proceedings, and to transfer the right which he might claim in future to the said woods, so that I may be maintained and continued in the possession thereof, agreeably to the memorandum I have already sent you. De Chaulnes has promised me in his last, that he will pay what I owe you out of the moneys he shall receive, which I will shortly pay him again. As to my house at Fontainebleau, respecting which Ruisseau spoke to me in your behalf, believe me, had it been at my disposal, I would most willingly have made you a present of it; but it is nearly three months since I promised it, through my ambassador, who wrote to me about it, to my cousin M. de Guise, who, I think, before this will have settled himself there, although it is very small.

Let the sum of forty crowns be given to the daughter of the Laird of Grange, who is over there, to enable her to return into Scotland, as her mother has refused my proposal of sending her to France, and getting her an appointment: and I see no likelihood of having her about me; and let them not wait longer over there for an answer, if they have no other occasion for staying. I thank you for the favours and courtesies which the said du Ruisseau informs me that you have shown him on my account, and for which he feels greatly obliged. Be assured that, whenever an opportunity presents itself of making a return, I shall heartily avail myself of it. In the mean time, I pray God to have you, Monsr. du Mauvissière, in his holy and worthy keeping. Written at the manor of Sheffield, in England, the second of September, 1582.

Your very best friend,

MARY.

1582. *October* 5. The change in the calendar from the old to the new style is introduced into France, but not adopted in England and Scotland until 1752.

The Queen of Scots to M. de Mauvissière.

Sheffield, October 8th, 1582.

Monsieur de Mauvissière,—Since my despatch herein enclosed, kept ready ever since the beginning of last month, the Sieur du Ruisseau has been apprehended in this country by the Earl of Shereusbury, at the same time that he laid a fresh restriction on my liberty, and he has since refused me permission to write to the Queen of England, madam my good sister, or to you. I am astonished beyond measure at this proceeding, knowing in my conscience how little occasion I have given for it, having taken particular pains, during the whole of the past time, to accommodate myself as much as possible to all that I thought agreeable to the said queen. And besides, I can answer for it that neither the said du Ruisseau, nor any other of his company, would ever furnish cause for their confinement, and indeed the Earl of Shereusbury has not been able to allege any. I have made my complaints on this subject to the said queen in my letter herein enclosed, which I have commissioned the said Sieur du Ruisseau to present to her in my name ; and, in case the court should be far from his road, and he cannot do so, I request you to undertake the office, urgently requiring from her a declaration of her intentions regarding my said restriction, which I think she would not continue without occasion ; and, in case she should be persuaded of any, let me be apprized of it, that I may explain the matter to her. Such harsh treatment has contributed greatly to impair my health, as the said du Ruisseau can more particularly inform you : referring to him on this point, and for other news from this place, I shall add nothing further but my commendations to your good grace, praying God to have you, Monsieur du Mauvissière, in his holy keeping. Written at Chefeild, this viii day of October, 1582.[1]

Monsieur du Mauvissière, you will see by my letters to the Queen of England the complaint which I make about a thing which is so great an innovation that I cannot help feeling great alarm respecting the conclusion of so new a reformation ; for, since I have been in England, whatever disturbances there might be in this country or elsewhere, or whatever might have happened, I have never before been forbidden to complain to her, and to represent what might be agreeable to her, or to allege whatever I thought proper in my defence when I was falsely accused : now I am ill, I am prohibited, not knowing wherefore, or by whom, unless it be for the pleasure of the Earl of Shereusbury, to write to you or to her, whatever necessity I may have ; if this continues

[1] This letter thus far is in the handwriting of Mary's secretary ; what follows is her own.

without reprehension, it is exposing me to death, at the pleasure of any one who shall choose to make use of her name. If these letters are delivered to you, I beg you to provide in some other way for the safety of my life, remonstrating with the said lady my good sister, feeling assured that, for the sake of the king, who has an interest in this matter, she will attend to it. The bearer will inform you of my state.

Your very obliged and best friend,

MARY R.

The Queen of Scots to the Duchesse de Nemours.[1]

Sheffield, Nov. 6, 1582.

My aunt,—It is now a long time since I have commended myself to your good grace, not because I desired not its continuance, but because of being so closely searched, by their finding amiss the thickness of my packets, and the number of my letters, telling me that I write to too many people, and that I have but too much intelligence; it may be well if they do not open all, and retain those that they chuse, but to my thinking, it vexes them as much that I remind any one that I am in this world, as that I am still here. It may be, as I am here, and you have power, that you will please to do a good turn to the estate[2] of a poor prisoner, who is captive and in adversity, but as much your niece as any you have belonging to you. This I supplicate you to do, and to impart to me your good news, and that of my uncle, Monsieur de Nemours, to

[1] Bethune MS., No. 8702. Bibliothèque du Roi, Paris. Autograph.

[2] Regarding her dowry in France, about which she was often in trouble, and often beholden to the good offices of the Duke of Nemours.

whom I pray you to permit me to recommend myself here affectionately, and· to all my cousins, your children, and having kissed your hands, I pray God to give you, my aunt, in health, a very long and happy life.

From Sheffield this 6th of November, 1582.

Your very affectionate and obedient good niece,

MARY.

To the Duchesse de Nemours, my aunt.

The Queen of Scots to Queen Elizabeth.[1]

Sheffield, November 8, 1582.

Madam,—Upon that which has come to my knowledge of the last conspiracies executed in Scotland against my poor child, having reason to fear the consequence of it, from the example of myself, I must employ the very small remainder of my life and strength before my death to discharge my heart to you fully of my just and melancholy complaints ; of which I desire that this letter may serve you as long as you live after me for a perpetual testimony and engraving upon your conscience, as much for my discharge to posterity as to the shame and confusion of all those who, under your approbation, have so cruelly and unworthily treated me to this time,

[1] Blackwood, whose history of the sufferings of Mary was published so early as 1587, says :—" The queen, at the reported seizure of her son by Lord Gowry, having received an intimation of her son's captivity, fell so sick that she thought she should die, as the English physicians reported she would to their mistress, who wanted nothing better, having the son already in her power, or, which was the same, in the hands of the people who were devoted to her; with which the poor mother, being greatly agitated in her mind, after she had addressed her prayers to God, put her hand to the pen, thinking to obtain favour from and to soften the heart of her cousin by this address." The French original of this celebrated letter is in the British Museum, Cotton lib. Calig. c. vii. 51.

and reduced me to the extremity in which I am. But as their designs, practices, actions, and proceedings, though as detestable as they could have been, have always prevailed with you against my just remonstrances and sincere deportment; and as the power which you have in your hands has always been a reason for you among mankind; I will have recourse to the living God, our only judge, who has established us equally and immediately under him for the government of his people.

I will invoke him till the end of this my very pressing affliction, that he will return to you and to me (as he will do in his last judgment) the share of our merits and demerits one towards the other. And remember, madam, that to him we shall not be able to disguise anything, by the point and policy of the world; though mine enemies, under you, have been able, for a time, to cover their subtle inventions to men, perhaps to you.

In his name, and before him sitting between you and me, I will remind you that, by the agents, spies, and secret messengers, sent in your name to Scotland while I was there, my subjects were corrupted and encouraged to rebel against me, to make attempts upon my person, and, in a word, to speak, do, enterprize, and execute that which has come to the said country during my troubles; of which I will not, at present, specify other proof than that which I have gained of it, by the confession of one, who was afterwards among those that were most advanced for this good service, and of the witnesses confronted with him. To whom, if I had since done justice, he had not afterwards, by his ancient intelligences, renewed the same practices against my son, and had not procured for all my traitorous and rebellious subjects, who took refuge with you, that aid and support which they have had, ever since my detention on

this side ; without which support I think the said traitors could not since have prevailed, nor afterwards have
stood out so long as they have done.

During my imprisonment at Lochleven, the late
Trogmarton [Throckmorton] counselled me on your
behalf to sign that demission which he advertised me
would be presented to me, assuring me that it would
not be valid. And there was not afterwards a place in
Christendom, wheie it was held for valid or maintained
except on this side, [where it was maintained], even to
having assisted with open force the authors of it. In
your conscience, madam, would you acknowledge an
equal liberty and power in your subjects? Notwithstanding this, my authority has been by my subjects
transferred to my son, when he was not capable of exercising it.

And, since I was willing to assure it lawfully to him,
he being of age to be assisted to his own advantage, it
is suddenly ravished from him, and assigned over to two or
three traitors; who, having taken from him the effec·
tiveness of it, will take from him, as they have from me,
both the name and the title of it, if he contradicts them
in the manner he may, and perhaps his life, if God does
not provide for his preservation.

When I was escaped from Lochleven, ready to give
battle to my rebels, I remitted to you, by a gentleman
express, a diamond-jewel, which I had formerly received
as a token from you, and with assurance to be succoured
against my rebels, and even that, on my retiring towards
you, you would come to the very frontiers in order to
assist me; which had been confirmed to me by divers
messengers.[1]

This promise coming, and repeatedly, from your
mouth (though I had found myself often deceived by

[1] See her letter from Dundrenan, which accompanied this jewel.
Vol. i.

your ministers), made me place such affiance on the ef-
fectiveness of it, that, when my army was routed, I had
come directly to throw myself into your arms, if I had
been able to approach them. But, while I was planning
to set out, there was I arrested on my way, surrounded
with guards, secured in strong places, and at last reduced, all shame set aside, to the captivity in which I
remain to this day, after a thousand deaths, which I
have already suffered from it.

I know that you will allege to me what passed between the late Duke of Norfolk and me. I maintain that
there was nothing in this to your prejudice, or against
the public good of this realm, and that the treaty was
sanctioned with the advice and signatures of the first
persons who were then of your council, under the assurance of making it appear good to you. How could such
personages have undertaken the enterprize of making
you consent to a point, which should deprive you of life,
of honour, and your crown, as you have shown yourself
persuaded it would have done to all the ambassadors and
others, who speak to you concerning me?

In the mean time, my rebels perceiving that their
headlong course was carrying them much farther than
they had thought before, and the truth being evidenced
concerning the calumnies that had been propagated of
me at the conference to which I submitted in full assembly of your deputies and mine, with others of the
contrary party in that country, in order to clear myself
publicly of them; there were the principals, for having
come to repentance, besieged by your forces in the castle
of Edinburgh, and one of the first among them poisoned[1]
and the other most cruelly hanged;[2] after I had twice
made them lay down their arms at your request, in hopes
of an agreement, which God knows whether my enemies
aimed at.

[1] Secretary Maitland.   [2] The Laird of Grange.

I have been for a long time trying whether patience could soften the rigour and ill-treatment which they have begun for these ten years peculiarly to make me suffer. And, accommodating myself exactly to the order pre-scribed me for my captivity in this house, as well in re-gard to the number and quality of the attendants which I retain, dismissing the others, as for my diet and ordi-nary exercise for my health, I am living at present as quietly and peaceably as one much inferior to myself, and more obliged than with such treatment I was to you, had been able to do ; even to the abstaining, in order to take from you all shadow of suspicion and diffidence, from requiring to have some intelligence with my son and my country, which is what by no right or reason could be denied me, and particularly with my child ; whom, instead of this, they endeavoured by every way to persuade against me, in order to weaken us by our division.

I was permitted, you will say, to send one to visit him there about three years ago. His captivity, then at Sterling, under the tyranny of Morton, was the cause of it, as his liberty was afterwards of the refusal to make a like visit. All this year past I have several times entered into divers overtures for the establishment of a good amity between us, and a sure understanding be-tween these two realms in future. About ten years ago com-missioners were sent to me at Chatsworth for that pur-pose. A treaty has been held upon it with yourself by my ambassadors and those of France. I myself even made last winter all the advantageous overtures con-cerning it to Beal that it was possible to make. What return have I had from them ? My good intention has been despised, the sincerity of my actions has been neg-lected and calumniated, the state of my affairs has been traversed by delays, postponings, and other such like

artifices. And, in conclusion, a worse and more unworthy treatment from day to day, in spite of any thing
which I am obliged to do [to deserve the contrary, and
my very long, useless, and prejudicial patience, have
reduced me so low that mine enemies, in their habits of
using me ill, now think they have the right of prescrip-
tion for treating me, not as a prisoner, which in reason I
could not be, but as some slave, whose life and whose
death depends only upon their tyranny.

I cannot, madam, endure it any longer ; and I must
in dying discover the authors of my death, or living
attempt, under your protection, to find an end to the
cruelties, calumnies, and traitorous designs of my said
enemies, in order to establish me in some little more
repose for the remainder of my life. To take away the
occasions pretended for all differences between us, banish
from your mind, if you please, all that has been reported to you concerning my actions ; review the depositions of the foreigners taken in Ireland; let those
of the Jesuits last executed be submitted to you ; give
liberty to those who would undertake to accuse me
publicly, and permit me to enter upon my defence : if
any evil be found in me, let me suffer for it ; it shall be
patiently, when I know the occasion of it ; if any good,
allow me not to be worse treated for it, with your very
high commission before God and man.

The vilest criminals that are in your prisons, born
under your obedience, are admitted to their justification ; and their accusers and their accusations are always declared to them. Why, then, shall not the same
order have place towards me, a sovereign queen, your
nearest relation and lawful heir ? I think that this last
circumstance has hitherto been on the side of my enemies the principal cause of all their calumnies, to make
their unjust pretensions slide between the two, and keep

us in division. But, alas! they have now little reason
and less need to torment me more upon this account.
For I protest to you upon mine honour, that I look
this day for no kingdom but that of my God, whom I
see preparing me for the better conclusion of all my
afflictions and adversities.

This will be to you [a monition] to discharge your
conscience towards my child, as to what belongs to him
on this point after my death ; and, in the mean time,
not to let prevail to his prejudice the continual practices and secret conspiracies which our enemies in this
kingdom are making daily for the advancement of their
said pretensions ; labouring, on the other side, with our
traitorous subjects in Scotland, by all the means which
they can to hasten his ruin ; of which I desire no better
verification than the charges given to your last deputies
sent into Scotland, and what the said deputies have
seditiously practised there, as I believe, without your
knowledge, but with good and sufficient solicitation of
the earl my good neighbour at York.[1]

And on this point, madam, by what right can it be
maintained that I, the mother of my child, am totally
prohibited not only from assisting him in the so urgent
necessity in which he is, but also from having any intelligence of his state ?   Who can bring him more care-
fulness, duty, and sincerity, than I ?   To whom can
he be more near?   At the least, if, when sending to
him to provide for his preservation, (as the Earl of
Cheresbury [Shrewsbury] gave me lately to understand
that you did,) you had been pleased to take my advice
in the matter, you would have interposed with a better
face, as I think, and with more obligingness to me.
But consider what you leave me to think, when, forgetting so suddenly the offence you pretended to have

_____
[1] The Earl of Huntingdon, then lord president, at York.

taken against my son, at the time I was requesting you that we should send together to him, you have dispatched one to the place where he was a prisoner, not only without giving me advice of it, but debarring me at the very time from all liberty, that by no way whatever I might have any news of him.

And if the intention of those, who have procured on your part this so prompt visit to my son, had been for his preservation and the repose of the country, they needed not to have been so careful to conceal it from me, as a matter in which I should not have been willing to concur with you. By this means they have lost you the good-will which I should have had for you. And, to talk to you more plainly on the point, I pray you not to employ there any more such means or such persons. For, although, I hold the Lord de Kerri [Cary, Lord Hunsdon] too sensible of the rank from which he is sprung, to engage his honour in a villainous act, yet he has had for his assistant a sworn partisan of the Earl of Huntingdon's, by whose bad offices, an action as bad has nearly succeeded to a similar effect. I shall be contented, then, if you will only not permit my son to receive any injury from this country, (which is all that I have ever required of you before, even when an army was sent to the borders to prevent justice from being done to that detestable Morton,) nor any of your subjects to intermeddle any more, directly or indirectly, in the affairs of Scotland, unless with my knowledge, to whom all cognizance of these things belongs, or with the assistance of some one on the part of the most christian king my good brother, whom, as our principal ally, I desire to make privy to the whole of this cause, notwithstanding the little influence that he can have with the traitors who detain my son at present.

In the mean time, I declare with all frankness to you

that I hold this last conspiracy and innovation as pure treason against the life of my son, the good of his affairs, and that of the country ; and that, while he shall be in the state in which I understand he is, I shall consider no message, writing, or other act that comes from him, or is passed in his name, as proceeding from his free and voluntary disposition, but only from the said conspirators, who are making him serve as a mask for them, at the risk of his life.

But, madam, with all this freedom of speech, which I can foresee will in some sort displease you, though it is but the truth itself, you will think it still more strange, I am sure, that I importune you again with a request of much greater importance, and yet very easy for you to grant. This is, (that not having been able hitherto, by accommodating myself patiently for so long a time, to the rigorous treatment of this captivity, and, carrying myself sincerely in all things, yea, even in such as could concern you ever so little, in order to give some assurance of my entire affection for you, all my hope being taken away of being better treated for the very short period of life that remains to me,) I supplicate you, for the sake of the painful passion of our Saviour and Redeemer, Jesus Christ, again I supplicate you, to permit me to withdraw myself out of your realm, into some place of repose, to seek some comfort for my poor body, worn out as it is with continual sorrows, that, with liberty of conscience, I may prepare my soul for God, who is daily calling for it.

Believe, madam, (and the physicians whom you sent this last summer are able sufficiently to judge the same,) that I am not for a long continuance, so as to give you any foundation of jealousy or distrust of me. And, notwithstanding this, require of me whatever just and reasonable assurances and conditions you think fit. The

greatest power rests always on your side to make me
keep them ; though on no account whatsoever would
I wish to break them. You have had sufficient experience of my observance of my simple promises, and
sometimes to my prejudice ; as I showed you upon this
very point about two years ago. Recollect, if you
please, what I then wrote to you; and you will never
be able to bind my heart to you so much as by kindness, though you keep my poor body languishing for
ever between four walls ; those of my rank and nature
not suffering themselves to be gained or forced by any
rigour.   •

Your imprisonment, without any right or just ground,
has already destroyed my body, of which you will shortly
see the end, if it continues there a little longer ; and my
enemies will not have much time to glut their cruelty
on me: nothing is left of me but the soul, which all
your power cannot make captive   Give it, then, room
to aspire a little more freely after its salvation, which
is all that it now seeks, rather than any grandeur of
this world.   It seems to me that it cannot be any great
satisfaction, honour, and advantage to you for my
enemies to trample my life under foot, till they have
stifled me in your presence.   Whereas, if in this extremity, however late it be, you release me out of their
hands, you will bind me strongly to you, and bind all
those who belong to me, particularly my poor child,
whom you will, perhaps, make sure to yourself by it.

I will not cease to importune you with this request
till it is granted.   And on this account I beg you to
let me know your intention ; having, in order to comply
with you, delayed for two years till this time to renew
my application for it.   In the mean time, provide, if
you please, for the bettering of my treatment in this
country, that I may not suffer any longer, and commit

me not to the discretion of any other whatever, but only your own self, from whom alone (as I wrote to you lately) I wish for the future to derive all the good and the evil which I shall experience in your dominions. Do me this favour, to let me, or the ambassador of France for me, have your intention in writing. For, to confine me to what the Earl of Scherusbery [Shrewsbury] or others shall say or write about it on your behalf, I have too much experience to be able to put any assurance in it; the least point which they shall capriciously fancy being sufficient to make a total change from one day to another.

Besides this, the last time I wrote to those of your council, you gave me to understand that I ought not to address myself to them but to you alone ; therefore, to extend their authority and credit only to do me hurt could not be reasonable ; as has happened in this last limitation, in which, contrary to your intention, I have been treated with much indignity. This gives me every reason to suspect that some of my enemies in your said council may have procured it with a design to keep others of the said council from being made privy to my just complaints, lest the others should perhaps see their companions adhere to their wicked attempts upon my life, which, if they should have any knowledge of them, they would oppose, for the sake of your honour and of their duty towards you.

Two things I have principally to require at the close : the one, that, near as I am to leaving this world, I may have with me for my consolation some honest churchman, to remind me daily of the course which I have to finish, and to teach me how to complete it conformably with my religion, in which I am firmly resolved to live and die.

This is a last duty which cannot be denied to the

meanest and most abject person that lives: it is a
liberty which you grant to all the foreign ambassadors,
and which all Catholic kings give to your ambassadors
—the exercise of their religion. And even I myself
have not heretofore forced my own subjects to any
thing contrary to their religion, though I had all power
and authority over them. And that I should be
deprived in this extremity of such freedom, you cannot
in justice require. What advantage will accrue to
you, if you deny it me? I hope that God will forgive
me, if, oppressed by you in this manner, I render him
no other duty than what I shall be allowed to do in
my heart. But you will set a very bad example to the
other princes of Christendom, to act towards their
subjects with the same rigour that you will show to
me, a sovereign queen, and your nearest relation, which
I am, and shall be as long as I live, in spite of my
enemies.

I would not now trouble you concerning the increase
of my household; about which, for the short time I
have to live, I need not care much. I require then from
you only two bed-chamber-women to attend me during
my illness; attesting to you, before God, that they are
very necessary to me, now that I am a forlorn creature
among these simple people. Grant these to me for
God's sake, and show, in this instance, that my enemies
have not so much credit with you against me as to exercise their vengeance and cruelty in a point of so little
importance, and involving a mere office of humanity.

I will now come to that which the Earl of Scherusbery has charged me, if such a one as he can charge
me, which is this: that, contrary to my promise made
to Beal, and without your knowledge, I have been ne-
gotiating with my son, to yield to him my title to the
crown of Scotland, when I had obliged myself not to

proceed in it but with your advice, by one of my servants, who should be directed by one of yours in their
common journey thither.   These are, I believe, the very
words of the said earl.

I will tell you upon this, madam, that Beal never had
an absolute and unconditional promise from me, but,
indeed, conditional overtures, by which I cannot be
bound, in the state in which the business is, unless the
stipulations which I annexed to it are previously executed ; and so far is he from having satisfied me about
this, that, on the contrary, I have never had any answer from him, nor heard mention of it since, on his
part.   And on this point, I well remember, that the
Earl of Scherusbery, about Easter last, wishing to
draw from me a new confirmation of what I had spoken
to the said Beal, I replied to him very fully, that it was
only in case the said conditions should be granted and
consequently fulfilled towards me.   Both are living to
testify this, if they will tell the truth about it.   Then,
seeing that no answer was made to me, but, on the contrary, that by delays and neglects my enemies continued
more licentiously than ever their practices carried on
ever since the sojourn of the said Beal with me, in
order to thwart my just pretensions in Scotland, so that
the effects have been well witnessed there, by these
means a door was left open for the ruin of myself and
my son ; I took your silence for a refusal, and discharged
myself, by express letters, as well to you as to your
council, from all that I had treated upon with the said
Beal.

I made you fully privy to what monsieur the king,
and madame the queen, had written to me, with their
own hands, on this business, and I asked your advice
upon it, which is yet to come, and on which it was in
truth my intention to proceed if you had given it me

in time, and you had permitted me to send to my son, assisting me in the overtures which I had proposed to you, in order to establish between the two realms a good amity and perfect intelligence for the future. But to bind myself unconditionally to follow your advice before I knew what it would be, and, for the journey of our servants, to put mine under the direction of yours, even in my own country, I was never yet so simple as to think of it.

Now I refer to your consideration, if you knew of the false game which my enemies in this country have played in Scotland, to reduce things to the point at which they stand, which of us has proceeded with the greatest sincerity. God judge between them and me, and avert from this island the just punishment of their demerits!

Take no heed of the intelligence which my traitorous subjects in Scotland may have given you. You will find, and I will maintain it before all the princes of Christendom, that nothing whatever has passed there on my side to your prejudice, or against the welfare and tranquillity of this realm, which I affect not less than any councillor or subject that you have, being more interested in it than any of them.

There was a negociation for gratifying my son with the title and name of king,[1] and for ensuring as well the said title to him as impunity to the rebels for their past offences, and for replacing every thing in repose and tranquillity for the future, without innovation of any kind whatever. Was this taking away the crown from my son? My enemies, I believe, had no wish whatever that the crown should be secured to him, and are therefore glad that he should keep it by the unlawful

[1] It appears from a subsequent portion of the correspondence' that Mary carried this intention into effect.

violence of traitors, enemies from times of old to all our family. Was this then seeking for justice upon the past offences of the said traitors, which my clemency has always surpassed ?

But an evil conscience can never be assured, carrying its fear continually in its very great trouble within itself. Was it wishing to disturb the repose of the country to grant a mild pardon of every thing past, and to effect a general reconciliation between all our subjects? This is the point which our enemies in this country are afraid of, much as they pretend to desire it. What prejudice would be done to you by this? Mark then, and verify, if you please, by what other point. I will answer it, upon my honour.

Ah! will you, madam, suffer yourself to be so blind to the artifices of my enemies as to establish their unjust pretensions to this crown after you are gone, nay, perhaps, against yourself? Will you suffer them in your lifetime, and look on, while they are ruining and so cruelly destroying those so nearly connected with you both in heart and in blood? What advantage and honour can you hope for in allowing them to keep us, my son and me, so long separated, and him and me from you ?

Redeem the old pledges of your good-nature; bind your relations to yourself; let me have the satisfaction, before I die, of seeing all matters happily settled between us; that my soul, when released from this body, may not be constrained to make its lamentations to God for the wrongs which you have suffered to be done it here below; but rather that, being happily united to you, it may quit this captivity, to go to him, whom I pray to inspire you favourably upon my very just and more than reasonable complaints and grievances. At

Sheffield, this 8th of November, one thousand, five hundred, eighty-two.

> Your very disconsolate nearest kinswoman,
> and affectionate cousin,
>
> MARY R.

1582. *December* —. Henry III. sends Messieurs de la Mothe Fénélon and Menneville to Scotland, to assist the young king in regaining his liberty.

December 15. Elizabeth charges Davison to accompany M. de la Mothe Fénélon, and accredits him to James VI. to assist Bowes, her ambassador in Scotland, to counterbalance the influence of France

1583. *January* 17. The Duke of Anjou, baffled in his attempt to gain possession of the principal towns in Flanders, flies to France.

Monsieur de Mauvissière to King Henry III.

London, January 17, 1583.

Sire,—I have deferred, until the present, acknowledging the receipt of the despatch which it pleased your majesty to send me by Hervé; and as I have received all the instructions it pleased you to give me respecting my journey into Scotland, as well as the kind letters written by your own hand to the queen of Scotland and to the king her son, your little nephew, wherein you express your great sincerity towards them, and your wish to see them in unity and good understanding with each other; as also of interposing your authority to reconcile all dissensions which the time past, adversity, and circumstances have occasioned, and to bind yourselves all together by a good and firm friendship, and to prevent all ill-will that might hereafter arise; whereupon I applied for an audience of the said queen of England, and presented to her the letters of your said majesty, as well as those of the queen your mother, which she appeared to me to receive with much pleasure, begging me to assist her in reading them ; and returning you infinite thanks for your good-will towards her, and assuring me she would correspond with you.

After informing her of all which it pleased your majesty to command me regarding my journey into Scotland, and inquiring if it was her pleasure to depute some person on her part to accompany me, that we might both join together in performing all the good offices necessary, she told me she would consult with her council upon this, and on the steps most proper to be taken in this affair with the young prince, with whom she is not much pleased, but of whom, on the contrary, she feels great distrust, as I judge from her language and manner. Nevertheless, she told me to await an answer from him, by which she will govern herself to your contentment, for my said journey to the king of Scotland. She then went on to say, that he had driven away, banished, or removed all his nobility, to call about him some who would cause his ruin, if he did not take care. After this, she said that, at the present moment, he did nothing but by the advice of the queen his mother, of whom she made great complaints, although she had but just assured me that she would send to her incontinently those commissioners to nego-ciate the treaty for her liberty, and bring it to an honourable conclusion, saying that she would be for the mother, but, as for the son, she would give herself no concern about his affairs, unless he changed his counsels.

She then said to me that your letter was full of great offers of friendship, as well as that of the queen your mother, except that, towards the conclusion, it made mention of the queen of Scotland, whose name seems to give her great vexation, saying that if she had had to

do with any other, she should long since not have been
living ; that she had held conference in England with
her rebels, another at Rouen, another in Paris, another
in Rome, another in Spain, and had set on foot intrigues
against her throughout all Christendom ; that she held
prisoners some of her couriers and messengers who had
disclosed most of her secrets, which were in the end to
take away her kingdom and her life, if she could, but
rather by means of the king of Spain than by yours;
and that she hoped your majesty would deliver up to
her all her traitors and rebels within your kingdom,
especially Lord Paget and his brother, and Lord
Arundel, and some others of their accomplices, and
that your said majesty would command me not to intermeddle any further in the affairs of the said queen of
Scotland, and that in future I should not be so curious
and inquisitive in observing the manners and customs
of this kingdom, or have such close connexion with her
subjects, lords, and others, as I had, in which I had
been too exact, and in watching all that passed in England, of which she should complain to your majesty ;
and that, had it not been for the particular affection she
had always entertained for me, she would not have allowed so much to another, nor have the affairs of the
said queen of Scotland to be treated at such length ;
and that, if another ambassador ever came hither from
France, he should not have the same liberty that I have
had in all things.

Whereupon I replied, that I had not acted like her
and her ambassadors, who had too many dealings and
communications with your bad subjects ; and we had a
long dispute thereupon, wherein, sire, I did not forget
to remind her of all the favours which she had bestowed
in her kingdom upon those who fled thither from yours,
and the assistance they had received from her and her

subjects to keep up the troubles in France, and that she had not delivered them up to you, but, on the contrary, had made a point of bestowing on them places and pensions, and encouraged them in their disobedience; for instance, the Vidame[1] de Chartres, who, during the first troubles, sold Havre de Grace to her; afterwards, Cardinal de Chastillon, the Count de Montgomery, and many others; and that her ambassador Throcmorton had withdrawn himself from the court of the late king your brother, to repair to the late Prince de Condé, the Admiral, and those who were at war with him; begging her to consider this conduct of these ambassadors towards your crown, when she had found means to keep up troubles, which she ought to be sorry for, as well as for the ill done to France since the death of the late king your father, and during the minority of your majesty, who have always rendered good for evil, and to whom she ought to feel grateful: and the said queen gave me occasion to say all these truths to her, as I saw that it was fitting to do so.

Upon this, I reminded her, that, after the taking of Havre de Grace, I had the pleasure, according to the command of your majesties, to take charge of the two ambassadors, Smith and Throcmorton, who had in every respect violated the law of nations, and who had acted rather as enemies than as ambassadors; that I began to treat for peace with them, out of the great affection borne her by the queen, your mother; that I had afterwards gone to Windesors to carry her the news and the articles, to her great contentment; that since that time I had always used my best endeavours to maintain peace, as I had actually shown during the eight years that I have been your majesty's ambassador

---

[1] The judge of a bishop's temporal jurisdiction

at her court, and, by several other equally cogent reasons and examples, made her acknowledge that she could not too highly praise your majesty and myself, having shut my eyes on many occasions, for fear of rousing too strongly your majesty's suspicions concerning her conduct; and likewise spoke to her explicitly and candidly on all that the Sieur de Segur attempted to negotiate with her, saying, "I knew her intention, which was to fish in troubled water, to take the course which she might think most advantageous to herself; and that, as she was determined to be absolute sovereign over her subjects, so would you be without colleague over yours."

The said queen, seeing that I spoke to her in this manner, and that I was so well acquainted with her affairs, from the many examples that I had adduced, said "she thought she had good reason to be angry with me, but that I complained most; that she had trusted to me as a brother, at the time when the marriage was under discussion, but that at present I was pursuing a totally different course; and she thought that, if your majesty were ever inclined to deliver up to her Lord Paget, his brother Charles Arundel, and her other subjects, whom she calls rebels, I would prevent you from doing so." I told her "I would, because you would act very wrong in doing so, after they had sought refuge in your kingdom; and it was a thing that would too sensibly affect your greatness and reputation;" but she said "she was certain you would deliver them up to her." I told her that "I was sure she would not make so uncivil a request."

I afterwards observed to her, "that she had very little occasion to complain of your majesties in regard to the queen of Scotland, as you have never done any thing for her beyond bearing her good-will, as you were

7

obliged by every law, divine and human, she being so nearly related to you, and what is more, your sister-in-law, and having once been your queen, whom you could not abandon without great injustice, and without causing yourself to be looked upon as a prince having but little affection for your friends and allies; and as to her liberation after so long an imprisonment on the part of her nearest relative, it was a circumstance depending on the treaty and agreement which they might make together, and that she ought to wish and be very glad that your majesty should interfere as the friend of both; also, that one friendship ought never to prevent another."

The said queen, seeing that I spoke to her in this fashion and with such truth, and with arguments so strong that she could not contradict any of them, begged me "to drop all these subjects, and to talk of something more agreeable," but I was resolved to draw one conclusion, "that she was greatly indebted to you and to the queen your mother, for the kind manner in which you have usually acted towards her, and that she ought peremptorily to reject all the proposals made by the Sieur de Segur and others of your subjects, who address themselves to her, without being authorized by your majesty, " which she promised me to do, as well as to consider the course to be adopted regarding my journey to Scotland, where I will not forget what it has pleased your majesty so particularly to command me in the little paper in the handwriting of Monsieur Pinart, and to do both here and there every thing that can be of service to you either now or hereafter.

I have heard, sire, that the gentlemen of your finances have ordered me only five hundred crowns for such a journey, and without sending me any ready money. I meant to spend no more than fifteen hundred, which is as much as they allowed Monsieur de la Mothe last year. I keep several servants, some of them going and coming to bring me news for the service of your majesty, and others in this quarter, who think that I ought to recompense them handsomely for their zeal in the service of your majesty. There is Archubal Duglas, who has asked me to lend him a thousand crowns, and so do several more here whom I detached from the Spanish party, which is the same as asking your majesty for money, and on these occasions I have spared nothing for your service. The said Archubel,[1] who is a man of quality, and very useful, has refused a pension of two thousand crowns from the queen of England; he is so clever that I can refuse him nothing that is in my power. The said queen of England gives six thousand crowns a year to the Ambletons,[2] for whom of late I have done what I could. I know, sire, that it is not by the desire of your majesty that the gentlemen of your finances have not ordered me more for the said journey into Scotland, of which I make more account than of all the wealth of the said sieurs of your finances, to whom I might reply, by leave of your said majesty, to what they say about my having the ordinary allowance for this country, which would be twenty livres a day, if I were duly paid, and I had no additional expenses for my journey to Scotland. Last year there was left an arrear of twelve hundred crowns of the said allowance, postponed to the present. And if this were paid me I should not have half sufficient, considering the high price of money, provisions, and all other things in this country, where it is more than a hundred years since this allowance was instituted, when every thing was two-thirds cheaper, without counting the recompences which the kings, your predecessors, gave their ambassadors, none of whom has for these forty years incurred so many expenses, ordi-

---

[1] Archibald Douglas, who affected to be in the interests of Mary, Queen of Scots.
[2] Hamiltons.

nary and extraordinary, as myself, who have never lived
half the year on your said allowance; and to say that
it would be sufficient to go to Scotland, having here a
large house, many servants, wife and children, is very
unreasonable; for, to make such a journey of high importance for the honour and service of your majesty,
and to be honourably accompanied, and to live in a
becoming style, as he will do who will go on behalf of
the queen of England, and who will spare nothing—
this cannot be done for a trifle; but, whatever the said
gentlemen of your finances deem for your service, I
will be the first to conform to, and to every thing that
it shall please your royal bounty to command me, humbly
beseeching you, that at the beginning of this year you
will please to pardon me if I make such just remonstrances, and to cause me to be paid what is due to me,
that I may be enabled to discharge large debts which I
have contracted for your service, without ever being
master of one inch of ground, excepting Concressault,
which is worth seven or eight hundred livres by the
year, and which I hold for the sum of thirty thousand
livres upon bond of the late king, your brother, and of
your majesty, for money which I furnished by your
commands to remove the German troops from your
kingdom. And Monseigneur your brother purposes to
seize the said Concressault, to unite it to his domain of
Berry, for which reason I shall most humbly beseech
your majesty to repay me the said thirty thousand
livres, as nothing more than reasonable; and that done,
I can say that I have no other retreat in your kingdom
but an hostelrie; but I will console myself for every
thing, with having faithfully served your majesty and
your crown, as I will continue to do all my life, and to
employ it wherever it shall please you to command me,
always praying to God, sire, to grant your majesty per-

fect health, and a long and happy life.   From London,
this xviith January, 1583 (N.S.).

[This letter, though not signed, is by Mauvissière, as
it is easy to perceive from the corrections, additions,
and interlineations, which are in his own handwriting,
on the draft from which it was transcribed by Brequigny, from whose collection it is taken.]

1583. *January* 27.   The King of Scotland recovers his liberty,
and resumes the reins of government.

The Queen of Scots to Monsieur de Mauvissière.

Sheffield, July 15, 1583.

Monsieur de Mauvissière,—I think before this you will
have been fully informed of the deliverance of my son
from the hands of those traitors who held him in
durance ; I need not, therefore, tell you the particulars
that I have heard respecting it, and will only beg you to
interpose with the king, monsieur my good brother, in
my name, in order that he may be pleased, necessity
requiring it, to assist my son for his preservation and
for the support of the good party which is now about
him. If, however, this queen attempts to assist the
rebels in any way, employ, if you please, the name and
credit of the king, monsieur my good brother, to prevent her. You have formerly, on the like occasions,
made the same remonstrances, which may be of service
on this. I know not how far the treaty for my liberty
will succeed, having received no news or answer since
the departure of the commissioners; strive with Beale
to discover the intentions of the said queen, and her
opinion of the late alteration in Scotland, and which I
affect not to know of in my last of the 10th, which I
addressed to you through Walsingham, seeing that he
has not written any thing about it, and lest it should

be discovered, that I have any secret correspondence. Endeavour, I beg you, but as if of your own motion, and not upon any new solicitation which I have made, to ascertain the final resolution of the Queen of England respecting the articles of the said treaty already agreed upon by me with her deputies; observing to her, that she cannot do less than set me at liberty, if she accepts my overtures and conditions. I also wish you to tell me what the high treasurer and Walsingham said at the conferences you had with them on this treaty.

The enclosed is to be forwarded to my ambassador; and if you receive any trunks from him, order them to be sent to me, if possible, without being searched; not that they contain any thing of importance, being merely clothes for my own use, which at this time I do not wish to be much handled. Having nothing more to write to you, I conclude, praying God to have you, Monsieur de Mauvissière, in his holy keeping.

From Sheffield, this xiith day of July, 1583.

Since writing the above, I have received your last of the xxiiid of this month, according to the New Style. I am surprised that you have not given me any particulars relative to the deliverance of my son, which makes me think that those of this council keep it secret and concealed. Please to thank, in my name, Archubald Duglas, for his good offices with the Sr. de Valsingham,[1] and beg him to continue his intercourse with him, that he may draw from him all he can ; taking especial care not to let him know that he holds any secret communication with me; and, to cover it the better, let him try to write to me through the ordinary channel, to inform me of the kind offers of the said Valsingham in my behalf, and persuading me to continue in the good opinion which he knows me to have for him ; for indeed,

[1] Sir Francis Walsingham.

if I were but sure that the said Valsingham was dealing
uprightly, I should be very glad to make friendship
with him, without prejudice to his duty towards his
mistress, looking upon him to be a plain, downright
man, and whose disposition would easily agree with
mine, if he were acquainted with it otherwise than from
the reports of my enemies. Adieu. This xvth day of
July.

[This letter is taken from a copy which had probably
been communicated to Walsingham. See the note at
the bottom of a letter, addressed to M. de Mauvissière,
the 26th February, 1584. (Note by Brequigny.)

The following is the note in question.

N.B. This letter is taken from a copy which appears to have been made by some person who was betraying the Queen of Scotland, and, probably, communicating to Walsingham the letters of this princess
to Mauvissière. On the back of this copy is still to be
seen a seal, with the impression of a fleur-de-lis within
a lozenge, and several holes in the paper through which
passed the strings that closed the said copy.

I have remarked that all the copies of the letters of
Mary Queen of Scotland to Mauvissière which are in
this register are in the handwriting of the secretary of
Mauvissière, and the same register contains several
minutes, sewed together, in the handwriting of Mauvissière himself.]

1583 *July* 27. Mary Stuart goes for the last time to the baths
at Buxton.

September 1. Walsingham arrives, on the part of Elizabeth,
at the court of Holyrood, to support the English party, but is
received with great coolness.

The partisans of Mary Stuart in France, but especially Charles
Paget and Morgan, the manager of her dowry, propose a new plan
for her deliverance, according to which the Duc de Guise is to

land with an army in the south of England, and James VI. to enter with his troops in the north.

Lord Seaton[1] to the Queen of Scots.[2]

Sept. 16, 1583.

Madam,—The 15th of this month, at the departure of the ambassador Walsingham, your son certified to me that he is determined to send me to France, in all haste. I perceive that he is fully bent to pursue the league and amity of this kingdom [with France,] and to follow in all things the counsel of the Duc de Guise, and complete the treaty begun between you and him.

Meantime, if you will give proper directions for that, I deem your affairs will soon be brought well into port. The poverty of your son is so great, that he cannot put into execution the least part of his designs. Wherefore, I entreat you to hold the hand, for means and counsel, towards M. de Guise and others, that he may be succoured. I am myself constrained to undertake this journey at my own expense, which I cannot well sustain if your majesty aids me not; for the principal motive which makes me undertake it is the advancement of your service. At the same time, I entreat that your majesty will make me understand in what particular manner your majesty desires I should employ myself

[1] George, sixth Lord Seaton. See Queen Mary's opinion of this most faithful adherent, in her letter to the King of France from Carlisle. He was ambassador extraordinary to France from Scotland. (Sadler papers, vol. ii., p. 374.) MS. from the Imperial Library, St. Petersburgh

[2] This letter was intercepted by Elizabeth, and deciphered by the decipherer Philps (Sadler Papers, vol. ii. p. 374), from whose copy it is now translated. It never reached Queen Mary; but corroborates James's pathetic assertion respecting the deep poverty which prevented him from aiding his mother.

there. Walsingham has been very ill received and entertained here.

I pray you, madam, answer me and send me intelligence with all speed.

From Seton, 16th September 1583.

SETON.

M. de Mauvissière to King Henry III.

London, November, 1583.

Sire,—I have received the despatch which it pleased
your majesty to send me by Courcelles, and learn by it
that you have seen mine, which I have forwarded to him,
as well relative to the arrival of the S^r· de Segur at this
court, as to his sojourn and his doings, the journey
of the S^r· de Walsingham to Scotland, what he was
charged to treat of there, the change made about that
time by the young king, for which the English, who were
enemies of the queen his mother and of himself, have
redoubled their hatred towards her and her son; whilst,
on the contrary, the Catholics and others less prejudiced
are more favourably disposed towards them. The said
S^r· de Walsingham has returned greatly dissatisfied with
the said King of Scotland and those who are at present
of his council, and he said to me all was owing to the
intrigues of the queen his mother, who, though very
ailing, was well enough to see the utter ruin of her son,
if he does not take to a different course. Some of the
most violent here were of opinion that the queen would
have taken occasion of some extremity for war against
the said King of Scotland; but I observed, in the remonstrances which I made to her, that she ought not
to undertake any thing against this young prince for
striving to regain his liberty, or for following the counsel of those of his subjects in whom he most confides;

but she had just reason to fear his calling in foreigners
to his succour, which the said Queen of England has
well considered, and, by the advice of her high treasurer,
has resolved not to declare war against the King of
Scotland upon any slight pretext or trifling occasion,
but allow him to proceed his own way, and sow his
wild oats, but she should be on her guard against him,
and if the Scotch should make any more incursions on
the English border, seek to adjust matters by gentle
means and justice: yet, at the same time, she is trying
more than ever, by means of those Scotch who are dis-
contented at present—noblemen and others, assisted by
ministers, always greedy—to wrest a part from the
said Scotland, and sparing no money to form a new
party for the purpose of placing the King of Scotland
in other hands, and with another council, if possible,
than that which he has at present, and to restore the
authority to those whom he lately dismissed, because he
considered them as stanch partisans of the English and
the Hamiltons; a thing against which the King of Scotland must be carefully on his guard, and against any
change being speedily made in his situation; about
which I warned him, as well as about the intrigues
which the said Sr de Walsingham left him in the said
Scotland, for which he thanked me. He also told me
that, seeing the good offices which I am in the habit of
doing him, those which I have done to the Duke of
Lennox, and the confidence which the queen his mother
places in me in all things, he begged me to be in the
same disposion towards them, and to inform him of anything of importance to them that might come to my
knowledge, and that he would acquaint me more fully
with all his affairs through an ambassador, named James
Melvil, whom he is going to send hither.

For my part, sire, I think that the best advice which

can be given to him at present is to accommodate matters as speedily as possible with all his subjects, and to
remove the suspicions they at present entertain, otherwise the ill-will which the nation bears him, and which
is further excited by the English faction, may reduce
him to great extremity, like his predecessors, most of
whom have been killed or come to a tragical end, as
well as those who governed them, as the said Duke of
Lennox at last experienced ; the Queen of Scotland, his
mother, is still suffering for it ; the which princess, sire,
has written to me several secret letters, in the last of
which, among others, she earnestly entreats me to write
to your said majesty, and beseech you not to abandon
your old alliance in Scotland, nor the mother and the
son, who both bear you the warmest affection, but to
defend them against their enemies and wicked subjects,
who would, if they could, reduce the son to a worse
state than the mother, in order to ruin them both afterwards by plots, which the English have and always will
have in the said Scotland, as well as with their enemies,
or permit messieurs, her cousins, of the house of Guise,
to assist them as far as lies in their power, in order that
the said king, her son, may never seek other means,
favour, or support, than those of your said majesty and
of your kingdom.   The said Queen of Scotland also desires that, in case I should be again spoken to about her
liberty, and about sending back the commissioners, I
should turn a deaf ear and make no reply ; for, as they
have not promptly come to a conclusion with her, she
has no wish to repeat the requests which she has made
to you by her ambassador, and to permit her to dispose
of some part of her dower, seeing the necessity she is in
and the losses she has sustained during the wars in her
said dower, that she may have a sum of money to pay
her debts, and to oblige her this once, her and her son,

by which you will bind them for ever to your majesty
on all occasions that may occur. I informed her, in
reply to this, that in my opinion it would not be proper
for me to write this in my own name to your majesty,
and, therefore, I entreated her to excuse me. Nevertheless, I have not dared to omit to represent to you all
that passes, that your majesty may command me, if you
please, what answer I must give, if she should write to
me again on this subject; as I have not and never shall
have anything in my thoughts or in my view but your
will and faithful service.

And as the Sr. Archibal Duglas has spoken to me
several times to prevail upon me to interpose, in the
name and with the authority of your said majesty, to
adjust all matters between the King of Scotland and his
subjects, and to render you the mediator for settling
the differences which prevail among them, and prevent-
ing what might happen worse through the English ;
he told me again, yesterday, that he thinks your majesty would perform an act worthy of your greatness,
and that you would gratify both parties much by interposing as mediator. I am informed, sire, that, two
days ago, the Queen of England received intelligence
from France, that your said majesty will not interfere,
nor permit any of your subjects to go thither ; this gave
her great satisfaction, and she is better pleased with
your majesty than she was before.

Upon this, and the despatch which you were pleased
to send me, I considered it my duty to see her, as I
have done, and to assure her of the desire you have of
cultivating her friendship in all things, if, on her part,
she does the like, and acts sincerely, which was very
agreeable to her, and she received me with great favour
and honour, saying, she daily found your said majesty
more and more kindly and sincerely disposed towards

her. Whereupon I did not let slip the opportunity of observing, "that your said majesty was a magnanimous and generous sovereign, and sincere and faithful in the friendship you promised to your friends and servants; that she ought to consider that you never had desired or sought any thing but her happiness and repose, and to see her reign happily over her subjects, as she ought to wish that you might reign over yours, and not to think that you had other kings in France, or colleagues, who ought or could send ambassadors or messengers without your permission, or that it was right for her to receive them." Whereupon she changed colour, and, asking "Why I had said this," I told her "that I alluded to the Sr. de Segur and other subjects of yours, some of whom were now with her, and others on their way, to whom she could not do a greater kindness than by advising them never to seek any other favour or protection in the world than yours." This she took in good part, as also when I seriously represented to her, quoting past examples, "that all her negociations with your subjects, princes, nobles, Huguenots, and others, without your majesties, had brought her nothing but a bad character and injury, and that she was in danger that God would retaliate upon her the evil she had done to another." She took this well of me, and gave me good words, wishing to remove the idea of her having treated with the said Sr. de Segur, against your said majesties, saying, "that he was more frequently at my house, he and his friends, and with me, than with her, or in any other place with any of her subjects." I replied "that this was in order to give greater colour to those practices, which I should soon discover;" and so I will, with the help of God, and all that he purposes doing on his journey, and will send all the secret intelligence that he has transmitted in writing to your kingdom; for I

have persons about him who never sleep ; and, in the
end, it will be found that they are on the point of concluding the league, concerning which I have written to
her, and will build it with great art and diligence, if
they can.   But, as for the negociation of your subjects,
princes, or others, here, I hope to frustrate their designs, as I did in time past similar factions of the Duc
de Casmir and Monsieur the Prince de Condé.

It is necessary, along with fair words of friendship
to this princess, to excite her fears and to represent to
her the greatness of your said majesty, and the means
you have of resenting any injuries and ill offices done
to you ; and I do not doubt, unless some great change
takes place, that I shall be able to keep this princess
and this kingdom in the utmost fear of offending you ;
and at least, if they do you not much good, that they
will not dare to do you harm ; for I know of means
of making them feel, and in their own country, through
their own subjects, whenever your said majesty may
please to command me, for they are well aware that I
am acquainted with the circumstances and disposition
of each, for I have spared nothing to entertain them.
And, in this place, I will again most humbly pray your
majesty to have pity on me, and cause the xxi^{m} [21,000]
livres which you have by your kind order assigned me,
to be paid me this year, that I may pay my debts ; and
that, through your royal generosity and bounty, I may
receive this particular favour without being under obligation to any body.   This, sire, will be greatly to your
service and honour ; because, in paying my debts, I
shall gain servants for you, and hold your enemies in
check, as well as be enabled to recompense those who
are of use to you here, and who give me the good information for which I spare nothing ; and I know not
how God has given me the means of subsisting so long,

without having had any benefit or recompense from
your majesty, who is so beneficent and liberal to all.
But I shall await your pleasure, and in the mean time,
very humbly beseech you to pardon me, if I take the
liberty of requesting so often that I may be paid at
least what is owing to me. It is a very singular circumstance that the Spanish ambassador, who has not
seen the Queen of England for these three years, and
never stirs from his house, who has no expenses, sees
no company, and has placed the affairs of his master in
this kingdom in a very bad position, should, nevertheless, receive from his master such numerous benefits,
having had two commanderies and other valuable re-
compenses given him, besides having all that he wants
for his ordinary pay, which is advanced to him every
quarter. But I will value more highly the favour of
your majesty, to whom I will always render most
humble and faithful service, than all the wealth of the
Indies.

We have news here that Signor Don Antonio[1] will
have come to an agreement with the said King of Spain,
on which subject there are different opinions. As for
the Sr. de Segur, he has gone to Flanders ; he will
thence proceed to Germany, to continue the journey
which I have mentioned to your said majesty, to the
princes whom he believes to be well disposed towards
his master, and to form as extensive a league as he can
with them for the preservation of the Protestants. But
I will send you a copy of it soon, God willing. The
said Sr. de Segur dined and supped at my house the
day before his departure, and made me a thousand fine
protestations that he would not do any thing contrary
to the interests of your said Majesty ; and likewise told
me, that he had had divers accounts that the King of

[1] The claimant of the crown of Portugal.

Navarre, his master, as well as all those of his religion, had more confidence in you than in any other person in your kingdom ; and that, if any ill befel them, they should be certain that it did not proceed so much from any ill-will on your part as from their own ill luck and other enemies, which they were resolved to remedy if they could, and he to seek what friends the King of Navarre could reckon upon, in case he needed them." I said the same to him that I had done to the said Queen of England ; namely, "that he did not want a better than your said Majesty." The Queen of England has furnished him with a good ship, to convey him over with his money ; but he found the wind very high and contrary, so that he was obliged to put into Dover. I shall be sure to hear of his proceedings, as I presume that your servants in Germany will give you information, particularly M. de Dansay, who is in Denmark, where the said Sr. de Segur is to treat upon several affairs, pecuniary and others, and of their protestant league.[1]

I have often said and written to your majesty, that it was in this kingdom that the first levies and capitulations of hired troops took place, when your subjects of the reformed religion determined to make war against you; but, since I have been resident here, I have prevented this, which I will always do, with God's aid, by my best and most zealous services. Praying God, sire, to give your Majesty perfect health and a long and happy life. From London, this . . . . [2] November, 1583.

P. S. If your majesty sends the mules and carriages which I have been promised, and which have been so long expected, they will not be badly employed.

[1] This Protestant league, of which the King of Denmark was a member, has been mentioned in the note to Bothwell's Death-bed Confession, vol. i.

[2] The date is blank in the manuscript.

[This letter is copied from a minute, the whole of which is in the handwriting of the secretary of Castelnau. It is full of erasures, corrections, and interlineations, by the hand of Mauvissière himself.]

The King of Scots to the Queen his Mother.[1]

Stirling, November 8, (supposed date,) 1583.
(Written in his seventeenth year.)

Madam,—I am startled at receiving no answer from you, touching the articles that I sent you so long ago by our cousin of Lenox. At times, I consider it proceeds from the troubles which have since prevailed in this country, of which I have, nevertheless, fully informed you, taking the opportunity by this ambassador, whom I sent to France to the king and our cousin of Guise. At all events, fail not, with as much diligence as possible, to send me your opinion on the said articles.

Be assured, that in all the adversities which I have sustained for love of you, I have never failed of, or been turned from, my duty and affection towards you; but, on the contrary, it greatly increases and augments with every trouble that I have: at any rate I would make appear to you that I know my duty to you, as much as any son in the world towards his mother.

Meanwhile, I pray you, without delay let me hear your opinion of the said articles, and at the same time employ me in aught I can do for your pleasure or service. At least, let me show you my goodwill; and if it pleases God to second our affairs and intentions, He will add also success. I pray send to our cousin of Guise, that he will use all his power with our ambas-

---

[1] Translated from the Sadler Papers, vol. ii , p. 374.

sador in our affairs. From Stirling, this 8th of November.

From your son,

JAMES.[1]

1583. *November* 24. Arden, a gentleman of Warwickshire, Sommerville, his son-in-law, with their wives and sisters, are tried, with Hall, a Catholic priest, for a pretended conspiracy against Elizabeth's life

December 20 Arden is executed in London. Sommerville, who was originally deranged, destroys himself before execution.

M. de Mauvissière to King Henry III.

London, December 19, 1583.

Sire,— Since the last despatch which I sent to your majesty, I have received that which it pleased you to address to me on the 25th ultimo, commanding me to transmit to you the negociations of the Sr. de Segur in this country, and what he has written over concerning it, and the answer which he has received, on which points I have completely satisfied you, through Hervé. Since then, I have several times seen the Queen of England, your good sister, whom I accompanied, with a party from this city, to a house of hers, called Hampton Court, where she stayed two days, and then returned to this city; the said lady having expressed great pleasure that I had seen her so privately; and I took suitable

---

[1] The unfortunate Mary never had the satisfaction of receiving this affectionate letter from her son; it was, with many more, intercepted and deciphered by the spies of Elizabeth, and remained shut up among her state papers. The letters James VI. wrote were nearly all thus intercepted, and only served to furnish information to those whose interest it was to sow dissension between the mother and son. This was thoroughly effected the succeeding year, as we shall soon plainly show by Queen Mary's agonizing letters regarding what she considered the unnatural conduct of James.

occasions (as I had done before) to tell her "that your majesty was not so ill informed, as not to be thoroughly acquainted with all the proposals made to her by the said Sieur de Segur, and what were the intentions of the King of Navarre and those of his religion, to seek to form leagues, as well with her as with the other Protestants, upon pretext of religion, tending some day, if they were the stronger, to overthrow the Catholic religion and the political state of your kingdom ; but that your majesty, having put good right on your side, would always take measures that such practices of your subjects and their adherents should turn to their own great confusion and injury." And I said to the queen, "that your majesty would not believe, nor I either, that she would ever meddle in so bad a cause as to take part with subjects against their king, but more especially in respect to you, who had always been, and would be, if she gave you occasion, the best brother, neighbour, and friend she could wish for," which is the same thing that I had said to her before ; and " that she ought to take care lest God should retaliate on her the evil she should bring upon her neighbours." Whereupon she gave me a very mild answer, saying, "God forbid that she should undertake any thing against you or your kingdom, which could offend you." So that she not only promised me not to do any thing of the kind that could displease you, but begs me "not to give you any alarm, especially since I assure her, from day to day, of your friendship, of which she confesses " that she had a striking proof, when you would not permit forces to go from your kingdom to Scotland, strongly as you were solicited to do so, and which she promises to repay."

And in regard, sire, to the schemes of the said Sieur de Segur here, I hope to make them pass off in smoke ; besides, the said Queen of England and her council have

at present business enough at home, without meddling
in the affairs of others; the said queen having confessed
and declared to me, quite in detail, "that she has discovered, and was discovering every day, great conspiracies
against her; and that there were more than two hundred men of all ages who had conspired, at the instigation of the Jesuits and those of the seminary of Rheims,
where there are several Englishmen, to kill her; that
the execution was to have taken place either last month
or this; and that several of the conspirators were in
this city, and sometimes at her court, and others dis-
persed in different parts of her kingdom; which circumstances were miraculously coming to light every day,
by the grace of God, to whom she was ready to yield
up her soul whenever it might please Him to call her
by any death whatever; and she returned Him infinite
thanks for having permitted her to reign thus far so
happily, to the great quiet of her subjects, who had
always appeared perfectly contented until now." She
then said, "that it had been reported in Spain that she
was dead, and people had told this to several English
merchants, who were in that country on business, or
that she would die soon, at the same time expressing
great joy, which she thought to have originated with
her Jesuit subjects who have retired to the said Spain;"
and the said lady went on to talk to me, at great
length, very privately of such occurrences, and of the
conspiracies against her, which had entered into the
hearts of some of her Catholic subjects

Just at this moment, many people, in large companies,
met her by the way, and kneeling on the ground, with
divers sorts of prayers, wished her a thousand blessings,
and that the evil-disposed who meant to harm her might
be discovered and punished as they deserved. She fie-
quently stopped to thank them for the affection they

manifested for her; being, she and I alone, amidst her
retinue, mounted on goodly horses, she observed to me,
that she saw clearly that she was not disliked by all.   I
then said " that, in general, and on particular occasion,
your majesty would take her part against all her enemies;" at the same time paying her all the compliments
calculated to keep up your friendship, not forgetting, as
it was fitting, to remind her, " that it is not right to furnish subjects with the means of attacking their sovereigns, who ought to be held sacred;" and that, " as your
majesty reprobated such wickedness on your part, she
ought to do the same on hers, and not henceforth give
audience to subjects of yours, who may address themselves to her with the intention of disturbing your kingdom."

She then touched upon the language of several of
her subjects, who had withdrawn to France, Rome,
and Spain, where they had hatched all their conspiracies
against her; therefore it was not without occasion that
she had so often besought your majesty to expel them
from your kingdom. I did not fail to remind her " that
she had been the first to sin on this point, not only by
harbouring Frenchmen in England, but by giving them
a church, with full liberty to write, compose, treat and
manage affairs of state, prejudicial to yours; to fit out
ships; as Montgomery and several others had found aid
and assistance here for making war upon you, which
had turned to their confusion; as all that she might do
at the solicitation of the Sieur de Segur and others of
your subjects would also do."

Thus, sire, in going to and returning from the said
Hampton Court, did we advert to many things for your
service, which I discussed more familiarly than in an
audience.   I also slightly touched upon my journey into
Scotland by the authority and command of your ma-

jesty, and she acknowledged that this would be sufficient to place the affairs of that kingdom in a better
state, and to unite you both for that purpose, and to
keep that young prince[1] in safety, and in peace with his
subjects. I likewise spoke to her of the Queen of Scotland, and repeated the substance of the letter which she
wrote to me, and which I sent to you; this she took in
very good part, promising me to return an answer as
soon as she had seen an ambassador, whom the King
of Scotland is to send to her. The Bishop of St. André,
Primate of the said Scotland, arrived here four days
ago, on his way to France, whither he pretends to be
going for the benefit of his health, as well for the use of
baths at the moment as to consult some eminent physicians for the future. And he was directed by the King
of Scotland to wait in passing upon the Queen of England, to assure her of his good-will, and to sound her
as to her sentiments towards him.

The said bishop informed me, that he was charged
to call to see me on behalf of the King of Scotland, to
speak to me on several subjects, as having confidence in
me, and begged me to excuse him for not coming
sooner, on account of the great suspicion he perceived
in the English, who narrowly watched every motion of
himself and his people. I have been told "that the said
bishop was a friend of the late Duke of Lenox, and that
he was charged by the Earl of Arran, about whom I
lately wrote to you, to assure the said Queen of England and her council that, if she wished it, he, the said
Earl of Arran, would render the King of Scotland
entirely devoted to her in any way she wishes, and so
as to do only just what she pleases:" but I know not
if she can place any confidence in this. It is thought
that he is going to France, to negociate some affair,
under the pretext of recovering his health; but the

[1] James VI.

queen told him "that it was very possible to do that here, and that there are very excellent baths in England." She manifested great jealousy because Lord Seaton was ambassador in your kingdom.

The son of the said Duke of Lenox has arrived in Scotland, and is so much beloved by the young king that he cannot live without him, caressing him with great affection from morning till night. The queen of England assured me of the same thing, saying " that she wished to gratify the Queen of Scotland ;" and that, " in regard to her son, she would behave towards him as he should to her." Nevertheless, the said Queen of Eng-land is treating very secretly and assiduously for his marriage with the daughter of the King of Sweden, in order to attach him on that side, and to prevent him from having favour and succour through any other alliance, as she fears he will turn Catholic, in order to marry the daughter of the King of Spain. And I have been assured that the said queen has offered to the King of Sweden to pay the whole expense of his daughter's marriage. On this subject I shall learn more, that I may inform your majesty.

Meanwhile, I must not omit to tell you that a great many persons are committed to prison on account of this conspiracy ; and that Lord Paget, Charles Arundel, and several more noblemen and principal gentlemen of quality in this kingdom, fled four or five days ago, and embarked by night on board a vessel at Arundel, which still more astonished the queen and those of her council. I have written to the Queen of Scotland what your majesty was pleased to command me, touching the succours that she might require of you, she and her son, to inquire if they needed any, either soldiers, *or other munitions.*[1]   I shall be very sorry to intermeddle

---

[1] These words are underlined in the minute.

if things should not turn to your majesty's honour and service. The despatch which will be necessary in this case, would be a power and plenty of blank papers, signed by your said majesty, to be filled up whenever the said King of Scotland might have occasion; such as were formerly given to me by the late king, your brother, when I made a like agreement with the Queen of Scotland and her subjects, at the time when all her bastard brothers were against her, and when she solicited assistance from France to make war upon them, and upon England, which took part with them; but I put a stop to this by the said agreement and reconciliation between them. It would also be necessary that your majesty should write a very civil letter, with your own hand, to the said Queen of England, to assure her that your majesty is impelled solely by a friendly and laudable desire to see things in a good state among them; and if you interfere as a third party, it is as the best and most faithful friend they can have. It would be advisable to write the same to the Queen of Scotland and her son.

And, in regard to the expence, sire, to which I shall be put by my journey, I hope that your majesty will provide for it as befits your honour and service, that I may go honourably, as those do who go on the part of the said Queen of England, and who display there the grandeur of their mistress; which I will leave to the consideration of your majesty, as well what is necessary for my journey, as how much shall be paid to me of what is due to me, and not to that of the gentlemen of your finances, who (what faithful services soever I have done you, or what ordinary or extraordinary expences soever I may from necessity have incurred) have never yet found that there was any money for me. So I suppose that they judge my intention and duty to be what they really are, to value your faithful service above all the riches in the world.

I must not forget to inform your majesty, that there are at present two principal persons in Scotland who govern there ; namely, Colonel Stuart, who has pushed his fortune so successfully during the last six months since he has been ambassador there, that he has become rich, with the certainty of being created Earl of Boucan [Buchan.] There is another also, of the name of Stuart, called Earl of Arran,[1] made such by the Duke of Lenox, who has quarrelled with every one with whom he has had any dealings, as he did with the said Duke Lenox, and afterwards with the Queen of England; he took her money and laughed at her ; and did not keep his promise to the noblemen of the country, with whom he agreed to return with the said Duke of Lenox; and he has always been very fickle, and only keeps on good terms with those whom he supposes to possess most power and favour. It is necessary, sire, to hold out fair hopes and promises on the part of your majesty to these two ; for I understand that the Queen of England is endeavouring to gain them over, whatever it may cost her. And the said Earl of Arran gives her hopes that he will do what she pleases, and place the King of Scotland entirely at her disposal ; but she dare not trust him.

There is another thing which would be of great importance, which is to obtain some appointment for the Sieurs Hamilton, if possible. Your majesty would have the honour of re-establishing them by the same means; but, as the said Earl of Arran holds their earldom, and as he would rather see all Scotland ruined, than

[1] The character of this most profligate man is delineated in a subsequent letter to the queen of the Scots, by a friend at her son's court,, who seems to have known him well.

give it up without being recompensed with the like dignity, it would be necessary to find means to obtain for him another earldom, to induce him to relinquish that of the said Hamiltons, that they might owe this obligation to you; and, in case the said King of Scotland and the said queen his mother should die without heirs, the said Hamiltons would always be at your disposal and service, for which they have very often expressed a desire and anxiety to me, and that your majesty would take them under your protection, rather than the queen of England, who allows them a very handsome maintenance. It is but a few days since she gave three thousand crowns to him who was in France, and she gave him two thousand when he arrived. Here I shall pray to God, sire, to give your majesty perfect health and a long and very happy life. From London, the xix December, 1583.]

[This paper is copied from a minute full of erasures and interlineations, most of them in Mauvissière's handwriting.]

Henry III. to the Queen of Scots.

St. Germain en Laye, Dec. 20, 1583.

Madam my sister,—It is unnecessary to represent to you the vexation and displeasure which I have received, and still suffer, from your long detention and captivity. The friendship, affinity, and close alliance between us must give you sufficient testimony and assurance of this, and enable you to conceive what are my feelings; but my chief care and anxiety is to bring about and facilitate by my good and fraternal offices your deliverance and liberty. I have also a particular desire to see my nephew, the King of Scotland, your son, reign happily and peaceably, as I know you to be guided by the like affection, and that he should be respected,* served, and obeyed by the lords and subjects of your kingdom, as it is their natural and bounden duty.

For these considerations and purposes, I have ordered the Sieur de Mauvissière, my councillor and ambassador in England, agreeably to what I have seen in the letter which you wrote to him, that you wish him to interfere and to make use of my name, as well with the Queen of England as with my nephew, your son, and the said lords of your kingdom, to proceed thither; being certain that I could not have made choice of a better person than the said Sieur Mauvissière, not only because he is zealous in the matter, but because he will be more agreeable and better liked than any other for the management and negociation of the said affairs.

I am sure also that he will acquit himself faithfully and worthily, according to my intention and yours; and, in order that he may be more particularly acquainted with the latter, I have written to him to call to see you in my name on his way, and to deliver to you this letter with my most affectionate and cordial recommendations to your good graces, by the permission of the Queen of England, madam my good sister and cousin, who, in my opinion, cannot but approve the office that I am undertaking in this case, which is praiseworthy in itself, and must be well pleasing to God, whom I pray to have you, madam my sister, in his holy and worthy keeping. Written at St. Germain en Laye, the xxth day of December, 1583.

[This letter is transcribed from a copy, which appears to be in the handwriting of Mauvissière's secretary. It is endorsed, " Copy of the letter of the King to the Queen of Scotland."]

1583. *December.* Walsingham, having received information of the projects of Morgan and Paget, apprehends Francis and George Throgmorton, and summons the Earls of Northumberland and Arundel before the Council.

1584. *January* 1. The latter succeed in exonerating themselves, but Francis Throgmorton, on being put to the torture, confesses that the Duc de Guise and Mendoça, the Spanish ambassador in London, had communicated to him the plan of an invasion.

The Queen of Scots to her godchild the daughter of the Sieur de Mauvissière, Ambassador from the King of France.[1]

Date unknown, but after 1574.

My child and *mignonne,*—I am glad to perceive in your letters, proofs of the perfections with which God has endowed you in your early youth. Seek, mignonne, to know and serve Him who has given you such grace, and He will multiply blessings upon you. I earnestly implore that He will do so, and grant you His benediction. I send you a little token from a poor prisoner, to remind you of your godmother; it is but a trifle, but I send it you as a pledge of my affection for you and for your family. It was given me by the late king (Henry II.) my kind and revered father-in-law, while I was but young, and I have kept it to the present hour. Think of me kindly, and look upon me as a second mother, for so I would wish to be.

Your very affectionate,

MARY.

Sheffield, January 26.

[1] The original of this letter is to be seen in French in the Memoirs of M. de Castelnau, who is the same person as Mauvissière. Mary sends a message to this young lady, her god-daughter, March 9, 1585; it appears she was then in London with her father and mother.

The Queen of Scots to M. de Mauvissière.[1]

February 26, 1584.

I have been unable to reply to your letters in the usual manner, because I am informed that your house is surrounded day and night with spies, who watch every one that enters or comes out, and that all the agents of my correspondence with you have been discovered. Some suspect that your servants are bribed, and that is my own supposition ; therefore, I earnestly implore that you permit none but your most trusty servants to communicate with the persons whom I may send to you. Do not let them communicate with those in your dwelling, but meet in the city, as if by accident. You can easily appoint time and place, and keep it secret from every other person, or I shall not be able to find any agent who will dare to undertake our matters.

I have twice informed you minutely of the scandalous reports, which have been circulated of my intimacy with the Earl of Shrewsbury ; these have originated with no one but his good lady herself. If the Queen of England does not cause this calumny to be cleared up, I shall be obliged openly to attack [*probably meaning prosecute*] the Countess of Shrewsbury herself. I have been restrained by two reasons from making use of the advantages I have over her, [the countess,] whenever I choose to make known to the Queen of England and her councillors how she has behaved to me, and in respect to me, regarding the Earl of Leicester and other noblemen in this kingdom.

Firstly, I will preserve my reputation for good faith and firmness in the opinion of all my partizans, showing that I do not readily accuse them, even when they turn

---

[1] MS. Harl. No. 1582. This letter very evidently fell into Burleigh's possession.

against me, and do not act against them, excepting in the last extremity.[1]

Secondly. If I accuse that wretched woman of the various arrogant speeches and intrigues against the queen, [Elizabeth,] myself, and some of the nobility of this realm, I apprehend that her husband might be injured. besides, I might be strangely reflected on for listening to such particulars. Altogether, I am afraid lest those who disclosed them to me, if not called to account, may remain objects of suspicion. Yet whatever may befal, there is nothing that I would not venture to clear my honour, which, to say nothing of my exalted station, is more precious to me than a thousand lives.

Most earnestly I entreat you to pursue diligently all means to extirpate this infamous calumny, that I may obtain full satisfaction by public notice throughout the whole kingdom, (which you are especially to insist on,) or by the exemplary punishment of the authors of the scandal. Should you be called on to name these, answer" Charles and William Cavendish,[2] incited thereto by the Countess of Shrewsbury;" or require at least, that they may be examined on this matter.

One of the [privy] council, I know, in the presence of four or five persons of distinction, acknowledged that

[1] The MS. is here illegible, but this seems her meaning. This letter and the succeeding one appears to have given rise to the fabrication of the extraordinary one full of accusations against the Countess of Shrewsbury, printed in the Murdin Papers. No person who was as considerate as Mary appears in this letter would have written the other

[2] The sons of the Countess of Shrewsbury by a former husband, brothers of her daughter, Lady Elizabeth, wife of Lord Charles Lenox, and uncles to his little daughter, Lady Arabella Stuart, whose interest, as heiress of the crown, they were upholding against the title of the Queen of Scots.

they[1] all believed the story to be false, but that its propa-
gation was serviceable to prevent my marriage with the
King of Spain, which God knows, neither I, nor probably that king, ever thought of.

All this confusion originates with Leicester and Walsingham, who (as I have been informed for a certainty)
sent the Countess of Shrewsbury a copy of some lost
letters which I had written to you.

It may not be unadvisable to complain to the queen,
[Elizabeth,] as if you had learned these matters elsewhere, that the Countess of Shrewsbury is the enemy
who has raised these false and scandalous tales, and that
she is secretly instructed, advised, and supported by
men, who, were it only for the honour of the queen
herself, as my near relative, ought to uphold mine no
less than that of her own. For I cannot govern my
affairs myself in a state of restraint, as if I had the
liberty of speaking and acting.

You can likewise observe to the Earl of Leicester, as
if the thought originated with yourself, and as your own
advice, that if he is not more cautious, all this confusion
will be ascribed to him, for all concerned in it are his
domestics, or dependents, among whom, you may safely
say, " that you have heard that one named Laiselles,
[Lascelles,] and another named Topliffe, [probably Top-
cliffe,] have entered into a very close understanding with
the Countess of Shrewsbury and her children."[2]   If he
[Leicester] would have me conceive a good opinion of
him, and of the renewal of his promises, which you
mention in your last letter, he must confirm such by his
deeds, and remove every appearance to the contrary,

---

[1] Meaning probably, by *they*, the privy council.
[2] Evidently the Cavendishes, whose interest was connected with
the rights of Lady Arabella (their niece) to the English crown, as
the next in blood to Mary and James VI.

which arises from the conduct of his dependents and servitors. Now, were it practicable, I should not be sorry if you said to him plainly, " that he seemed rather to wish to be considered the chief of my enemies ;" and so, by his conduct, he was generally taken to be, not only by my son, [King James,] and my relations and friends in Christendom, but by my adherents in this realm, from whose minds I have endeavoured to remove, as far as in me lies, their suspicious and bad opinion of him.

The Earl of Shrewsbury, I understand, is more than ever resolved to visit the court, in order to inquire into the accusations of his enemies ; I doubt not he will prove his innocence, to their confusion and his own honour.

Should, however, anything be said of removing me from this place, you are decidedly to oppose it, partly for the security of my life, which the king, my good brother,[1] cannot hold to be secure in any other hands; and partly because, after the scandalous report spread concerning me and the earl, a removal from hence would tend to my dishonour.

You may safely intrust your letter to the bearer of this. Write to me as often as possible, how affairs go on. With respect to M. de la Tour, the Earl of Northumberland and Lord Henry Howard,[2] I hope God will pre-

---

[1] Henry III., of France, that is, Mary prompts his ambassador to say, as if from Henry III., that he only considers her life secure in the guardianship of the Earl of Shrewsbury.

[2] Camden offers a valuable illustration on Mary's letter, though he knew not of its existence : see his Life of Elizabeth, p. 497.— White Kennet's edition.

" Counterfeit letters were now sent privately in the name of the Queen of Scots, and left at the Papists' houses, and then spies were sent up and down the country to take notice of their discourse and lay hold of their words. Hereupon many were brought into suspicion, and among the rest Henry, Earl of Northumberland

serve them, by demonstrating their innocence. If you can come directly, or indirectly, at Throckmorton,[1] or Howard, (for with the third I have no sort of connexion,) assure them, in my name, that their affection, and the great suffering which they endure on my account, shall never be effaced from my heart, and that I take no less interest in them than one of their relatives could, and I

Philip, Earl of Arundel, the eldest son of the Duke of Norfolk, was confined to his own house, and his wife committed prisoner to Sir Thomas Shirley's house. Lord William Howard, (the celebrated Belted Will,) Lord Henry Howard, (one the youngest son, the other brother to the beheaded Duke of Norfolk,) were several times examined relative to letters from the Queen of Scots, and from Lord Charles Paget" The Earl of Northumberland, who was fierce and untameable, shot himself through the heart with a loaded pistol, brought him to his prison in the Tower in a meat-pie. This suicide was to prevent his attainder and preserve his estate to his descendants, who now enjoy it. Before he did this act he was heard to exclaim, bestowing, at the same time, a canine appellation on Queen Elizabeth, which we will not repeat, "That she should not have his estate!"

He succeeded to his title and property on the execution of his brother Thomas, Earl of Northumberland, against whom he took so decided a part in the rebellion in the north, raised in 1569, for the restoration of the Roman Catholic religion and the liberation of Mary Queen of Scots, that Earl Thomas, an ignorant but sincere man, said before he laid his head on the block, "Simple Thom must be headed to make way for cruel Henry."—See Sir Cuthbert Sharpe's valuable History of the Northern Rebellion.

Yet here we see the same Henry following the steps of the victim, and dying violently in the same cause, but by his own desperate hand. Queen Elizabeth and her ministers had the credit of murdering Earl Henry in the Tower, which was just what he intended. His example was avowedly followed by the Earl of Essex in the time of Charles II As to Lord Arundel, his imprisonment only ended with his life, but Belted Will, his brother, and Lord Henry Howard, escaped with better fortune.

[1] See Chronological Summary, January 1st, 1584, vol. ii. p. 85.

pray to God that He will enable me one day worthily to
reward them.

Sheffield, 26th of February, 1584.

P.S.—I earnestly entreat you to keep all this a pro-
found secret, in order that the ambassador[1] may not
perceive anything of it, for I would not for all the trea-
sures in the world that it should be discovered, on
account of the disgrace it would bring on me. Yea,
and not merely the disgrace, but my life depends on it,
which, however, I care not for equal to the disgrace,
since I must die at all events.

[The scandal to which Queen Mary refers in this
letter is best explained by the following notice,[2] in a
letter of Serjeant Fleetwood, by which it appears that
the punishment she so earnestly demanded might be
wreaked on her slanderers fell upon an obscure knot of
suburban gossips at Islington, persons far enough removed from the elevated circles in which the report was
concocted. "At this sessions, Michaelmas, 1584, one
Cople and one Baldwin, my Lord of Shrewsbury's
agents, required of me that they might be suffered to
indict one Walmesley, an innkeeper at Islington, for
scandilation of my Lord of Shrewsbury their master."

The effect of it all was, that the innkeeper Walmesley
had told his guests openly at table, "that the Earl of
Shrewsbury had had a child by the Scottish queen, and
that he knew where this child was christened; further
adding, that Lord Shrewsbury would never be permitted

[1] It is difficult to discover who the ambassador is whose knowledge she dreads; she is here writing confidentially to the French
ambassador. Perhaps it was the Scotch ambassador.

[2] Queen Elizabeth and her Times. By T. Wright, Esq., vol. ii.,
p. 241. Letter of Serjeant Fleetwood.

to go home to his own country again." " An indictment," adds Fleetwood, was " drawn by the clerk of the
peace, the which I thought good not to have published,
or that evidence should be given openly, and therefore I
caused the jury to go into a chamber, and heard the
evidence given, among whom, one Merideth Hammer,
a doctor of divinity, and vicar of Islington, had dealt as
evilly towards Lord Shrewsbury as the innkeeper
Walmesley. This doctor regardeth not an oath, surely
he is a very bad man; but in the end the indictment
was indorsed *billa vera* [true bill]." Here, however, is
an end of the whole *scandalum magnatum*, for Serjeant
Fleetwood speaks no more of the matter in his succeeding letters.

There is in the State Paper Office a declaration by the
Countess of Shrewsbury and her sons, that they considered the reports relative to the Queen of Scots having had two children by the Earl of Shrewsbury, false,
scandalous, and malicious, and that they were not the
authors of the said reports.]

The Queen of Scots to Lord Burleigh.[1]

March 2, 1584.

I shall send an ambassador to Scotland to come to a
final decision with my son. This treaty is the only
thing in this world which can ease me either in body or
mind; for I feel so depressed by my seventeen years'
captivity, I can bear it no longer. Again I earnestly

---

[1] MS. Harl., 4651, p. 138. According to the desire of Mauvissière, Mary wrote to the Lord Treasurer Burleigh, making
known some of her requests,¹ great and little, comprising, at the
same time, the commencement of the treaty of arbitration between
England, France, and Scotland, for her restoration to her crown
and to liberty, and—a supply of groceries from the next town.

entreat that an end may be put to it before I die a lingering death.

I am greatly obliged to the queen, my good sister, for the care she is now pleased to take for my honourable treatment, but nothing is done without the sixteen horses,[1] which I have asked for, without them I am shut up, and cannot enjoy the fresh air to recover or preserve my health, as those who have hitherto guarded me can testify.

I must trouble you with another matter, namely, that my servants may be permitted to purchase grocery and other articles for me in the neighbouring town, under a sufficient guard, because I cannot always have at hand such like trifles when I want them.

[The letter of Mary, Queen of Scots, now following in chronological order, deserves great attention, because, with that of the previous 26th of February, some analogy seems to exist relative to the extraordinary scandal-letter on Queen Elizabeth, purporting to be by Mary, Queen of Scots, which is printed in French in that portion of Lord Burleigh's correspondence called the Murdin State Papers. That letter details all the scandals on Queen Elizabeth which ostensibly were narrated by the Countess of Shrewsbury to the Queen of Scots during the early years of her captivity, when the closest intimacy was maintained between them. The scandal-letter is, however, so different in its style and contents from any undoubted specimen of Mary's pen, that its

[1] Mary never was suffered to ride out or take the air without being surrounded by a mounted guard; and when horses were not provided for a sufficient number, she was restrained from exercise. (See Shrewsbury Correspondence, vol. II., Lodge's Illustrations, many assages.)

authenticity has been greatly doubted by most historians. A most improbable story, too, was repeated by Carte relative to the discovery of the scandal-letter, as for instance, that it was found rolled up in woollen, and buried in a stone chest in the garden at Hatfield, two feet from the surface, by which process it would infallibly have been destroyed by damp in a very few weeks. From these dubious circumstances, as well as from the odious nature of its contents, the scandal-letter is not printed in this collection; yet, if a fabrication, it belongs undoubtedly to the times in which Mary lived.

From the following letter, and from the preceding one, it is evident that Mary wished to recriminate on the Countess of Shrewsbury the endeavours that lady had made to ruin her, from the moment of the birth of Lady Arabella Stuart. For this scion of the royal blood of England being, at the same time, grand-daughter to the ambitious Countess of Shrewsbury, and the third in degree to the English crown, the countess thought that if Mary was destroyed Arabella's chance of the succession was greater. Such appears the real cause of the enmity between Queen Mary and the Countess of Shrewsbury, and not jealousy of the earl, as Lady Shrewsbury affirmed. For of course such jealousy would have occurred before the birth of Arabella, when Queen Mary's beauty was brighter. It is certain that these letters never reached their destination—the hands of the French ambassador—but fell into the possession of Burleigh and Walsingham, who probably fabricated the scandal-letter, to make the breach wider between the house of Shrewsbury and the Queen of Scots; for it is the opinion of most of our historical antiquaries, that Queen Elizabeth never saw the scandal-letter, or heard any of the representations which her unfortunate captive, in the present letters, prompts the French ambassador to pour into her ear against the Countess of Shrewsbury, as retaliation of the scandalous stories that lady had levelled against her reputation. Moreover, the accusations which the Queen of Scots wished to communicate to Elizabeth against her inimical hostess were former plans and treasons in her favour, before the birth of a grand-daughter of royal blood turned the current of interest against Mary's title to the throne. It is evident by an existing document that Nau, Mary's confidential secretary, was recommended by Elizabeth, and was too probably the creature of her ministers; therefore, no person can wonder that Queen Mary's letters were constantly betrayed and intercepted, years before her final tragedy.]

The Queen of Scots to M. de Mauvissière.[1]

March 21, 1584.

Monsieur de Mauvissière,—As I shall write to you by the usual channel more fully to-morrow, respecting what the Earl of Shrewsbury has signified to me in the name of the Queen of England, his mistress, it will suffice to send you to-day a copy of my answer to the earl. You must now do your utmost to get leave to go to Scotland, and take with you a plenipotentiary from the Queen of England, and one from me. I have been unwilling to write too urgently myself on the subject, not to excite suspicion, and give ground for a refusal; but if any one is to intervene in the name of my good brother the King of France in any treaty between the Queen of England and myself, I desire that it may be you, as you are so much better acquainted than any other person with all the circumstances between us.

[1] MS. Harl., 1582, fol. 313. Both Raumer and Mademoiselle de Keralio have edited this letter.

I assure you, on my word and honour, that if the Queen of England would act sincerely towards my son and me, and give us the necessary securities for our preservation, I would be the first to oppose, for instance, even my own son, if he should wrongfully, and contrary to the stipulations of the treaty, undertake anything against her; so far am I from intending, (after the conclusion of an equitable treaty,) not to restrain my ministers from all enterprizes which might tend to the prejudice of Elizabeth and her realm; but, as I lately wrote to you, I fear that the partizans of my *good* neighbour the Earl of Huntingdon,[1] will never permit any kind of friendship betwixt us, as they would then have less power and ability to ruin us, which I believe to be their design.

To leave this frequently-discussed matter, I entreat that you will more distinctly show to Queen Elizabeth the treachery of my honourable hostess, the Countess of Shrewsbury. I would wish you to mention privately to the queen, (obtaining, if possible, her promise neither to communicate it to any one, nor make any further enquiry,) that nothing has alienated the Countess of Shrewsbury from me but the vain hope which she has conceived of setting the crown of England on the head of her littlegirl Arabella,[2] and this by means of marrying her to a son of the Earl of Leicester.[3] These children are also educated in this idea ; and their portraits have been sent to each other. But for the notion of raising

[1] Alluding to Hastings, Earl of Huntingdon, as a formidable competitor for the throne, as the representative of George, Duke of Clarence.

[2] Lady Arabella Stuart, the grand-daughter of the Countess of Shrewsbury, by her daughter, Elizabeth Cavendish, wife of Lord Charles Lenox, brother of Darnley.

[3] His little son Robert, by Lettice, Countess of Leicester, who

one of her descendants to the rank of queen, she would never have so turned away from me. for she was so entirely bound to me, and regardless of any other duty or regard, that if God himself had been her queen, she could not have showed more devotion than she did to me. Say to the queen, that you heard from Mademoiselle Seton,[1] (who went to France last summer,) that a solemn promise was given me by the Countess of Shrewsbury, that if ever my life should be in danger, or orders given to remove me to another place, she would find means for my escape : and, being a woman, she should easily avoid all peril of punishment; that her son, Charles Cavendish, she assured me, in his presence, rested for no other purpose in London, but to acquaint me with everything that passed there; that he had constantly two swift horses ready to communicate to me as soon as it occurred, the death of Queen Elizabeth, who was at that time ill ; and that Walsingham had invited the Earl of Huntingdon to hasten to London, with which proposal he had immediately complied.

The countess, as well as her son, Charles Cavendish, at that time took all possible pains to convince me that, in the hands of [her husband] the Earl of Shrewsbury I was in the greatest possible danger, for he would deliver me into the hands of my enemies, or suffer them to surprise me ; so that I should be in a very bad condition without the aid of the said countess [of Shrewsbury].

At this time, I will send you only these little in-

died soon after It was a curious idea to exchange portraits between these infants ; it shows how these juvenile engagements were carried on between the little lovers

[1] Mary had a fair damsel of the name of Seaton as her attendant long after her sojourn in England, not exactly the Kate Seaton of Sir Walter Scott, for her name was Mary.

stances, that the Queen of England may judge of the
rest, and see what has been carried on by the countess
regarding me in past years. I could also, if I pleased,
bring her into great trouble, as her people have, by her
express orders, brought me ciphers, and she has also
delivered me some with her own hands. It will be
sufficient if you tell the Queen of England that you
heard these particulars from Mademoiselle Seton, and
that you were convinced that, if she would cause me to
be asked quietly and privately about the Countess of
Shrewsbury, I could disclose to her things of much
greater importance, and in which several of those about
her would be deeply implicated.

However, prevail upon her to keep this secret, and
never to mention your name. Say that you have been
induced to make this communication from the interest
you take in her welfare; and, that she may know what
confidence is to be placed in the Countess of Shrewsbury, add that you are firmly persuaded the said countess
could be gained by me whenever I pleased with a bribe
of 2000 crowns.

You have done me a kindness by sending copies of
my letters to France and Scotland, in order that the
truth of these misunderstandings may be known, which,
I am persuaded, arise from the countess and her son
Charles Cavendish. But the witnesses by whom I could
prove this fear to incur the displeasure of Queen Elizabeth, therefore I am obliged to defer coming to a public
enquiry and explanation till I can find others.

I recommend to you, as far as possible, the unhappy
De la Tour[1] and all belonging to him. I daily lament

[1] This man is called Latour in history; he was suspected as an
agent for Mary, Queen of Scots, sent to the Tower, and cruelly
tortured by the ruthless Walsingham, till he confessed, not only
what he had done, but whatever was demanded of him—such were

their misfortune, and would willingly sacrifice a part of my blood to deliver them.   Also, if you can find means of doing it, I would have you remit ten or twelve pounds sterling to Edward Moore in the Tower, for he is said to be in great distress.

I thank you for the intelligence you sent me respecting my son, for whose preservation I know no way of providing, but by the aid of the king my good brother [Henry III.], and of my relations and my servants in France, to whose judgment I entirely refer as to doing whatever is needful.   If 15,000*l* or 20,000*l*. were distributed among the chief men of Scotland, they would be wonderfully confirmed in their loyalty; but hitherto I have not received one penny from the king, nor have been able to obtain leave from him to sell part of my estates.   On the contrary, by the late costs and unjust proceedings, I have lost almost three-quarters of my marriage portion, but I trust God will not leave me thus distressed.

From Sheffield, March 21st, 1584.

———————

April 12, 1584.

[*The following letter to the Queen of Scots, being inter-cepted by Elizabeth's spies, was sent to Mr. Sommer, one of Mary's castellans, that he might aid in guessing the persons alluded to in it, accompanied by the following letter from Walsingham :*

the usual fruits of the diabolical system of torture, which was an infringement on the ancient laws of this country   (See the Works of Sir John Fortescue, the learned judge who wrote in the time of Henry VI.)

[1] Sadler Papers, edited by Arthur Clifford, Esq , vol ii p 375 to 379.   It is here translated from the French, in which it was sent for the inspection of Queen Elizabeth, into whose hands it unfortunately fell.   The intelligence respecting the invasion of England

*Sir,—I send, by her majesty's commandment, a copy
of a cypher [letter] sent out of Scotland unto the Queen
of that realm [Mary].   It hath been decyphered by
Phillips, but not fully to her majesty's contentment   It
is written in French, and is all in one letter, though
in the decyphering paper it may seem two.   It should
seem to be written in March last.[1]   The matter is of
great weight, and therefore worthy of travail, which
I recommend to your wonted good care.   At the Court,
the 22nd of April, 1584.*

Your assured friend,

Fra. Walsingham.]

*A Gentleman of rank (name unknown) in the household
of James VI. to Mary, Queen of Scots.[1]*

Madam,—Necessity obliges me to endeavour most
sedulously to renew the intelligence so long extinct between the king your son and your majesty, the means of
which, thanks to God, I have found by an honest Englishman, who will make himself known to your majesty
by this letter, in which, I believe, he will testify the
opinion he has of the king my master, who, having heard
his tidings, was very glad to visit your majesty with these
three or four lines[2] from his hand, as much to assure
your majesty of his obedience and filial affection, as to
learn news of you by your reply; as also to testify how
greatly his majesty approves of the design of M. de Guise,

by the Duke of Guise is alluded to by Mr. Sommer in his curious
conversation with Mary, quoted at the end of this volume. Sommer
had seen this letter.

[1] A mistake of Walsingham's, since the writer dates it *ce
deuxième d'Avril.*

[2] King James's letter to his mother perhaps reached her, as it is
not enclosed.

his cousin, touching his enterprise in England, the more
so that he deems it will tend to the liberty of your
majesty ; which he considers far beyond any increase ot
greatness, and desires more than the utter freedom of
his own person and state; both of which, truth to say,
have been for these three months past in very great
danger.   For his bad subjects, nurtured by the *good*
Queen of England, seek daily some opportunity or
other to get his person into their treacherous hands.
This, we others [*i. e.* who are loyal], strive by all means
to obviate.   Altogether, our enemies are so vigilant,
and the wicked ministers [Calvinist preachers] so careful to accomplish their intentions, that we consider the
sole means against all these machines [machinations] ot
the Queen of England would be the achievement of the
aforesaid enterprise.   For his majesty [James] has deliberated to treat of the person of his cousin as his
own.

And the better to do so, as his majesty has had long
experience of the counsel of Colonel Stuart,[1] his majesty
has communicated to him the whole of this enterprise;
and the said Colonel Stuart thinks higher of it than
of thousands of other things in this world : because it
will not only increase the grandeur of the king his master,
but it will revenge on the Queen of England the breaking
of all her fine promises last year, and withal tend to the
service of your majesty.

In particular he has promised, as much as in him lies,

[1] Colonel William Stuart was a kinsman of King James's, and
commander of his guard of gentlemen ; he was brave and faithful,
but rather wild and rough in manner, yet he was far superior to
his profligate and discreditable relative, Stuart, Earl of Arran,
whom King James, or, rather the dominant faction, had invested
wrongfully with that title, which belonged of right to the house
of Hamilton.

the attestation of which I have sent you, written and subscribed by his hand. In truth, I advised the king to communicate this to him, because at present he can do more than any man in Scotland for the preservation of the person of his majesty, seeing that he is the captain of his guard. Besides, madam, the king has sounded for a long time those of his nobility, whom he esteems the most faithful, such as [Maxwell] Earl of Morton, Lord Herries, and Ogilvy, to whom he has communicated all, and the Sieur [Sir] Robert Melville But to speak frankly of all the three to whom his majesty communicated the said enterprize, Colonel Stuart is the most vigilant and careful; for since he has known of it he has rejected all the idea that he had of any other.

Madam, the gentleman of his majesty's guard that I have sent last to France, to monsieur your cousin [the Duke of Guise], is not yet heard of, neither any news of the money that I sent in quest of, for the payment of his [the king's] guard, if so be that his majesty is obliged to make a levy of three hundred soldiers to abide near his majesty, at all events. But, madam, as already said, there is no other remedy, to deliver your majesty and the king your son from all peril than the success of these affairs about England, which induced his majesty to liberate and send William Hault, an Englishman made prisoner in the castle of Lisleburgh, to monsieur your cousin [the Duke of Guise], on these two principal points: to desire him to accelerate all things, because the Queen of England is about to kill the king your son by very extraordinary means, thinking thus to cut off and traverse the plans of La Mothe Fenelon . . . . and of your cousin, monsieur the Duke of Guise; as for your majesty, you are always at her mercy. The other occasion of the journey of this Englishman is, that M. de la Mothe Fenelon may, if possible, be sent again in

embassy, and that the twenty thousand crowns may be
delivered to him, which M. de Guise promised me, to
raise soldiers at the time he makes his preparations. For
without doubt [his majesty's] bad subjects, and those
colleagued with our preachers, as soon as they see the
king and all his other subjects take up arms, will raise
against them some new animadversion, such as, in time
past, used to be practised in your majesty's case;
so that it is the more necessary that the aforesaid sum
be sent with all diligence.

Madam, the king your son entreats you to take in
hand to write, by the first opportunity, to monsieur your
cousin, to make out whether it is not possible for the
said M. la Mothe Fenelon to obtain the embassy. His
majesty desires, affectionately, some of his cousins of the
house of Guise may come to advise him at this time in
all his actions, appearing merely as if they came to visit
him; this they will agree to very willingly, if it will please
your majesty to give your opinion in favour of it.

Madam, the king [James] commands me, on his
part, to entreat you to take good care of your personal
safety, that he may be aided by your advice at this time;
for, without the preservation of that, he will not be able
to do aught for his great estate or the increase of his
grandeur, nor any other good that might happen to
him in future. But of this your reply will assure him;
as also what you know of your friends in England, and
how much you can depend on them and hope for their
aid.

Fearing, madam, that you are o'er wearied by my dis-
cordant discourse, I supplicate your majesty to spare
[excuse] him who will never spare his life to perform
his humble service to you, and who desires to give some
ample proof of loyal intention in receiving your commandments, which I will obey also with faithful affection,

as humbly as I pray God, madam, that he will give your
majesty in very excellent health a long and prosperous
life, with the accomplishment of all the projects you
most desire.   This twelfth of April,

From your majesty's very humble

And very obedient servant,

$x:$[1]

*Private letter to the Queen of Scots, added by the writer
of the above, as postscript, unknown to King James.*

Madam,—In my letter I have omitted the principal
point, not daring to show it to the king.   There is here
a gentleman, the Earl of Arran,[2] and his wife.   In them
the king [James] confides more than in any other, yet
he himself confesses that they are, as to you, very impudent.   The said earl is a noted enemy to all Catholics in general, but to your majesty and all yours especially, labouring always indirectly to impair the amity
between your majesty and the king your son; for instance, a few days since, he practised, at the instigation
of the Queen of England, regarding the marriage of the
king your son and a daughter of the King of Sweden.

And on this he has had some *angelats*, which the
king knows well himself; but in that, and in all other
proceedings of this wicked man, the king is blind.

Wherefore, madam, as your majesty desires the pre-

_____

[1] By this cipher, the name of the writer is indicated.

[2] Arran was James Stuart, second son of Lord Ochiltree, and
one of the instruments of Morton's fall.   He was rewarded by
the king—or rather by himself, for James was a mere boy—with
the earldom and estate of the insane Earl of Arran, which he had
previously got possession of, as guardian of that unfortunate nobleman's person.   His influence lasted scarcely two years, when another wild revolution, led by Patrick Gray, displaced him; he was
forced, ultimately, to give up his usurped title, and died in great
obscurity.

servation of his life, warn him to take better heed of the actions of this earl, and leave not everything to this roisterer, who is equally despised by the nobles and the people, as a man who, for his evil habits, is not at all desirable for the common weal. For the bruit [public report] runs, that his majesty is totally governed by his lies, and bewitched by the *diablerie* of his wicked and audacious wife.[1]

Besides, madam, he [Arran] is master of the wardrobe ; and there are some others of his majesty's chamber who have been put there by enemies, which the king will not alter for any advice of us others. It is needful, madam, that you write to him your opinion. Add your maternal authority, and make him believe that your majesty learns all this elsewhere.

I remain, waiting the reply of your majesty.

Mr. Sommer to Sir Francis Walsingham.

Right Honorable,—Herewith I do return to you for her majesty [Elizabeth], the [de]cyphered letter you sent and brought me upon Thursday last by John Puttrell, messenger, and my little travail to make it somewhat plainer. By the discourse you shall find it cometh from a principal person about the Scottish king, as the Earl of Arran,[2] or Colonel Stuart. From a

[1] The abducted Countess of March, a most infamous character.

[2] It could not be Arran, because that person's character, so severely described in the secret postscript, has been identified by the general voice of history, public and private ; and of course he could not draw this black portrait of his own conduct, which was far more infamous for debauchery and all vileness than the indignant writer of this salutary warning to young James's mother has described. The guesses of Queen Elizabeth's ministers as to the writer of this letter were singularly unfortunate, for it is endorsed

Scotchman it is, as his orthography and articles of the genders shew in many places, which in the extract I have only a little holpen, referring to her majesty, as you shall perceive by comparing Mr. Phillips' extract with this. As to the significative notes,[1] some I have voted [quoted] in the end of this extract, the rest I leave to your judgment, who by further acquaintance can guess at them.

April 13. The Earls Gowry, Angus, &c., put themselves at the head of a body of Scotch insurgents.

April 18 Gowry is made prisoner, after an obstinate battle with the royalist army; the other insurgents seek refuge in England.

May 4. Earl Gowry executed in Scotland.

—" It was written by the Master of Gray, by the king's (James's) commandment " But the subsequent conduct of that most treacherous of all poor Mary's enemies is not in accordance with the tone that breathes in this postscript. It is no little honour to Mary to find Arran (to whose corrupting influence her son owed his tendency to inebriety and all the ill in his disposition) in the ranks of her avowed enemies, while in the ranks of her friends, in the worst of times, we find the three admirable Melvilles, Protestants though they were, and those manly and devoted nobles, Herries, Fleming, and Seaton From some gentleman in the king's household this despatch evidently came ; even if Gray had been sufficiently friendly, he could not have been the writer, because the author of this letter seems a much older man.

[1] Merely his surmises as to the persons indicated by certain capitals and Greek letters in the cypher. Mr Sommer was an honest-hearted country gentleman, who much desired to make peace between Elizabeth and her captive, which did not suit Walsingham and his party The letter was not sent for his feeble aid in guessing state secrets, but merely to inflame his patriotism, with the idea of a Scotch and French invasion The letter should be read in conjunction with Sommer's curious conversation with the captive queen, quoted subsequently in this volume, as they cast light on each other.

The Queen of Scots to M. de Mauvissière.

Sheffield, April, 1584.

Monsieur de Mauvissière,—I should have answered before this your last of the 29th of March, 1st, 6th, and 17th of April ult., but for the arrival here of Seneschal Maron, who having assured me that you are minutely informed of what passed during his short stay in this country, as well with himself as with the Sieur Wade, I will not enter into any repetition. I did not neglect, agreeably to your advice, to explain and earnestly recommend my just grievances and complaints to the said Maron of the wrongs which have been done me, and which I am daily suffering, in regard to the disposal of my dower, and I told the other as plainly what were my conceptions relative to the present situation of my son in Scotland, and to my own in this captivity, purposely that he may make his mistress acquainted with it. I should have gone deeper into the matter with him, especially about the renewal of the proposed treaty for my liberty, had he not repeatedly assured me that he had no order, or charge, or commission, from his mistress, but merely to accompany the said Maron. I can testify that, in all his conversation and remonstrances, he proved himself to be as partial an Englishman, and as ill affected towards the king, my good brother, as it is possible to be ; whereupon Nau did not fail to rebuke him severely for it, and especially because he alleged " that a French gentleman, who is charged to conduct the affairs of the said king, monsieur my good brother, in this kingdom, [putting his finger upon you,][1] had said, on showing him some of my letters, that it would cost the said king, monsieur my good brother, more than four millions before I or my son should ever attain the crown of Eng-

[1] i. e. Maron insinuated that Mary's friend, the ambassador Mauvissière (to whom she is now writing), had made this speech.

land." I, however, earnestly entreat you not to betray
the least knowledge of this, inasmuch as it could only
come from this quarter, and would greatly injure me, as
well as the said Nau, to whom he went so far as to observe that, being the servant and subject of the king,
monsieur my brother, and treating him so harshly, he
could not be so faithful to me if he interfered to give me
any good advice or council for the benefit of this kingdom and mine, since my interest and that of the king
were directly opposite. However, at last, he went away
quite contented and satisfied. I have forwarded by him
a pacific letter to the Queen of England, to soften her as
much as lies in my power.

If they proceed to the said treaty for my liberty, I
earnestly wish that you might be appointed on behalf of
the king, monsieur my good brother, as I request of him,
in my letters inclosed herein to my ambassador, by Monsieur de Seton. If the Earls of Angus, Mar, Gohory
[Gowry], and others of the conspiracy, have already
proceeded so far as you tell me, there is no longer any
possibility of entering into negotiation with them, as
Archibald Du Glas [Douglas] proposed to you, in order
to bring them back to my interest; therefore I would
not, in any way whatever, serve them for a shield against
my son, as they formerly boasted that he did for them
against me; and of course there is no other means of
treating with them but their submission to my son, estrangement and rupture with our enemies in this kingdom and all others, and assurances of their true and
complete amendment: upon these conditions I promise
to do all that lies in my power to obtain their pardon and
reinstatement, which will be better secured to them in
this way, than if gained by force.

And if Archibald Du Glas should persevere in going
into Scotland, contrary to the advice I sent him through
you, charge him to strive to prevail upon the earls and

rebels to lay down their arms, and to obtain permission from the Queen of England for me to send to my son, in company with one of her own people and with your-selves, if possible, that, under the authority of the king, monsieur my good brother, hers, and mine, all affairs may be adjusted in that quarter into some solid peace and firm union of our subjects with one another, and of them with my said son, and for this purpose I could re-commend the said Du Glas, and do for him all that she shall require; but, above all, let him not know, in any way whatever, that you hold the slightest secret commu-nication with me; for I perceive, that the negotiations which Walsingham keeps up with you have no other object but to discover, from the replies you make in my name, if you still have any secret means of communicat-ing with me; and, therefore, never admit, if you please, either to the said Archibal or to any other person what-ever, that you write to me any longer in this manner; but leave them to judge and imagine what they please, how you become acquainted with my intentions.

My host[1] is more than ever in doubt and suspense respecting leave to go to court; yet his desire to do so increases daily, thinking, as I imagine, to exculpate him-self from the calumnies of his enemies, and force himself to be acknowledged what he is. The worst I fear from this journey is that, during his absence, I may be re-moved hence, or even that he may be persuaded to consent to it; it is, therefore, very important that you should prevent this, if you please; and, at any rate, take care that I may not be put into a hostile and suspicious hand, as I was before. I have informed you of the inter-pretation put upon the meeting between the Earl of Rut-land and my host, which originates only with the good lady of Chatisiorth, who has ever been an enemy to the said

[1] The Earl of Shrewsbury.

Earl of Rutland, (own nephew to my host by his first wife,) the proximity of this relationship being of itself a sufficient and plausible reason for the said meeting, without its being imputed to me. I hear that Lord Talbot was there likewise, but more in body than in heart; or, if his heart went thither, it was only the half, as it is not his nature to give the whole, or ever to stop in one place.

It is not in my power to enlighten you on what has been represented to the Queen of England respecting the language made use of by young Seton, when at Bordeaux about a marriage between the Catholic king and me ; as I was not even aware that the said de Seton had been in Spain, and much less on what errand he went thither, so that I can with truth disavow all he may have said or done.

I commit to your prudence the safeguard of my secret despatches, promising to reimburse you, whatever you may pay on this account, to couriers and others, whom you may employ, whatever it may be ; and, therefore, henceforward charge it to my account under the head of gold or silver thread sent to me.   From Sheffeil, this last day of April, 1584.

What follows is from Nau to M. de Mauvissière.

Sir,—I hope that Monsieur de Joyeuse[1] has lately received the despatch forwarded to him by M. Marron,[2] and that he will, with as frank and good affection, urge the king for some redress of the affairs of her majesty, which have great need of his favour and influence.   A report has reached us that monsieur the duke is dead ; but I shall not believe it, until we receive advice of it from you.   Monsieur Vade and I commenced our ac-

---

[1] The favourite of Henry III. and his brother-in-law.
[2] The same as Maron in the beginning of the letter.

quaintance rather roughly, on account of the blows that
he struck at our France, and at you in particular, which
I thought it was my duty at least to parry; and I did
so, and will do while I live, whatever may happen, as it
is impossible for me to be either in heart, or in words,
other than I was born. The conclusion was very calm
and friendly; we became sworn brothers; for which reason, I beg the more earnestly, that he may never know
that you have had wind of his behaviour here.

I have paved the way to your overture respecting the
disposal of the county of Chaumont, and hope to
bring it to bear, if Monsieur de Joyeuse will in good
earnest loosen his purse-strings. Without wishing for
the death of another, I should be glad to see you peaceable possessor of your bailiwick, as I think you will be
shortly.

Pardon me for not having sent you the letter of Madame de St. Pierre; the departure of the said Marron
and Vade having been so sudden that I was obliged to
sit up all night about their despatch. If you write to
Monsieur de Joyeuse, I beg you to assure him of my
desire to pay him my most humble service.

The following is a Postscript by the Queen of Scots.

Monsieur de Mauvissière,—Since writing the above,
I have received intelligence, that the Queen of England
has the intention to despatch shortly the Earl of Derby
and some other lords to the king monsieur my good brother, that, under colour of conveying to him the garter
of the order of this country, they may negotiate with
him a league, offensive and defensive, against all other
kings and princes of Christendom; and, in case it should
be carried into effect, I beg you to represent on my
behalf to the king the just cause I shall have to think
myself neglected and abandoned by him, as the said

7

Queen of England, on many occasions, and recently by
Vade, would fain have persuaded me, if I and my son be
not included in the said league, and if provision be not
made for my liberty and for the safety of my son's person and crown in Scotland; and if, by the said league,
any thing be agreed upon and stipulated to the prejudice of the ancient league between France and Scotland,
for the renewal of which Monsieur de Seton is, as I
have heard, charged to treat. I will not enter into a
detail of the many cogent reasons which ought to with-
hold the king monsieur my good brother from so close a
friendship, believing him to be too discreet to act otherwise than his conscience and the general good of the
Church shall dictate. I will only say that, if monsieur
the duke my brother-in-law is dead, as report says, this
league will but tend to strengthen and secure the King
of Navarre against the king monsieur my good brother,
who can himself derive but little fruit or advantage from
it. There is a report of the apprehension of the Earl of
Gohory [Gowry] in Scotland. I beg you to inquire into
the truth of this, and to do all that lies in your power to
make this queen give up the scheme.

1584. *June* 10. Execution of Francis Throgmorton in London,
death of the Duke of Anjou in France.

June —. Henry Percy, Earl of Northumberland, apprehended

The Queen of Scots to M. de Mauvissiere.

Sheffield, May 31, 1584

Monsieur,—Since writing the enclosed, Beale has left
this place, and, having written you by him so amply
about the obstacles which have occurred, I will not
repeat any thing to you, unless that the report, which he
has made of my replies and negotiations with him has
been most maliciously wrested and misconstrued, by

some of this council. He has not been less angry than myself, for I never said those things as they have been taken, nor did he ever report or represent them in that way. Walsingham has done, I believe, like all his fellows in matters of religion : he has garbled and falsified the text. Prosecute your journey to me, and hence to Scotland, with those whom this queen and myself shall depute to accompany you ; which is the only plan that I can approve for the said journey, which, if thus performed, will be very agreeable to me, and place me under great obligation to you; otherwise, it would be highly prejudicial for several reasons, some of which I have made you acquainted with; and, if there were no others but the reinstatement of the rebels to be effected by my intercession and not without me, it would be sufficient to induce me to prevent their said reinstatement, were I not of the party. Speak of this on my behalf to Archibal Du Glas, and promise him in my name that, if he can bring this journey to bear in that manner, I will exert all my efforts in favour of the Earl of Anguis [Angus] and himself.

I recommend to you once more the S^r. de la Tour, for whose life, as I have already written to you, I will answer, as also the pardon of the said Earl of Anguis; but it is necessary, that this should be managed skilfully, and in an indirect manner, without my name being either made use of or insinuated, and as if it originated with the said Archibal Du Glas or you. From Sheffield, this last of May, 1584.

N. B. The copy from which this letter is transcribed is in the hand-writing of Mauvissière's secretary. It appears to be the copy of a letter from the Queen of Scots to Mauvissière.

1584. *September* 20. The Scottish parliament, in spite of the intercession of Elizabeth, confiscates all the property belonging to the Scottish rebels who have taken refuge in England.

The English faction in Scotland being reduced to a state of impotence, Elizabeth appears disposed to come to an accommodation with Mary Stuart. Gray goes to London on the part of James VI., and Nau on behalf of his mother, to treat on the subject, under the mediation of the French ambassador.

The Queen of Scots to the same.

Supposed September, 1584.

Monsieur de Mauvissière,—Although, on account of the uncertainty in which I remain respecting the treaty with the Queen of England, I cannot give you any certain information about it ; still, I will not omit to advise you, by the brief summary herewith inclosed, what has taken place between the deputies of the Queen of England and myself; but, as they have required me not to mention it to any one, and most especially neither to the king, monsieur my good brother, nor to you, I beg you to keep it as secret as you can, until matters are further advanced, either to a rupture or a conclusion; so that they may not have it in their power to charge me with having divulged anything contrary to their desire and request. Nevertheless, you can confide it to my brother, to whom I have enclosed a letter, sending him in this the ring, respecting which, to my great regret, he has expressed himself displeased with you.

I am informed for certain, that Captain Stuart[1] has been expressly charged by this queen to persuade my son to break off all alliance with France, and to enter into a league with this queen, proposed and urged very strenuously by the secretary Dunfermiling, upon pretext of supporting their religion; but I have written very

---

[1] Captain of James VI.'s guard, formerly mentioned as Colonel Stuart. See p. 101 of this vol.

firmly to the contrary, as well to my said son as to the principal persons of the good party who are about him; so that I hope it will come to nothing. The convention was to have been held on the 26th of last month, to consult on the negotiations with which the said Stuart was charged on his return from this country. It is said that my son has determined upon setting himself at liberty, and disbanding his new guard as soon as he shall find himself in a place of safety.

I beg you to intercede on my behalf with the king, monsieur my good brother, that he may be pleased to favour the children of the Duke of Lenox, in particular the eldest, especially for the journey which he is about making to Scotland : rely upon it, that, young as he is, he will be able greatly to strengthen the French faction, if the estates of his late father be secured to him. It would also be well if the king, monsieur my good brother, would confer some pension or gratuity on Lord Haumilton, the machinations and intrigues of this queen with him and his brother aiming, upon pretext of their restoration, to attach them to her party.

Tell Archibal Du Glas from me that I have been informed on good authority that this queen has no intention to send him to Scotland; and, therefore, it is my opinion, that he may accept any appointment he can get from her, striving by all possible demonstrations to persuade Walsingham that he is well affected towards the Queen of England,[1] that, if possible, he may discover their intention respecting me and my son ; and henceforward desire him, in my name, when in conferring with the said Walsingham the conversation turns upon the treaty for my liberty, to sound what opinion he holds ; and, if he discovers any thing, inform me of it, if you

[1] Archibald Douglas took this advice thus far, and finding Elizabeth paid the best, he betrayed Mary and became one of the most active agents in bringing her to the scaffold.

please, by the first opportunity. I beg you also to favour me with your good advice respecting the terms of the said treaty, as you have long had great experience such matters in this country. Nevertheless, if you find that the business is likely to be spun out to a great length, insist urgently, according to my last by Beale, on a final arrangement one way or the other, and, if this cannot be effected within the time mentioned, let it, at least, be done immediately afterwards, without further delay, for I will no longer be deceived by vain hopes.

The honour of monsieur the duke, and the sincerity of Monsieur de Biron, have been much compromised in this last defeat of the English in the Low Countries. Let me know what answer you have from the said S^r. duke, as respects his reconciliation with his Catholic majesty, and what has become of his brother Charles.

This letter is transcribed from a copy in the hand-writing of Mauvissière's secretary. It has no date; but the subjects of which it treats prove it to have been written in the year 1584.

M. de Mauvissière to the Queen of Scots.

Madam,—Since writing last evening to your majesty, thinking that this letter would go off incontinently, but being now in doubt whether it will ever reach you, I have dined familiarly with the Earl of Lestre¹ and his wife,¹ of whom he he is very fond, and both of them treated me most kindly, offering to renew our former friendship, and requesting that his said wife and mine might be friends, to which I assented. After dinner the said earl took me out to walk, and disclosed to me his whole heart towards your said majesty, protesting that he had never been adverse, but that he had now lost all credit with his mistress, with France, and with your

¹ The Earl of Leicester and his second wife.

majesty; and that, as for the Earl of Hontinton [Hun-
tingdon], he would be the first to make war upon him,
and to spend all he has to prevent him from undertaking
any thing against your majesty ; that he would be always
ready, in case his mistress should die, to render you
signal service, as would likewise all his relatives and
friends, and he begged me, if I had the means, to assure
you of this, but to let no one else know it, otherwise it
would be his ruin; and, further, that the said queen is
going to give you some answer, and to come to an arrangement with your majesty, if your son behaves
affectionately to you Nevertheless, the said Queen of
England is very jealous of those in this kingdom who
are attached to both : and it is on this account that the
S^r. de Walsingham had like to have got into trouble, which
is the reason why he disguises the good-will which he
entertains for you. The said earl [Leicester] also told
me, that, as to the Earl of Cherosbery [Shrewsbury] and
the countess his wife, they are continually writing hither
the worst they can of each other, and that your majesty's
interest suffers in consequence, and he said that he
ardently desires nothing more than your comfort, and not
to quarrel with the said earl, if the matter can be adjusted
between them. In short, madam, the said earl [Leices-
ter] never promised more for the service of your majesty
than at present, and the way to keep him in this favourable disposition is to entertain his wife, and to assure
them that you will be their friend

Inform me if you wish to keep them in the disposition
to serve you, for, if he is not a very great hypocrite, he
seems to me to have the inclination to do so, but desires
that no person living may know of it, not even the said
Walsingham. This is what I have hastily added to
my letters, and to what I have desired Courcelles to write
to you respecting the deposition of the S^r. de la Tour.

This letter is copied from a minute, which is entirely
in Mauvissière's hand-writing.

M. de Mauvissière to the Queen of Scots.

Madam,—This epistle is to acquaint your majesty,
that I have been informed that the Queen of England
has manifested extreme jealousy on hearing that Lord
Talbot, the Earl of Roteland [Rutland], and all the nobility in your neighbourhood, had met a few days ago,
and promised firm friendship, not only for the present
but for the future; and this has excited in the said
queen such suspicion and anger, that if she could ruin
the whole of them she would do it, thinking that it is on
your account they have associated. On the other hand,
it is reported here that Lord Talbot is adverse to you
I have also been assured that the said queen has resolved upon removing you, at any rate, from the custody
of your host, and, under pretext of recommencing a
treaty for your liberty, to send Mildemay [Mildmay]
and the chevalier Revel to conduct you to Herford
[Hertford] castle, which is twenty miles distant from
hence [i. e. from London], and to send for your host and
his wife to this court, under colour of giving them some
appointment and reconciling them,[1] and to give you, at
the said Herford, a new household, new servants, and
keepers, and to remove you from those who are thought
to be too good friends to you in the vicinity of Chefie
[Sheffield] and towards the north.

I shall make further inquiry on this subject, and go
to-morrow to the Queen of England to speak to her
about it, and to remonstrate that it is neither right nor
reasonable, to subject you to a new change, or to remove

---

[1] The Countess of Shrewsbury had for some time been jealous of
the Queen of Scotland.

you from the custody of a nobleman who has always been so faithful to her; and I will try whether I can in some way or other prevent this blow. Write about it also, in your own name, to the said queen and her council. I have been told that the said Midlemay and Revel beg to decline this commission. These people here are so false and double-faced in all they say, that it is impossible to put any faith in them.

For my part, madam, I consider your majesty cannot be removed from your present keeper to the custody of any other in this kingdom, whoever he may be, without danger, great annoyance, and inconvenience, whereupon I can only say, I will do all that lies in my humble power to render you good and faithful service, and in executing all that you shall ever be pleased to command me. I must not forget to inform you that the King of Spain has written a letter, with his own hand, to Don Bernardin de Mendosse,[1] approving all that he has done here, and still refusing to see W . . . .,[2] who had been sent to him from this country, saying that he would have nothing to do with that heretic; and he has sent to the said Don Bernardin a bill of exchange for four thousand ducats, ordering him to await his commands, which he should forward by another courier.

Take care, on your part, madam, not to fall into the hands of your enemies. I will do all I can on mine. Write to the high treasurer, and send me the letter. He is, after all, the best, and listens to reason.

1584. *October* —. Creighton, the Jesuit, and Abdy, a Scotch priest, are taken at sea by an English cruiser, and carried to the Tower of London. On being put to the torture, they disclose all

[1] Mendoça, ambassador of Philip II.
[2] This name is torn in the manuscript.

the particulars of the projected invasion for the deliverance of the Queen of Scotland . all negociations are again suspended

October —. Mary Stuart is removed to Wingfield.

Discourse between the Queen of Scots and me, [*Mr. Sommer, son-in-law to Sir Ralph Sadler,*] *on our journey from Sheffield Castle to Wingfield Castle, September 2nd,* 1584.[1]

After the Scottish queen had uttered her grief of her long imprisonment, having spent her years from twenty-four to past forty, and by cumber and infirmity become old in body, she delivered the like grief as she had done three days past to my Lord of Shrewsbury and Mr. Chancellor of the Duchy, saying, " That the queen's majesty had no confidence in her words, when she told the truth to Sir William Mildmay and Mr. Beale, as things have happened since in Scotland, whereof and of Mr. Secretary's[2] evil usage and reception in Scotland, going thither without her recommendation;" adding, " she had foretold it, but could not be believed. And now that her majesty, having found her true in that, if her highness would trust, she hath means and credit to do her good service."

I told her, (as I had done the other day,) " That upon further proof of her leaving to practise and have unfit [underhand] intelligence with her son, and some evil ministers about him, to the trouble of her majesty [Queen Elizabeth] and of her state, she might find her majesty to be her good friend, an' that[3] writings which

---

[1] This document is modernized from the ancient orthography, in which it may be seen. Sadler Papers, vol. ii. pp. 389, 390.

[2] Walsingham. See Lord Seaton's Letter to Queen Mary, of September the preceding year.

[3] The antique conjunction *an*, well known in Shakspeare, is frequently mistaken for *and* in documents of this date

are come to her majesty's knowledge, wherein are spoken of an enterprise in England, tending for her liberty and increasing her son's greatness, and meant to come to her the [Queen of Scots], had not both greatly offended her majesty, and given her cause to think that she is a party in that enterprise, whatever it is."

"As for having intelligence with my son," replied the Queen of Scots, "and esteeming them, whom he maketh account of as his good servants, and so doth recommend them to me, I must needs do that, for, should I leave my son, who is more to me than anything in this world, and (solely) trust to the queen my good sister's favour, (which I cannot get,) I might thus be without both, and then what would become of me? And as for my son, nothing can ever sever me from him, for I live for him and not for myself; and therefore, I must trust to the one." "But," added she, "if I might be assured and trust to the queen my good sister's favour—an' that she would trust me in the points which I have long offered, and now lately moved, and in other good offices that I would do, she would find good cause to think better of me than she hath done. For I have my son's own hand to show that he offers to be ordered altogether by me in all things; he hath also sent me certain things to have mine opinion of them, for which he hath long called for answer, but I have of purpose stayed it yet, and done nothing thereunto, hoping that the queen, my good sister, would have employed me in the good motions I have made. Therefore, if it would please her majesty to be served by me, it is time; for in good faith, Mr. Sommer, I fear my son will take another course shortly without my direction, wherein I shall not be able to stay

by modern editors. Thus, this passage is not sense without it; the meaning is, Elizabeth would be Mary's good friend *an that* (if) writings, &c. &c.

him, as I am sure I can do yet. And as to the enter-prise you spoke of, by my troth, I know not, nor heard anything of it: nor, so God have my soul, will ever consent to anything that should trouble this state, whereof I seek the quiet with all my heart; for if any unquietness [commotion] should happen here, it would be laid to my charge, and so I might be put in greater danger."

And as to another point, I told her then, of an in-struction *given* to[1] . . . . to be sent to the Duke of Guise, that he should hasten things, because the queen's majesty [Elizabeth], as was there written, was about to cause the young King of Scotland to die by an extraor-dinary death; which was so great an indignity and irre-parable a wrong done to the queen's majesty, my sove-reign, and most false and far from her majesty's thought.

She replied, " That indeed my Lord Ruthven had told the king her son so; but, so God have her soul, she suspended her judgment therein."

" Well, madam," quoth I, " you hear what evil minis-ters do, thinking to do you and your son good service, but it is far otherwise. But seeing you disavow the knowledge of these things, and you offer to do good offices for her highness' [Queen Elizabeth's] service, and to have her favour, may I be bold to ask your grace what you have thought of the matter particularly, and what you would do to have her majesty's favour?"

" Marry," said she, " to persuade my son to enter into a good mutual league, offensive and defensive, with the queen my good sister, if she would so like of it, and

---

[1] Some words are here unintelligible. Sommer's speech seems to relate to some intercepted paper which Phillips, Queen Eliza-beth's decipherer, could not make out. As Lord Ruthven's name is mentioned, it probably alluded to the time when the young king was his prisoner, in 1572.

therein to comprehend the King of France, in respect of the ancient league between France and Scotland. And as I know," continued she, "the French king hath commanded his ambassador, M. de Mauvissière, to have special care of that, if any treaty should be talked of between England and Scotland. And such a league would be better for England than for Scotland, because England lieth nearer those that have been dangerous to it than Scotland doth; and so shall these two realms live long in peace, seeing no foreign prince doth claim any thing in them."

"This seemeth a very good notion," quoth I, "and a thing which the princes of both realms have often sought by alliances, and other ways; but hath been oft empêched [hindered] by foreign practices and the ambition of some, as namely, fresh in memory, the motion of a match between Edward VI. and yourself."

"Therefore," replied the Queen of Scots, "it is good to look to it now, whilst it may be holpen," adding that her son would harken shortly abroad for a *parti* [matrimonial alliance], as he did already.

"Madam," quoth I, "what other thing have you thought of in this matter, for you have had good leisure?"

"In good faith," replied she, "Scotland is poor, not able to maintain a king, and therefore England must give good pensions,[1] for surely my son is so offered in other places. And thereby the queen my good sister shall gain much, for by this means she should [would] save greatly in her charge in Ireland, where, if she needed, my son would help me with his folk, to get her good obedience, and she should not need—these two

---

[1] It is well known that James was pensioned by Elizabeth in the latter years of her life, a circumstance which probably arose from these words of his mother.

realms being thus united in amity—to spend her money
to maintain war in another country to keep her own in
quiet;" meaning what the Queen of England had done
in France, and in the King of Spain's countries, viz.,
Holland and Flanders.

"Besides that," continued the Queen of Scots, "all
my kinsfolk would be her majesty's faithful friends,
whom now she doth suspect;" and then commended she
highly the Duke of Guise, "for his valiantness and
faithfulness to his friends. There is another thing,"
added she, "to be done in this case, which must be my
care; that is, the pope's bull against all those of the
religion Protestant, which I will take in hand to deal in
—that in respect of me being a Catholic queen, the
same shall not touch my realm, though my son be a
Protestant, and then none will dare to touch the one
realm for religion without offending both. Thus, Mr.
Sommer," quoth she, "I speak plainly to you, that you
may testify of my good-will to do good, if it please the
queen to trust me. And I would to God the queen my
good sister knew my heart, which, in good faith, she
shall never find false to her, so that I and my son may
have her favour, as appertains, being of her blood and
so near."

"Madam," quoth I, "if you mean thereby any claim
after her majesty, as you have been plain with me, so I
beseech you give me leave to be plain with you; that is,
if you or your son speak [publish] anything in the world
of that matter [the claim to the English succession],
either in that treaty you desire, or by any other discourse or message that you may make or send to her
majesty Queen Elizabeth, I know you will greatly displease her and her people, and do yourself no good;
therefore, whatsoever you or your son do think thereof,
leave off to deal therein, and leaving all to God's good-

will,[1] be content with her majesty's favour otherways, if you hope to have it of her !"

She knoweth, by dear experience, what it is to offend her majesty [Queen Elizabeth] in great things. She thanked me for my plainness and good advice, and said, "she would not offend her majesty therein;" although desiring " that she might have at least like favour and estimation, as other of her blood had had at her majesty's hands."[2]

Then did I ask her opinion "where she thought the king her son had a fancy to match?" adding, "that I had heard of the Princess of Lorraine."

She replied, "There was such a notion, but thought it would not be;" and said, "that the Duke of Florence had offered his daughter, being fourteen or fifteen years, and a million of crowns with her."[3]

" Why, madam." quoth I, " do you think the duke would send his daughter from that warm and dainty country of Tuscany into the cold realm of Scotland?"

"Yea, I warrant you!" answered she. She also said, " that there was a motion made for a daughter of Denmark,[4] with great commodity of money and friendship;

[1] This honest and kind advice of Mr. Sommer (who seems as true-hearted as his relative, Sir Ralph Sadler, so much esteemed by the poor Queen of Scotland), was to warn Mary against aggravating Elizabeth's jealousy by claiming to be recognised as her successor.

[2] This probably alluded to Lord Darnley, her husband, who, before his marriage with the Queen of Scots, took precedence at the English court as first prince of the blood-royal, according to Melville's Memoirs, who was eye-witness of this fact.

[3] This must have been Marie de Medicis, married afterwards to Henry IV. of France

[4] Elizabeth, eldest daughter of Frederic II , King of Denmark and Sophia of Mecklenburgh The treaty was, in 1588, renewed for Anna, the younger princess of Denmark, whom King James married in 1589.

but the crown of Denmark, going by election [being elective], her son was not sure of longer influence than the life of the reigning king,[1] and, therefore, had no great fancy that way."

Then did I ask her of any offer of Spain, she answered merrily,

" So as my son might have the Low Countries withal; but who can warrant that ?   But I am sure my son will marry as I shall advise him !"

Here falling into other talk, she asked " Whether I thought she would escape from me or not, if she might ?"

I answered plainly.   " I believed she would, for it is natural for every thing to seek its liberty, that is kept in strait subjection."

" No, by my troth !" quoth she, " ye are deceived in me; for my heart is so great that I would rather die in this *sort* [state] with honour, than run away with shame." —I said, " I would be sorry to see the trial."

Then she asked me, " If she were at liberty with the queen's majesty's [Elizabeth's] favour, whither I thought she would go ?"

" I think, madam," quoth I, " you would go to your awn, in Scotland, as in good reason and command there."

" It is true," replied the queen of Scots; " I would go thither, indeed; but only to see my son, and give him good counsel; but unless her majesty [Elizabeth] would give me countenance and some maintenance in England, I would go to France, and live thenceforth among my friends, with the little portion I have there, and never trouble myself with government again, nor dispose my-

[1] The father of Frederic II., Christian III., had been elected to the throne on the deposition of Christian II., who had only female heirs, the Salic law being prevalent in Denmark.

self to marry any more, seeing I have a son who is a man; but I will never stay long there [*i. e.* in Scotland], nor would I govern, where I have received so many evil treatments." "For her heart," she added, "could not abide to look upon those folk that had done her that evil, being her subjects, whereof there are many yet remaining." I had told her that they were almost all dead.

Ever in her talk she beseeched her majesty to make trial of her, that, with some honourable end, she may live the rest of her days out of this captivity, as she termeth it.

This I have thought it meet in duty, to let be known to the queen's majesty, because here are some very material points.

The Queen of Scots to M. de Mauvissière.

Wingfield, Oct. 30, 1584.

Monsieur de Mauvissière,—I sent you a very long despatch on the last day of the past month, and, since that, another on the 18th of the present, to demand that I may be cleared and exculpated by a public examination and declaration of the Countess of Shereusbury, from the false reports she has circulated respecting me and her husband. If the whole has not been delivered to you, apply for it, that you may have occasion to proceed as I desired you, and remonstrate in my name. The principal point that I have now to write to you upon is my removal from this place, which, I am told, is resolved upon, either into the custody of that good man, Sir Raff Saddler, or . . . . Be this as it may, I beg you, in the name of monsieur the king, monsieur my good brother, and on my own behalf, to insist as strongly as you can, without relaxing on account of any excuse they may allege, that, before I am taken out of the hands of the said Earl of Shereusbury, I may, as I have desired, be fully satisfied and cleared from the said reports, which I will not have tacitly confirmed in the public opinion by my separation from the said earl. 2ndly. That he, in whose custody I may be placed, shall not be one of the pretenders against me or my son to this crown, nor a dependent of theirs, as my life would not be safe in such hands. 3rdly. That he be a person of such authority, influence, and power, that, in any event, either of the death of the Queen of England, or any other, he may be capable of protecting me against my enemies. 4thly. That the name of him who shall be appointed be notified to me, to know whether I have any objection to make against him on the ground of my personal safety. And in case that the said queen, my good sister, should desire to have the whole left to her choice, as knowing better than I her own subjects and those whom she can trust, it may easily be urged in reply, that she may perhaps be deceived by the representations of my enemies about her, and that, after she shall have heard my remonstrances, I will leave the final determination to her. 5thly. That my said new keeper shall deliver to me letters, by the hand of the said queen, conveying an express declaration of her intentions touching my said removal, and that she answer for their integrity and duty, and for the safety of my life in such custody; for I will not, in such an innovation, especially affecting my life and my condition, and consequently those of my son, suffer myself to be governed by any person but the said queen herself. Otherwise, she may be assured beforehand that she shall never take me hence but by force. 6thly. That I must know, if possible, before the said removal, what has been finally resolved upon in regard to the treaty for my liberty, whether it be a positive refusal and entire rupture, or an assured determination of proceeding and coming speedily to a final resolution. There can now be no plea for delaying this any longer, for Mr. Gray having been heard on behalf of my son, they cannot expect any more particular answer or explanation of his intention or mine on this subject. Meanwhile hasten, I beg you, with all the diligence you possibly can, the journey of Nau, and speak of it in particular, and in my name, to . . . . reminding him . . . .

I recommend to you the said Gray and all his negotiations, and that in any thing, wherein he may need your aid and assistance, and the intercession of the king monsieur my good brother, you would help him; and especially, if, in the next parliament, the right of succession to this crown be discussed, deliver to him a copy of the remonstrances which I formerly sent you on this subject, so that he may make representations with you on the part of my son, in our common name. If he obtains permission to come to me, I should be very glad if you could send Courcelles along with him, and in this case do not forget to inform the said Courcelles of all your ideas, opinions, and good counsels on my situation and affairs . . . . .

Do, if you please, all the good offices you can for that poor Jesuit, who, I hear, has been recently taken; not that I am afraid of his disclosing any communications of mine with him, as I have never had any upon any subject whatever, but for the preservation of the privileges and rights of foreign nations, it being a proceeding of too great consequence, that the subjects of a friendly king passing on the seas should be taken and so treated, as even to be put to the torture; the king monsieur my good brother being bound by the ancient league between France and Scotland to assist us in this affair. And,

this being all that I can say to you at present, as I am
in haste to send off this despatch, I will conclude with
my affectionate recommendations, praying God to have
you, Monsieur de Mauvissière, in his holy keeping.
Winfield, this xxxth day of October, 1584.

1584. *October.* An association is formed in England for bringing
to condign punishment not only the persons who may conspire
against Elizabeth but those in whose favour such plots may be
framed

October 31 The statement relative to this association is read to
Mary Stuart, who proposes to join it.

December —. Parry, a secret agent of Burleigh's, having gained
the confidence of Morgan in Paris, returns to London, and informs
against him and his accomplices.

1585. *January* 5 Mary Stuart signs an engagement, by which
she declares that all persons who make attempts against the life or
the power of Queen Elizabeth should be prosecuted by her unto
death.

January 13. She is removed from Wingfield to Tutbury.

The Queen of Scots to M. de Mauvissière.

Tutbury, Feb. 6, 1585.

Monsieur de Mauvissière,—I think it very strange to
be so long without hearing from you, particularly after
the last despatch which I sent you, which makes me
doubt whether it has been delivered to you with the
necessary diligence. I am now writing to the Queen of
England, madam my good sister, for permission to send
into Scotland, otherwise I am not sure to receive any
information respecting the intentions of my son, as my
letter, which I sent to obtain this, agreeably to the order
that was given me, was so tardily forwarded to him, that
it cannot be of any avail against the persuasions to the
contrary, which there will meanwhile be abundant opportunity to give my son. I therefore beg you affec-

tionately to urge, as warmly as you can, that my request respecting the said mission to Scotland may be complied with, having no other means so certain and expeditious of learning the state of affairs in that quarter, because upon this depends all that we have begun to treat of here.

I beg you also not to forget the attendants that I have again applied for, namely, two ladies for my chamber, two gentlemen, and two valets de chambre, that I may be sure of their passports, as I shall bring them either from France or Scotland; but, above all, the establishment of a small stud of twelve horses, besides my coach, it being impossible for me to take the air without them, since I am unable to walk fifty paces together. I told you before, how greatly I stand in need of money, which again compels me to importune you to forward to me, as early as you possibly can, whatever my treasurer may remit to you, either by bank or otherwise, having written to him earnestly on this subject in the enclosed despatch, which I beg you to send to him by the first opportunity. I hope you have received the order to send the xi^c [1100] livres; but, to this moment, nothing has yet arrived here; it would help me on the road, as they say. Remember me to my *commère*, your lady, and remind her to send me an answer to what I lately asked of her; that is, to engage me a lady of middle age, and one younger, if she knows any one that will suit me. Meanwhile, I pray God to have you, Monsieur de Mauvissière, in his holy and worthy keeping. Tutbury, this vith February, 1585.

M. de Mauvissière, I beg you to inquire diligently concerning him, or them, who are to supersede those in whose custody I now am. I dare say you perfectly recollect the remonstrances which, in such a case, I formerly desired you to make to the queen, madam my good

sister, and conformably with which the king monsieur
my brother-in-law, and the queen madam my mother-in-
law, were pleased to charge you to make solicitation in
their name.   You know of what importance this may be
to me.   I hope you will not be less assiduous than formerly.   I am so pressed to get the despatch ready for
sending off, the courier being on the point of setting out,
that I am writing this whilst at dinner, which will serve
for my excuse until the first opportunity.

Your much obliged and best friend,

MARY R.

1585. *February* —.   Parry himself is apprehended, and brought
to trial on the accusation of Nevil, another agent of the English
ministry.

February 25.   Sentence of death pronounced upon Parry; he is
executed a few days afterwards.

March 9   Elizabeth sends the Order of the Garter to Henry III.,
and demands the delivery of Morgan.   The king, not daring to
refuse altogether, orders him to be confined in the Bastille, and all
his papers to be given to the English ambassador.

The Queen of Scots to M. de Mauvissière.[1]

Tutbury, March 9, 1585.

Monsieur de Mauvissière,—Since my last was closed,
I have received yours of . . . day of February, with the
packet of my ambassador [Archbishop of Glasgow],
which has in part removed the pain in which I was, for
having been so long without receiving any letters from
France.   Now in the said packet I have found no letters
from the people of my council [*for her dowry as queen-
dowager of France*]; if you have any, send them if you
please, so that I may have them with diligence.

[1] Des Mesmes MS., No. 9513, tome iii. (99).   Bibliothèque du
Roi, Paris.

Meantime, I recommend to you again, and pray you most earnestly to insist on it, by all means, to obtain [leave] for your passage into Scotland and to me, with the son of M. de Pinart,[1] since it has thus been resolved; and come with those delegated on the part of the Queen of England, madam my good sister; this being the true and only way of arranging with my son all things solidly, and to clear up all from the very grounds, and to form a last deliberation to regulate the future. For who will proceed on a simple message, such as I am constrained to send, if you go not there? Nor can you be denied, understanding as you do these affairs, else I fear greatly that the whole will not come to the good end promised me on the one part and the other. And above all this, that you will send me word when the Justice-Clerk is expected [from Scotland]. I have made my request to the queen to let him come here to me, either going or returning; as much to have the consolation of hearing from him of the state of my son's health as to inform him myself of the intentions I had regarding this treaty with my son. I pray you to urge this, and send me the answer as soon as possible. And present two letters which I have written with my hand to the queen [Elizabeth], madam my good sister, for in them I have frankly informed her of the whole of my intention.

As to the accident which has occurred to the wretched and detestable Parry, I thank God infinitely for the grace he has shown, in that the said queen my good sister has so happily discovered his hateful design, on which I congratulate her myself in my letters, yet I beg you to do so yourself on my part, as I most sincerely do

---

[1] Pinart was private secretary to Catherine de Medicis. Mary expected she should have been included in the treaty between her son and Elizabeth; in three days she was aware of her disappointment.

in my heart, relying on her wisdom, if from this any of my enemies should take advantage to involve me in this adventure, which very prudently she had sent to me about, for which I thank her. She would know enough regarding it to ascertain the truth ; and, on my part, I ask no better, save that they [Elizabeth's ministers] should proceed with the most rigorous inquisition they can, to discover all those who are mixed up in this design, and in what mode they proceeded.[1] Well I remember the reply made me touching Sommerfield,[2] "that to excuse before being accused was a sign of a guilty conscience ;" and therefore I leave all to the prudence of the said queen my good sister, and wait the worst that my enemies choose to make of this affair; yet I pray, Monsieur de Mauvissière, omit not to defend my innocence and just cause.

I am thinking of writing to the king, my good brother, regarding what my ambassador spoke to him about, touching the state of my affairs and dowry. Nor can I help complaining of you, to yourself, for having despised the gift I made you of my town of Vittry, before

[1] It is a fact worth remarking that, whenever any treaty seemed in a favourable way of progressing towards the liberation of the unfortunate Mary, some assassination plot was always discovered by the ministers of Elizabeth against the life of that queen, by which they played on her fears and resentment to break the treaty When the trials of these assassins are examined, it will be found that they were worked on by mysterious agents, whom they knew little about ; and the assassins themselves were generally crackbrained persons, like this Sommerfield (or Sommerville) and Parry. These attempts were always attributed to the Queen of Scots, though they were sure to occur at a time so disastrous for her that, had they been concocted by her direst enemies (as she affirmed they really were), they could not have befallen more opportunely for her ruin.

[2] The leader of one of the numerous plots ostensibly made against the life of Elizabeth ; he killed himself in prison, and had been insane.

that the Sieur de Sommievre or any other, could have
spoken about it to the king; for so soon as those who
have my affairs in hand in Champagne (who were then
at Troyes) sent me word that the Sieur d'Armancourt
was condemned, I made them expedite my *lettres de
provision*, thinking that it might be agreeable to you to
have it. Although you have treated it with a negligence
which is prejudicial, saying, " that you cannot accept
it but by the express commandment of the king your
master," yet I greatly appreciate your moderation. It
is a long time since I wrote to my ambassador for him to
solicit the king about it; yet he found he could do little
concerning it during the long audience he had, neither
about the bad state of my other affairs. I cannot persuade myself that they would hold me for an utter
stranger in France, nor take from me the means of
exercising the rights that appertain to me there over my
dowry, in behalf of one towards whom I am so much
obliged as I am to you, by your performing the commissions you have so often done for me from the king
my good brother, your master, for these ten years, which
makes me greatly regret the little value of this present
from me to you—a thing so just and reasonable as it is;
which makes me so much astonished at the reply given
to my ambassador, that I am inclined to suppose that it
arises from some evil report that has reached the king
my good brother, rather than that he, whom I hold as
my only support and protector, would refuse me anything so very reasonable as the power of rewarding your
signal services.[1]

[1] On reference to her letter from Chartley, one twelvemonth
afterwards, viz., March 31, 1586, she again mentions the present of
her feudal rights in the town or bailiwick of Vittry. The moderation she justly praises in this letter, which made Mauvissière so loth
to accept anything from her poverty, is perfectly consistent with the

I pray you, while you stay on this side [of the water], which you will till my gossip your wife is put to bed, do not omit to aid me. I must ask you to negociate for me two thousand crowns at London, by some banker who can do it, and I will send for them a letter at sight on Chaulnes, my treasurer, without fail, for he has funds to do this ; which will be the case, as well, when I recommend myself to your good heart, and to that of my gossip [Madame de Mauvissière], and my god-daughter, whom I have an extreme desire to see, so virtuous as they say she is; and I pray God, Monsieur de Mauvissière, to have you in his holy and worthy keeping.

From Tutbury, this 9th day of March, 1585.

Your very good, obliged, and best friend,

MARY R.

[This letter is endorsed, Copy of a letter written by the Queen of Scotland to Monsieur de Mauvissière.]

The Queen of Scots to M. de Mauvissière.

Tutbury, March 11, 1585.

Monsieur de Mauvissière,—The principal object of this despatch is, to beg you to make more urgent representations than ever, in order to the prosecution of your journey to Scotland and of two others with you, on behalf of the Queen of England, madam my good sister, and myself, to remove completely all the difficulties in that quarter, which might prevent or delay the advance of the treaty begun between us ; for, till I know for certain, from the lips of my son himself, his intentions touching

character his brother historians have given him, as being one of the best good men of France. It is necessary to observe, that it appears by a subsequent document, that Mauvissière lent her the 2000 crowns she asks for here , and the documents in the succeeding pages refer to them and other loans.

his association to the crown of Scotland and conjunction
with me to the said treaty, I shall adhere to my original
determination not to pass and enact anything without
him, or to receive, through any other channel whatsoever, anything that shall come from him by message or
in writing, as his, and as proceeding from his own
movement and inclination. I never will do it, having,
in time past, had too much proof and experience of his
entire duty and good disposition towards me to be
lightly persuaded that he can now be so much changed
by the practices and the persuasions of my enemies, as
well in this country as about him. I have written freely
what I think on the subject to the said queen my good
sister in my enclosed letters, which I request you to
deliver to her from me, urging as much as I can that
journey, and representing to her how necessary your
prudence is there, for upholding the said association as
made, and principally upon the advice and counsel of
the king your master, monsieur my good brother, and of
the queen my mother-in-law, they having been the first
and the only persons who persuaded me to it.

Exert yourself, on your part, by all means in your
power, to bring about your said journey to Scotland,
and, if possible, to this place; but it is necessary to be
expeditious, lest things in Scotland should become irre-
mediable. Meanwhile, if you learn that it is in con-
templation to make a change in my keeper, I beg you to
interpose the name and credit of my said lord and
brother to prevent it, so that no alteration be made till
the said queen my good sister has taken a final resolution touching the treaty, as it cannot be otherwise but
that in two months, at latest, things must be sufficiently
settled both in Scotland and elsewhere, for a speedy end
to be put to them, as the state of my health, so impaired
by an imprisonment of seventeen years, requires more

than ever. I place entire confidence in the said queen my good sister, whose good disposition I perceive, and learn to know better from day to day, by her honourable conduct towards me in what proceeds from her own movement; but, on the other hand, I must confess that I am grieved to the heart by the crosses which I have to endure, but especially by the estrangement of my son from me and his being set against me; praying God to let me die rather than learn for certain that such a thing can be.

It would not be amiss, I think, if, by the first opportunity you have of writing to Scotland, you would intimate to my son, that I have requested you, in case he refuses the legitimate title and authority of king in association with me, as he has written to the Queen of England madam my good sister, to cease to give him that title in all negotiations in this country, and that I will take steps to cause the same course to be followed in all parts of Christendom to which my influence extends; nay, even give him my everlasting malediction, and deprive him, as far as in me lies, of all the grandeur which he can claim in this world in my right, leaving him only that of his father to enjoy; for I think no punishment, divine or human, can equal such enormous ingratitude, if he is guilty of it, as to choose rather to possess by force and tyrannically that which justly belongs to me, and to which he cannot have any right but through me and of my goodwill and free gift. Moreover, I request you to thank the said queen my good sister, in my name, for the honourable care which she demonstrates to me that she takes that I should be well accommodated in this country, both in regard to servants and other necessary things; but, as the principal thing that can contribute to the recovery and preservation of my health is to take the air abroad, which I can now only do on horseback, I must employ your solicitation to procure me some order for the sixteen horses, for which I have already applied, as well for myself as for some of my women and others of my servants, who will have to accompany me : the expense cannot be great; and this I should esteem the principal gratification in my whole treatment from this time forward.

As for the new servants that have been granted me, I thank Mr. de Walsingham for them. You will once more request him, if you please, to give you assurance of their passports when they arrive, agreeably to the enclosed memorandum, for I cannot specify their names, because that depends on the choice made by my ambassador and others, to whom I shall address myself in France. Learn, in particular, if Nau's brother will be permitted to come hither from Scotland, where I think he still is at present; and, in this case, I beg you to send to him the enclosure, which I have written to him, desiring him to come. His good qualities and the assistance which his brother will receive from him in matters relating to my service and his office make me the more desirous of this, and I shall feel an especial obligation to the said de Walsingham for it.

I am very sorry for the tardiness and delay of my treasurer in paying the money you have lent me, it being purely and entirely his fault; for, as I have arranged my affairs, he cannot, on any occasion whatever, plead in excuse that he has not funds for such demands as are for my own person, and which he ought to discharge every year before any others, whatever they may be. In the month of May last, when I received by Beale the remainder of that sum of fifteen hundred crowns, since increased by three hundred, which he remits for payment, I signified to him, in a letter in

my own hand, the receipt of the said sum, and ordered
him most expressly to discharge it without delay, according to the order for the purpose delivered at the
time to Bauldwyn, because he had been the bearer of
part of the said sum, and Wade even declared lately,
in the presence of Nau and Courcelles, that he recol-
lected that such an order was found among the papers
of the said Bauldwyn. Now, Monsieur de Mauvissière,
in order to repay all that I have hitherto received from
you, I have written a line to my said treasurer, in language as positive and peremptory as I can, as you may
see yourself; and you may be assured that I am highly
displeased to find myself so ill obeyed in that quarter.
Let, I request you, payment be obtained from Mazzy,
the banker, of the two thousand crowns which the said
Chaulnez has remitted through him, and find means to
forward them to me, with the xi^c [1100] crowns, either
by means of M^r. Walsingham, or by the next carrier,
whom you may find to be coming to this quarter; for I
cannot do without them any longer. In a month's
time, several servants of Sir Raff Sadler's are coming
hither from London; the money might be sent by them;
or, that way failing, M^r. de Walsingham might order it
to be paid here by one of the receivers of the queen my
good sister in these parts, which would be the most
prompt, easy, and safe method. I thank you for the
choice you give me of your people to come hither to
serve me, and will make up my mind about it between
this and my next despatch. I have been much pleased
with the head-dresses which my *commère*, your good
wife, has sent me. God grant her a happy delivery,
and have you both in his holy and worthy keeping.
Tutbury, the xith day of March, 1585.

Your entirely best friend,

MARY R.

1585. *March*—. Sir Amias Paulet appointed keeper of Mary Stuart.

The Queen of Scots to M. de Mauvissière,[1] *Ambassador in England from Henry III.*

Tutbury, March 12, 1585.

Monsieur de Mauvissière,—I have just received, by Sommer, a letter said to be from my son, but so far in language and reality from his former promises, and from the duty and obligation that my said son owes to me, that I cannot receive it for his own, but rather for the act of Gray,[2] who, full of impiety and dissimulation, as much towards God[3] as towards man, thinks this letter a *chef d'œuvre*, which is to screen what he is undertaking in this country, to wit, the entire separation of my son from me. Therefore, I implore you, as you will do me a kindness in a matter of the last importance, and which touches me so nearly, that you will request the Queen of England that I may speak to the Justice-Clerk[4] [lately sent to her], in order to let me understand by him more fully of the truth of my son's intention, and at the same time send him my final resolution in this case, which, if she permits not, I shall have great reason to impute to her bad ministers, before all Christendom,

[1] Des Mesmes MS., No. 9515, fol. 158. Original State Letters. Bibliothèque du Roi, Paris.

[2] For the character and conduct of this man, see the supplementary part of this volume.

[3] By this expression, we find Mary was aware that Gray's profession of her religion was a mere mask.

[4] M. de Mauvissière has noted,—"This Justice-Clerk was a young ambassador sent from Scotland, who would not go to the Queen of Scots without express commands." The office of Justice-Clerk was a situation, the second in rank in the legal department of the Scottish government.

this evil conduct, and first division between my son and me: because, before they intermeddled between us, we had always been in good and perfect amity, such as God and nature required. But since that (on the assurances which they have given us), I have consented to walk in their way, nothing has prospered but all impiety, in the which if men think to make advantage politically, as perhaps our common enemies intend, I hope that God, the all-just, will avenge himself sooner or later

The second point, on which I would have you labour, is to draw a clear and final resolution from the said queen my good sister, in case she holds as the intention of my said son the contents of this letter, that she will make me, if she pleases, plainly and particularly understand whether she means to treat with me or not; and how she determines to proceed in it, without holding these things as occasion of vain delay and putting off; for she has not yet sent in her definitive reply, deferring it purposely till I knew these excuses of my son. In the mean time, that my son may feel to what the ways of his good friends and councillors here [*i. e.* in this country] have conducted him and will lead him hereafter, I pray you, immediately and for the future, to take from him the name of king, since he will not hold it of me; and, until he makes this recognition, I am assured that the king [Henry III.] my good brother, who is the author of the association [1] between us (and has been

---

[1] This passage alludes to a curious point of secret history between Mary and her son, best developed by an attentive perusal of these letters. Mary had entered into an agreement (called by her an *association*) with her son, whom, after the revolution, called the Raid of Ruthven, made by the Calvinist republicans, she found too weak to support his regal authority without the aid of her faithful friends. It appears by the present letter, that the King of France was a party to this wise measure, by which Mary surrendered her regal rights to her boy, and effected a coalition of her friends with his, on condi-

himself a signal example in the present age, and to all
posterity, of the rare piety of a son to a mother),[1] will
not countenance or maintain him in this enormous ingratitude.   And I entreat you at this time, or at any future
time, name not my son as king in any negotiation that
you carry on with him.

I wish also that the queen [Elizabeth] would declare
to you, if she means to maintain the usurpation of my
said son in the fashion to which, it seems, he pretends,
or what is her opinion in this case.   My son has sent
to me, " that the reason he cannot join with me in this
treaty is, because I am held captive in a desert."   The
queen my good sister can exonerate me when she pleases
from this objection, and put me at once in a free state to
serve her, as I would sincerely desire, if she would but
give me an opportunity.

God give me consolation, and have you, Monsieur de
Mauvissière, in his holy and worthy keeping.

From Tutbury, the 12th day of March, 1585.

tion, that he should acknowledge that he received the title of king
from her voluntary resignation, and not from her forcible deposition
by her rebels.   Hence her extreme anguish at the ungrateful treatment, of which she complains here, and in the subsequent grand,
but imprudent, letter to her persecutor, Elizabeth.   All the parties
treated her with neglect, her reproaches were never suffered to
reach her son, who was virtually as much a captive as herself, but
with a tether long enough to allow him to follow the chase and take
personal exercise.   It was strange that Mary, who knew by experience to how low an ebb the personal power of a Scottish sovereign
had dwindled, should for one moment have considered her son a
responsible agent in the matter   Her good sense clearly shows her
at once whose work it is, and yet her heart is pierced with maternal
anguish, and she cannot refrain from reproaching James, who was
then only in his seventeenth year.

[1] To Catherine de Medicis, whom he permitted to be his prime
minister, though he was of full age to govern for himself, and to
rule his kingdom to their mutual tribulation.

" *What follows is in the handwriting of the Queen of Scotland,*"—*such is the indorsement on the manuscript.*

Monsieur de Mauvissière, — I am so grievously wounded and cut to the heart, by the impiety and ingratitude my child has been constrained to commit against me in this letter, dictated to him by Gray, being both in terms and in substance quite similar to one which he wrote to me in cipher, whilst he [Gray] staid in London. But if my son persists in this, you can assure him by the Justice-Clerk (in reply to the fine message he has brought me on his part), that I will invoke the malediction of God on him, and will give him not only mine, with all circumstances that may touch him to the quick, but say also that I will disinherit him, and deprive him, as an unnatural son, who is ingrate, perfidious, and disobedient, of all the grandeur that he can have through me in this world; and rather in such case will I give my right (be it what it may) to the greatest enemy that he may have, before ever he shall enjoy it by usurpation, as he does my crown, to which, save by my act, he has no right, as I will show that he himself confesses under his own hand.

I cannot persuade myself that the queen my good sister would ever favour and support so enormous and detestable an impiety, nor refuse me to clear up the whole with the Justice-Clerk, for one echo cannot suffice for such a report as this! At least, she could untie my hands, and let me treat with my child as required, seeing that he excuses himself by reproaching me with my long captivity in a desert! And this reward for having done all that I could to obey and please him.

But if they would let me have a little explanation

with the Justice-Clerk,[1] I could more patiently receive
the good or evil that would result, without attributing ill
to any other than to the ministers of the queen [Eliza-
beth] my good sister; so much of passions, malice, and
enmity, have I experienced from them on less occasions
than this affair.   And because Archibul Duglas has had
many secrets together with this Gray, who has so falsely
comported himself towards me, I wish you would tell
him that I cannot but suspect him, unless he gives me
some good proof of the fidelity he has so often sworn to
me; for, if he comports not himself as he ought to me, I
shall disavow him as mine [agent], for he need not
reckon to be on both sides; he may consider it enough
to be favoured in the country here, and with my lost
child. Believe not, I entreat you, anything that these
persons may show in outward semblance of affection
towards my service; and if he [Archibald Douglas]
would be for me, let him declare it in plain terms, as
he has offered before now.[2]

    Abandon not, I implore you, Monsieur de Mauvis-
sière, the justice of my just cause; aid me with your

---

[1] Her passionate requisition of the conference with this minister,
whose official title must be so undignified to English readers, was
evidently to learn from him, whether the political manœuvre of
leaving her name out of a treaty ostensibly opened with France,
England, and Scotland, for her freedom, arose from her son's personal cruelty towards her, or was a mere state trick of the dominant
faction in Scotland.   Her son, in his manuscripts, earnestly af-
firms, that he was as much a prisoner at the time, and long after,
as she was herself.

[2] She was perfectly right in her suspicions of this traitor; she
had disavowed him for her agent some time previously to this
period, as appears by the Sadler Papers, vol. ii.   Patrick Gray and
Keith threw all the blame regarding the death of Mary on Archibald Douglas. And it was said at the court of Scotland, "that
this man had now compassed the deaths both of the king's mother
and father."   He died, nevertheless, a prosperous nobleman.

accustomed firmness and prudence, since you alone can
do much for me, by means of the authority and name
you have near the queen my good sister, that before
your departure [from England] I may know my best or
my worst.

    Your very affectionate and obliged friend,

                      MARY R.

The Queen of Scots to Queen Elizabeth [1]

Tutbury, March 23, 1585.

    Madam, my good sister,—Since I cannot obtain per-
mission to send to my son, or speak to any one coming
on his part to this country, to clear up, as I have so
many times required, all that is ill interpreted and traversed between him and me; by which I see, more and
more, the little that remains for me to hope, my enemies
being, meantime, suffered to continue their old practices, in the case of my misled child, to sever him from
me as they have laboured so earnestly for a long time
past, I have therefore come to a resolution, which I will
not longer defer making you understand that, since my
ill-advised son is so unhappy, and abandoned by the
Spirit of God, that he permits himself to be led and
persuaded to refuse to hold of me[2] that of which,
without me, he could not be legitimately possessed; it
may please you at once to bring to a conclusion the
treaty for my liberty, and to permit me to retire, with
your good grace, out of this isle into some solitary place,
as much for the repose of my soul as of my body. And
I offer you anew not only those terms which have been
lately tendered by my secretary but all other things I

---

[1] MS. Des Mesmes, No. 9513. Bibliothèque du Roi, Paris.
[2] His title to the throne of Scotland.

will give up without any reserve, save honour and safe conscience, that you may be entirely satisfied, and I out of this slavery, or " *desert* captivity," (which is my reproach.)

I would, as much for myself as my posterity, renounce and quit for ever all rights that I or mine can pretend to in this kingdom after you, (whom God preserve,) which will at once take away altogether all motive for my enemies to cause you to distrust me and make you forget the others.

I shall, by this means, no more serve for a pretext, to whomsoever they may be, who do or attempt, under my name or pretence to my favour, anything to your prejudice or annoyance ; for since of late he[1] has failed me and deceived me, for whose sole advantage (I take the living God to witness) I have suffered and strove in this my captivity to uphold and preserve the grandeur which appertained to me and was my lot in this world, having held *his* preservation much more dear to me than my own, he shall no more descant on what is to befall him and me in the future; in short, he shall no longer experience that the greatest pleasure I have in this world is his advancement, but rather, it will be to leave him to all posterity a signal example of God's just vengeance on him and his supporters, for tyranny, ingratitude, and impiety.

You may remember, madam, how it pleased you to send to me, that you had never recognized him for king by letter written with your own hand, before I myself had so called him; but I did not so, neither did I require other princes to do the same, excepting on his consent and promise to enter into a bond of agreement, by him requested and since sent to him, as I desired,

[1] Her son, James VI.

perfect.[1]   On his side he acknowledged that he had
neither right nor security in the possession of the crown,
but by my voluntary acceptance of his duty and my
abdication of all government, the which I myself then
remitted to him, contenting myself with the honours and
the name which was my due, without any hindrance to
his ambition, sanctioned by my agreement.[2]   And in
truth, he could neither hold [his crown] legitimately and
in security by any other way; or it would be extremely
prejudicial to all princes in Christendom, and in consequence, to you among them; although, some among
your subjects, very near to you, dare publicly to affirm
and uphold the election and deposition of kings   Be
not, I entreat you, one of those who open the door to
such extraordinary violences, and instead of being my
protectress to whom I have utterly committed myself,
suffer not, under the shelter of your name and countenance, such impiety to be established and maintained,
contrary to all law, divine or human.

It has happened sometimes that brothers and other
near relatives have, in regard to one another, forgotten
all in the ambition of reigning, but alas ! was ever a
sight so detestable and impious, before God or man, as
an only child, and one to whom all has been yielded and
given up at will, not only despoiling his mother of her
crown and royal estate, (for as to the crown, he cannot
be debarred from it even if it were in debate—which it
is not—for I have willingly given it to him, and ask but

---

[1] She means *perfectly executed;* this was the voluntary deed of
abdication in favour of her son, which was a most sensible measure
for Mary to take in her situation, but the gist of the matter is,
that she chooses to endow him of her own free will.   `

[2] This explanation shows why Lord Herries, Seaton, and a large
body of true and loyal Scotch nobles, transferred their allegiance
to King James; they only did so by her express orders.

honour and liberty of conscience, without ever desiring to set foot in Scotland.) But otherwise infatuated by sinister and partial counsel, he would prefer rather to detain it by usurpation and the violence of his subjects, (though of daily occurrence to himself under his own eyes,) than by my frank, liberal, and pure consent. For God's sake, madam—you are his godmother, and much have I desired you to be his other mother, as at a former time I left him to you, when I thought myself about to die, and would have it so still—make him then reflect—with your natural inclination to all that is just, and with your accustomed prudence — what good or honour can at the end revert to you from such counsel, (which I know well others than you have given him), of joining, by any league or treaty of amity with my child separated thus from me, for lack of liberty of being enlightened of the truth. Be not the means, then, by countenancing him, of confirming him more in his ingratitude and neglect towards me.

He will come to have proof, (as without doubt he will, if I persist in giving him for ever my malediction, and of depriving him, as much as he can be by me, of all benefit and grandeur he thinks to pretend to, through me, in Scotland and elsewhere,) that in all Christendom I shall find enough of heirs, who will have talons strong enough to grasp what I may put into their hand.[1]   And

[1] In this bitter denunciation against her son, whom cruel mischief-makers had misrepresented to her, Mary follows the idea which at that era prevailed throughout the world, (excepting with some bold reformers,) that kingdoms were like estates, not only to be enjoyed at the pleasure of the possessor, but liable to be left with the good-will and blessing of parents to their heirs, if dutiful; while, on the contrary, if the heir gave offence, he could be disinherited, and the kingdom and people left to a stranger by will. The great stress Queen Elizabeth had laid on a bequest of this kind, obtained from Mary, when a child, by Henry II., must have

rather than retract from it, let them [her son and his
counsellors] make my corpse the shortest way, if they
please, to their ends, for this will be to me more welcome.   And for my resolution, assure yourself that, if,
after having sincerely opposed, and, as far as was permitted me unto the present, done and performed whatever in me lay to rank myself entirely with you, and
lead my said son with me; and surely, if I am left and
put after him, and if he thinks to treat with you, supposing under your name that our enemies will yield to
him, as he persuades himself—there is a long time to
that, as he himself sent to me by Gray—but assure
yourself, sooner than this I will disavow him for my
son, lay on him my malediction, and disinherit him, not
only from what he holds now, but from all that, through
me, he can pretend to elsewhere,[1] abandoning him to his
subjects to do to him as he has been instigated to do to
me, and also to strangers to invade and punish him for
his fault.   At least, I assure myself, that he will not
enjoy without trouble anything that may come to him
with the strength and support he has.   And I will take
from him—and with good right—the protection of God,
who will not, against the promise of his word, favour to

confirmed this queen in thinking, that the threat which she offers
above would be formidable to Queen Elizabeth and her son, who,
it seems, (by the intrigues of Patrick Gray,) were concluding the
treaty, opened ostensibly for Mary's liberation from her doleful
prison, without the slightest heed to her miseries, and worse than
that, Patrick Gray, she had been most truly told, was conspiring
her death.   Among other accusations against James, he has been
blamed for the banishment of Patrick Gray from court, and the
detestation in which he ever held him after his mother's execution;
but had he ever seen the letters that passed between that traitor and
Archibald Douglas, he would not have been content with such
light inflictions.

[1] The English throne.

the end, the like impiety and injustice! Thus, whoever may treat with him will have in it little honour, merit, or security, nor will my enemies draw from him such advantages as they may think; if indeed, they are not merely trying to ruin him by his own means, which I believe they are essaying to do. Receive not, I supplicate you, regarding this, the evil interpretation of mine enemies; for I proceed simply, and with open heart, to show you in like case what I am resolved to do, in order that afterwards you may not find any fault, or blame me for having done aught without your knowledge, or ask more than a *yes* or a *no* in all this affair. You could have me assuredly all your own to serve you, as I have offered in all which pertains to your good, your preservation, and your contentment; but this being only accepted with the loss of my child, I have no more to leave to you or him but my poor body, to do with it what it would appear (save the will of God) that my enemies have been wishing and urging so long; but as to any fear or apprehension of such like accident, I would not take a single step or say a single word more or less; for I had rather die and perish with the honours such as it pleased God I was born to, than by pusillanimity to disgrace my life, by prolonging it with anything unjust and unworthy of myself and of my race.

It pleased you to promise me by my secretary [Nau], being, as he said, your last words at his departure, that after you should have replied to Scotland, you would send me plainly your last resolution touching this treaty for my liberty. At this moment I pray and require you, as affectionately and earnestly as possible, that you will no longer delude the rest of my miserable days with vain hope, and that I may, for the last time (as

I have already said), have power to attend to my affairs at this good season of Easter, before taking my course of medicine.

Moreover, on this, that the French ambassador has lately imparted to me, about one Parry and of Morgan, I will only say, taking it on my honour and conscience, that you will not find me mixed up with anything of the sort, abhorring more than any other in Christendom such detestable practices and horrible acts. For, to speak freely, madam, I believe that those who attempt your life would do as much on mine, and indeed, at this moment, mine wholly depends on yours, for well I know that, if yours should be cut off, you have near you those of these new Associates[1] who would soon cause me to follow you; but I would far rather go before than live with such a burden, with which I think I shall not be laden. God, then, and my conscience will be sufficient to exonerate me in this case, and I will trouble you no more, that I may not give cause to my enemies to say, as they did when I wrote on a similar occasion about Sommerfield, "that very often those who defend themselves before they are charged with aught accuse themselves." But you will find that I bear a heart far enough from any such wicked intention, and that more than ever (if I had no more from you to complain of) I would respect you, love you, obey you, and serve you faithfully and sincerely in all I could, in return for that

[1] Of a celebrated Association in which each member took a pledge to defend the life of Queen Elizabeth, and revenge, to the utmost of his power, any attempts on it. Mary Queen of Scots herself offered to become a member, though it was confederated peculiarly for her destruction by Burleigh and his party, of which she gives a hint here.

liberty, which I yet demand of you at the conclusion of this letter, in tears and oppressed with grief.

    At Tutbuiy, this 23rd of March, 1585.

        Your humble and very affectionate, but desolate sister and cousin,

                    MARY R.

[On the back of this letter is written, in the hand of M. de Mauvissière, *Copy of a letter of the Queen of Scots to the Queen of England, 23rd March*, 1585.]

March 24. The Queen of Scotland, being informed that Gray, her son's envoy, was betraying her interests, resolves to deprive James VI. of all rights which he holds from her.

The Queen of Scots to M. de Mauvissière.

                      Tutbury, May 15, 1585.

Monsieur de Mauvissière,—You have seen by my last, which I forwarded by Monsieur Sommers, how much I was grieved to be so long without receiving any news from you. The same day that he left this place arrived a packet from you, addressed to Nau, in which I found a single letter for me, of the xxvi[th] of April, making mention of another large despatch that I have not yet received. I beg you will urge that it be speedily forwarded to me, as I am in expectation to have news by it concerning the business of my dower. And I will defer writing to those of my council in France, until I receive the said despatch. I should, moreover, be glad to know particularly how you have proceeded with the Queen of England, madam my good sister, relative to the points, which I some time since recommended to your attention, not having heard any thing on the subject through any channel whatever. I have given to the aforesaid Sommer a memorial, which he will show

                        H 5

to you, that you may, if you please, have the matter followed up, being sure that he will need your assistance. Above all, persist in this my determined importunity to be clearly resolved of the intention of the said queen my good sister relative to my deliverance or detention in this captivity, not desiring to remain altogether bound by offers and conditions so strict as I proposed in the utmost sincerity, and by orders, rules, and regulations more precise and rigorous than ever in this new prison; for, no doubt, it will be very difficult for good-will and force ever to unite in me; and the said queen my good sister will never find, not only as regards myself but in all other things which may depend on me elsewhere, so much security in the close custody of any one whatever to whom she may commit my body, as in my heart, my faith, and my promises, none of which I have ever yet broken; being, I protest to you, more grieved, vexed, and uncomfortable, to find that, do what I will, I cannot induce her to place any confidence in me, than on account of my imprisonment itself and the severities by which she thinks the better to secure me.

I thank you affectionately for your loan of two thousand crowns, which you sent me by the S^r· Darell, and for the reimbursement of which sum I enclose you an order on my treasurer, which I have drawn for the wages of my officers, whom I found to be in such great need that I was obliged to give them that. For the satisfaction of my said treasurer, you will see the note that I have written with my own hand, under the aforesaid order. I am greatly displeased that Gozzy has of late been so negligent in his correspondence. I believe you have seen what I have written at different times to my said treasurer, to obviate such severities and abatements which he ought not to practise in any thing that concerns my own person. Wherefore I am afraid to importune you further, and to contract more debts over there, though my revenue for the whole of this year is in arrear; the which if you receive from my said treasurer, or if you can assist me by obtaining money from the French merchants, with their convenience, as you wrote to me, try to prevail on Mr. High Treasurer, or Mr. Walsingham, to write to Sir Amyas Paulet, to draw as much as you may deliver over to them from abroad from the hands of the receiver of this province, and to pay it to me here; about this, I think, they will not make any difficulty, as it would cause them neither loss nor inconvenience that I can apprehend.

Moreover, among other innovations made here, I complain through you to the queen madam my good sister that the said Sr. Paulet would not permit me, a few days since, to send some trifling alms, according to my means, to the poor of this village; which, indeed, I cannot but impute to very strange rigour, as it is a pious work, and one which no Christian can disapprove of; and in which the said Sr. Paulet might take such precautions, and send with my man such of his servants or soldiers as he pleases, or even the constable of the village, as to leave no cause or ground for complaint or suspicion; so that, having by these means provided for the safety of his charge, it appears to me wrong to debar me from a christian work that might afford me consolation amidst sickness and affliction, without giving offence or being prejudicial to any person whatever. Remonstrate about this, I beg of you, in my name, with the queen my good sister, and request her to command Sr. Paulet not to treat me in this manner, as there never was a criminal or prisoner, however vile, low, or abject, to whom this permission has ever been by any law denied.

I am very sorry to learn from you the likelihood of

fresh troubles in France, and still more that my relatives are so deeply involved in them; but I hope that
the king, monsieur my brother-in-law, who is a prince,
full of zeal for his religion and of love for his subjects,
will find means to put a stop to them, and timely, with
the prudence of the queen, madam my mother-in-law,
as nothing can result from such divisions but a great
convulsion of their kingdom. But my present personal
misery presses upon me so heavily and so long as to
give sufficient occupation to my thoughts, without my
thinking on the evils that threaten others. Wherefore,
leaving all to the inscrutable providence of God, before
whom the wisdom and the designs of men are but a mere
illusion, I pray him to grant the king my said lord and
brother a happy continuation of his reign, and to have
you, M. de Mauvissière, in his holy and worthy keeping.
From Tuthbury, the xvth day of May, 1585.

Your much obliged and very best friend,

MARY.

---

*Memorial addressed by the Queen of Scots to Queen
Elizabeth.*

Sent by M. Sommers.

The Queen of Scotland beseeches the Queen of England her good sister to give her an answer to the three
last letters which she has written to her, especially
touching a final and clear determination on the treaty
for her liberty, respecting which, for reasons she has
amply explained to the said Sr. Sommer, she begs more
earnestly than ever that it may please the said Queen
her good sister to negociate separately with her, without
any intervention on the part of Scotland.

That, to settle those matters which formerly led to
differences between her and her son, she may be per-

mitted to send some one to him, accompanied by the French ambassador, agreeably to the most express commission which he has to this effect from the king his master.

That the ordinary communication which she has hitherto had with the said ambassador may be continued; and, accordingly, directions given for the more diligent despatch of their packets, as well on the one part as the other; nothing passing between them that can in any way prove prejudicial to this kingdom.

That her household establishment here be determined upon and fixed; in order that, as the said Queen, her good sister, has been pleased to assure her, she may take her into her own keeping and into her own house: also, that from her alone she may receive her allowance in this country.

That a second house may be granted her to remove to on finishing her course of diet, or next autumn, at latest; it being quite impossible, without great detriment to her health, to live in winter in the two rooms which she has here for the whole of her lodgings, which are built of wood, old, full of holes, and tumbling down on all sides, and having no sheltered place whatever to walk in or retire to.

That, in regard to the servants allowed her, and that they may not have the trouble of travelling hither in vain, it be declared whether she shall be permitted to bring over any she may choose, as she might select some from the household of Guise, having no other acquaintance in France through whom to get them.

And that, as for ordinary varlets, her servants may be permitted to employ Englishmen, so as to avoid the frequent coming and going of such persons, whom it is difficult to retain.

Done at Tuthbury, the xth of May, 1585.

This memorial is to be found in Castelnau (de Mauvissière) vol. i. p. 627. It is introduced here as connected with the foregoing letter, and as completing the instructions of the Queen.

The Queen of Scots to M. Antoine de Chaulnes.

Tutbury, May 15, 1585.

The Queen of Scotland, Dowager of France.

Monsieur Antoine de Chaulnes, treasurer and receiver-general of our finances, we command you to pay and deliver, in ready money, to M. de Mauvissière, chevalier of the order of his most Christian king, our very dear and much honoured brother-in-law, and his ordinary ambassador in this kingdom, the sum of two thousand crowns, in repayment of the like sum, which we certify to have been furnished and sent by him to this place, Tuthbury, for the payment of wages of the officers about our person for the year ending the last day of December m.v^{c}iiii^{xx} and four ; and, on delivery of this our present order, with the receipt of the said M. de Mauvissière, we will that the said sum of two thousand crowns be passed and allowed in the statement of your accounts by our dear and faithful counsellors, the auditors, whom we command to do this without any difficulty. For such is our pleasure. Given at the castle of Tuthbury in England, the xvth of May, 1585.

MARY R.

NAU.

I have ordered this sum to be applied to the payment of wages of my officers who are here, for the last year, preferring their necessities to my own ; and, in future, do not fail to send in time and apart what is appropriated for them, agreeably to the particular statement which you will receive. That which has been received for the last year has not been without very urgent necessity. Give orders that I may, with all diligence, be furnished, as heretofore I desired you, with the two thousand crowns for myself, and the five hundred for my stable.

MARY R.

1585. *June* 20. The Earl of Northumberland commits suicide in the Tower of London.

The Queen of Scots to M. de Mauvissière.

Tutbury, July 12, 1585.

Monsieur de Mauvissière,—Since my last letter, I have heard, that you have obtained for me over there xv^c [1500] crowns, and that you will send me as much as three thousand on my furnishing you with an order for that amount; considering, on the other hand, the extreme need I have of it at present, not having yet received anything from my treasurer for the whole of this year, I have resolved to send you an order for the sum of iii^m iii^c xxxiii [3333] crowns, the which my said treasurer ought to furnish me for myself for this said year, according to the account which I send to him with the present despatch, and that out of the first clear moneys he shall receive, and on the authority of this, so that your reimbursement will not be on any account delayed. But I shall not fail to remember the particular obligation I owe you, and to return it the very first opportunity that shall present itself. And as this has no other object, I shall pray God, M. de Mauvissière, to have you in his holy and worthy keeping. Tuthbury, xiith of July, 1585.

Your much obliged and best friend,

MARY R.

1585. *September.*   M. l'Aubespine de Chateauneuf succeeds
M de Mauvissière as French ambassador.

---

*The Queen of Scots to M. de Mauvissière and M. de
Chateauneuf.*

Tutbury, September 5, 1585.

Gentlemen,—Foreseeing that your answer to my last
will be some time before it reaches me, I have thought
it best, without waiting for it, to impart to you my just
complaints concerning what Sir Amyas has been directed
to signify to me, touching the memorial which I have
sent you, which amounts, in fact, to an absolute refusal
of the principal requests contained in it, namely, those
relating to the change and conveniences of dwelling,
intelligence concerning the affairs of my dowry by the
Sieur de Cherelles, and the increase of the number of my
servants—things, though trifling and of no importance
to the Queen of England madam my good sister, yet so
necessary for the preservation of my life and health, so
mainly contributing to the few comforts that are left me
in this world, and to my consolation between these four
walls (where I perceive more clearly from day to day
that they are determined to reduce me to the last
extremity), that, but for the very urgent need I have
of them, I could not have stooped to beg for them
with such earnest and persevering supplications, that I
think I could not have bought them at a dearer rate;
regretting exceedingly that, for all the duty I have im-
posed upon myself to please the said queen in every
thing and in every place, so little consideration and respect is paid to my honour and content in the matter of
my state and treatment here.

To give you, then, ocular proof of the situation in
which I find myself in regard to dwelling in the first

place, and that you may remonstrate in my behalf on the subject with the said queen (who, I presume, has never been accurately informed about it), I will tell you that I am in a walled enclosure, on the top of a hill, exposed to all the winds and inclemencies of heaven. Within the said enclosure, resembling that of the wood of Vincennes, there is a very old hunting-lodge, built of timber and plaster, cracked in all parts, the plaster adhering nowhere to the wood-work, and broken in numberless places; the said lodge distant three fathoms or thereabouts from the wall, and situated so low, that the rampart of earth which is behind the wall is on a level with the highest point of the building, so that the sun can never shine upon it on that side, nor any fresh air come to it; for which reason it is so damp, that you cannot put any piece of furniture in that part, without its being in four days completely covered with mould. I leave you to think how this must act upon the human body; and, in short, the greater part of it is rather a dungeon for base and abject criminals than a habitation fit for a person of my quality, or even of a much lower.

I am sure that there is not a nobleman in this kingdom, nor even one of those who, being inferior to noblemen, wish to reduce me beneath themselves, who would not deem it a tyrannical punishment, to be obliged to live for a year in so straitened and inconvenient a habitation as they want to force and constrain me to do; and the only apartments that I have for my own person consist—and for the truth of this I can appeal to all those who have been here—of two little miserable rooms, so excessively cold, especially at night, that, but for the ramparts and entrenchments of curtains and tapestry which I have had made, it would not be possible for me to stay in them in the daytime; and out of those who have sate up with me at night during my illnesses, scarcely one has escaped without fluxion, cold, or some disorder. Sir Amyas can bear witness that he has seen three of my women ill at once from this cause alone; and my physician himself, who has had his share of it, has several times positively declared "that he will not take charge of my health, during the next winter, if I am to remain in this house." As for replastering or in any way repairing or enlarging it, you may conceive how wholesome it would be for me to live in such new pieces of patchwork, when I cannot endure the least breath of damp air in the world; and on this account it is of no use whatever to offer me to make any repairs or any new conveniences against the winter.

As for the house to which it is proposed that I should remove during the said repairs, it is a building attached, as it were, to this; and my keeper can testify that it is not in his power to lodge the few servants I have; and, without them, I have too many reasons to be afraid of living thus apart, whereof at this time I will say no more. If I must proceed to my conveniences, I have not, as I heretofore informed you, any gallery or cabinet to retire to occasionally alone, excepting two paltry holes, with windows facing the dark surrounding wall, and the largest of them not above a fathom and a half square. For taking the air abroad, on foot or in my chaise (there being no vacant spot on the top of that hill), I have only about a quarter of an acre of ground contiguous to the stables, which Sommer had dug up last winter, and enclosed with a fence of dry wood; a place, to look at, fitter to keep pigs in than to bear the name of garden: there is not a sheep-pen amidst the fields but makes a better appearance.

As for taking exercise on horseback, during the whole winter, as I experienced, sometimes snow, sometimes rain, break up the roads in such a manner, that

there is no house containing so many people of the lower sort as this does, which can be kept clean long, whatever pains may be taken with it. Then, again, this house, having no drains to the privies, is subject to a continual stench; and every Saturday they are obliged to empty them and the one beneath my windows, from which I receive a perfume not the most agreeable. And if to the above I may be permitted the opinion which I have conceived of this house, a thing to be considered in the case of persons inferior in station to me when in ill health, I will say that, as this house has been my first prison and place of confinement in this kingdom, where from the first I have been treated with great harshness, rudeness, and indignity, so have I always held it since to be unlucky and unfortunate, as last winter, before coming hither, I caused to be represented to the said Queen of England; and in this sinister opinion I have been not a little confirmed by the accident of the priest, who, after having been grievously tormented, was found hanging from the wall opposite to my windows,[1] about which I wrote to you, Monsieur de Mauvissière; and, then, four or five days afterwards, another poor man was found who had tumbled into the well; but this I did not mean to compare with the other. Then I have lost my good Rallay, who was one of the chief consolations of my captivity; another of my servants is since dead, and several more have been sorely troubled with illness.

So I cannot have any convenience or enjoyment here; and, but for the express assurances which the said queen my good sister gave me of honourable treatment, and

[1] The Catholic priest here mentioned had been persecuted on account of his religion; and, to escape further hardships, he hung himself in the manner described by Mary, who, on the occasion, addressed to Elizabeth an eloquent letter on the duty of permitting toleration, which is to be found in Laboureur's work.

which caused me to wait for it with patience till now, I would never have set foot in this place ; sooner should they have dragged me to it by force, as I now protest that nothing but the force of constraint makes me stay here, and that, in case my life should be cut short by illness, from this time I impute it to the deficiency of my dwelling, and to those who are determined to keep me there, with the intention, it would seem, to make me wholly despair for the future of the good-will of the said queen my good sister in matters of importance ; since in such reasonable, ordinary wants I am so ill used, and promises made to me are not kept. To allege that the season of the year is already too far advanced, and the time too short to provide a new habitation for me (as if I had not long ago made remonstrances on the subject) is to forget, that at the time my secretary was there, he spoke about it very urgently to the queen my good sister, and left a memorial at his departure for Mr. Walsingham. Since then, the point has been urged anew by Sommer, as well by a message from my own lips as by a memorial which was given to him ; whereupon I am told that the memorial was delivered to you, Mr. de Mauvissière, and that the fault lies in your not having followed it up ; nevertheless, I have written to you several times, and myself solicited Sir Amyas about it, so that no trouble has been spared on that head.

As for the inconveniences of removal at this season, and for the provisions requisite to be made, they did not stand last year upon such ceremony, when they obliged me to leave Sheffield for Winkfeild, and Winkfeild for this place in the depth of winter, when I was scarcely able to turn in my bed, which I had kept for nearly three months before. This house, which had not been inhabited for the space of fifteen or sixteen years, was at that time prepared in less than five weeks, and, such as it was, they lost no time in bringing me to it, no matter whether with or without my consent. However, I affectionately beg you both to insist more urgently and perseveringly than ever, in the name of the king monsieur my good brother and on my own behalf, on my removal from this house and the conveniences, which from the foregoing you may judge necessary in the new one that shall be appointed for me; and do not be put off, if you please, with excuses, evasions, or fair words that may be given you, if they are not to the effect that is capable of satisfying and contenting me in this matter.

Insist, also, by all means, I beg you, on permission for the Sieur de Cherelles to come to me, reminding the said queen my good sister how she was pleased, till last winter, to allow me to have some one over every year, to give me an account of my affairs, as it is very requisite, and more than reasonable, especially considering the state in which they are at present, from the attacks that are daily made upon my rights and the hindrances and annoyances that are given me in the enjoyment of the little which is left me of my dowry, one-third of which and more has been already wrested from me piecemeal; and it is not in my power to apply a remedy and set things to rights unless I can be minutely informed of the particulars by some trusty person, who, it is well known, would not attempt to write to me by letters which must pass through so many hands, neither would I thus openly inform them of my intentions. There is no criminal or prisoner, however mean, who is not permitted to receive accounts of his private affairs, and to manage them as he pleases, prisons having never been designed for the punishment of malefactors but only for safe custody; and it seems, on the contrary, that as for me, born a sovereign queen, who sought refuge in this kingdom upon the assurance and promise of friendship, they wish to make this imprisonment drive me from affliction to affliction to the very last extremity, as if it were not sufficient, that, after seventeen of the best years of my life spent in such misery, I have lost the use of my limbs and the strength and health of the rest of my body, and that various attacks have been made upon my honour, but they must persecute me into the bargain, and abridge me as much as possible of the property and conveniences yet left me in this world.

Learn, then, if you please, gentlemen, if the queen my good sister intends to treat me in future like a condemned criminal, and to keep me in perpetual imprisonment, as it would appear from the severity with which I am used, without getting rid of me altogether by giving me my liberty (from which, agreeably to the conditions which I offered, she would derive more advantage than she ever will from my detention or death), or, on the other hand, affording me occasion to accommodate myself to her satisfaction in captivity. My requests are not made for pleasure but from necessity, not against her safety but for her honour, and such I may say as I have more than justly merited. What encouragement to do better can it be to me to see myself, after the entire voluntary submission to which I made up my mind, more harshly and rigorously treated than ever, and with more demonstration, in appearance and reality, of ill-will, suspicion, and mistrust!

I had more servants, when I was with the Earl of Shrewsbury, than I have now, when I have more need of them, especially in my chamber, on account of the aggravation of my bodily ailments. Reckon up those whom I have discharged or who have died, without my having as yet any others in their place, and that family of my embroiderer who is about to leave me; the number of those, whom I require will not be much greater, nor su-

6

perior even in quality, excepting the Countess of Athol, for whom also I applied as a favour, because I had about me here in this solitude, as I represented, no companion worthy of my rank and my age, which would be highly proper and suitable. Seton and my good Rallay formerly supplied the want of better, and I cannot imagine any sufficient reason, for denying me the said countess in their stead, unless they are fearful that she may give me some consolation by bringing me tidings of my son; whether in this there be any respect for humanity, I leave all those to consider who have really felt parental love for their children, which is the more fervent in me, because my separation from my son is accompanied by so rigid a prohibition of all communication between him and me, that I am debarred even from hearing about his state and health. I will not hereupon call to mind that the said queen promised me, last winter, that if the answer of my son to the letter which I was writing to him did not satisfy and content me, I should have permission to send to him again, and to learn more precisely his intentions relative to those matters which had been in doubt between him and me. Nevertheless, this has hitherto been peremptorily refused and denied me, without consideration that such conduct tends to confirm the intimation given me formerly by the said Gray, that in this quarter people were only striving to produce division and a total separation between my son and me.

With respect to the other servants whom I have applied for, such as Fontenay and Thomas Levingston, I cannot discover any ground for the refusal made me, unless it be that, as formerly the said Gray, at the time of his journey to this country, and the Countess of Shrewsbury assured me, the right way to cause anything whatever to be denied me was to signify that it would be particularly agreeable to me, and then I must never expect to have it, but just the contrary to what I desired. They do not approve of my employing English, in order to make it appear more plainly that I am looked upon as an absolute foreigner in their country; at least they ought to allow me to have my own subjects or French people, such as I like, and to receive from their faithful service some consolation between these four walls; where, being confined and watched so closely as they are accustomed to be, I know not what just suspicion can be conceived of them, when once shut up here. However, I beg you to make very urgent application that I may be permitted to send for those whom I have demanded, as well from France as from Scotland, according to the promise made me by the lips of the said queen my good sister herself that I should have an increase and supply of servants; a promise confirmed to my secretary by Mr. Walsingham, and since in his name by Wade, having given it in writing to my said secretary, and again by Sir Raff Sadler and Sommer when there, and lately by my present keeper, being assured in these very words " that I might send to France and Scotland for such servants as I thought proper, but that I must not have English on any account "

If they are afraid lest, by means of the said servants whom I desire to bring over from France, I should receive news of the affairs of that country, it is a vain apprehension, for I have nothing wherein to intermeddle there; and, if I had any interest, it is very certain that those who might be well affected towards me and have compassion on my condition here will not take one step less, either forward or backward, because they are deprived of the means of receiving news from me and I from them; on the contrary, that would spur them on still more, apprehending the danger from death to be greater than peradventure it is.

This is, for the present, what I have to communicate to you on the sudden, concerning the just dissatisfaction I feel on finding myself so unworthily used and treated; wherefore, hoping through your favourable intercessions and good offices to find some remedy, I shall only apologize for having troubled you about such bagatelles, and especially for being obliged to make known to you my real state here, which otherwise might be disguised from you; so awaiting your answer about all this, I pray God to have you, gentlemen, in his holy and worthy keeping. Written at the Castle of Tuthbury, in England, the vth September, 1585.

Your entirely best friend,

MARY R.

Gentlemen, I am ashamed to be under the necessity of representing to you so particularly, my miserable situation here, but the evil presses me and constrains me to declare it to you, in order that they may not put you off yonder with words, without affording me any relief, of which I have no hope whatever, since I see nothing at this time that tends to realize that honourable treatment which has been so much talked of. Sir Amyas had already signified to me the reply to my memorial, and an hour ago I received your last, and, on considering both, I find, in fact, no cause for content either in the one or the other, which makes me entreat you more earnestly than ever to follow up the contents of the above letter.

1585. *September.* Before leaving, M. de Mauvissière obtains a promise that Mary Stuart shall be removed from Tutbury to some more healthy and more commodious place.

1586. *January.* She is removed from Tutbury to Chartley Castle, in the county of Stafford.

The Queen of Scots to M. de Mauvissière.

Chartley, March 31, 1585.

Monsieur de Mauvissière—I thank you most affectionately for the trouble you have taken, since your departure from this kingdom, in giving me news of France; this has afforded me singular pleasure, as I receive but very little intelligence from any other quarter. I shall ever feel, both in heart and affection, deeply interested in the weal and woe of that crown, as it is my bounden duty to be. As for yourself, you have seen that thus far I have done all that lay in my power, to validate my gift to you of the *baillage* of Vittry, about which I have written again by this despatch to those of my counsel, desiring them to speak in my name to the Dukes de Joyeuse and d'Espernon, not being able to write to them myself, nor even to the king and the queen madam my mother-in-law, as I have great need to do, concerning my affairs, owing to an inflammation of my right hand. Assist me in thanking the said Sr. Duke d'Espernon, for the kind assurance which you say he has given you of his good-will towards me, which I receive with the obligation to repay it on the first opportunity that offers.

I have already disposed of the seignorial rights which you apply for in favour of the Sr. de St. Belin, upon the express recommendation made to me by the said queen my mother-in-law; finding myself in such need, from the heavy losses and wrongs which I have suffered and which are daily done me, in regard to the enjoyment of my dower, without being able to obtain any redress, that I am obliged in my present situation to avail myself of the little that is left, and to do violence to my inclination to reward those who deserve it.

As to what you requested of me for the son-in-law of

M. Badins, your valet de chambre, and partly your secretary, you shall be satisfied. I have commanded, likewise, an order to be sent you for the final settlement of the account betwixt us. Since the commencement of February I have suffered greatly from defluxions, but have kept mending since the departure of Cherelles from hence, so that only this defluxion on my right arm is now left; it is an inheritance acquired by seventeen years imprisonment, which, I fear, will never end but with my life. Meanwhile, I pray God to grant me the necessary patience, and to have you, Monsieur de Mauvissière, in his holy and worthy keeping. Charteley, in England, the last day of March, 1586.

Your much obliged and best friend,

MARY R.

The Queen of Scots to M. D'Esneval Sieur de Cour-celles, Ambassador from Henry III. to James VI.[1]

April 30, 1586.

Monsieur D'Esneval, — On the reception of your letters, dated the 20th of February (which came to my hands but the 22nd of this present month), I could not help testifying the satisfaction I feel at the good choice it has pleased the king, monsieur my brother-in-law, to make of you to reside near my son, and at the same time, at the express commandment that he has given you in favour of my affairs in that country [Scotland].

I assure myself that you have found (and will in the future more and more discover) good inclinations there to cultivate our ancient alliance with France, which I recommend to you with all the affection possible.

I shall receive an especial pleasure if you will inform

[1] Des Mesmes MS, tome iii., fol. 318. Lettres Originales d'Etat Bibliothèque du Roi, Paris.

me from time to time, according as opportunity and convenience permit, of the health and state of my son, towards whom my extreme affection as a mother has never failed,[1] although his bad ministers have made him so much forget my sufferings. Meantime, expecting that this means [of communication] may be so well established, as to give me an opportunity of writing to him and to you more amply, I will not make this longer, excepting to assure you, that should I ever have the means of acknowledging the obligations I have had from your father-in-law, and hope to have from your own good offices there, I will do so with a very thankful heart.

Praying God that he will have you, M. D'Esneval, in his holy and safe keeping.

Written at Chartley, in England, the last day of April, 1586.

I beg you to send me a whole length portrait of my son, as large as life, drawn from his own person.

Your entirely good friend,

MARY R.

[In the same collection of the President de Mesmes, in the Bibliothèque du Roi, is a minute of the answer of M. D'Esneval, from Scotland, to Mary Queen of Scots; he tells her "that he has given orders to a painter, the only one who was at Lislebourg,[2] to make a portrait of the king her son, not indeed from the life, but from a good portrait lately painted of him, and that her son seemed greatly obliged by this mark of affec-

---

[1] In this letter the unfortunate queen resumes the maternal feelings for her son, which had been outraged the preceding year by the machinations of Patrick Gray and his colleagues in iniquity.

[2] If Lislebourg indeed means Edinburgh, then must the Scottish capital have been strangely destitute of artists.

tionate regard in his mother." In a letter from D'Esneval, dated " Falkland Palace, June the 3rd, 1583," the
reconciliation between the mother and son was rendered
more complete by the good offices of this French ambassador. He found James alone, he said, " excepting the
presence of his most confidential household servants;"
and he took the opportunity of telling him, " that he
had just received a letter from his mother the Queen of
Scotland, who named him with great kindness, and that
she bade him tell James, that her extreme affection for
him had never been impaired." To which the young
king listened very willingly, and said, " that he was
always desirous of being her very dutiful son, and would
have served her effectually if he had had but the means."
James then told the French ambassador " that he had
written letters to his mother, expressing his affection,
and when he was sure of not being seen, had tendered them
to the care of Fontenay,[1] who had refused to take them,
on account of the bad terms on which his mother was
with him," " which were, indeed," added the young king,
" wholly owing to the English, with whom he was obliged
to dissemble, but that he would never hold faith with
them;" and he entreated D'Esneval, " if he wrote letters expressive of the natural duty and love he bore
the queen his mother, and could hand them to him
without being seen, that he would take care of them,
and forward them to her, if she would excuse the regular
formalities."

There is some reason to believe, from the letter writ-

[1] It appears the person called Fontenay in the French ambassador's despatch, who made serious mischief between Mary Queen of
Scots and her son, is the same designated by Walsingham as " Le
Fountaine, brother to Nau, sent into Scotland by the said queen "
(Sadler Papers, vol ii., p 46). He told James " that his mother
commonly said, that if she recovered her throne, she would reduce
him to the fortune and degree of his father, Lord Darnley."

ten by Queen Mary after her condemnation to death in
the ensuing October, to Queen Elizabeth, that these
letters from her son had never reached her ; yet it will
be perceived that she speaks of him in a very different
spirit from that of the bitter denunciations wrung from
her by maternal anguish, in her correspondence of
March, 1585.]

1586. *April and May.* Gifford, Maude, Greetly, and Pooley,
agents of Walsingham, find means to discover the secrets of Morgan and John Ballard, and, through them, enter into a communication with Mendoça, ambassador of Spain in France, and with
Savage and Babington, who are conspiring in England to save
Mary Stuart.

The Queen of Scots to Don Bernard de Mendoça.

Chartley, May 20, 1586.

Monsieur l'ambassadeur of France,[1]—By your last of
the tenth of February and the twenty-sixth of July,
1585, which were not delivered to me till the twentieth
of April last, I have been rejoiced to learn the good
choice which the Catholic king, your master, monsieur
my good brother, has made, by appointing you to reside
in France, agreeably to the request which I formerly
made to him. I have been so strictly guarded during
the last eighteen months, that all secret intelligence
failed me down to last Lent, when Morgan transmitted
this alone to me; I am in the same ignorance at present, not knowing what has been done for the advancement of our preceding designs. I am, therefore, quite
at a loss what course to take here. I have directed
William to communicate to you some overtures in my
name, on which I beg you to impart to him freely what
you think he will be able to obtain from the said sieur

[1] She thus addresses him because he was ambassador from Spain
to France.

king your master, that he may not be importuned about these matters, should you imagine them not likely to succeed.

There is another subject which I have reserved to write about to you alone, and which I wish you to communicate to the king, so that no other person but himself, if possible, may have cognizance of it. It is this, that, considering the obstinacy and perseverance of my son in heresy, and which I assure you I have deplored and lamented day and night more than my own calamity, and, foreseeing the eminent injury which will result to the Catholic church, if he should succeed to the throne of this kingdom, I have come to a determination, in case my said son should not embrace, before my death, the Catholic religion (of which I must confess to you I see little hope so long as he remains in Scotland), to cede and give by will my right to the said succession to this crown to the said sieur king your master,[1] begging him, on such condition, to take me henceforward under his special protection, and likewise the state and affairs of this country, the which, for the discharge of my conscience, I think I cannot place in the hands of a prince more zealous in the cause of our religion, or more capable in every respect to re-establish it here, which is a point of great importance to all the rest of Christendom, considering myself more bound to regard herein the general good of the Church than, with detriment to that, the particular greatness of my own posterity.

[1] Robertson, in his History of Scotland, vol. iii , gives the substance of the will of Mary Stuart made at Sheffield in 1577, in which this clause occurs. He says that the document was copied from the original by the Rev. Mr. Crawford, that part of it is in the handwriting of Nau, and the remainder in the queen's own hand. It may be observed that Mary only does in her despair, what she had distinctly declared to Queen Elizabeth in her letter of March 23rd, 1585, previously printed in this volume.

Once more I beg you to keep this intention most secret, for, were it to be divulged, it would cause me in
France the loss of my dowry, in Scotland a complete
rupture with my son, and in this country my total ruin
and destruction. Thank, if you please, for me, the said
sieur king my good brother, for the favours and liberality
he has shown towards Lord Paget and his William, which
I beseech him most affectionately to continue, and also
to reward, for my sake, with some pension poor Morgan,
who has suffered so much, not for me only but for the
common cause, being able. from the experience I have
had of him, to assure you of his entire fidelity, and that
he has always conducted himself as an upright man in
all matters that I have hitherto entrusted him with. I
likewise recommend to you Foliambe, whom you know,
that you may procure him some further aid beyond the
salary that I have assigned him according to my scanty
means, regretting that they are inadequate to provide
for those persons in the manner I desire and they have
deserved. May God have you, monsieur l'ambassadeur,
in his holy and worthy keeping. From Chartleau, in
England, the xxth May, 1586.

The Queen of Scots to Don Bernard de Mendoça.
Chartley, July 2, 1586.

Monsieur l'ambassadeur,—These lines are principally
to acknowledge the receipt of your last, dated the 4th
of April, and to assure you that I do not, in the least,
impute the delay of our designs to any failure on the
part of his Catholic majesty, your master, monsieur my
good brother, for I have always seen him walk with such a
firm step, as well in the general cause of religion as in
every thing that I have solicited for myself, that I should
deem myself ungrateful were I to entertain any other

opinion. Since it is the will of God that I should suffer, I am ready to yield and to bow my neck to the yoke; and, in my conscience, I do not regret this delay so much on my own account, as for the misery and affliction in which I have seen, and see daily, so many good people of this kingdom, feeling more keenly the public calamity than my particular misfortune.

I have charged my ambassador to speak to you in my name respecting some moneys advanced, nearly three years ago, by the Sieurs Paget, Arundel, and Morgan, on the assurance given them of reimbursement in the name of his holiness and the aforesaid sieur king your master. I beg you to do all that lies in your power to satisfy them, as it is most reasonable, and also of consequence, not only for the payment of the agents who engaged in the business on their behalf, but likewise for my safety here. May God have you, monsieur l'ambassadeur, in his holy and worthy keeping. The second of July, 1586.

1586. *July* 5. A treaty signed between England and Scotland.

July —. Babington corresponds with Nau and Curle, secretaries of the Queen of Scotland, but under the supervision of Walsingham.

Thomas Philips is employed to decipher the letters, and Arthur Gregory to counterfeit the seals.

August 4. Ballard is apprehended, and discloses the whole plot.

The Queen of Scots to Don Bernard de Mendoça.

Chartley, July 27, 1586.

Monsieur l'ambassadeur,—You will have learned from my last letter that I have received those you forwarded to me by William; since then, yours of the 19th of May has been delivered to me, by which I perceive, with extraordinary satisfaction, that the Catholic king monsieur my good brother has begun to resent the designs and machinations of the Queen of England against him, not only on account of the good which you give me reason to hope may result from this circumstance alone, but principally for the upholding of his reputation in Christendom, for which, in particular, I feel deeply bound to be solicitous. You cannot believe how much the appearance of the exploits of the Earl of Leicester[1] and Draques[2] have elated the hearts of the enemies of the said sieur king throughout all Christendom, and how much his very long patience with this Queen of England has diminished the confidence which the Catholics of this country have always had in him. For my own part, I freely confess to you that I was so much discouraged from entering into any new schemes, seeing the futility of the past, that I have turned a deaf ear to several overtures and proposed enterprises made to me during the last six months by the said Catholics, it not being in my power to give them any positive answer.

As to all the news that I have lately received respecting the said king's good intentions towards this quarter, I have amply explained to the principal of the said Catholics a plan, which I sent to them with my opinion on each point, that they may consult together on the execution of it, and, to gain time, I desired them to dispatch with all diligence one of their party, sufficiently informed, to treat with you agreeably to the general offers that have already been made to you, concerning all the things that they will have to require in this affair from the said sieur king your master, assuring you, upon the faith and

---

[1] Leicester, commanding the English troops in the Low Countries, had gained some advantages over the army of Philip II.

[2] Sir Francis Drake, the celebrated English navigator, who had just come from the Cape de Verde islands and the West Indies, and plundered and burnt several Spanish settlements.

promise which they have given me, that they will faithfully and sincerely perform, at the hazard of their lives, all that they shall promise by their deputy, and hereby I beg you to place the same confidence in him as if I had sent him myself. He will inform you of the means of escaping from hence, which I take upon myself to effect, provided I am in the first place assured beforehand of assistance being ready. Thank God, my health is at present better than it has been for the last three months.

I thank you most affectionately for the kind offices you rendered me with the said sieur king your master, for the 12^m [12,000] crowns with which he has been pleased to supply me for my said deliverance, for which purpose they shall be employed and for no other. I greatly regret that the twelve thousand for Scotland have been of so little benefit. I have had intelligence from London, which informs me that the Sieur Tassis was appointed to act in this business, but, without very urgent necessity, I am unwilling to importune any one about such things, and therefore value the more the trouble you have taken, and to which I acknowledge myself to be principally indebted for the grant of these sums.

You will assist me, if you please, to express to the said sieur king, monsieur my good brother, the obligation which I protest I owe him, and my wish to return it, if I should ever have it in my power to do so; and, as to yourself, I hope that I shall not be ungrateful. I have charged my ambassador to receive what you may please to deliver him, and to send it to me with all diligence, and by the secret channel which I have mentioned to him. May God have you, monsieur, &c. &c.

From Chartley, 27th July, 1586.

Postscript.

Monsieur l'ambassadeur,—I was on the point of sending you the enclosed when I received yours of the 7th of July. Thank God our communication has commenced so favourably, and is so safely established, that henceforth you can, if you please, write to me whenever you have occasion. May it please God to restore the king monsieur my brother to health, preserve his children, and grant him that happiness, content, and prosperity, which he deserves for his sincere piety and the care he takes for the welfare of Christianity : and to this end he shall have my daily prayers, if I cannot serve him in any other manner.

I thank you for the great punctuality you have shown in communicating to him the contents of the letters which I wrote to you in May last, not only as to what concerns myself, in which I feel fully convinced you will act according to your promise, but also for those poor English gentlemen, whom I cannot refrain from recommending to you again, especially the release of Morgan, and some pension, if you can by any means assist to obtain it. I have answered you concerning the money which you have obtained for me, and hereby beg you will consult with my ambassador as to the best means of remitting it to me, along with whatever is yet to come.

I shall therefore conclude this, praying God, &c.

From Chartley, August 2nd, 1586.

N B.—Gifford and Maude, secret agents of Walsingham's, having obtained, in April 1586, the confidence of Morgan and Ballard, the two latter introduced them to Mendoça, Spanish ambassador in France, and afterwards to Babington and Savage. The consequence was, that all this correspondence passed under the eye of

Walsingham, until the moment when he conceived that he had sufficient proof to compromise the Queen of Scotland. Then, on the 4th of August, two days after Mary had written the above letter, he caused Ballard to be apprehended, and on the 8th of the same month Sir Amias Paulet unexpectedly removed the queen, from Chartley to Tixal, and took possession of all her papers and jewels.

1586. *August* 8 Mary Stuart is taken from Chartley to Tixal, where all her jewels and papers are seized.

August 28. Sir Amyas Paulet brings Mary Stuart back to Chartley.

September 20. Babington and five of his accomplices are executed.

September —. The Queen of Scots is removed from Chartley to Fotheringay Castle, in Northamptonshire

October 6. Elizabeth appoints a commission of forty-seven peers and members of the Privy Council to try Mary Stuart, and writes to her on this subject.

October 7. Burghley and Walsingham are authorised by Elizabeth to hold a secret conference with Mary Stuart, to persuade her to answer before the commissioners.

October 11. Thirty-six members of the commission assemble at Fotheringay.

October 12. First and second meeting of the commission. The Queen of Scotland protests against all that they do, but afterwards replies to several charges which are preferred against her.

October 13. Third meeting. Mary Stuart renews her protestations, and denies, with great vehemence, the proofs which are brought against her from Babington's letters.

Burghley receives a letter from Elizabeth, dated 12th October, which enjoins him not to permit the sentence to be pronounced against Mary Stuart before the commission returns to London.

October 14. The commission adjourns to Westminster.

Lord Burleigh to Secretary Davison.[1]

Fotheringay, October 15, 1586.

Mr. Secretary,—Yesternight, upon receipt of your

[1] MS. Cotton. Calig., c. ix. fol. 433.

letter dated on Thursday, I writ what was thought would be this day's work. This Queen of the Castle [Mary at Fotheringay] was content to appear again afore us in public to be heard, but in truth, not to be heard for her defence, for she could say nothing but negatively, that the points of the letters that concerned the practice against the queen's majesty's person [Elizabeth] were never by her written, nor of her knowledge ; the rest for invasion, for escaping by force, she said she would neither deny nor affirm. But her intention was, by long artificial speeches, to move pity, to lay all the blame upon the queen's majesty, or rather upon the [privy] council, that all the troubles past did ensue, avowing her reasonable offers and our refusals ; and in these her speeches I did so encounter her with reasons out of my knowledge and experience as she had not that advantage she looked for ; as I am sure the auditory did find her case not pitiable, her allegations untrue, by which means great debate fell yesternight very long, and this day renewed, with great stomaching.[1]

And we find all persons here in the commission fully satisfied, as by her majesty's order, judgment will be given at our next meeting, but the record will not be provided in five or six days, and that was one cause why, if we should have proceeded to judgment, we should have tarried five or six days more ; and surely the country could not bear it by the waste of bread specially,

---

[1] It is some consolation to find that the *whole* of the junta of English nobles sent down to Fotheringay, for the purpose of condemning a helpless woman, (suffering with severe ill-health, and without legal aid, or any means of defence, but what her own eloquence afforded,) were not base enough to sentence her without a sharp opposition. This fact is plain from the above words of the wily veteran Burleigh, though he asserts the contrary in the same sentence, yet the truth is glaringly apparent.

our company being there and within six miles above 2000 horsemen, but by reason of her majesty's letter, we of her [privy] council, that is, the Lord Chancellor, Mr. Rich, Mr. Secretary and myself only, did procure this prorogation for the other two causes.

And so, knowing that by my Lord of Cumberland her majesty [Elizabeth] shall, sooner than this letter can come, understand the course of the proceeding, I will end.

Your assured loving friend,
W. BURGHLEY.

15th October, 1586, *at Burghley.*[1]
To the Right Honourable my very good friend,
        Mr. Secretary Davison.

[The intrigues of Patrick Gray, the ambassador sent by the Scotch government to the court of Elizabeth, against the life of Mary Queen of Scots, are now well known matter of fact. His principal agent in mischief was Archibald Douglas, resident ambassador from Scotland, a spy of Burleigh, who, under pretence of being an exile from Scotland, kept up an intriguing correspondence with all parties, but was in reality a deadly enemy of Mary. He had been represented, however, to the young king as a person of great influence at Elizabeth's court, and, at the same time, as a friend of his mother, who had certainly been deceived into employing him in her affairs. It is evident that some circumstance had given the young King of Scotland some suspicion of this person's real line of conduct, for he addressed to him the following straightforward letter,

[1] Although dated Burghley, it is done by mistake, for he is evidently at Fotheringay, since the Queen of Scots was not removed from that castle.

when he found that the tendency of the English politics was to take his mother's life.]

King James VI. to Mr. Archibald Douglas.[1]

Reserve up yourself no longer in the earnest dealing for my mother, for ye have done it too long; and think not that any of your travails [labour] can do good if her life be taken, for then adieu with my dealing [negociating] with them that are the special instruments thereof. And therefore, if ye look for the continuance of my favour towards you, spare no pains nor plainness in this case, but read my letter written to William Keith, and conform yourself wholly to the contents thereof; and in this request let me reap the fruits of your great credit there, either now or never. Farewell.

JAMES R.

1586. *October* 25. The commission pronounces sentence of death against the Queen of Scotland.

October 29. The English Parliament confirms this sentence.

November 12. Petition of the two Houses, praying a speedy execution.

November 12. Thomas Sackville, Lord Buckhurst, and Beale, arrive at Fotheringay, and communicate the sentence to Mary Stuart

November 24. Buckhurst and Beale permit the Queen of Scots to have an interview with Préau, her chaplain, to whom she secretly delivers her last letters to the Pope, the Duke of Guise, Mendoça, and Mons. A., a French gentleman.

Henry III. to M. de Courcelles.[2]

St. Germain en Laye, November 21, 1586.

Courcelles,—I have received your letter of the 4th of

[1] MS. Cotton. Calig., c. ix., fol 432, written wholly in the hand of King James.

[2] M. de Courcelles, French ambassador in Scotland, had been previously employed in London under M. de Mauvissière.

October last past, wherein you inform me of the conversation that passed between you and the King of Scotland, on your expressing to him the sincere affection I bear him, by which he seems to have an earnest desire to correspond with me entirely; but I wish that letter had also informed me that he were better disposed towards the queen his mother, and that he had the heart and the will to do every thing to assist her in her present affliction, considering that the captivity, in which she has been unjustly held for eighteen years and more, might have induced him to listen to the many proposals which have been made to him for obtaining her liberty, which is naturally most desirable to all men, but more particularly to those who are born sovereigns and to command others, who are more impatient of being thus detained prisoners. He ought also to think that, if the Queen of England my good sister should follow the advice of those who desire her to imbrue her hands in the blood of his said mother, it will be a great stain on his reputation, inasmuch as it will be thought that he has withheld the good offices which he ought to render her with the said Queen of England, which might be sufficient to move her if he had employed them as early and as warmly as natural affection commanded. It is much to be feared that, in case of the death of his said mother, there may hereafter be some scheme for acting the same violent part towards him, to render the succession to the throne of England more easily attainable by those who have it in their power to secure it after the said Queen of England, and not only to deprive the said King of Scotland of the right that he may claim to it, but render doubtful that which he has to the crown of Scotland.

I know not in what state the affairs of my said sister-in-law may be when this letter reaches you; but I desire you will endeavour to excite the said King of Scotland by these remonstrances and any others that can bear upon this subject to take up the defence and protection of his said mother; and tell him in my name that this is a thing for which he will be highly praised by all other kings and sovereign princes, and that he may be assured, if he fails in this, great blame will attach to him, and perhaps great injury ensue to himself.

As to the state of my affairs, you must know that the queen madam my mother is very shortly to see the King of Navarre, to confer with him respecting the pacification of the troubles in this kingdom, and, if he be as sincere in this matter as myself, I hope that things will soon be satisfactorily arranged, and that my subjects will enjoy some respite from the great evils and calamities which the war has brought upon them.

Beseeching the Creator, Courcelles, to have you in his holy keeping. Written at St. Germain en Laye, the xxist day of November, 1586.

Signed, HENRY; and, lower down, BRULART.

The Queen of Scots to Don Bernard de Mendoça.

Fotheringay, Nov. 23, 1586.

My very dear friend,—Having ever found you zealous in the cause of God, and desirous of my welfare and deliverance from captivity, I have always communicated to you all my intentions upon that subject, begging you to make them known to the king my good brother. For this reason I now write to bid you a last adieu, notwithstanding the little leisure I have, being about to receive the stroke of death, which was announced to me on Saturday last; I do not know when, or in what manner; but at least you may praise God for me, that, through his grace, I have had the heart to receive this unjust sentence of heretics with resignation, on account of the happiness which I esteem it to shed my blood at the requisition of the enemies of His church, who do me the honour to say that it cannot be subverted while I am alive, and also that their queen cannot reign in safety in the same predicament.

As for these two conditions, I have accepted without contradiction the high honour which they confer upon me, as one most zealous for the Catholic religion, for which I have publicly offered my life; and, as for the other, although I have never committed either act or deed tending to take off her who was on the throne, unless it be that they make a crime of my right to the crown, which is acknowledged by all Catholics, yet I would not contradict them, leaving them to think as they please. This annoyed them much, and they told me that, whatever I may say or do, it will not be for the cause of religion that I shall die but for having endeavoured to murder their queen. This I denied, as being utterly false, having never attempted any such thing, and leaving it to God and the church to dispose of this island in what relates to religion.

The bearer of this has promised to relate to you how rigorously I have been treated by those here, and how ill served by others, whom I did not expect to have shown so great a fear of death in so just a quarrel.[1] They have not been able to draw any thing from me but that I am a queen, free, Catholic, and obedient to the church; and that, not being able to effect my deliverance by fair means, I was compelled to seek it by those which presented themselves. Nau has confessed all; Curle has in a great measure followed his example: so that every thing turns against me. I am threatened, if I do not beg pardon; but I say that, " as they had already destined me to die, they may proceed with their injus-

---

[1] It is evident she here alludes to her secretaries, whom she thus considers as cowards rather than as betrayers.

tice, hoping that God will recompense me in another world;" and, out of spite, because I will speak, they came yesterday (Monday) and took down my canopy,[1] saying that I was no more than a dead woman, and without any rank. They are at present working in my hall—erecting the scaffold, I suppose, whereon I am to perform the last act of this tragedy. I die in a just cause, and am happy in having made over my rights to the king, your master. I have said that I consider him, should my son not return into the bosom of the church, as being a prince the most worthy to govern and protect this island. I have written to the same purpose to his holiness, and I beg you to assure him that I die in the determination which I have communicated to you, and also another, whom you know to be his dearest and most intimate friend, and a fourth, and these above all others I bequeath to the protection of the king, beseeching him in God's name not to abandon them, and entreating them to serve him in place of me. As I cannot write to them, greet them in my name, and pray to God, all of you, for my soul. I have asked for a priest ; but I do not know if my request will be granted. They have offered me one of their bishops; but I positively refused him. You may believe all that the bearer of this shall tell you, and also those two poor girls who have been immediately about my person; they will tell you the truth, which I beg you to make public, as I fear that a very different interpretation will be given. Order a mass to be said for deliverance and repose of my soul —you know the place I mean—and let the churches in Spain remember me in their prayers. Keep the name of the bearer of this secret : he has been a faithful servant to me. God grant you a long and happy life ! You will receive from me, as a token of my remem-

---

[1] A cloth of state, or a sort of throne.

brance, a diamond, which I have held very dear, having been given to me by the late Duke of Norfolk as a pledge of his troth, and I have always worn it as such: keep it for my sake. I do not know if I shall have leave to make a will. I have applied for it, but they have all my money. God be with you! Excuse what I write in sorrow and trouble, not having any one to help me to make my rough draughts and to write for me. If you cannot read my hand, the bearer will read it for you, or my ambassador, whom he knows.

Among other accusations, that of Criton [Crighton] is one which I know nothing of. I fear greatly that Nau and Pasquier have hastened my death, having kept some papers, and they are men who will turn on any side for their own advantage. Would to God Fontenay[1] had been here! he is a young man of great knowledge and resolution.

Once more adieu. I recommend to you my poor (and henceforth destitute) servants, and pray for my soul.

From Fotheringay, Wednesday, the 23rd of November, 1586. I recommend to you the poor Bishop of Ross, who will be wholly destitute.

Your very obliged and perfect friend,
MARY R.

Received at Paris, 15th October, 1587.

The Queen of Scots to the Duc de Guise.

Fotheringay, Nov. 23, 1586.

My good cousin,—You, whom I hold most dear in the world, I bid you farewell, being on the point of being put to death by an unjust judgment, such a one as never any belonging to our race yet suffered, much less one of

---

[1] He was the brother of Nau, but whether better in principle is somewhat doubtful.

my rank. But praise God, my good cousin; for, situated
as I have been, I was useless to the world in the cause
of God and his church; but I hope that my death will
bear witness of my constancy in the faith, and my readiness to die for the support and restoration of the Catholic
church in this unfortunate island. And though executioner never yet dipped his hand in our blood, be not
ashamed, my friend; for the judgment of these heretics
and enemies of the church, and who have no jurisdiction
over me, a free queen, is profitable before God to the
children of his church, which had I not adhered to, this
stroke had been spared me. All those of our house have
been persecuted by this sect; witness, your good father,
with whom I hope to be received in mercy by the just
Judge.

I recommend then to you all my poor servants, the
discharge of my debts, and the founding of some annual
obit for my soul; not at your expense, but to make such
solicitation and arrangements as shall be requisite to
fulfil my intentions, which you will be informed of by my
poor disconsolate servants, eye-witnesses of this my last
tragedy.

May God prosper your wife, children, brothers, and
cousins, and especially our head, my good brother and
cousin, and all belonging to him! May the blessing of
God, and that which I should give to my own children,
be upon yours, whom I commend to God not less sincerely than my own unfortunate and deluded son! You
will receive tokens [rings] from me to remind you to
have prayers said for the soul of your poor cousin, destitute of all aid and counsel but that of God, who gives
me strength and courage to withstand alone so many
wolves howling after me; to God be the glory! Believe,
in particular, a person who will give you, in my name,
a ruby ring, for I assure you, upon my conscience, that

this person will tell you the truth agreeably to my desire, especially as to what concerns my poor servants,
and the share of each. I recommend to you this person
for her sincerity and honesty, in order that she may be
put into some good place. I have chosen her as being
the most impartial, and as one who will most simply
report my commands. I beg you not to let it be known
that she has said anything to you in private, for envy
might injure her.[1]

I have suffered much for the last two years and upwards, but have not been able to inform you of it for an
important reason. God be praised for all things, and
may he give you grace to persevere in the service of his
church so long as you live, and may that honour never
depart from our race, that all of us, both males and
females, may be ready to shed our blood in the defence
of the faith, regardless of all other worldly interests!
For my own part, I think myself born, both on the father's
and the mother's side, to offer up my blood for it, and have
no intention to degenerate. May Jesus, crucified for us,
and all the holy martyrs, render us, by their intercession,
worthy of the free-will offering of our bodies for his glory!
From Fotheringhaye, Thursday, this 24th November.

Thinking to degrade me, they took down my canopy,
and my keeper afterwards came and offered to write to
the queen, saying that this act had not been done by her
command but by the advice of some of her council. I
showed them, on the said canopy, in place of my coat of
arms, the cross of my Saviour. You will be informed
of all that was said; they have since been more indulgent.

Your affectionate cousin and perfect friend,

MARY R. of Scotland,

Dowager of France.

[1] As *personne* is a feminine noun in French, it is doubtful whether the person alluded to in this passage was male or female.

1586. *November* 27. M. de Pomponne de Belliévre, sent by Henry III. to remonstrate with the Queen of England upon the sentence of death pronounced against Mary Stuart, obtains his first audience at Richmond ; but without any result.

December 4. Elizabeth signs the sentence pronounced against Mary Stuart.

December 5. M. de Belliévre goes again to Queen Elizabeth ; but, as she refuses him any respite, he demands his passport.

December 6. The sentence is published in London with great ceremony ; bonfires are made, and the bells rung the whole day.

The same day Messrs. de Belliévre and de Chateauneuf write to Elizabeth, to demand a respite until such a time as they receive an answer from the King of France.

December 9. The queen sends them a verbal intimation that she will grant twelve days.

The Sieurs Belliévre and Chateauneuf, the French Ambassadors, to Henry III. of France, relating to their interviews with Queen Elizabeth on the subject of the Queen of Scots.[1]

London, December 18, 1586.

Sire,—We had audience with the Queen of England the 7th of this month, the letters of your majesty having been presented to her. She received us in public, in her chamber of presence, attended by most of the nobles of her nation, the lords of her council, and many others besides were present. When we began to explain to her that which it had pleased your majesty to command us to say, she made the Earl of Leicester retire, who was near enough to her ; the other lords of her council, when they heard her tell him to fall back, withdrew themselves also, and she alone heard that which was represented to her on the part of your majesty. She interrupted the

[1] "Lettres Originales d'Etat," Des Mesmes Collection, No. 9513, tome iii. fol. 399, Bibliothèque du Roi.

i

address many times, and made an answer, general enough, speaking so loud that she could be heard all over the saloon. The substance of what she said is, " That your majesty is ill-informed as to what has passed touching the affairs of Scotland, and that she [Queen Elizabeth] has always borne herself in your cause with so much amity and affection, that she merited some acknowledgment." She burst into invectives against the Queen of Scots, recounting the evil that she had received from that princess, and the good offices she had rendered to her; " but that she had been compelled to come to the resolution which has been taken, because it was impossible," she said, " to save her own life, and preserve that of the said queen ; but that if we knew any means whereby she could find security for herself in preserving the Queen of Scots, she would be under great obligations to us, never having shed so many tears at the death of her father, of her brother, King Edward, and of her sister Mary, as she had done for this unfortunate affair." She left us to make her an answer in four days. The day before she gave us audience, the Lord Buckhurst was sent to Fotheringay, where he had to pronounce the sentence of death to the Queen of Scotland; and it has been said many times in this city of London that it is certain that they have put the said queen to death.[1]

The audience that was granted us for Thursday has been deferred till the Monday following. We having sent divers days to the high treasurer,[2] that he should confer with us, this he did last Saturday, accompanied by Lord Hunsdon, lord-chamberlain, and the secretary, Walsingham, to whom we propounded again, " that your majesty would demand, in friendship, of the

---

[1] This was a false report.
[2] Lord Burleigh.

Queen of England, the wise reasons which moved her to
do this." Their reply was long in support of the judgment
that had been given against the Queen of Scotland, saying,
" they could see no way of . . . .¹ that they did not
wish to lose the queen their mistress, and . . . ." After
a long discourse, they told us that " she could not give
us audience till Monday next." The said lady queen
had, however, sent to inquire of her parliament if any
means could be found of saving her life and preserving
that of the Queen of Scotland. It was answered, " that
there were none; and they prayed her to cause judgment
to be executed on the said queen."

The said lady [Queen Elizabeth] gave us audience on
the appointed day, Monday, in her chamber of presence.
We recommenced the same prayer with all the urgency
that was possible, and spoke in such a manner that we
could not be heard save by her principal councillors.
But she rejoined in so loud a tone that we were put in
pain, because we were using prayer, (as the necessity
of the affair required,) and by her answers they could not
but understand that our plaint was refused. After she had
continued long, and repeated many times the same language, she adverted to Morgan, and said, " Wherefore
is it that, having signed a league which I observe, he
[the King of France] also does not observe it in a case
which is so important to all princes?" assuring us, " that
if any of her subjects—ay, those that were nearest of
kin (naming at the same time and showing us my lord
the chamberlain,² who is her cousin-german) had enterprised things to the prejudice of your majesty's life, she
would have sent him to you for purgation." To which
we answered, " that he had not . . . . that if Morgan,
having been on her sole account, for a long time detained

¹ Here a hiatus occurs in the MS.
² Lord Hunsdon, the son of her aunt, Mary Boleyn.

8

in a strong prison in France, had plotted a little against
her majesty, he could not do her any harm, as he was
in ward; that the Queen of Scotland has fallen into such
a miserable state, and has found so many enemies in this
kingdom, that there was no need to go and search for
them in France to accelerate her ruin; and that it would
be deemed a thing too monstrous and inhuman for the
king to send the knife to cut the throat of his sister-in-
law, to whom both in the sight of God and man he owed
his protection." We could not believe, but that we had
satisfied her with this answer, but she abandoned the
subject of Morgan, and flew to that of Charles Paget,
saying, " Wherefore is he not sent ?"

We replied "that we did not consider that Paget
was in your majesty's power, as Paris was a great
forest; that your majesty would not refuse to perform
any office of friendship that could be expected, but that
she must please to reflect, that you could not always do
as you would wish in the present state of your realm;
for your majesty had been censured at Rome and elsewhere for the detention of Morgan, which was done
solely out of respect to her." On which she said to us,
"that the said Paget had promised to Monsieur de
Guise to kill her, but that she had means enough in
Paris to have him killed if she wished."

She said this, on purpose, so loud, that the archers of
her guard could hear; " and as to Morgan, that he had,
within three months, sent to her, ' that if she would
please to grant him her pardon, he would discover all
the conspiracy of the Queen of Scotland;'" adding,
"that he was very ill-guarded in the Bastille, for the
Bishop of Glasgow had spoken more than twenty times
to him; and that he was also free to converse with
whomsoever he thought proper." Then the said lady,
lowering her voice, told us, " that she would wish us to

K 2

be well advised, desiring the good of your majesty; and that you could not do better than to give shortly a good peace to your subjects, otherwise she could foresee great injury to your realm, which a great number of foreigners would enter, in such sort that it would not be very easy to find a remedy to the evil."

On this we took upon ourselves to tell her, "that your majesty desired nothing more than to see his country in a happy repose, and would feel obliged to all princes, his neighbours, who had the same wish, if they would counsel his subjects to that effect when they addressed themselves to them; that the queen, your mother, at her age, had taken the trouble to seek the King of Navarre for this good purpose; and that it was our opinion that they would now enter into a treaty; that the king, your majesty, and all good people, desired much the preservation of the King of Navarre; but that it was impossible for you to assist him if the aid was not reciprocal on his side; that, knowing the respect which the said King of Navarre had for her, we thought the good counsel she might give him would greatly tend to accelerate the blessing of peace." While holding this discourse to her, it seemed to us, considering her countenance, that we talked of a thing that was distasteful to her, for she turned away her head as not wishing to proceed with the topic, and said to us in Latin, "He is of age."

We observed to her, "that she talked much of leagues and of armies; but she ought to wish that your majesty, who has never willingly consented to any thing which was prejudicial to his realm, were delivered from these unhappy civil wars, and to consider that she could not take the same assurances of all other princes;" on this she said, "that we might perhaps mean the King of Spain, but that their [Queen Elizabeth and Philip II.]

enmity had never begun but by loves, and that we ought
not to think, that they could not be well together whenever *she* wished." And in truth, sire, we believe that
she might very easily enter into such relations as she
chose with that king. As far as we can judge, she has
not the means needful for sustaining a war against so
powerful a prince, being infinitely sparing of her money,
and her people very desirous of a peace with Spain, as
they have lost all their commerce on account of the war.
It seems that this queen has determined rather to accord
with Spain than continue the war; and we understand
she has sent several missions to the Duke of Parma.
As to the disposition of this princess, touching the
peace of your realm, we have written to you what she
has said to us upon it; her councillors hold no other
language to us; but, from what we can gather from the
gentlemen of this country and the French refugees
here, all the council of England consider that the tran-
quillization of France would be their ruin, and they fear
nothing so much as to see an end of the civil wars in
your kingdom.

Her majesty returned to the subject of the Queen of
Scots, saying, "that she had given us several days to
consider of some means whereby she could preserve that
princess's life, without being in danger of losing her
own; and not being yet satisfied on that point, nor
having yet found any other expedient, she could not be
cruel against herself, and that your majesty ought not to
consider it just that she, who is innocent, should die, and
that the Queen of Scotland, who is guilty, should be
saved." After many propositions on one part and the
other on this subject, she rose up. We continued the
same entreaties, on which she said to us, " that in a few
days she would give us an answer."

The next day we were apprized that they had made

proclamation through this city that sentence of death had been given against the Queen of Scotland. She has been proclaimed a traitress, incapable of succeeding to the crown, and worthy of death.

The Earl of Pembroke, the Mayor and Aldermen of the city of London, were present at this proclamation, and the same instant all the bells in this city began to ring; this was followed universally throughout the realm of England, and they continued these ringings for the space of twenty-four hours, and have also made many bonfires of rejoicing for the determination taken by their queen against the Queen of Scotland. This gave us occasion to write to the said lady [Queen Elizabeth] the letter of which we send a copy to your majesty. Not being able to devise any other remedy, we have made supplication that she would defer the execution of the judgment, till we could learn what it would please your majesty to do and say in remonstrance.

The said lady sent word to us, "that on the morrow morning she would let us know her answer, by one of her councillors of state." The day passed, and we had not any news. This morning the Sieur Oullé,[1] a member of her council, came to us on the part of the said lady queen, with her excuse, that we had not heard from her yesterday on account of the indisposition of her majesty; and, after a long discourse on the reasons which had moved them to proceed to this judgment, he said that out of the respect she [the queen] had for your majesty, she was content to grant a delay of the term of twelve days before proceeding to the execution of the judgment, without pledging herself, however, to observe such delay, if in the interim anything should be attempted against her, which might move her to alter

---

[1] Probably Sir Thomas Woolley.

her mind, and the said lady has granted a like delay to the ambassadors of Scotland, who have made her a similar request. They have declared to this queen ".that if she puts to death the Queen of Scotland, the king, her son, is determined to renounce all the friendship and alliance that he has with England, and to advise with his friends how he shall proceed in her cause;" at which she put herself into a great fury.

You see, sire, the pitiable state to which the Queen of Scots is reduced; her life is in the greatest danger, and we have no news of her save that she is very strictly guarded, and that they have only left her four women and two servants. The sentence of death having been communicated to her in the presence of Lord Buckhurst, we have not learned that she said anything but this, "that she could not have believed that the queen her sister would have exercised such inhumanity towards her."

When they had ordained the said proclamation of the judgment that had been given against her, we are told that they proceeded to take away the *dais* which was in her chamber, and deprived her of all other marks of royal dignity. Her chamber and her bed have been hung with black. They have offered a minister for her consolation, and she has refused to confer with a Protestant, although he came to her. She means to die Catholic.

Your majesty will be pleased to consider if there be not some way, through your favour and authority, whereby there may be a hope of saving her life, of which, may it please you to let us understand, within the said term, your good will and commandment; and that you will hear the Sieur de Genlis, the present bearer, to whom we have given credence to you touching the state of your affairs.

Sire, we supplicate the Creator to give to your majesty very happy and very lengthened life.

This from London, this 18th day of December, 1586.

Your very humble and very
obedient servants,
BELLIEVRE,
DE L'AUBESPINE CHASTEAUNEUF.

[In a letter from the Earl of Leicester to Walsingham, extant in the British Museum, (MS. Harl., No. 285,) occurs the following extraordinary passage in allusion to the following beautiful letter from Mary, Queen of Scots, to Queen Elizabeth, after sentence had been pronounced upon her, which, it is well known, was done three months before her execution.

Leicester says to Walsingham, " There is a letter from the Scottish Queen *that hath wrought tears* (viz., drawn tears from Elizabeth), but, I trust, shall do no further herein ; albeit, *the delay is too dangerous*." A mangled abstract, translated from the Latin of Camden, is all hitherto known of this last letter from Mary to Elizabeth ; it is here presented to the reader as literally rendered from the original French, in which poor Mary wrote it, as the idioms of the two languages admit.]

The Queen of Scots to Queen Elizabeth.[1]

Fotheringay, December 19th, 1586.

Madam, — Having, with difficulty, obtained leave from those to whom you have committed me to open to you all I have on my heart, as much for exonerating myself from any ill-will, or desire of committing cruelty, or any act of enmity against those with whom I am connected by blood ; as also, kindly to communicate to you

[1] Des Mesmes MS., No.9513, Collection of Original State Letters, Bibliothèque du Roi.

what I thought would serve you, as much for your weal and preservation, as for the maintenance of the peace and repose of this isle, which can only be injured if you reject my advice, you will credit, or disbelieve my discourse as it seems best to you.

I am resolved to strengthen myself in Christ Jesus alone, who, to those invoking him with a true heart, never fails in his justice and consolation, especially to those who are bereft of all human aid; such are under his holy protection; to him be the glory! He has equalled my expectation, having given me heart and strength, *in spe contra spem* [in hope against hope], to endure the unjust calumnies, accusations, and condemnations (of those who have no such jurisdiction over me) with a constant resolution to suffer death, for upholding the obedience and authority of the apostolical Roman Catholic Church.

Now since I have been on your part informed of the sentence of your last meeting of Parliament, Lord Buckhurst and Beale having admonished me to prepare for the end of my long and weary pilgrimage, I beg to return you thanks on my part for these happy tidings, and to entreat you to vouchsafe to me certain points for the discharge of my conscience. But since Sir A. Paulet has informed me (though falsely), that you had indulged me by having restored to me my almoner [1] and the money that they had taken from me, and that the remainder would follow; for all this I would willingly return you thanks, and supplicate still further as a last request, which I have thought for many reasons I ought to ask of you alone, that you will accord this last favour, for which I should not like to be indebted to

---

[1] De Préau: he remained at Fotheringay, but was forbidden to see his royal mistress. Her letter to him is comprised in this series.

any other, since I have no hope of finding aught but cruelty from the puritans, who are at this time, God knows wherefore, the first in authority, [1] and the most bitter against me.

I will accuse no one; may I pardon, with a sincere heart, every one, even as I desire every one may grant forgiveness to me, God the first. But I know that you, more than any one, ought to feel at heart the honour or dishonour of your own blood, and that, moreover, of a queen and the daughter of a king.

Then, madam, for the sake of that Jesus to whose name all powers bow, I require you to ordain, that when my enemies have slaked their cruel thirst for my innocent blood, you will permit my poor disconsolate servants altogether to carry away my corpse, to bury it in holy ground, with the other queens of France, my predecessors, especially near the late queen, my mother; having this in recollection, that in Scotland the bodies of the kings my predecessors have been outraged, and the churches profaned and abolished; and that, as I shall suffer in this country, a place will not be given to me near the kings your predecessors, [2] who are mine as well as yours; for according to our religion, we think much of being interred in holy ground. As they tell me that you will in nothing force my conscience nor my religion, and have even conceded me a priest, [3] refuse me not this my last request, that you will permit free sepulture to this body when the soul is separated, which when united could never obtain liberty to live in repose, such as

---

[1] With no little greatness of soul, Mary treats Elizabeth, not as her murderess, but as a person controlled by a dominant faction.

[2] This implied wish of burial in Westminster Abbey, her son James afterwards fulfilled.

[3] In this she was deceived; her chaplain was not suffered to see her, though in the castle.

you would desire procure for yourself,—against which repose, before God I speak, I never aimed a blow; but God will let you see the truth of all after my death.

And because I dread the tyranny of those to whose power you have abandoned me, I entreat you not to permit execution to be done on me without your own knowledge, not for fear of the torment, which I am most ready to suffer, but on account of the reports[1] which will be raised concerning my death unsuspected, and without other witnesses, than those who should inflict it, who, I am persuaded, would be of very different qualities from those parties whom I require (being my servants) to remain spectators and witnesses of my end, in the faith of our sacrament, of my Saviour, and in obedience to his church. And after all is over, that they together may carry away my poor corpse (as secretly as you please), and speedily withdraw, without taking with them any of my goods, except those which in dying I may leave to them . . . . . which are little enough for their long and good services.

One jewel[2] that I received of you I shall return to you with my last words, or sooner if you please.

Once more I supplicate you to permit me to send a jewel and a last adieu to my son, with my dying benediction, for of my blessing he has been deprived, since you sent me his refusal to enter into the treaty from which I was excluded by his wicked council; this last point I refer

[1] She here dreads the imputation of suicide, a crime which is considered with peculiar horror by Catholics, as rendering impossible the rites which their creed deems it essential that the dying should receive

[2] This was probably a diamond ring which Elizabeth sent her as token of amity when she first came to England. " It was," says Melville, " an English custom to give a diamond, to be returned at a time of distress, to recal friendship." Many instances exist in history of this custom.

to your favourable consideration and conscience, as the others; but I ask them, in the name of Jesus Christ, and in respect of our consanguinity, and for the sake of King Henry VII., your grandfather and mine, and by the honour of the dignity we both held, and of our sex in common, do I implore you to grant these requests.

As to the rest, I think you know that in your name they have taken down my *dais* [canopy and raised seat], but afterwards they owned to me that it was not by your commandment, but by the intimation of some of your privy council; I thank God that this wickedness came not from you, and that it serves rather to vent their malice than to afflict me, having made up my mind to die. It is on account of this and some other things that they debarred me from writing to you, and after they had done all in their power to degrade me from my rank, they told me, " that I was but a mere dead woman, incapable of dignity." God be praised for all !

I would wish that all my papers were brought to you without reserve, that, at last, it may be manifest to you that the sole care of your safety was not confined to those who are so prompt to persecute me; if you will grant this my last request, I would wish that you would write for them, otherwise they do with them as they choose. And, moreover, I wish that to this my last request you will let me know your last reply.

To conclude, I pray God, the just judge, of his mercy, that he will enlighten you with his Holy Spirit, and that he will give me his grace to die in the perfect charity I am disposed to do, and to pardon all those who have caused or co-operated in my death. Such will be my last prayer to my end, which I am happy to think will precede the persecution that I foresee threatens this island, where . God is no longer seriously feared and revered, but vanity and worldly policy rule and govern all—still will I accuse no one, nor give way to presumption—yet, while leaving this world and preparing myself for a better, I must remind you, that one day you will have to answer for your charge, and for all those whom you doom, and I desire that my blood and my country may be remembered in that time. For why? From the first days of our capacity to comprehend our duties, we ought to bend our minds to make the things of this world yield to those of eternity!

From Forteringhay (Fotheringay), this 19th December, 1586.

Your sister and cousin,
Prisoner wrongfully,
MARIE (ROYNE.[1])

December 24. M. de Belliévre receives a reply from Henry III., and demands an audience for taking leave.

December 27. He is at length admitted into Elizabeth's presence at Greenwich Palace. He renews his remonstrances, and concludes by intimating that the king, his master, had charged him to declare that he felt particularly offended at the little attention she had paid to his entreaties and remonstrances.

1587. *January* 4. M. de Belliévre sets out for Dover, not being able to obtain his passport until the preceding evening.

The same day Stafford, brother to the English ambassador in Paris, calls on Destiappes, secretary to M. de Chateauneuf, and takes him to see a prisoner confined for debt, who proposes to take the life of Elizabeth. Destrappes, indignant at such audacity, immediately informs M. de Chateauneuf, who orders Stafford to quit his house, forbidding him ever to enter it again.

[1] In the days of her prosperity, Mary merely signed her name Marie, but after her captivity, she was careful to add R. or Royne, for Regina, for the purpose of asserting the royalty, of which she declared she had been deprived by violence and hard restraint, at Lochleven.—Egerton Papers.

January 6. Patrick Gray, Robert Melville, and Keith, ambassadors of James VI., obtain an audience of Queen Elizabeth, and make several proposals to save the life of Mary Stuart, but obtain nothing

The same day Destrappes, on his way to join M. de Bellhévre at Dover, is apprehended at Rochester by order of the Queen, brought back to London, and confined in the Tower.

January 7. The English Ministers announce the discovery of a new conspiracy, in which they pretend that M. de Chateauneuf is concerned

January 8. The ports of England are closed, and the couriers of the French ambassador stopped

---

Statement for M. de Villeroy of the transactions of M. de Belliévre in England, relative to the affairs of the Queen of Scotland during the months of November and December, 1586, and January, 1587.— N.S.

Monseigneur,—I have received the letter which you were pleased to write to me on the 17th of last month, by which I learn, that you have received and read the propositions made by M. de Bellhévre to the Queen of England, but that you desire to be further informed what judgment has been given against the Queen of Scotland, and of his success. I will, therefore, relate to you all that has happened, and all that I have been able to learn and collect as accurately as I can.

My said Seigneur set out from Paris on his journey to England, on the 17th day of November, and arrived at Calais on the 27th, where he received letters from M. de Chateauneuf, begging him to make all the haste that he could, as the Queen of England and the states of her kingdom were proceeding with the greatest despatch to the trial of the said Queen of Scotland. Of this, Monseigneur was more particularly informed by the Sieur de Callery, a near relative to M. de la Brosses, and a native of Lyons, a very respectable gentleman, who is about de Chateauneuf, who had come express from him in London to the said Calais, to bring thither an English vessel to carry my said Seigneur to Dover; the said vessel having arrived with a fair wind, which was, of course, a contrary one for us, we were, therefore, obliged to wait two or three days at the said town of Calais for the convenience of the wind. But though the wind was contrary and the risk great, my said Seigneur, from the great desire he had to arrive before any thing had been resolved upon relative to the said Queen of Scotland, embarked on Friday, the 28th of the said month of November, at midnight; and we arrived at Dover next day, about nine o'clock in the morning ; but not without suffering greatly from sea-sickness, all of us excepting my said Seigneur, who remained at the said Dover the whole of the said day, that the gentlemen who accompanied him, and who were shaken by the sea, might rest themselves. On Sunday morning, the 30th of the said month, he got into a coach, which my said Seigneur de Chateauneuf had sent for him by M. de Brancaléon, whilst we of his suite were mounted on post-horses, which are easily obtained and in great number all along the road from the said Dover to London, distant from each other twenty-five French leagues, which generally take two days to travel.

My said Seigneur, with all his company, arrived in London on Monday, the first of December, at noon. On the morrow, he sent M. de Villiers, one of the gentlemen of his suite, to the Queen of England, who was holding her court at the palace of Richemont [Richmond], distant from the said London three good French leagues, to request her to grant him audience ; and, as the malice of that queen is infinite, she wished to defer seeing my lord for some days. Meanwhile, she caused her estates

and parliament to proceed secretly with the extraordinary trial of that poor princess, the Queen of Scotland,
and an evil report to be spread, in order to put off the
audience of my said Seigneur, which he warmly urged,
and, moreover, taking two occasions, and making use of
false pretences, purposely to gain time, and to take advantage of these delays and inventions, to finish the said
trial.

In the first place, she caused a report to be raised at
her court and in London that all the company of my
said Seigneur was full of contagion, that three or four
had died of the plague at Calais, and that others had
been left ill on the road ; another report generally circulated was that he had in his company some unknown
men, and that they had come expressly to kill her.
These two false reports never ceased for the space of
eight days, but, on the 7th of December, in the morning, madam the said queen sent to fetch my said Seigneur, who went to her after dinner to the said town of
Richemont, accompanied by all the gentlemen who had
come from France with him.

On entering the presence-chamber, he found the said
lady sitting on her royal seat, accompanied and surrounded by great lords and gentlemen of the kingdom.
After my said Seigneur and M. de Chateauneuf had
paid their respects, he began to make such remonstrances to her, on the part of the king, as are contained in the paper which I sent to you some time since;
to which she replied, nearly point by point, and in good
terms, and in the French language. and, as if seized
with some passion which appeared in her countenance,
she represented "that the Queen of Scotland had been
continually persecuting her, and that it was the third
time she had endeavoured, by an infinite number of
means, to take away her life ; that she had too long

borne this with great patience; and that nothing had
ever touched her heart so keenly as this last circumstance, which had cost her more sighs and tears than the
loss of all her relatives had done, and, so much the more,
because the said Queen of Scotland was her nearest
kinswoman, and so nearly allied to the king;" and, as in
the said remonstrance Monseigneur had put forward several examples drawn from history, she observed "that
she had read much and seen many books in her lifetime,
and more than a thousand others of her sex and rank,
but never had she met with or heard talk of such an
act as that which had been planned against her and prosecuted by her own kinswoman, whom the king, her
brother-in-law, could not and ought not to support in
her malice, but rather aid her in bringing speedily to
justice as an example;" adding "that she had, in good
proof and experience of this world, known what it was
both to be subject and sovereign, what it was to have
good neighbours, and sometimes to have to remonstrate
with such as were evil disposed ; that she had sometimes
found treason where she had placed the utmost confidence; that she had seen great benefits scarcely acknowledged, and, in place of gratitude, schemes to thwart
her;" telling Monseigneur de Belhévre "that she was
very sorry he had not been deputed on some better occasion ; and that in a few days she should send to the
king her good brother, whose health she inquired after,
as also that of the queen his mother, who had taken
great pains to restore peace in France, which, as far as
she could judge, was necessary."

This said, she retired to her apartment, and my said
seigneur returned that day to London, where he remained some days awaiting the answer of the said queen,
whom he urged incessantly for it, as also the lords of her
council, who, nevertheless, always put off all business

relating to the poor Queen of Scotland; which occasioned my said seigneur to return to the Court at Richemont, to make fresh remonstrances to the said Queen of
England about the measures which he had learned to
have been resolved upon and determined respecting this
poor princess.

It was on the 15th of December that he begged and
entreated her, "as she had proceeded so far as to cause
even sentence of death to be passed upon her, and there
was no need for him to make a longer stay in England,
to give him his safe-conduct to return to the king," which
she promised to do in the course of two or three days;
and he returned to London that same day, which was
Monday.

On the morning of Tuesday, the 16th of the said
month, all those of the states and of the parliament of
the kingdom were assembled at the palace of Westminster, where also were present the principal lords of the
said kingdom, and of the council of the said kingdom;
in which place, and in the presence of the above-said,
was proclaimed and pronounced in open court the sentence of death against that unfortunate princess, as was
done also with great solemnity and ceremony in all the
public places and streets of London, and consequently
throughout the said kingdom; and on this proclamation
the bells of the said city were rung for twenty-four
hours without ceasing; and the inhabitants were commanded to make bonfires, each before his own door in
the streets, as is done in France on the eve of St. John
the Baptist.

On the following day, the said sentence of death was
carried and read to the said Queen of Scotland, and
some of the principal of the council of the kingdom,
accompanied by all the officers of justice, proceeded
to the Castle of Faldsinzay [Fotheringhay], ten leagues

distant from London. It is said that this poor princess was not much surprised, but with great firmness said to them, "that all the contents of the said sentence were nothing but falsehoods and suppositions invented against her; and that they had proceeded against her in the same manner as did the Scribes and Pharisees against Jesus Christ; that she was not subject nor amenable to the laws and statutes of the kingdom, as she had before protested, when, by compulsion, she had spoken and answered before them;" which answers and interrogations, at least the few I have been able to collect, I have transcribed below; and, after the evident proclamations, which my said seigneur had seen and heard, he resolved to write the following letter to the Queen of England:—

"Madam, we left your majesty yesterday, expecting, as you were pleased to tell us, that we should have in a few days your good answer to the request which we made to you on the part of the king our good master, your brother, in behalf of the Queen of Scotland, his sister-in-law and ally; but though this morning we have been informed that the sentence passed upon the said queen has been proclaimed in this city of London, while we were promising ourselves a different result from your clemency, and from the friendship you bear our said lord the king your good brother, yet, not to omit anything that we consider to be our duty, and according to the wish of his majesty, we have not failed to write you this present, by which we again beseech you very humbly not to refuse his majesty the very urgent and very affectionate request which he has made to you, and that you would be pleased to spare the life of the said Queen of Scotland, which our said lord the king will receive as the greatest pleasure that your majesty or any other person can do him; whereas, on the contrary, there could not happen anything that would cause him greater displeasure, or wound his heart more, than if severity were exercised towards the said queen, being what she is to him.

"Wherefore, madam, as the said king, our master and your good brother, when he despatched us for this purpose to your majesty, did not imagine that it was in any way possible for such execution to be so promptly resolved upon, we most humbly beseech you, madam, before you permit anything further to be done, to grant us some time, during which we may apprise him of the state of the affairs of the Queen of Scotland, in order that, before your majesty takes a final resolution, you may hear what it shall please his most Christian majesty to say and to remonstrate upon the most important matter which, in our memory, was ever submitted to the judgment of men. The Sr. de St. Cir, who will deliver these presents to your majesty, will, if you please, be the bearer of your good reply. From London, the 16th of December, 1586."

It was on the 16th of December, that the said Sr. de St. Cir and other French gentlemen proceeded to the said court of the said Queen of England at Richemont, to present to her the aforesaid letter, which bore the signature of my said lord and M de Chateauneuf; but the queen would not be seen that day, excusing herself upon the plea of indisposition; and the said letter was left with the Sr. de Walsingham, her chief secretary of state, who promised to send the answer of the queen on the morrow; but it was two or three days before the said answer was verbally delivered by two gentlemen, who came to London to my said seigneur without any letters; for it is not customary with the English to negotiate any business in writing, but only by word of mouth. The message which they delivered to my said lord, on the part of their queen, was to this effect—that, according to the letter, which he had written to her a few days before, expressing a wish that she should grant a delay of some days to enable them to acquaint the king with the state of the affairs of the Queen of Scotland, the said Queen of England granted a delay of twelve days only, during which he might send to the said king, and advise him of the aforesaid things ; whereupon Mr. de Sanlis [Genlis], eldest son of M. Bruslard, was incontinently sent to France; and, in addition to the ample despatch which he carried to his majesty on this subject, he was expressly charged to report to him, as he did faithfully, every circumstance that he had witnessed during his sojourn in England relating to the affairs of the Queen of Scotland His majesty thereupon resolved to send a sudden express, which arrived in London two days after the expiration of the twelve which were granted. My said lord sent immediately to the said Queen of England, who was at a palace called Grenuche [Greenwich], a league from London, where she was keeping the Christmas holidays, according to the old almanac, begging her to be pleased to grant him audience, but which he could not obtain for four or five days, on account of the said holidays.

At last, on the 6th of January, my said lord was sent for by her, and went thither on the same day. On entering, with the Sr. de Chateauneuf, a hall in the said palace of Grenuche, which they call the presence-chamber, and in which was the said queen, having saluted her, he made the remonstrances and the second propositions, which you have seen, and to which the said queen listened very patiently, until nearly the concluding and last words of them, which made her say very abruptly, and almost angrily, " M. de Bellièvre, have you had orders from the king my brother to hold such language to me ?" He replied, " Yes, madam, I have the express commands of his majesty." She then replied, "Have you this power signed by his own hand?" He again said, "Yes, madam; the king my master, your good brother, has expressly ordered and charged me, by letters signed with his own hand, to make the above remonstrances." She said to him, "I must have the same signed by yourself," which my said lord sent to her the same day. She then ordered all those who were in the chamber to withdraw, and there remained with her only my said Seigneurs de Bellièvre and Chasteauneuf and one of her's, where they continued in conference for a good hour; nevertheless I do not learn that my said lord was able to draw from her any assurance of the life of the Queen of Scotland; but she assured my said lord, that she would send to the king an ambassador of her own, who should be in Paris as soon as he, and by whom she would send to his majesty her resolution respecting the affairs of the Queen of Scotland.

On Sunday, the 6th of January, my said lord left the said queen, in her palace of Grennche, having taken leave of her and the lords of her court, intending to set out two days afterwards, which was Tuesday, the 8th of January, when we were all prepared and booted, to commence our journey to France; but the said queen sent on that day two of her gentlemen to my said lord, begging him to wait two or three days longer; whereupon, to obey her, he stayed till the 13th of January, when she sent him his passport, and gave orders to her admiral to hold one of her ships in readiness at Dover, to carry my said lord over on his return.

After passing through Rogester and Canterberitz, two of the principal towns and bishoprics of the kingdom, we arrived at the said Dover on Saturday, xvijth of January; and on Sunday morning, at nine o'clock, the wind was so favourable that, after embarking, we found ourselves happily arrived in port, in the road of Calais, the same day, at one o'clock in the afternoon, and, thank God, without any sea-sickness, which we all experienced on our passage from the said Calais to England.

What happened since, and the very day of our departure from England, was the commencement of a strange tragedy. An English gentleman, calling himself Sieur Stafor,[1] brother to the ambassador residing in France for the said queen, came and addressed himself to M. de Trappes, saying, that there was a certain person imprisoned in London, for debt only, who desired to communicate to M. de Chateauneuf an affair of importance for the service of the king, and which likewise concerned the Queen of Scotland; which information my said lord would not despise; not suspecting any evil design, he resolved to send the said Sieur de Trappes to the said prisoner, to hear what he had to say. On the arrival of the said Sieur de Trappes, the prisoner began by saying, that he was detained there merely for the sum of a hundred or a hundred and twenty crowns; and if M. de Chateauneuf would be pleased to lend him that sum, he could render a signal service to the Queen of Scotland by the resolution which he had formed to kill the Queen of England. The said Sieur de Trappes, on hearing this proposal, was astonished, and observed to the said prisoner and to the said Stafor, who had accompanied him thither, that he was a very bad man if he had resolved upon so wicked an act; and that he could assure him that M. de Chateauneuf would highly disapprove all his undertakings, nor would he participate or meddle in any of them. He left him without saying any more; and having returned to the said Sr. de Chateauneuf, he related to him all that the said prisoner had said; then the said Sr de Chateauneuf said to Stafor, "that he

[1] Stafford.

thought this mode of proceeding most extraordinary, and was sure that it was an artifice; and that this snare had been laid to bring him into trouble;" and asked "why he had applied to him upon so base and wicked a business," and remonstrated with him in the strongest terms, and told the said Stafor "to leave his house immediately, and never again to enter it," advising him to fly, "as he saw plainly that he was a lost man;" and he went away quite amazed.

Next day the said Staffor went again to the said Sr. de Trappes, who was to set out for France, and who had prepared himself to make the said journey with us, and the said Staffort begged the said Sr. de Trappes to do him the favour to assist him to cross the sea. This the said de Trappes represented to M. de Chasteauneuf, who said to the said de Trappes, "Go and tell the said Staffort that I have forbidden him my house, and I desire him to leave it forthwith; and that, if it were not for the respect I have for his family, I would instantly inform the queen of his designs." He immediately left the said house, and was taken up the same day. The said de Trappes, setting out the same day by post for Dover, where he was to wait for us, to cross the sea with my said lord, when he was only two posts from London, was apprehended, brought back prisoner to the said place, and put into the Tower. The said de Trappes, after having been interrogated by the council of the queen, it was found that the said interrogations and answers were all contrary to 'and different from the truth; these fine councillors of England having forged, falsified, and composed just such papers as they pleased, respecting this fact by them invented and planned; for, be it remarked, they never produce the original papers signed by parties, but only copies, in which they insert or omit what they please and what is favourable to their ordinary inventions.

On the following day, or two days, after the imprisonment of the said de Trappes and Staffort, my said Seigneur de Chasteauneuf was summoned before the council of the queen, to which the said Staffort was brought and confronted with him : he asserted strange things, saying that he and the said de Trappes had treated with the said prisoner about the death of the Queen of England : but the said Sr. de Chasteauneuf knew well how to reply and to defend himself against such dangerous inventions, of which the English are so full, and which they employ against all those who displease them, as does my said Seigneur Chasteauneuf, because he is too upright a man, and performs his duty to his master as a very good and faithful servant of his majesty; this fine queen of England having, in order to colour all her schemes and proceedings, sent to France an ambassador, who arrived eight or ten days after us, bringing (as I supposed) to the king, some favourable reply on the affairs of the Queen of Scotland, which she had deferred when my said lord left her, promising to make him acquainted with her final resolution on this point. Instead of giving him this satisfaction, she [Elizabeth] made new complaints of his ambassador to the said queen, who, she said, participated in the designs of those who aimed at taking her life, without apprising her of it, and making many other charges full of calumny, falsehood, and artifice.

This invention, so maliciously conceived, being circulated throughout all England, has so excited and embittered the people of the said kingdom against the said Sr. de Chasteauneuf and the poor Queen of Scotland, that, in short, the said Queen of England, to consummate and crown her artful scheme, has taken advantage of this new occasion to manifest her high displeasure at this circumstance recently brought about by her, and projected also by the aid and pure malice of her creatures, so that the whole odium of it has fallen upon the head of that poor, unfortunate princess, whom she has by her artifices brought to such a cruel death, as you may see by a brief account, which I have collected from those who can vouch for the truth.

The trial of the said Queen of Scotland has been got up and instituted on grounds, which the Queen of England has pretended and pretends to have been proved and verified: that the said Queen of Scotland had conspired against her person, her state, and kingdom, and sworn her death, which she had endeavoured to effect by means of those whom she had brought to execution; the principal of fourteen gentlemen, executed in London, was called the Seigneur de Babinton.

The said Queen of England, in order to obtain evidence of the above, resolved, with her council, that the said Queen of Scotland should be examined, and should answer by word of mouth, on the facts and articles deduced and resulting from the trial of the persons executed: whereto she was compelled, on account of the incessant persecutions and threats employed against her, though she held out for some days, and resolved neither to appear nor to answer in any way: however, rather than that this silence should afford occasion to think that she might be guilty of that which was laid to her charge, she at last determined to appear before the said commissioners deputed by the said Queen of England, and made this speech, which I have received from good authority.

The aforesaid lady being seated at the end of the table in the hall, and the said commissioners around her, the Queen of Scotland began to speak in these terms:

" I do not consider any one of you, who are here assembled, either as my equal or my judge, to examine me upon any facts; therefore, what I now do, and what I say to you is of my own free will, taking God to witness that I am innocent, pure, and clear in my conscience of all the accusations and calumnies which are laid to my charge."

She then went on to protest that she was a free-born princess and queen, not subject to any but to God, to whom she had to render an account of her actions; and therefore she again protested that her appearance before the said commissioners should not be prejudicial to her, or to the kings, princes, and potentates, her allies, or to her son, and desired that her protest should be registered, and demanded a copy of it.

The chancellor, one of the commissioners, began and protested, on the contrary, that the said protest of the Queen of Scotland could not hurt or prejudice the majesty of the Queen of England or her crown.

The said chancellor ordered their commission to be read in the presence of the said Queen of Scotland, as being founded on the statute and law of the kingdom.

The said Queen of Scotland replied, that she protested anew, that the said statute and law were insufficient and suspicious, and that she could not submit to them, being in no way amenable, as the said law and statute were not made for her.

The said chancellor insisted that the law was sufficient for proceeding against her; but she answered and said to the said chancellor that that law and statute were not for those of her rank.

The said chancellor declared that the commission authorised the proceeding with her trial, even though she refused to answer, and that he could pass on to the evidence, and he represented to the said queen that she had offended against two branches of the said statute and of the law, both in the conspiracy against the queen and on the present occasion, and that she had herself planned and devised it. The said Queen of Scotland replied that she had never even thought of such a thing.

Thereupon the letters which they alleged to have been written by her to Sr. de Babinton, and the answer of the said Sr. de Babinton, were read to her.

The said lady replied, "that she had never seen Babinton, nor had she any conference with him, nor received any letters from him; that she could not prevent him or any other man from crossing the sea; but that there was not a person who could assert and maintain with truth that she had ever done any thing to the harm or prejudice of the said Queen of England; that, being so strictly guarded, cut off from all communication, separated from and deprived of all her friends, surrounded by enemies, destitute of all counsel, it was impossible she could have participated in or consented to such practices as she was charged with; and that many persons wrote letters to her whom she did not know, and that letters were sent to her without her knowing whence they came."

The confession of Babinton being read to her, she replied "that she had never seen any such letter."

Her letter to Babinton being read, she said "that if Babinton or any others had said any thing, whatever it might be, against her, they were liars." She then said, "Now produce and show me my own letter, in my own writing and with my signature, which you say I wrote to Babinton; you show me only falsified copies, which you have filled with such language as you have thought proper;" and she asserted that she had never seen the said letter.

The letter of Babinton to her she again said, she had never seen; she was told that she must have seen it, as that was proved by her answer. She said, " I know nothing whatever of that answer. If you will show me my letter and signature containing what you say, then I will admit what you charge me with; but thus far you have produced nothing worthy of belief, mere copies which you have invented and augmented as you thought proper." She then said, weeping, " If I have ever planned or consented to such schemes affecting the life of my sister, I pray God that he may never grant me mercy. I confess, indeed, that I have written to several, that I have begged them to assist in delivering me from my miserable confinement as a captive and ill-treated princess for nineteen years and so many months; but never did I either wish or write such things against the queen. I have indeed written for the deliverance of several persecuted Catholics, and, could I have saved them from punishment with my own blood, I would have done and would yet do it, and I will always do every thing in my power to prevent their destruction."

The said lady then addressed the Secretary Walsingham, as if in anger, saying, "that he had always been her greatest enemy, as well as her son's, and that he had tampered with certain persons against her to her prejudice." The said Walsingham replied, " Madam, I protest before God, who is my witness, that I have never done any thing to your prejudice, as a private man unworthy of a man of honour, or a public man of my rank; and I say this before God, and, as a man anxious for the welfare of my mistress, I have been careful of it."

This is all that was done in this matter for that day

on the morrow, she was again compelled to appear before the said commissioners, and, having seated herself
at the end of the table in the hall, and the said commissioners around her, she began thus, in a loud voice :
" You are not ignorant that I am a queen, a sovereign,
crowned and anointed in the church of God, and cannot,
and ought not, for any cause whatever, to be summoned
before you, and examined, and judged by the laws and
statutes which you put forth, because I am a free
princess, and owe to no prince more than he owes to me;
and as to all the offences against my sister which you
lay to my charge, I can give you no answer, unless I am
assisted by my counsel; and if you will choose to proceed, do what you please, but in regard to all your
proceedings, I renew my former protest, and appeal to
God, who is the true and just judge, and to the kings
and princes, my allies, friends, and confederates."

Her protest was again registered, as she desired.
She was then told "that she had, besides, written several
malicious letters to the princes of Christendom, prejudicial to the Queen of England and to her kingdom."
She replied, " I do not deny it, and if it were yet to do,
I would do the same again, with a view to recover my
liberty.   Consider and remember that there is not either
man or woman in the world, of lower rank than I am,
who would not seek the aid of friends to obtain release
from such a captivity as mine.   You charge me with
certain letters of Babinton's; I do not deny it; but
show me in these letters, if you can, one single word
which refers to the queen my sister; you will then have
occasion to prosecute me.   I wrote to him, who wrote
to inform me that he would set me at liberty, that, if he
could do so without risking the life of both, he was to
make the attempt, and that is all."

The said lady also said : " Respecting the charge you

bring against me on account of my servants, and even my secretaries, you have treated them very roughly; therefore they cannot and ought not to be made and produced as witnesses against me. And as for the words of traitors, they are of no account; now that they are dead, you can say whatever you think fit: let them believe them who choose."

Several charges were brought against her, but without sufficient proofs. Thus much is to be collected from the proceedings against the said Queen of Scotland, having been taken from a translation made from English into French.

1587. *January* 10. The ambassadors of the King of Scotland obtain another audience of Elizabeth, which, like the former, leads to no result.

Memorial addressed by the Master of Gray to the King of Scotland.

It will please your majesty, I have thought meeter to set down all things as they occur, and all advertisements as they came to my ears, than jointly in a letter.

" I came to Vere [1] the 24th of Dec. and sent to Wm. Keith, and Mr. Archibald Douglas, to advertise the queen of it, like as they did at their audience. She promised the queen your majesty's mother's life should be spared till we were heard. The 27th, they came to Vare to me, the day which Sir Robt. came to Vare, where they shewed us how far they had already gone in their negociation, but for that the discourse of it is set down in our general letter, I remit me to it, only this far I will testify unto your majesty, that Wm. Keith hath used himself right honestly and justly till our coming,

[1] Probably Ware.

respecting all circumstances, and chiefly his colleague in his dealing, which indeed is not better than your majesty knows already.

The 29th day of Decr. we came to London, where we were no ways friendly received, nor after the honest sort it has pleased your majesty to use her ambassadors; never man sent to welcome or convey us. This same day, we understood of Mr. de Believre his taking leave, and for that the custom permitted not, we sent our excuses by Mr. George Young.

The 1st day of Jan^{ry}, W^m. Keith and his colleague, according to the custom, sent to crave our audience. We received the answer contained in the general letter, and could not have answer till the 6th day; what was done that day your majesty has it in the general, yet we was not out of expectation at that time, albeit we received hard answers.

The 8th day we speak with the Earl of Leicester, where our conference was, as is set down in the general. I remarked this, that he that day said plainly, the detaining of the Queen of Scotland prisoner was, for that she pretended a succession to this crown. Judge then by this what is thought of your majesty, as ye shall hear a little after.

The 9th day we speak with the French ambassador, whom we find very plain in making to us a wise discourse of all his proceedings, and Mr. de Believre's: we thanked him in your majesty's name, and opened such things as we had to treat with this queen, save the last point, as more largely set down by our general.

It is thought here, and some friends of your majesty's advised me, that Believre his negociation was not effectual, and that the resident was not privy to it, as indeed I think is true, for since Believre his parting, there is a talk of this Chasteauneuf his servants taken with his whole papers and pacquets, which he was sending in France, for that they charge him with a conspiracy of late against the queen here her life.   It is alledged his servant has confessed the matter, but whom I shall trust I know not, but till I see proof, I shall account him an honest man, for indeed so he appears, and one (without doubt) who hath been very instant in this matter.   I shew him that the queen and Earl of Leicester had desired to speak with me in private, and craved his opinion : he gave it freely that he thought it meetest, I shew him the reason why I communicate that to him, for that I had been suspected by some of her majesty's friends in France to have done evil offices in her service, that he should be my witness that my earnest dealing in this should be a sufficient testimony that all was lies, and that this knave Nau, who now betrayed her, had in that done evil offices; he desired me, seeing she saw only with other folks' eyes, that I should no ways impute it to her, for the like she had done to himself by Nau his persuasion.   I answered he should be my witness in that.

The 9th day we sent to court to crave audience, which we got the 10th day; at the first, she [Queen Elizabeth] said, ' A thing long looked for should be welcome when it comes, I would now see your master's offers.'   I answered, 'No man makes offers but for some cause; we would, an like your majesty, first know the cause to be extant for which we offer, and likewise that it be extant till your majesty has heard us.'—'I think it be extant yet,' she said, ' But I will not promise for an hour,[1] but you think to shift in that sort !'   I answered, ' We mind not to shift, but to offer from our sovereign all things that with reason may be; and in special, we

[1] Meaning she would not answer that Mary Stuart was not put to death.

offered as is set down in our general: all was refused and thought nothing.' She called on the three that were in the house, the Earl of Leicester, my lord admiral, and chamberlain, and very despitefully repeated all our offers in presence of them all. I opened the last part, and said, 'Madam, for what respect is it that men deal against your person or estate for her cause?' She answered, 'Because they think she shall succeed to me, and for that she is a papist.' 'Appearingly,' said I, 'both the causes may be removed.' She [Queen Elizabeth] said, 'she would be glad to understand it.' 'If, madam,' said I, 'all that she has of right of succession were in the king our sovereign's person, were not all hope of papists removed?' She answered, 'I hope so.' 'Then, madam, I think the queen his mother shall willingly demit all her rights in his person.' She answered, 'She hath no right, for she is declared unable.' 'Then,' I said, 'if she have no right, appearingly the hope ceases already, so that it is not to be feared that any man attempt for her.' The queen answered, 'But the papists allow not our declaration.' 'Then let it fall,' says I, 'in the king's person by her assignation.' The Earl of Liecester answered, 'She is a prisoner, how can she demit?' I answered, 'The demission is to her son, by the advice of all the friends she has in Europe; and in case, as God forbid, that any attempt cuts the queen here [Elizabeth] away, who shall parly with her to prove the demission or assignation to be ineffectual, her son being opposite party, and having all the princes her friends for him, having bonded for the efficacy of it with his majesty of before?' The queen [Elizabeth] made as she could not comprehend my meaning, and Sir Robt. [Melville] opened the matter again, yet she made as though she understood not. So the Earl of Leicester answered, 'That our meaning was, that the king should be put in his mother's place.' 'Is it so,' the queen [Elizabeth] answered, 'then I put myself in a worse case than of before; by God's passion,[1] that were to cut my own throat, and for a duchy, or an earldom to yourself, you, or such as you, would cause some of your desperate knaves kill me. No, by God, he shall never be in that place.' I answered, 'He craves nothing of your majesty but only of his mother.' The Earl of Leicester answered, 'That were to make him party to the queen my mistress.' I said, 'He will be far more party, if he be in her place through her death.' She [Elizabeth] would stay no longer, but said, 'she would not have a worse in his mother's place.' And said, 'Tell your king what good I have done for him in holding the crown on his head since he was born, and that I mind to keep the league that now stands between us, and if he break it shall be a double fault;' and with this minded to have bidden us a farewell; but we eschewed. And I spake craving of her that her life may be spared for fifteen days; she refused. Sir Robert [Melville] craved for 'Only eight days,' she said; 'Not for an hour;'[2] and so *geid* her way. Your majesty sees we have delivered all we had for offers, but all is for nothing, for she and her counsel has laid a determination that they mind to follow forth, and I see it comes rather of her counsel than herself, which I like the worse; for without doubt, sir, it shall cut off all friendship ye had here. Although it were but once they had meaned well to

[1] It is well known that the maiden queen, like her impetuous father, did not scruple to give increased emphasis to her language by an oath.

A similar instance occurs in Chateauneuf's despatch of the 13th of May, 1587, which follows.

[2] The presence of Sir Robert Melville obliged James's treacherous ambassadors to give a correct report of this most extraordinary interview with Elizabeth.

your majesty, yet remembering themselves that they have meddled with your mother's blood, good faith they cannot hope great good of yourself, a thing in truth I am sorry for; further your majesty may perceive by this last discourse of that I proponit, if they had meaned well to your majesty, they had used it otherwise than they have done, for reason has bound them. But I dare not write all. I mind something to speak in this matter, because we look *shurly* [surely] our letters shall be *troucit* by the way.

For that I see private credit nor no means can alter their determination, although the queen again and the Earl of Leicester has desired to speak with me in particular; I mind not to speak, nor shall not; but assuredly shall let all men see that I in particular was no ways tied to England, but for the respect of your majesty's service. So albeit, at this time, I could not effectuate that I desired, yet my upright dealing in it shall be manifested to the world. We are, God willing, then to crave audience, where we mind to use sharply our instructions, which hitherto we have used very calmly, for we can, for your honour's cause, say no less for your majesty than the French ambassador has said for his master.

So I pray your majesty consider my upright dealing in your service, and not the effect, for had it been double by any I might have here had credit, but being I came only for that cause I will not my credit shall serve here to any further purpose. I pray God preserve your majesty and send you of true and sincere friendship. From London, 12th of Jan. 1586-7.

I understand the queen is tosend one of her own to your majesty.

1587. *January* 17. The Scottish ambassadors take leave of queen Elizabeth, and in the name of their king protest against all that she might do to the prejudice of Mary Stuart.

William Stanley, governor of Deventer, in Flanders, dreading the fate of Babington, who had been his friend, gives up the place to the Spaniards, and enters, with 1300 men, into the service of Philip II.

[In justice to James VI., the urgent letter he wrote to Queen Elizabeth, when he found his mother's life was in jeopardy, ought not to be omitted in a collection of documents illustrative of her career and death. The crabbed orthography in which it is shrouded, has concealed its manly and earnest tenor from all but the historical antiquary, while the blame with which general historians have loaded the memory of the son of Mary of Scotland, is read universally. Much discussion has likewise been thrown away on the question of whether James VI. appointed Patrick Gray, with the evil intent of urging Elizabeth to destroy his mother. The truth is, that whether Patrick Gray went with malevolent or benevolent intentions against poor Mary, the young king was equally powerless in his appointment; for he was, as he most emphatically declared, nearly as much a prisoner as his unfortunate mother. Queen Elizabeth well knew that he was utterly helpless in the hands of the dominant faction of his kingdom. " I was unable," he says himself, "to revenge the heinous murder committed against my dearest mother by the old enemies [the English] of my progenitors, realm and nation. First, in respect of my youth, not trained up in dexterity of arms either to withstand injury or to conquer my own right, *being at all times bygone detained in captivity.* Next, my excessive want of money, being obliged to live from hand to mouth, having sufficient *patrimony* and *casualty* [land and expectations] without anything in store.   Then the divers factions of spiritual and temporal estates, every one regarding himself, and not one me."

Those who doubt this statement, so forcible in its unvarnished simplicity, should compare it with the actual facts of James's situation, and they will find it will bear the severest scrutiny.   It is drawn from a paper called the " King's Reasons," extant in his own handwriting, among the Cottonian Manuscripts, Julius F., fol. 70.]

King James VI. of Scotland to Queen Elizabeth.[1]

January 26th, 1586-7.

Madame and dearest sister,—If ye could have known what divers thoughts have agitated my mind, since my directing of William Keith unto you for the soliciting of this matter, whereto nature and honour greatly and unfeignedly bind and oblige me—if, I say, ye knew what divers thoughts, and what just grief I had, weighing deeply the thing itself, if so it should proceed, as God forbid!—what events might follow thereupon—what

[1] MS. Cotton. Caligula, c. ix., fol. 146.   Entirely in the young king's hand.   See Ellis's Original Letters, vol. ii. p. 18, for this letter, in the original orthography.   The unfortunate Mary never had the consolation of knowing that her son had pleaded so earnestly for her life as he did in this letter to Queen Elizabeth.   The murderous intrigues of his ambassador, Patrick Gray, against her had been duly detailed to her by the French ambassador, as we have shown by her preceding letters; and if she did not lay her head on the block with bitterness in her heart against her only son, the contrary must have been effected by the strongest exertion of Christian charity.

number of straights I should be driven unto—and, amongst the rest, how it might peril my reputation amongst my subjects. If these things, I yet say again, were known to you, then doubt I not but ye would so far pity my case, as it would easily make you at the first, to resolve your own hest[1] unto it.

I doubt greatly in what fashion to write on this purpose, for ye have already taken so evil my plainness, as I fear, if I persist in that course, ye will rather be exasperated into passions[2] by reading my words, than by the plainness thereof to be persuaded to consider rightly the simple truth. Yet, justly preferring the duty of an honest friend to the sudden passions of one who, how soon they be past, can wislier [more wisely] weigh the reasons than I can set them down, I have resolved, in few words and plain, to give you friendly and best advice, appealing to your ripest judgment to discern thereupon. What thing, madame, can more greatly touch me in honour, both as a king and as a son than that my nearest neighbour, being in strictest friendship with me, shall rigorously put to death a sovereign prince and my natural mother?—she being alike in sex and in state to her that so uses her!—albeit subject, I grant, to a harder fortune, touching her too so nearly in proximity of blood? What law of God can permit that justice shall strike upon them, whom he has appointed supreme dispensers of the same under him,

[1] The young king's meaning is · If you knew how unfortunate my case is, pity for me would influence your *hest*, or decision, on the fate of my mother.

[2] Ellis's Collection of Original Letters contains a violent rating given by Elizabeth to James, in 1582, when he was only fifteen, on account of one of his letters which she had taken ill He now plainly tells her, that he fears to rouse her angry passions by saying all he feels for his mother.

whom he hath called gods, and therefore subjected to the censure of none on earth, whose ,anointing by God cannot be defiled by man, unrevenged by the author thereof?[1]—they being supreme and immediate lieutenants of God in heaven, cannot therefore be judged by their equals on earth. What monstrous thing it is that sovereign princes themselves should be the example-givers of the profaning of their own sacred dia- dems! Then what should move you to this form of proceeding, (supposing the worst which, in good faith, I look not for at your hands,) honour or profit? Honour were it to you to spare, when it is least looked for! Honour were it to you—which is not only my friendly advice, but my earnest suit—to make me and all the princes in Europe eternally beholden to you, in grant- ing this my so reasonable request! And not—I pray you pardon my free speaking—to put princes to straits of honour where, through your general reputation and the universal, almost all, misliking of you, may danger- ously peril, both in honour and utility, your person and state. Ye know, madame, well enow, how small differ- ence Cicero concludes to be betwixt *utile* and *honestum* in his discourse thereof, and which of them ought to be framed to the other.

And now, madame, to conclude, I pray you so to weigh these few arguments, that as I ever presumed of your nature, so the whole world may praise your subjects for their dutiful care of your person, and yourself for your princely pity—the doing thereof only belongs to you—the performing thereof only appertains to you—and the praise thereof only will ever be yours.

---

[1] This strain of argument, however obsolete at the present day, was wonderfully cogent with her to whom it was addressed, and was wisely enforced by the young king, then under age

Respect then, good sister, this my first so long continued and so earnest request, and despatch my ambassadors with such a comfortable answer as may become your person to give, and as my loving and honest[1] . . . . unto you merits to receive.

But in case any do vaunt themselves to know further of my mind in this matter, than my ambassadors do (who indeed are fully acquainted therewith), I pray you not to take me to be a camelion, but by the contrary, them to be malicious imposters.

And thus praying you heartily to excuse my rude and longsum [lengthy] letter, I commit you, madame and dearest sister, to the blessed protection of the Most High, who must give you grace to resolve in this matter as may be honourable for you and most acceptable to him.

From my palace of Holyrood-house, the 26th day of January, 1586-7.

Your most loving and affectionate
Brother and cousin,
JAMES R.

[Superscription, A madame ma très chère sœur et cousine la Royne d'Angleterre.]

[The following highly-wrought letter from Queen Elizabeth is so caressingly worded, that it must excite wonder how Sir Amias Paulet avoided the snare laid for him in Walsingham's letter, which will be immediately quoted.]

---

[1] Here is an hiatus in the MS.

Queen Elizabeth to Sir Amias Paulet.[1]

Amias, my most faithful and careful servant, God reward thee treblefold for thy most troublesome charge so well discharged.[2] If you knew, my Amias, how kindly, besides most dutifully, my grateful heart accepts and prizes your spotless endeavours and faultless actions your wise orders and safe regard, performed in so dangerous and crafty a charge.[3] it would ease your travails and rejoice your heart, in which I charge you place this most just thought, that I cannot balance in any weight of my judgment the value that I prize you at, and suppose no treasure to countervail such a faith. If I reward not such deserts, let me lack when I have most need of you;[4] if I acknowledge not such merit, *non omnibus dictum.*

Let your wicked murderess [*his prisoner, Mary, Queen of Scots*] know how, with hearty sorrow, her vile deserts compel these orders, and bid her, from me, ask God forgiveness for her treacherous dealings towards the saviour of her life many a year, to the intolerable peril of my own, and yet, not contented with so many forgivenesses, must fault again so horribly, far passing woman's thought, much less a princess; instead of excusing whereof, not one can sorrow, it being so plainly confessed by the authors of my guiltless death.[5]

Let repentance take place, and let not the fiend

---

[1] MS. Harl., 4649

[2] His custody of Mary, Queen of Scots.

[3] Mary.

[4] He did so when she proposed the assassination of his prisoner, for which this letter was meant as a preparation.

[5] Elizabeth meant to say, "there is no occasion for showing any sorrow in regard to Mary's condemnation to death, since the conspirators confessed they meant to take my guiltless life."

possess her, so as her better part may not be lost, for which I pray with hands lifted up to Him that may both save and spill.

With my most loving adieu and prayer for thy long life, your most assured and loving sovereign, as thereby by good deserts induced.

Walsingham and Davison to Sir Amias Paulet and Sir Drue Drury.[1]

February 1, 1586—7.

After our hearty commendations, we find by a speech lately made by her majesty [Queen Elizabeth], that she doth note in you both a lack of that care and zeal for her service that she looketh for at your hands, in that you have not in all this time (of yourselves without other provocation) found out some way of *shortening the life of the Scots' queen*, considering the great peril she [Queen Elizabeth] is hourly subject to *so long as the said queen shall live;* wherein, besides a kind of lack of love towards her, she wonders greatly that you have not that care of your own particular safeties, or rather the preservation of religion and the public good and prosperity of your country that reason and policy commandeth, especially having so good a warrant and ground for the *satisfaction of your consciences towards God,*

[1] These letters, though known to antiquaries, require a place in the direct current of the original documents, in order that the reader may well perceive the assassination that Elizabeth was endeavouring to practise, in order to obviate the scandal of putting her cousin to death, so much deprecated in the interview with the French ambassador. In Mary's noble letter of the 19th of December, it may be observed that she does not once ask her life of Elizabeth, but only that she may not be murdered privately, and this is the manner in which Elizabeth answered that piteous appeal.

and the discharge of your credit and reputation towards the world, as the oath of association, which you have both so solemnly taken and vowed, especially the matter wherewith *she* [Mary] standeth charged being so clearly and manifestly proved against her.

And therefore *she* [Elizabeth] taketh it most unkindly, that men, professing that love towards her that you do, should in a kind of sort, for lack of discharging your duties, cast the burden upon her, knowing as you do her indisposition to shed blood,[1] especially of one of that sex and quality and so near her in blood as that queen is.

These respects, we find, do greatly trouble her majesty, who we assure you hath sundry times protested, "that if the regard of the danger of her good subjects and faithful servants did not more move her than her own peril, she would never be drawn to the shedding of blood."

We thought it meet to acquaint you with these speeches lately passed from her majesty, referring the same to your good judgments. And so we commit you to the protection of the Almighty.

Your most assured friends,

FRA. WALSINGHAM,
WILL. DAVISON.

London, Feb. 1, 1586-7.

[If Walsingham thought he had to deal with men simple as the Gournays, the Maltravers, and the Extons of the middle ages, who did foul deeds for their betters, and reaped the odium alone as their reward, he was the more mistaken. History had not told her tale in vain to the astute castellans of Fotheringay; they had heard

---

[1] Meaning publicly, private murder she preferred.

of sovereigns who, when a black assassination was effected, talked of liking the work but hating the unfortunate agents who had effected it.

Davison's mind misgave him as soon as this murderous scroll was despatched, and he sent a special messenger, urging Sir Amias Paulet to make a heretic of the former letter and burn it. Sir Amias Paulet did no such thing; he preserved all the documents so carefully that they are at this day indisputable testimony of historical truth. He answered Walsingham's incentive to make him the cat's-paw in Mary's murder by the following epistle]:

Sir Amias Paulet to Secretary Walsingham.

Sir,—Your letters of yesterday coming to my hands this present day, at five post meridian, I would not fail, according to your direction, to return my answer with all possible speed, which I shall deliver to you with great grief and bitterness of mind, in that I am so unhappy as living to see this unhappy day, in which I am required, by direction from my most gracious sovereign, to do an act which God and the law forbiddeth.

My goods and my life are at her majesty's *disposition* [disposal], and I am ready to lose them the next morrow if it shall please her, acknowledging that I do hold them as of her mere and most gracious favour, and do not desire to enjoy them but with her highness' good liking. But God forbid I should make so foul a shipwreck of my conscience, or leave so great a blot to my poor posterity, as to shed blood without law or warrant.

Trusting that her majesty, of her accustomed clemency, and the rather by your good mediation, will take this my answer in good part, as proceeding from one who never will be inferior to any Christian subject living in honour, love, and obedience towards his sovereign, and thus I commit you to the mercy of the Almighty.

Your most assured poor friend,

A. POWLET [PAULET.]

From Fotheringay, the 2nd of February, 1586-7.

P.S.—Your letters coming in the plural number, seem to be meant to Sir Drue Drury as to myself, and yet because he is not named in them, neither the letter directed unto him, he forbeareth to make any particular answer, but subscribeth in heart to my opinion

D. DRURY.

[Davison, Queen Elizabeth's private secretary, who was deluded, to his ruin, into despatching the warrant for the death of Mary Queen of Scots, has, in his narrative of exculpation, given us some insight regarding the manner in which Queen Elizabeth received this answer of her Fotheringay castellans to the proposal of assassination. " When her majesty had read it, she fell into some terms of offence, complaining of the dainty perjury of Sir Amias, who, contrary to his oath of *association*, would lay the whole burden of this death on her. Then she took a turn or two on her gallery whither Davison followed her, she renewing her former speech, blaming the niceness of " that precise fellow Paulet," for so she called him now, instead of her former caressing epithets of " Amias, my most careful and faithful servant." " For," she added, " in words he would do much, but in deeds perform nothing," and concluded, " She would have it done without them, naming one Wingfield, who, she assured Secretary Davison, would with some others undertake *it* "—viz. the private assassination of the Queen of Scots. She did not, however, find it so easy in England to obtain agents for private murder.

" For," says Davison, " the next time I had access to her, she swore it was a shame to them all (her ministers and privy council) that it was not done."] [1]

February 1. Elizabeth signs the warrant for the execution of Mary Stuart, which Davison lays before her, and orders it to be forwarded to Walsingham, the chancellor.

Warrant of Queen Elizabeth for the Execution of the Queen of Scots.

Elizabeth, by the grace of God, Queen of England, France, and Ireland, &c. To our trusty and well-beloved cousin, George Earl of Shrewsbury, Earl Marshall of England, Henry Earl of Kent, Henry Earl of Derby, George Earl of Cumberland, and Henry Earl of Pembroke, greeting, &c.

Whereas, sithence the sentence given by you, and others of our Council, Nobility and Iudges, against the Queen of Scots, by the name of Mary, the Daughter of James the Fifth, late king of Scots, commonly called the Queen of Scots, and Dowager of France, as to you is well known; all the States in the last Parliament assembled did not only deliberately, by great advice, allow and approve the same sentence as just and honourable, but also with all humbleness and earnestness possible, at sundry times require, solicit, and press us to direct such further execution against her Person, as they did adjudge her to have only deserved; adding thereunto, that the forbearing thereof was and would be daily certain and undoubted danger, not only unto our own life, but also unto themselves, their posterity,

[1] We refer the reader for further particulars on this act of the tragedy to Sir Harris Nicolas' Life of Davison.

and the public estate of this Realm, as well for the cause
of the Gospel and true Religion of Christ, as for the
peace of the whole Realm; whereupon we did, although
the same were with some delay of time, publish the
same Sentence by our Proclamation, yet hitherto have
forborn to give direction for the further satisfaction of
the aforesaid most earnest requests, made by our said
States of our Parliament; whereby we do daily understand, by all sorts of our loving Subjects, both of
our Nobility and Council, and also of the wisest, greatest,
and best-devoted of all Subjects of inferior degrees,
how greatly and deeply, from the bottom of their hearts,
they are grieved and afflicted, with daily, yea hourly
fears of our life, and thereby consequently, with a
dreadful doubt and expectation of the ruin of the present happy and godly estate of this Realm, if we should
forbear the further final execution, as is deserved, and
neglect their general and continual requests, prayers,
counsels, and advices, and thereupon, contrary to our
natural disposition in such case, being overcome with
the evident weight of their counsels, and their daily intercessions, imparting such a necessity, as appeareth,
directly tending to the safety not only of our self, but
also to the weal of our whole Realm; we have con-
descended to suffer justice to take place, and for the
execution thereof upon the special trusty experience and
confidence which we have of your loyalties, faithfulness
and love, both toward our Person and the safety thereof,
and also to your native countries, whereof you are most
noble and principal Members, we do will, and by Warrant hereof do authorize you, as soon as you shall have
time convenient, to repair to our castle of Fotheringay,
where the said Queen of Scots is in custody of our right
trusty and faithful servant and Counsellor, Sir Amyás
Powlet, Knight; and then taking her into your charge,

After our very hartie Commendations &c &c to yu greate yu truble forth
privileges devised for drawing your forces... &c... with youre Castell of
England &c our good L of Shrewsbury... L... at... for your
... all forces... endure to the saftie of your... ...ion and peril fall
...gevance of her noble Realme at by yu said... un... your shall appere...
...unto yor Lp & &c have thought good to send the same by this bearer our
Robert Beale a person of greate trust and experience first to be advised
... un... and afterwards to be by him conveyed to the Earle of Shrewsbury
from whome wee doubt not but... he shall also receive find whereof and...
what... her Lp and your maie most convenient lye... to...
for by... given of... &c... drawing... and in... manner to...
Lp... and... ... ...full... it to have the
...

Yor assured lovinge ffreendes

W Burghley   H Derbye   R Leicester

h H Ward   H Hunsdon   W Cotham

                    Fr Knollys

Chr Hatton   Fra Walsingham   W Dawson

to cause by your commandment execution to be done
upon her person, in the presence of yourselves and the
aforesaid Sir Amyas Powlet and of such other officers
of justice as you shall command to attend upon you for
that purpose; and the same to be done in such manner
and form, and at such time and place, and by such persons, as to five, four, or three of you shall be thought
by your discretions convenient, notwithstanding any
Law, Statute, or Ordinance to the contrary: And these
our Letters Patents, sealed with our Great Seal of England, shall be to you, and every of you, and to all persons that shall be present, or that shall be by you commanded to do any thing appertaining to the aforesaid
Execution, a full sufficient Warrant and discharge for
ever. And further, we are also pleased and contented,
and hereby we do will, command, and authorize our
Chancellor of England, at the requests of you all and
every of you, the duplicate of our Letters Patents, to
be to all purposes made, dated, and sealed with our
Great Seal of England, as these Presents now are.

In witness whereof, we have caused these our Letters to be made Patents. Given at our Manor of
Greenwich, the 1st day of February, in the twenty-
ninth year of our Reign.

---

*Warrant of the Privy Council for the Execution of
Mary Queen of Scots.*[1]

To THE EARL OF KENT.

After our very hearty commendations to your Lord-

[1] Cotton M.S. Calig. c. ix. f 156. See fac simile opposite
It may be matter of satisfaction to the reader to examine the mysterious order of Elizabeth's privy council, which caused the execution of Mary The contents of this document in modern ortho-

ship, Whereas her majesty hath privately directed
her commission under her hand and great seal of
England, to our good Lord of Shrewsbury, your Lordship and others, for her special service tending to the
safety of her royal person and universal quietness of
her whole realm, as by the said commission shall appear to your lordship, We have thought good to send
the same by this bearer, Mr. Robert Beale, a person
of great trust and experience—first to be shewed to
your lordship, and afterwards to be by him carried to
the Earl of Shrewsbury, from whom we doubt not that
your lordship shall very speedily hear, at what time
his lordship and you may most conveniently meet together for the execution of the said commission.[2]   And
in the mean time your lordship shall understand by this
bearer, how needful it is to have the proceedings herein
to be kept *very secret*, and upon what occasion no
*more of the lords in commission are at this time used
herein.* [1]   Referring your lordship therefore to his
sufficiency for the rest, we heartily bid your lordship
farewell.   At the court at Greenwich, this third of
February, 1586 (7.)

    Your Lordship's loving friends,
        W. Burghley,   H. Derby,   R. Leicester,
          C. Howard,   H. Hunsdon,   W. Cobham,
                  Fr. Knollys,
      Chr. Hatton, Fra. Walsingham, W. Davison.

graphy are presented to the reader above.   The warrant signed
by Elizabeth herself, which she averred was only to be kept in
terrorem, was by this instrument of the privy council set in
activity.

    [2] i. e. putting to death Mary, Queen of Scots.
    [1] The passages in italics acquit the rest of the English no-
bility and nation of the foul stain of Mary's murder, and in
justice limit the disgrace to the men whose autographs are here
appended.

[Endorsed in another hand, 3 February 1586 (7). Copy of a letter from the Honourable of her Majesty's council to the Earl of Kent touching the execution of the Scottish queen.]

1587. *February* 4. Beale, secretary to the council, is despatched to Fotheringay, to carry the order, and take the necessary measures of precaution.

February 7. The Earls of Shrewsbury and Kent, accompanied by Sheriff Andrews, arrive at Fotheringay, and inform Mary Stuart that she is to be executed the next day.

The Queen of Scotland begs permission to see her confessor, which is refused her.

The Queen of Scots to her Almoner, De Préau, written the evening before her execution. [1]

February 7, 1587.

I have striven this day for my religion, and against receiving my last consolation from the heretics; you will hear from Burgoin [*her physician,*] and the others that, at least, I made protestation of my faith in the which I will die. I required to have you, to make my confession, and to receive from you my sacrament. This has been cruelly refused to me, as well as permission to carry away my body, and the power of leaving by will, freely, or of writing anything except it pass through their hands, and by the good pleasure of their mistress.

I must therefore confess my grief for my sins in general, as I had intended to do to you in particular, imploring you in the name of God, this night to watch for me, praying that my sins may be remitted, and to

[1] Jebb, vol. ii., p. 303. This is a translation from the original French, printed in that collection.

M 2

send me your absolution and pardon, if at any time I may have offended you.

I shall endeavour to see you,[1] though in their presence, as they have accorded to me my *maître d'hôtel*, [Melville]; and if it is permitted me, before them all, on my knees, I will ask your benediction.

Advise me as to the most proper prayers for this night and for to-morrow morning. The time is short, and I have no leisure to write, but I will recommend you with the rest [*of her household*]; above all, your benefices shall be assured to you, and I will recommend you to the king [of France.]

I have no more leisure. Advise me of all that you can think of for my soul's health by writing. I will send you a last little token.

1587. Feb. 7-8. Mary passes the night in prayer, and in writing her testamentary arrangements.

----

[1] De Préau, the almoner, or domestic chaplain of the Queen of Scots, had always been under the same roof with her, though debarred from her presence since October, 1586, the time of her mock trial. The following notice of this priest occurs in Sir Ralph Sadler's information concerning the routine of Mary's household, in November, 1584. "Her two secretaries, Nau and Curle; the master of her household, Andrew Melville; her physician, Burgoin, and De Préau, have separate chambers, and so always have had." Again, "the secretaries, Melville, Burgoin, and De Préau, eat at a mess of seven or eight dishes." In some accounts given of Mary's death, an old man is said to have been present, with the rest of her servants, and, as Mr. Tytler says, her almoner was present, this old man must have been De Préau.

The Will of the Queen of Scots.

COPY OF THE WILL and of a memorandum made by the late queen, Mary Stuart, Queen of Scotland and Dowager of France. The said copy, taken from the original of the said will and memorandum, entirely written and signed by the queen's own hand on the evening before, and on the day of her death, which was the 8th of February, 1587.

In the name of the Father, of the Son, and of the Holy Ghost, I, Mary, by the grace of God, Queen of Scotland and Dowager of France, being on the point of death, and not having any means of making my will, have myself committed these articles to writing, and I will and desire, that they have the same force as if they were made in due form.

In the first place, I declare that I die in the Catholic, Apostolic, and Romish faith. First, I desire that a complete service be performed for my soul in the church of St. Denis in France, and another in St. Peter's [church] at Rheims, where all my servants are to attend, in such manner, as they may be ordered to do by those to whom I have given directions, and who are named therein.

Further, that an annual obit be founded for prayers for my soul in perpetuity, in such place, and after such manner, as shall be deemed most convenient.

To furnish funds for this, I will that my houses at Fountainebleau be sold, hoping that the king will render me assistance, as I have requested him to do in my memorandum.

I will that my estate of Trespagny be kept by my cousin de Guise for one of his daughters, if she should come to be married. In these quarters, I relinquish half of the arrears due to me, or a part, on condition that the other be paid, in order to be expended, by my executors in perpetual alms.

To carry this into effect the better, the documents shall be looked out, and delivered according to the assignment for accomplishing this.

I will also that the money which may arise from my lawsuit with Secondat be distributed as follows :

First, in the discharge of my debts and orders hereafter mentioned, and which are not yet paid ; in the first place, the two thousand crowns to Courle,[1] which I desire to be paid without any hesitation, they being a marriage portion, upon which neither Nau nor any other person has any claim, whatever obligation he may hold, inasmuch as it is only fictitious, and the money is mine, and not borrowed, which since I did but show him, and afterwards withdraw it, and it was taken from me with the rest at Chartelay;[2] the which I give him, provided he can recover it, agreeably to my promise, in payment of the four thousand francs promised at my death, one thousand as a marriage portion for an own sister, and he having asked me for the rest for his expenses in prison. As to the payment of a similar sum to Nau, it is not obligatory, and therefore it has always been my intention that it should be paid last, and then only in case he should make it appear that he has not acted contrary to the condition upon which I gave it him, and to which my servants were witnesses.

As regards the twelve hundred crowns, which he has placed to my account, as having been borrowed by him for my use, six hundred of Beauregard, three hundred from Gervais, and the remainder from I know not whom, he must repay them out of his own money, and I must be quit, and my order annulled, as I have not received

---

[1] Curle, her secretary.   [2] Chartley.

any part of it, consequently it must be still in his possession, unless he has paid it away. Be this as it may, it is necessary that this sum should revert to me, I having received nothing; and in case it has not been paid away, I must have recourse to his property. I further direct, that Pasquier shall account for the moneys that he has expended and received by order of Nau from the hands of the servants of Monsieur de Chasteauneuf, the French ambassador.

Further, I will that my accounts be audited and my treasurer paid.

Further, that the wages and sums due to my household, as well for the last as for the present year, be paid them before all other things, both wages and pensions, excepting the pensions of Nau and Courle, until it be ascertained what there is remaining, or whether they have merited any pensioning from me, unless the wife of Courle be in necessity, or he ill-treated on my account; the wages of Nau after the same manner.

I will that the two thousand four hundred francs which I have given to Jeanne Kenedy[1] be paid to her in money, as it was stated in my first deed of gift, which done, the pension of Volly Douglas shall revert to me, which I give to Fontenay[2] for services and expences, for which he has had no compensation.

I will that the four thousand francs of that banker's be applied for and repaid; I have forgotten his name, but the Bishop of Glascou will readily recollect it; and if the first order be not honoured, I desire that another may be given on the first money from Secondat.

[1] Jane Kenneday, sometimes called Jane Kennet, who afterwards married Sir Andrew Melville, and was drowned by accident at Leith, having been appointed by James VI. first lady to his expected bride, Anne of Denmark. (Melville's Memoirs.)

[2] The brother of her secretary Nau

The ten thousand francs which the ambassador has received for me, I will that they be distributed among my servants who are now going away, viz.

First, two thousand francs to my physician.

two thousand francs to Elizabet Courle.

two thousand francs to Sebastien Paiges.

two thousand francs to Mairie Paiges, my god-daughter.

to Beauregard a thousand francs.

a thousand to Gourgon.

a thousand to Gervais.

Further, that out of the rest of my revenue, with the remainder of Secondat's and all other casualties, I will that five thousand francs be given to the foundling hospital of Rheims.

To my scholars, two thousand francs.

To four mendicants such sum as my executors may think fit, according to the means in their hands.

Five hundred francs to the hospitals.

To Martin, *escuyer de cuisine*, I give a thousand francs.

A thousand francs to Annibal, whom I recommend to my cousin de Guise, his godfather, to place in some situation, for his life, in his service.

I leave five hundred francs to Nicolas, and five hundred francs for his daughters, when they marry.

I leave five hundred francs to Robert Hamilton, and beg my son to take him, and Monsieur de Glascou, or the Bishop of Rosse.

I leave to Didier his registership, subject to the approbation of the king.

I give five thousand francs to Jean Landor, and beg my cousin of Guise, or of Mayne, to take him into their service, and Messieurs de Glascou and de Rosse to see him provided for. I will that his father be paid his wages, and leave him five hundred francs.

I will that one thousand francs be paid to Gourgeon, for money and other things with which he supplied me in my necessity.

I will that, if Bourgoin should perform the journey, agreeably to the vow which he made, for me to Saint Nicolas, that fifteen hundred francs be paid to him for that purpose.

I leave, according to my slender means, six thousand francs to the Bishop of Glascou, and three thousand to him of Rosse.

And I leave the gift of casualties and reserved seignorial rights to my godson, the son of Monsieur de Ruisseau.

I give three hundred francs to Laurenz.

Also, three hundred francs to Suzanne.

And leave ten thousand francs among the four persons who have been my sureties, and to Varmy the solicitor.

I will that the money arising from the furniture which I have ordered to be sold in London shall go to defray the travelling expenses of my servants to France.

My coach I leave to carry my ladies, and the horses, which they can sell or do what they like with.

There remains about three hundred crowns due to Bourgoing for the wages of past years, which I desire may be paid him.

I leave two thousand francs to Melvin [Sir Andrew Melville], my steward.

I appoint my cousin, the duke of Guise, principal executor of my will.

After him, the Archbishop of Glascou, the Bishop of Rosse, and Monsieur de Ruissieu, my chancellor.

I desire that Le Préau may without obstacle hold his two prebends.

I recommend Marie Paiges, my god-daughter, to my cousin, Madame de Guise, and beg her to take her into her service, and my aunt de Saint Pierre to get Moubray some good situation, or retain her in her service, for the honour of God.

Done this day, 7th February, 1587.

Signed,   MARY, Queen.

In the copy from which this will is taken, the following memorandum is on the same sheet.

MEMORANDUM

of the last requests which I make to the King.

To cause to be paid me, all that is due to me, of my pensions, as also of money advanced by the late queen, my mother, in Scotland, for the service of the king, my father-in-law, in those parts; that at least an annual obit may be founded for my soul, and that the alms and the little endowments promised by me may be carried into effect.

Further, that he may be pleased to grant me the benefit of my dowry for one year after my death to recompence my servants.

Further, that he may be pleased to allow them their wages and pensions during their lives, as was done to the officers of Queen Alienor.[1]   Further, I entreat him

[1] Leonora or Eleanora of Austria, sister of Charles V. and second queen of Francis I.

to take my physician into his service, according to his promise to consider him as recommended.

Further, that my almoner [Préau] may be replaced in his profession, and for my sake have some trifling benefice conferred upon him, so that he may pray to God for my soul during the rest of his life.

Further, that Didier, an old officer of my household, whom I have recompensed by a registership, may be permitted to enjoy it for his life, being already far advanced in years. Written on the morning of my death, this 8th of February, 1587.

Signed,   MARY, Queen.

Compared with the original paper, this 26th of April, 1638.—(Note of the time, in the same handwriting.)

Contemporary writers make frequent mention of this will; some of them even take notice of the exceptions made by Mary to the prejudice of Curle and Nau; still I am of opinion that it has never been printed, at least not in French. The original is supposed to be in the archives of the Vatican, but it must have been registered in France, since the parliament of Paris issued an *arrêt* relative to its execution. As for the memorandum, that has been frequently published, among others, by Jebb, ii., 303, and Keralio, v., 435.—(Note by Prince Labanoff.)

1587. *Wednesday, February* 8, *O.S.* (New Style, the 18th.) Mary Stuart is beheaded in one of the rooms in Fotheringay Castle. Henry Talbot, son of the Earl of Shrewsbury, is immediately despatched to inform Elizabeth of the event.

The scaffold being removed, Sir Amias Paulet causes the will of Mary Stuart to be read by her almoner, Préau, who had been separated from her ever since the 24th of November, and who had not permission to be present at her death.

The same day, the body of the deceased queen is embalmed, and placed in a leaden coffin, which was kept for six months in the said castle, where all her servants were likewise detained.

The last proceedings of the Queen of Scotland after she was admonished of her death till the hour thereof.[1]

On Monday the 7th day of February, my Lord Beale, one of the nobles who are about the Queen of England, was sent by her to Fotheringhay, where the Queen of Scotland was prisoner, with charge and commission from the said Queen of England to proceed to immediate execution of the sentence, which had been pronounced on the said Queen of Scotland, and command was sent to the Earl of Shrewsbury to be present at this execution, and also to some other gentlemen near neighbours to the Castle of Fotheringhay.

As soon as he arrived, the Lord Beale desired to visit the said lady queen, which he did the same day.

---

[1] Life of Egerton, Lord Chancellor, printed for private circulation by the Earl of Bridgewater, p. 109. This curious contemporary document appears to have been transmitted by the French ambassadors, with other reports of the transactions of that period, to their master, Henry III of France. Besides this original narrative, and the one following edited by Prince Labanoff, there are two others, one by a French eye-witness, the other by one of her Scottish servants, each enriched with little distinct particulars which had escaped the others; the principal variations are in her Life in French, published in 1670, by M. Pierre le Pesant, the other is printed in her Life by Sanderson, 1646.

[2] Meaning Mr. Secretary Beale.

About the eighth or ninth hour of the evening, he presented himself at her chamber door, which was immediately opened by one of her chamberers, of whom he demanded, " If the said lady were now going to bed ?" She replied, "that her majesty was making herself ready for it, having already taken off her mantle." She then hastily re-entered the chamber of the said lady, and told her "that Beale had already entered her antechamber, and desired to speak to her."

The queen called for her mantle which she had thrown off, and bade them open the chamber door. He entered, and having made his salutation, said, " Madame, I could well have desired, that some other, than I, had had to announce such evil tidings, as those I have now to tell you on the part of the Queen of England, but being her faithful servant, I can do nothing less than obey the commandment that she has given me, which is, madame, to admonish you, as I now do, to dispose and hold yourself ready, to-morrow at the tenth hour of morning, to suffer the execution of the sentence of death, which has been pronounced on you a little time ago."

The said lady replied to him with great firmness, and without betraying the slightest degree of fear.

" I praise and thank my God, that it pleases him to put an end by this to the many miseries and calamities that they have compelled me to endure; for, since nineteen years up to the present moment, I have been constituted a prisoner, and very evilly entreated by the Queen of England my sister, without having ever injured her, as God is my principal witness ; but I go to render up my spirit into his hands, innocent and with a pure heart, and conscience clear before his Divine Majesty of the crimes of which she has caused me to be accused ; and I shall now carry this same innocence boldly before his face, who is the sole judge of my past actions. And seeing that I must die a death so violent, brought about by the means of one so unjust, and by the iniquitous judgment of men to whom I could never be accountable, I will make myself known openly when I present myself there, which will be far better for me than to live on in the same calamity, and that martyr- dom in which they have made me languish so long; not having the least hope, from the evil nature of the queen —her mortal hatred and constant cruelty to me; and now, to please her councillors and others my ancient foes, she wills to make herself subservient to them, for the accomplishment of my ruin and my death, which I shall be seen patiently to endure, that I may be delivered from their continual persecutions, in order to reign per- petually, if it may please God, in a more happy resting- place than I have had the better part of my days, near so obdurate and cruel a relation; but since she is re- solved on such rigour, the will of God be done."

When the damsels and other persons, who were about the said lady heard and understood these doleful tidings, they began to scream and shed tears, and would have abandoned themselves to despair, but for the sweet con- solations which this poor princess gave them. She exhorted them on all the points of that patience which was shown for our example in the death and passion of our Lord Jesus Christ, whom she took and rested upon as the foundation of her salvation, begging her said damsels to watch and pray to God continually with her. This they did till an hour or two after midnight, when she wished to throw herself on her bed, where she re- mained only half an hour, and afterwards entered within a cabinet, which served her for an oratory, where she was accustomed to make her most particular orisons, entreating, however, those who were in her chamber to continue in their prayers while she was making hers, which she did till the break of day, when quitting her devotions, she said to her damsels these words:—

"My good friends, it gives me infinite regret that I have so little, wherewithal, to requite you, in effect, as I could much have wished, according to my good-will, for the good and faithful services that every one of you have rendered to me in my necessity. I have only one thing more to do, which is, to add a clause to the will that I have left, and ordain my son, the King of Scotland, to perform for me the duty of requiting and making to every one of you satisfaction and worthy contentment after my death. I will write to him on this, and some other things that I have particularly to say to him."

She re-entered her cabinet to write, having the pen in her hand during two hours. As she was on the point of concluding her letter, they came and knocked at the door,[1] which she would open herself to the Sieur Beale, who was accompanied by Sir Amias Paulet, the same who had had the said lady in his keeping, and whose office it was to conduct her to the place prepared for her last day. She prayed them, "to give her the delay of half an hour's time, to finish something that she had begun to write." This was granted, but the said Beale

---

[1] In another narrative of this scene, we find the following circumstances:—

Burgoin, her physician, having begged her to take a bit of bread and a glass of wine, she took it, and then fell on her knees to pray to God; after she had been some time in that posture they beat at her chamber-door a second time; this was the earl-marshal, with a great many attendants, who designed, as some have given out, to drag her to death by force if she had asked for longer time. But she no sooner saw them, than she declared her readiness to go along with them, and only desired "that one of her servants might be allowed to take a small ivory crucifix, which stood on the altar of her oratory." (Life of Mary, by M. Pierre le Pesant Sieur du Bois Guilbert.)

and Paulet remained all the time in her ante-chamber.

The said lady came soon after out of her cabinet, where she had left what she had written, and said to two of her damsels, " I beseech you, my good friends, not to forsake me, and be, if you please, near me at the hour of my death."

When she came out of her chamber, finding the said Beale and Paulet before her, she said to them, " If it is now that I ought to die, tell me, for I am all prepared for it, with as much of patience as it will please God to give me ; but in the mean time, I will intrust you to say and report to the Queen of England, my sister, from me, that she and those of her council have put on me the most iniquitous and unjust judgment that was ever given in this realm and all Christendom, without proof, assured form, or any order of justice whatsoever ; and I hold it for a certainty that the judgments of God will follow her so strictly and so closely that her own conscience will accuse her all her life, and God after her death, with my innocence, in which I will fearlessly render my spirit into his hands."

She then prayed that they would permit the approach of two damsels and her *maître d'hôtel*,[1] who took her under the arms to assist her in descending from her chamber to the great hall below in the castle of Fotheringay, which was full of people, who had been waiting there all the night for the purpose of witnessing this piteous spectacle. In the centre of this hall there was a high place, raised with five or six steps to ascend it ; thither she was assisted by her *maître d'hôtel* and the said damsels. The people, who were attentive throughout to observe her actions and her countenance, as well as to note all the words that proceeded from her mouth,

---

[1] Sir Andrew Melville was her *maître d'hôtel*.

fixed their eyes on this poor princess, whose countenance appeared of such great beauty that every one there marvelled at it.

The said lady being on her knees, her hands joined, and her eyes raised to heaven, she spoke in such wise that she did not seem like one compelled to her death, and on silence being accorded, she made this prayer:—

".My God, my Father, and my Creator, and his only Son, Jesus Christ, my Lord and Redeemer, who art the hope of all the living, and of all those who die in thee; since that thou hast ordained, that my soul must be separated from this mortal body, I supplicate very humbly of thy goodness and mercy not to abandon me in this extremity, but that I may be covered with thy holy grace, giving me pardon for all the negligences and faults that I have committed against thy holy ordinances and commandments, even as it has pleased thee of thine especial grace to make me born a queen, sacred[1] and anointed in thy church. I have, nevertheless, always well considered and believed, as I do now, that this greatness could not render me excusable for my faults towards thee, being of like condition with other mortals, subject to thy righteous judgments, and most certain, that they cannot be those which are from the heart and from the thoughts of men, inconstant and variable as they full often are, and of their own movements forgetful and reckless, for example, even of the misery that their pure ambition and envy have produced to me by the Queen of England, even to this bloody death, the which they have this long time premeditated and sworn against me.[2] I would not be ignorant, also, my God, but will freely say and confess, that I am, myself often very far from the

---

[1] Meaning *consecrated*.

[2] See Leicester's letter and other papers in the supplementary portion of this volume

right course of thy ordinances, for which, and for all
other faults, whatsoever they be, that I have committed,
I very humbly supplicate, my God, that thou wouldst
give me remission, even as I also, with a good heart,
pardon all those who have offended me and have condemned me, by their iniquitous sentence, to this cruel
death. Permit me, my God, that for my justification, I
may yet, without offence to thee, and in a few words, inform all those in whose presence I shall render up my
soul to thee, the rest of the realm, and the whole of
Christendom, of the protestation that I make ; which is,
that I never have concerted, willed, conspired, nor in
any sort given counsel nor aid, in any of the conspiracies
of death, for the which I am here so falsely accused and
so inhumanly treated, although I have often sought, with
the aid of my friends, Catholics of this realm and elsewhere, by means free from guilt and more suitable to
me, such as I could sanction, to effect my escape from
these miserable prisons, and to regain some liberty,
without in any way offending against thy divine majesty,
or troubling the peace of this kingdom. And if I have
had any other intention, in this place, I beseech thee,
that my soul may be deprived perpetually of the parti-
cipation in thy mercy and grace, and of the fruits which
she hopes and expects, from the death and passion of
thy very dear Son our Lord Jesus Christ; and being innocent of all such treachery, I remit all my other faults
and offences to the holy and divine justice, by the invo-
cation which I make to the glorious Virgin Mary, and
to all the saints, angels, and the blessed who are in
Paradise, that they will please to intercede now for me
to God, and that I may be partaker, and reign perpetually with them, in the celestial glory."

Having finished this prayer,[1] she took a white linen

    [1] " And now, being in her petticoat and kirtle prepared for

kerchief that she put into her mantle, and gave it to one
of her damsels who were near her, saying, " Hold, bind
my eyes with this linen, and abandon not my body, I
pray you, in my extremity, while I shall be employed in
the care of my soul." When her eyes were bound, she
was approached by a minister and the executioner—the
latter dressed in a habit of black velvet. The minister
wishing to give her counsel, began by saying, " Madame, the things of this world ought not to be thought
of, but God alone."

The said lady demanded quickly of one of her damsels, " Tell me, is not this that speaks to me a minister, hide it not from me ?"

The other replied, " Yes, madame."

Then she exclaimed, " Ah, my God, it makes me remember that Thou hast said, ' that we shall be some-

death, her maids *skreeking* and crying out with exceeding sorrow,
they crossed themselves and prayed aloud in Latin. The queen
crossed and kissed them, and desired their prayers without loud
moaning, adding, ' that she had passed her word for them :'
then she crossed her men servants, who stood without the rail,
weeping and crying out. She then kneeled down upon her
cushion, resolutely and undauntedly, and spoke aloud in Latin
the whole psalm, *In te Domine confido* " It was then, certainly,
that she expected, at every passing instant, the stroke of death.
" For," says the narrative by Pierre le Pesant Sieur du Bois
Guilbert, " she knelt upright some time, expecting her head to
be taken off with the stroke of a sword, as they do in France.
But the executioner and his servant, having waited some time,
placed her head on the block. The executioner then gave her
a stroke with an axe of the same shape of those which they
cleave wood withal, without doing any further harm than wound-
ing her scull, so awkward was he, then redoubling a second and
third stroke, he at last cut off her head." It appears, nevertheless, that the first stroke rendered her insensible ; for Sanderson's narrative declares " that she did not stir or move the
least, though it took two strokes to separate her head from her
body."

times assailed by the enemies of our souls at the hour of
our death.' " And thereupon shê uttered these verses
from the seven penitential psalms, " Depart from me all
ye who work iniquity, for my God has heard the voice
of my groaning, and he has received my prayer. My
God, delay not, and go not far from me; hasten to me,
my God, who art the author of my salvation."

Those who were there present, marvelled to behold
the great beauty and courage of this poor princess and
the patience that supported her. The executioner approached her to do his office, which was done according
to the fashion of this country, quickly enough. He
having cut off her head, took it in his hand, saying in a
loud voice, " Behold the head of Mary Stuart !" then
he replaced it near the body, which was immediately
covered by the said damsels with the black cloth which
was round about, and they were permitted to raise it up
and carry it into the chamber, where the said Queen of
Scotland had been accustomed to lie.

Most of the people present who had understood what
the said lady had declared at her death, considered that
she was innocent of everything that had been charged
and imputed to her; and if her execution had been
done in public, they were of opinion, which had been
greatly rumoured abroad, that the said lady would
have been succoured and delivered from this unjust
judgment.

The tidings of this execution were greeted in London
with their ringing of the bells in all the churches
during four and twenty hours, and in the evenings they
made bonfires in all the streets of the city, and in every
corner and cross-way, in token of rejoicing for their deliverance from the calamity, that had been predicted to
this realm.

The said lady, Queen of Scotland, spake as above, in

the English language, which has been translated and put in French.

February 9. The news of her execution reaches London, and bonfires and the ringing of bells are kept up all night.

Narrative of the Execution of the Queen of Scots. In a letter to the Right Honourable Sir William Cecil.

It may please your Lordship to be advertised, that, according as your honour gave me in Commaund, I have here sett downe in writing the trew order and mannor of the execucion of the Lady Mary last Q. of Scots, the 8 of February last, in the great hall within the Castle of Fotheringhay, togither with relation of all such speeches and actions spoken and done by the sayde Queen or any others, and all other circumstances and proceedinges concerning the same, from and after the delivery of the sayde Scottish Queen to Thomas Andrews, Esquire, High Sheriff for hir Majestyes County of Northampton unto the end of the sayde execucion: as followeth.

It being certyfied the 6 of Februarye last to the sayde Queen, by the right honorable the Earle of Kent, the Earle of Shrewsberry, and also by Sir Amias Pawlet, and Sir Drue Drurye, hir governors, that shee was to prepare hir self to dye the 8 of Februarye nexte, she seemed not be in any terror for aught that appered by any hir outward gesture or behaviour (other then marvelling shee should dye), but rather with smiling cheer and pleasing countenaunce, digested and accepted the sayde admonition of preparacion to hir (as shee sayde) unexpected execution, saying that hir death should be welcome unto hir, seeing hir Majestye was so resolved, and that that soule were too too farr unworthye the fruition of joyes of heaven for ever, whose bodye would not in this world be content to endure the stroake of the executioner for a moment. And that spoken shee wept bitterlye and became silent

The sayde 8 day of Februarye being comme, and tyme and place appoınted for the execution, the sayde Queen being of stature tall, of bodye corpulent, rownde shouldred, hir face fatt and broade, double chınned, and hazell eyed, hir borrowed haire aborne, hır attyre was this. On hir head shee had a dressing of lawne edged with bone lace, a pomander chayne and an *Agnus dei* about hir necke, a Crucifix in hir hande, a payre of beades att hir girdle, with a silver cross att the end of them. A vale of lawne fastned to hir caule bowed out with wyer, and edged round about with boane lace. Hir gowne was of black sattin painted, with a trayne and long sleeves to the grownde, sett with acorne buttons of Jett trymmed with pearle, and shorte sleeves of sattyn black cutt, with a payre of sleeves of puıple velvett whole under them. Hir kirtle whole, of figured black sattin, and hır petticoate skirtes of Crimson velvett, hir shooes of Spannish leather with the rough side owtward, a payre of green silke garters, hir nether stockinges worsted coulored watchett, clocked with sılver, and edged on the topps with silver, and next hır leg, a payre of Jarsye [Jersey][1] hose, white, &c. Thus apparreled she departed hır chamber, and willinglye bended hır stepps towardes the place of execution.

---

[1] All woollen knit-work waş originally named as ıf it belonged to eıther the ıslands of Jersey or Guernsey, and to show the tenacity of such names, the knitted woollen shıı ts worn by the poor, and often purchased as gıfts for them by the charitable, must be inquiı ed for by the appellatıon of Guernsey frocks, though now the produce of our manufacturıng towns.

As the Commissioners and divers other Knights were meeting the Queen comming forthe, one of hir servantes, called Melvin, [Sir Andrew Melville,] kneeling on his knees to his Queen and Mrs., wringing his handes, and shedding teares, used these wordes unto her. " Ah ! Madam : unhappy me, what man on earth was ever before the messinger of so important sorrow and heavines as I shall be, when I shall report that my good and gracious Queen and Mistris is behedded in England?" This sayde, teares prevented him of further speaking. Where upon the sayde Queen, powring forth her dying teares, thus answered him. " My good servant, cease to lament, for thow hast cause rather to joye than to mourne. For now shalt thow see Mary Stewards troubles receive their longe expected end and determinacion. For know" (sayde shee), " good servant, all the world is but vanitye, and subject still to more sorrow than a whole Ocean of teares can bewayle. But I pray thee" (sayde shee) "carry this message from me, that I dye a trewe woman to my religion, and like a trewe Queene of Scotland and Fraunce. But God forgive them" (sayde shee) "that have longe desired my end and thirsted for my bloud, as the harte doth for the water brookes. Oh God" (sayde shee), "thow that arte the author of truthe and truthe it selfe, knowest the inward chamber of my thought, how that I was ever willing that England and Scotland should be united togither. Well" (sayde shee), "commend me to my sonne, and tell him that I have not done any thinge prejudiciall to the state and kingdome of Scotland :" and so resolving hir self agayne into teares, sayde, " Good Melvyn, farwell;" and with weeping eyes, and hir cheekes all besprinkled with teares as they were, kissed him, saying once agayne, " Farwell, good Melvin, and praye for thy Mistres and Queen."

And then shee turned hir selfe unto the lordes, and tolde them shee had certayne requestes to make unto

them. One was, for certayne monye to be payde to
Curle, hir servant. Sir Amias Pawlet knowing of that
monye answered to this effect, "it shoulde." Next, that
her poore servantes might have that with quietnes which
shee had given them by hir will, and that they might be
favourably intreated, and to send them safely into their
countries. "To this" (sayde shee) "I conjure yow."
Last, that it would please the Lordes, to permitt hir
poore distressed servantes to be present about hir att hir
deathe, that their eyes and hartes maye see and wittnes
how paciently their Queen and Mistris would endur hir
execucion, and so make relacion, when they camme into
their country, that shee dyed a trew constant Catholique
to hir religion. Then the Earle of Kent did answer
thus : "Madam, that which yow have desired can not conveniently be graunted. For, if it should, it weare to be
feared least somme of them, with speeches or other behaviour, would bothe be grevous to your grace, and
troublesome and unpleasing to us and oure companye,
wherof we have had somme experience. For if such an
access might be allowed, they would not sticke to putt
somme superstitious trumperye in practise, and if it
were but in dipping their handkerchiffes in your Grace's
bloude, whereof it were very unmeet for us to give
allowance."

"My Lord," (sayde the Queen of Scotts,) "I will
give my worde, although it be but dead, that they shall
not deserve any blame in any the accions you have
named. But alas, (poore soules,) it would doe them
good to bidd their mistris farwell ; and I hope your
Mrs." (meaning the queen) "being a mayden queen,
will vouchsafe in regard of womanhood, that I shall have
somme of my own people about me att my deathe : and
I know hir majestye hath not given you any such streight
charge or commission, but that you might grant me a request of farr greater courtesie then this is, if I were a

woman of farr meaner calling then the Queen of Scottes."
And then, perceiving that shee could not obtayne hir request without somme difficultye, burste out into teares,
saying, " I am cosen to your queen, and discended from
the bloud roiail of Hen. the 7, and a marryed queen
of Fraunce, and an annoynted queen of Scotland " Then,
upon great consultacion had betwixte the two earles and
the others in commission, it was granted to hir what she
instantly before earnestly intreated, and desired her to
make choice of six hir best beloved men and weomen.
Then of hir men she chose Melvin, his apothecary, hir
surgeon, and *one old man more ;* [1] and of hir weomen,
those two which did lye in hir chamber.   Then, with an
unappalled countenance, without any terror of the place,
the persons, or the preparacions, she camme out of the
entrye into the hall, stept upp to the Scaffold, being two
foote high and twelve foote broade, with rayles rownde
about, hanged and covered with black, with a lowe stoole,
longe fayre cushion, and a block covered also with black.
The stoole brought hir, shee sat downe.   The erle of
Kent stood on the right hande, the erle of Shrewsberry
on the other, other knightes and gentlemen stoode about
the rayles.   The commission for hir execution was redd
(after silence made) by Mr. Beale, claike of the counseil;
which done, the people with a lowde voice, sayde, "God
save the Queen."   During the reading of this commission, the sayde queen was verye silent, listning unto it
with so careless a regard as if it had not concerned hir
at all, nay, rather with so merry and cheerfull a countenance as if it had byn a pardon from hir majestye for hir
life, and with all used such a straungeness in hir wordes

---

[1] The question is, was this old man Préau her almoner ?   Mr.
Tytler declares he was present ; Prince Labanoff denies it : see his
Chronological Summary in this volume, p. 252.

as if shee had not knowne any of the assembly, nor had
been any thing seene in the English tongue.

Then, Mr. Doctor Fletcher, Deane of Peterborough,
standing directly before hir without the rayles, bending
his bodye with great reverence, uttered the exhortacion
followinge.

"Madame, the queen's most excellent majestye,
(whome God preserve longe to reigne over us) having,
(notwithstanding this preparacion for the execution of
justice justly to be done upon you for your many tres-
passes agaynst hir sacred person, state, and government)
a tender care over your sowle, which, presently depart-
ing out of your bodie, must eyther be seperated in
the trew fayth in Christe, or perish for ever, doth for
Jesus Christe offer unto yow the comfortable promises of
God, wherin I beseech your grace, even in the bowells
of Jesus Christe, to consider these three thinges:

"First, your state paste, and transitory glorie.

"Secondly, your condicion present; of deathe.

"Thirdly, your estate to comme, eyther in everlasting
happiness, or perpetuall infelicitye.

"For the first, let me speake to your grace with
David the king; forget (Madam) your selfe, and your
owne people, and your father's howse; forget your
naturall birthe, your regall and princely dignitye, so shall
the King of kinges have pleasure in your spirittuel
bewtye, &c.

"Madam, even now, Madam, doth God Almightye
open yow a doare into a heavenly kingdome; shutt not
therefore this passage by the hardning of your harte, and
greeve not the spirit of God, which maye seale your hope
to a daye of redempcion.

The queen, three or four times sayde unto him, "Mr.
Deane, trouble not yourselfe nor me; for know, that I
am settled in the auncient Cautholique and Romaine re-

ligion, and in defence therof, by God's grace, I minde to spend my bloud."

Then sayde Mr. Deane, " Madam, change your oppinion, and repent yow of your former wickednes. Settle your faythe onlie upon this grownde, that in Christ Jesus yow hope to be saved." She answered agayne and agayne, with great earnestnes, " Good Mr. Deane, trouble not yourselfe any more about this matter, for I was borne in this religion, have lived in this religion, and am resolved to dye in this religion."

Then the earles, when they sawe how farr unconformable shee was to heare Mr. Deane's good exhortacion, sayde, " Madam, we will praye for your grace with Mr. Deane, that you maye have your mind lightned with the trew knowledge of God and his worde."

" My lordes," answered the queen, "if you will praye with me, I will even from my harte thanke yow, and thinke myselfe greatly favoured by yow; but to joyne in prayer with yow in your manner, who are not of one religion with me, it weare a sinne, and I will not."

Then the lordes called Mr. Deane agayne, and badd him saye on, or what he thought good els. The deane kneeled and prayed as follows:

" Oh, most gracious God and merciful father, who, according to the multitude of thy mercies, dost so put away the sins of them that truly repent, that thou rememberest them no more, open, we beseech thee, thine eyes of mercy, and behold this person appointed unto death, whose eyes of understanding and spiritual light, albeit thou hast hitherto shut up, that the glorious beams of thy favour in Jesus Christ do not shine upon her, but is possessed with blindness and ignorance of heavenly things (a certain token of thy heavy displeasure, if thy unspeakable mercy do not triumph against thy judgment), yet, O Lord our God, impute not, we beseech

thee, unto her those her offences which separate her
from thy mercy; and, if it stand with thine everlasting
purpose and good pleasure, O Lord, grant unto us, we
beseech thee, this mercy, which is about thy throne, that
the eyes of her heart may be enlightned, that she may
understand and be converted unto thee ; and grant her
also, if it be thy blessed will, the heavenly comfort of thy
Holy Spirit, that she may taste and see how gracious the
Lord is. Thou hast no pleasure, good Lord, in the
death of a sinner, and no man shall praise thy name in
the pit; renew in her, O Lord, we most humbly beseech
thy majesty, whatsoever is corrupt in her, either by her
own frailty, or by the malice of the ghostly enemy ; visit
her, O Lord, if it be thy good pleasure, with thy saving
health, as thou didst unto the offender at the side of
thy cross, with this consolation : This day shalt thou
be with me in Paradice. Say unto her soul, as
thou didst unto thy servant David, ‘ I am thy salvation ;’ so shall thy mercy, being more mighty, be
more magnified. Grant these mercies, O Lord, to us
thy servants, to the increase of thy kingdom and glory
at this time. And further, O most merciful Father, preserve, we most humbly beseech thy majesty, in long and
honourable peace and safety, Elizabeth thy servant, our
most natural soveraign lady and queen ; let them be
ashamed and confounded, O Lord, that seek after her
soul : let them be turned backward and put to confusion
that wish her evil ; and strengthen still, Lorde, we pray
thee, the hand and balance of justice amongst us by her
gracious government; so shall we, both now and ever,
rest under thy faithfulness and truth, as under our shield
and buckler, and bless thy name, and magnifie thy mercy,
which livest and reignest one most gracious God, for
ever and ever. Amen.”

. All the assembly, save the queen and hir servantes

sayde the prayer after Mr. Deane as he spake it, during which prayer, the queen satt upon hir stoole, having hir *Agnus Dei*, ciucifixe, beades, and an office in Lattyn. Thus furnished with superstitious trumpery, not regarding what Mr. Deane sayde, shee began verie fastly with teares and a lowde voice to praye in Lattin, and in the middst of hir prayers, with overmuch weeping and mourning, slipt of hir stoole, and kneeling presèntly sayde divers other Lattin prayers. Then she rose, and kneeled downe agayne, praying in English, for Christe's afflicted church, an end of hir troubles, for hir sonne, and for the queen's majestye, to God for forgiveness of the sinns of them in this islande: she forgave hir ennemyes with all hir harte that had longe sought hir bloud. This done she desired all saintes to make inter-cession for hir to the Saviour of the worlde, Jesus Christ. Then she began to kiss hir crucifix, and to cross hir self, saying these wordes, "Even as thy armes, oh, Jesu Christ, were spredd heer upon the cross, so receive me into the armes of mercye." Then the two executioners kneeled downe unto hir, desiring hir to forgive them hir death. Shee answered, "I forgive yow with all my harte. For I hope this death shall give an end to all my troubles." They, with hir two weomen helping, began to disroabe hir, and then shee layde the crucifix upon the stoole. One of the executioners tooke from hir neck the *Agnus Dei*, and shee layde hold of it, saying, she would give it to one of hir weomen, and, withall, told the executioner that he should have monye for it. Then they tooke off hir chayne. Shee made hir self unready with a kinde of gladnes, and smiling, putting on a payer of sleeves with hir owne hands, which the twoo executioners before had rudely putt off, and with such speed, as if shee had longed to be gone out of the worlde.

During the disroabing of this queen, shee never

altred hir countenance, but smiling sayde shee never
had such groomes before to make hir unreadye, nor ever
did putt of hir cloathes before such a companye. At
lengthe unattyred and unapparelled to hir petticoate
and kirtle, the two weomen burst out into a great and
pittiful shrieking, crying, and lamentation. crossed themselves, and prayed in Lattine. The queen turned towardes
them : *"Ne cry vous, j'ay preye pur vous ·"* and so
crossed and kissed them, and bad them praye for hir.

Then with a smiling countenaunce shee turned to hir
men servantes, Melvin and the rest, crossed them, badd
them farwell, and pray for hir to the last.

One of the weomen having a Corpus Christi cloathe,
lapped it upp three corner wise, and kissed it, and put
it over the face of hir queen, and pynned it fast upon
the caule of hir head. Then the two weomen departed.
The queen kneeled downe upon the cushion resolutely,
and, without any token of feare of deathe, sayde allowde
in Lattin the psalme, *In te, domine, confido*. Then
groaping for the block, shee layde downe hir head,
putting hir chain over hir backe with bothe hir handes,
which, holding their still, had been cut off, had they not
been espyed.

Then she layde hir self upon the blocke most quietly,
and stretching out hir armes and legges cryed out:
In manus tuas, domine, commendo spiritum meum,
three or four tymes.

Att last, while one of the Executioners held hir
streightly with one of his handes, the other gave two
stroakes with an Axe before he did cutt of hir head, and
yet lefte a little grissle behinde.

Shee made very smale noyse, no part stirred from the
place where shee laye. The Executioners lifted upp the
head, and bad God save the Queen. Then hir dressinge
of Lawne fell from hir head, which appeared as graye as
if shee had byn thre score and ten yeares olde, powled

very shorte. Hir face much altred, hir lipps stirred upp and downe almost a quarter of an hower after hir heal was cut off. Then sayde Mr. Deane: "So perish all the Queen's ennemyes." The Erle of Kent camme to the dead body, and, with a lower voice sayde, "Such end happen to all the Queen's and Gospell's ennemyes." One of the Executioners plucking of hir garters, espyed hir little dogg which was crept under hir cloathes, which would not be gotten foorth but with force, and afterwardes would not departe from the dead corps, but camme and layde between hir head and shoulders: a thing much noted. The dogg embrewed in hir bloud was carryed awaye and washed, as all thinges els were that had any bloud, save those thinges which were burned. The Executioners were sent awaye with mony for their fees, not having any one thyng that belonged unto hir. Afterwardes every one was commanded forth of the hall, saving the Sherife and his men, who carryed hir upp into a great chamber made ready for the Surgeons to imbalme hir, and there shee was embalmed.

And thus I hope (my very good Lord) I have certifyeth your honour of all accions, matters, and circumstances as did proceed from hir, or any other att hir death: wherein I dare promise unto your good Lordshipp (if not in somme better or worse woordes then were spoken I am sommewhat mistaken) in matter, I have not any whitt offended. Howbeit, I will not so justefye my dutye herein, but that many thinges might well have been omitted, as not worthie notinge. Yet, because it is your Lordshipp's faulte to desire to know all, and so I have certyfied all, it is an offence pardonable. So, resting at your honor's further commandment, I take my leave this 11 of February, 1586.

Your honors in all humble service
to command,

R. W.

⸝ To this paper Prince Labanoff has appended the following note:

" The despatch of M. de Chateauneuf gives in a great measure the same particulars, only this report is more circumstantial, and of very great weight, having been written by an English Protestant, who was an eye-witness. We know of two English accounts of the death of Mary Stuart, one by the Earl of Shrewsbury, the other by R. W. (Richard Wigmore, the secret agent of Burleigh.) I have not had time to ascertain positively whether this report is not a translation of one of those narratives; but I believe that it is not."

The prince is mistaken. The French narrative, which *he has given*, is evidently a translation of Wig-more's report, with some slight difference at the beginning, and the omission of the concluding paragraph.

Queen Elizabeth to King James VI.[1]

February 14, 1586-7, O. S.

My dear brother,—I would you knew (though not

---

[1] MS. Cotton. Calig. c. ix. folio 161. That great historical antiquarian, Sir Henry Ellis, whose intimate acquaintance with the fountain-springs of history is only equalled by the sound inferences he draws from his knowledge, has asked the question whether Elizabeth was not really betrayed by her ministers when the warrant for the death of Mary Queen of Scots was actually executed   The more the cruelty of Burleigh and Walsingham, and the treachery of Leicester (best seen in their correspondence) is unveiled, the more this supposition would gain ground on the mind ; were it not for the assassination-letters just quoted, which prove that the queen wished Mary to be privately murdered, and not publicly executed; if, indeed, Walsingham and Davison have not joined in bearing false witness against their queen.

felt) the extreme dolour that overwhelms my mind for that *miserable accident*,[1] which, far contrary to my meaning, hath befallen. I have now sent this kinsman of mine,[2] whom ere now it hath pleased you to favour, to instruct you truly of that which is irksome for my pen to tell you.

I beseech you—that as God and many *moe* know how innocent I am in this case —so you will believe me, that if I had bid aught, I would have abided by it. I am not so base-minded, that the fear of any living creature or prince should make me afraid to do that were just, or when done to deny the same. I am not of so base a lineage, nor carry so vile a mind. But as, not to disguise fits not the mind of a king,[3] so will I never dissemble my actions, but cause them to show even as I meant them. Thus assuring yourself of me, that as I know this was deserved, yet if I had meant it, I would never lay it on others' shoulders; no more will I *not*[4] damnify myself that thought it not.

The circumstances[5] it may please you to *have* [learn] of this bearer [Robert Carey]. And for your part, think not you have in the world a more loving kinswoman, nor a more dear friend than myself, nor any that will watch more carefully to preserve you and your state. And who shall otherwise persuade you, judge them more partial to others than to you. And thus in haste, I leave

[1] Cutting off the head of his mother—by accident!

[2] Sir Robert Carey, son of Lord Hunsdon.

[3] In this sentence, the use of the double negative, contrary to the rules of our language, has caused Elizabeth to contradict her evident meaning; she intends to say, "that disguise fits not the mind of a king," a precept certainly contrary to her own practice

[4] Again her double negative contradicts her own meaning.

[5] That is how Davison despatched the warrant, and how it was executed without Elizabeth's knowledge—as she said.

to trouble you, beseeching God to send you a long reign. The 14th of February.[1] 1586-(7).

Your most assured loving sister and cousin,

ELIZABETH R.

Report of the King's Affairs [King of France], from the departure of Monsieur de Bellièvre to the 25th of February, 1587, *N.S.*

On Friday, the second day after the departure of Monsieur de Bellièvre, the ambassadors of Scotland, namely, the Sieurs Gray, Melvin,[2] and Queth [Keith], had an audience, and took the same course as Monsieur de Bellièvre had done, in order to save the life of the Queen of Scotland, beseeching the Queen of England, in the name of their king, to spare her life; which the queen refused, alleging that she could not be safe so long as the said Queen of Scotland lived, with many very harsh expressions against the said Melvin, whom she considered as the principal adviser and instigator of the King of Scotland, to complain in behalf of his mother; and went so far as to say to the said Melvin, "that if she had such a counsellor as he, she would have his head cut off." To which the said Melvin replied, with great courage, "that he would never fail, even at the risk of his life, to give good counsel to his master,

[1] Six days after the execution of Mary. Elizabeth had thoroughly persuaded her kinsman and messenger, Robert Carey, of the fact, that she was half broken-hearted for the death of her victim; for, in a portion of his memoirs, written long after the death of both, he mentions the long-drawn sighs Elizabeth heaved just after the execution of Mary.

[2] Sir Robert Melville, brother of Sir James Melville, (who left memoirs of his times,) and of Andrew Melville, steward to the queen, and her faithful companion in captivity.

who had not one good servant but would advise him not to suffer his mother to be thus put to death."

Three or four days afterwards, they applied for an audience to hear her final resolution, and to take leave. The Queen of England referred them to her council, to confer upon the matter; which they positively refused to do, and sent to demand passports, that they might return. Upon this the queen sent for them and gave them audience, in presence of her council, as she had done the second time to Monsieur de Belliévre, and holding the same language as she had done to the said Sieur de Belliévre. And the queen having asked them what security they could give for her life, they replied, "that, in addition to the offers of the king, which had already been communicated to them, they offered the engagement of their master, the King of Scotland, and all the Scotch noblemen; and, moreover, if it pleased the queen to deliver her into the hands of her son, they undertook that the said Queen of Scotland should renounce, in favour of her son, all right which she claimed to the crown of England, without hope of ever succeeding to it, and with the surety of the King of France, and of all the other princes, her kinsmen, and friends, and they bound themselves also to keep her in safe custody."

To this the queen answered suddenly without consideration: "That would be arming my enemy with two claims—whereas, now he has but one—and increasing his power of injuring me." The said ambassadors took hold of this expression; upon which she changed colour, and said, in a milder tone, that she did not consider the said King of Scotland as her enemy, but it was a way of speaking. And, thereupon, in order to soothe them, she began to say, that if any way could be found for securing her life in sparing the Queen of Scotland, she much wished it, and begged the said Melvin to suggest it. And he, the said Melvin, having entered into a discussion with those of the council then present, in which the queen affected to be so satisfied with his arguments that she said to the High Treasurer that the said Melvin had adduced sound reasons. And the audience broke up, with hopes that the said lady would allow herself to be persuaded; nay, even when they were taking leave of her, with the view of urging her to come to a resolution, she told them that she would see them once more. This last audience was put off for five or six days; and, meanwhile, they saw in private the Earl of Leicester, the High Treasurer, and others; all of whom they found very hostile to the Queen of Scotland.

During this time, a gentleman of this court, in whom the Queen of England places confidence in important affairs, called upon Monsieur Gray, chief of this embassy, upon pretence of paying him a visit, and, speaking to him on this subject, said, "that in truth the queen would always be in danger so long as the Queen of Scotland was alive, and that all the English noblemen who had signed her sentence could not permit her to live, for they saw no security for themselves if she survived the Queen of England; that the renunciation which they proposed she should make in favour of her son was worth nothing; but that, perhaps, if the King of Scotland himself would renounce all the right that he claims to the crown of England, in case it should hereafter happen that there was any conspiracy against the life of the Queen of England, that might serve to satisfy the lords of this kingdom: otherwise, he did not see that there were any means of saving the Queen of Scotland." The said Gray peremptorily rejected this overture, asking, "if he had been ordered to hold such language:" the

other excused himself, saying, it was merely a suggestion
of his own.

At the last audience, the queen began by begging
them "to excuse the expressions she had before used,
saying that she did not mean them to be taken literally"
They then asked pointedly "what answer they were to
carry back to their master." She replied "that, after
having duly considered and consulted with her council,
she could not grant the life of the Queen of Scotland, seeing no security for herself." Whereupon they told her,
"if such were the case, they were charged by their master
to tell her that he protested all she had done against his
mother to be null, as done against a person over whom
neither she nor her subjects had any power." And
they declared to her that, on their return, he would assemble his estates, and send to all the Christian princes
to consult upon what was to be done.

The queen replied "that she did not think that they
had such a commission from their king." They offered
to give it her in writing. She said "that she would send
to the king their master, to learn the truth ; and, in the
mean time, desired them to remain in London." They
replied "that their master would not listen to any one
sent by her until their return."

When they had got back, they sent off to their master,
begging him "not to hearken to any one before they returned," and applied so urgently for their leave, that, five
or six days afterwards, it was granted; and the queen
informed them that she would send one of her council,
Monsieur Ouley [Woolley], immediately after them, to
acquaint the King of Scotland, and those of his kingdom more particularly with all the proceedings that
had taken place against the Queen of Scotland. They
then petitioned the Queen of England "to be pleased to
assure them, that the execution of the Queen of Scotland

should not take place till the return of the said Ouley ;" which she refused, saying, "that if she did this, the King of Scotland would be under the greater obligation to her." Monsieur the Earl of Leicester promised, in particular, to the said Monsieur Gray, that he would endeavour to prevail upon the queen to stay the execution till the return of the said Ouley.

Hereupon they had their leave, with presents, and set out from London the . . . .[1] of this month, having paid two visits in public to the Sieur de Chasteauneuf, and having always apprized him, day by day, of all that passed in their negociation

They have not been exempted from calumny invented by those who wish to keep alive the anger of the queen, and who gave her to understand that they were plotting against her. And having bought a good many pistols to give away, Monsieur Gray was sending a pair to my Lord *Huygby* who was at Court ; he who was carrying them, called the Baron of *Pruriougby*, cousin of the said Gray, was discovered with his pistols, and being apprehended, they were found empty, without any charge whatever ; he even mentioned the occasion which caused him to carry them. He was, nevertheless, in great trouble and danger of being imprisoned, if Monsieur Gray had not confirmed what he said ; and he was forced to stay at home without going out until the ambassador had departed. Many other reports were circulated against them and their suites.

After their departure, the lords warmly urged the queen to put the Queen of Scotland to death, and even prevented the said Ouley from being despatched. And in fact, the treason of Stanley occurring in Flanders just at this time, the queen, being irritated, suffered herself to be persuaded to sign the death-warrant. Accordingly,

[1] The date left blank.

on Saturday last, Monsieur Bele, clerk of the council, was despatched with an order to the sheriff of the county, to proceed to execution, and an order to the Earl of Sherosbery and three other noblemen of that neighbourhood to attend. On Tuesday, it was made known to her that it was the queen's pleasure she should die; whereunto she resigned herself. And on Wednesday, at nine o'clock in the morning, she was conducted from her apartment into the adjoining hall, where a scaffold had been erected, and there, in the presence of all the people of the village, and all the nobility of the county, four of her own servants, and two of her women, her head was cut off. Further particulars will be given when more at leisure.

As for the Low Countries, the States have sent hither four deputies, to confer with the queen on continuing the war next year, and complaining that the queen has not contributed to the expences of the war of last year, as she was bound to do. Some of the said deputies press her to accept the sovereignty of the said provinces; but when the conditions were stated, they could not agree; wherefore the said queen resolved to send over my Lord Bouchost [Buckhurst,] one of her council, to advise on the spot with those of the country upon what conditions they would accept her as sovereign. This is merely a delay on her part, to see if, in the mean time, she can make any agreement with the King of Spain.

At the time that Monsieur de Bellèvre was here, we were informed that a Flemish merchant, named Andrew de Bock, was treating at Antwerp about sending hither the Sieur de Champigny, or a person named Richardet. Immediately after his departure, a secret courier arrived here from the Duke of Parma, who was kept for three days shut up at Greenwich for fear the deputies of the estates should know it, and instantly sent back by way of Calais; those of the States being apprized of the circumstance were extremely urgent to have everything speedily settled, but the queen put them off till the return of my Lord *Bouchost.*

In the mean time, she is treating with the King of Spain, by way of Portugal, having six days ago sent a Portuguese merchant living here, named Bernard de Quys, to Lisbon, under pretence of traffic, but who carries letters from Monsieur de Walsingham to a person named Castille, formerly ambassador here for Sebastian, King of Portugal, but at present in the service of the King of Spain in that quarter. The letter of Walsingham is in reply to one written to him by Castille, at the commencement of the war, in which he offered to be mediator between the king, his master, and the queen, and since that time no answer had been given from this side.

There was a Spaniard here named Pietro Sarmento de Gamboa, who, having been prisoner here all last summer, was returning through France, when he was apprehended near Bordeaux and taken to la Rochelle. He had, whilst here, two interviews with the queen, and treated with those of the council concerning the means of reconciling these two sovereigns (as I informed the king last summer). They appeared much vexed; and the queen had so much confidence in his negociation, that she has sent a gentleman express to the King of Navarre, to obtain his release; and those of the council have spoken of it here to Buzanvil in very harsh terms. They say very generally that the Catholic King is anxious for peace, and that M. de Champigny will shortly be here.

As to the affairs of the King of Navarre, he has sent hither the Sieur de la Roche Gisard, of Brittany, who had, on Wednesday, an audience of the queen, at which, as I have been told, he explained to her the necessity to which the said king is reduced, which will compel him to yield to make peace, unless he is succoured by her in good earnest. Whereupon, she promised to give him an answer in a few days, at the same time representing the danger which the said king would incur, if he laid down his arms without good security, especially when the succours from Germany were so near at hand, and which he could not obtain another time. The said lady expects news from the Duke of Parma, if she sees any likelihood of coming to an accommodation with the Catholic king.

Ships are equipping here in haste, to oppose to the naval forces of the said king. At present, there are but six of the queen's ships and ten belonging to private persons at sea, and it is very evident that there is a great want of seamen.

Done at London, the xxvth February, 1587.

This paper did not reach the king till after the receipt of the following despatch, which is dated two days later.

M. de Chateauneuf to King Henry III.

Sire,—Your majesty will, no doubt, be astonished to learn the news of the death of the Queen of Scotland by common report, which will have reached Paris before receiving information of it from me; but, sire, your majesty will be pleased to excuse me, when I tell you that the ports of this kingdom have been so strictly closed, as to render it impossible for me to despatch a single messenger; and, what is more, that, having a passport under a different name from my own, he, whom I sent, was apprehended at Dover with his passport, where he still remains, although I despatched him on the 19th of this month, in the afternoon.

On Saturday, the 14th, Mr. Bele, brother-in-law of Mr. de Walsingham, was despatched towards evening with a commission, signed by the queen's own hand, for beheading the Queen of Scotland, and an order to the Earls of Sherosbery, Kent, and Roteland, with many other gentlemen of the neighbourhood of Fotheringay, to attend the said execution. The said Sieur Bele took with him the executioner of this city, who, I have heard, was dressed entirely in black velvet, and they set off very secretly on Saturday night: he arrived there in the evening of Monday the 16th, and on Tuesday, messengers were sent to the said earls and gentlemen. In the evening of the same day, Mr. Paulet, keeper of the Queen of Scotland, accompanied by the said Bele and the sheriff of the county, (that is the person who performs the office of provost marshal, or criminal judge in each bailiwick,) waited upon the said queen, and communicated to her the will of Queen Elizabeth, who was compelled to put in execution the sentence of her parliament. It is reported that the said lady showed great firmness, saying " that, though she never had believed that the queen, her sister, intended to come to this, yet for the last three months she had found herself reduced to such extreme misery, that she looked upon death as a happy release, and was ready to receive it whenever it pleased God :" they proposed to leave with her a minister, but she would not have him.

There is a spacious hall in the said castle, where was erected a scaffold covered with black cloth, with a cushion of black velvet. On Wednesday, at nine o'clock, the aforesaid earls, with her keeper, went to fetch the said lady, whom they found very firm, and, having dressed herself, she was led into the said hall, followed by her steward, Mr. Melvin, her surgeon and her apothecary, and another of her servants: she desired her women to attend her, which they were permitted to do, but all the rest of her servants had been kept in confinement since Tuesday evening. It is said she took some refreshment before she left her apartment. On reaching the scaffold, she desired Mr. Paulet to assist her up the steps, saying it would be the last trouble she should give him. There, upon her knees, she conversed for a long time with her steward, commanding him to go to her son, whom she felt assured he would always serve as faithfully, as he had done her, and who would recompense him, which she had not been able to do while living, for which she was very sorry; and she charged him to carry him her blessing (which she pronounced at the same time:)[1] she then prayed to God in Latin with her women, as she would not allow an English bishop who was present to come near her, declaring that she was a Catholic, and that she would die in that religion. After that, she asked Mr. Paulet "if the queen, her sister, had approved the will which she had made a fortnight before, in favour of her unfortunate servants." He replied "that she did, and that she would take care that all her directions relative to the distribution of the money should be fulfilled." She spoke of Nau, Curl, and Pasquier, who are in prison, but I have not yet heard for certain what she said about them: she then began to pray again, and even to comfort her women who were weeping, and prepared for death with great fortitude; one of her women then bandaged her eyes, she laid her head upon the block, and the executioner, having cut it off, held it up to the view of all present; for more than three hundred persons of the village and other neighbouring places had been admitted

---

[1] James carefully fulfilled these requests of his mother, transmitted to him through Melville.

into the said hall.   The body was immediately covered
with a black cloth, and carried back to her apartment,
where I have heard that it was opened and embalmed.
The Earl of Sherosbery immediately despatched his son
to the queen, to carry her the news of this execution,
which took place on Wednesday, the 18th of this month,
at ten o'clock in the morning, and on Thursday morning,
at nine o'clock, the said messenger arrived at Grenwich.
I know not if he spoke with the Queen [Elizabeth,] who on
that day rode out on horseback, and on her return had a
long interview with the King of Portugal [Don Antonio].
The same day, Thursday, I sent off a messenger to your
majesty, to bring you these tidings, which were not long
kept secret, for at three o'clock in the afternoon all the
bells in the city began ringing, and bonfires were made
in every street, with feasts and banquets, in token of
great rejoicing.

    Such, sire, is a true account of all that took place.
The servants of the said lady are still prisoners, and will
not be released for a month, being more closely guarded
than ever in the said castle of Fotheringhay ; the three
others are still in prison in this city, and it is not yet
known whether they are to suffer death, or to be set at liberty. Since the said execution, Mr. Roger[1] and I have sent
every day to apply for a passport, that we might apprize
your majesty of the death of the said lady, but this has
been refused, saying " that the queen did not wish your
majesty to be informed of this execution by any other
than the person whom she herself would send to you;"
in fact, the ports have been so strictly guarded for the
last fortnight, that no one has left this kingdom with the
exception of a person named Pintre, whom the queen

----
[1] Valet de chambre of the king, sent by Henry III. with letters for Queen Elizabeth and instructions for M. de Chateauneuf.

has despatched to Mr. de Stafort [Sir E. Stafford.] to
acquaint your majesty with the said execution.   The
rumour is that the said lady, when dying, persisted in
declaring herself to be innocent; that she had never
thought of compassing the death of the queen; that she
prayed to God for the Queen of England; and that she
charged Melvin to tell the King of Scotland, her son,
"that she begged him to honour the Queen of England
as his mother, and never to forfeit her friendship."

I have told you above, that young Cherosbery arrived at
Grenvish [Greenwich] at nine o'clock on Thursday morning; that by noon we were all acquainted with the news;
that all the bells began ringing at three, with bonfires in all
the streets, so that the people in this quarter even came to
my house to ask for wood for the fire that was made in
my street.   On Friday those of the council sent the
clerk of the signet to speak to me relative to the seizure
which they alleged to have been made at Dieppe of the
queen's packets, saying that on that day Jean Musnyer,
courier of Calais, had been brought to the court, bearing
several letters from your majesty and others for me, the
which they had detained, having resolved not to deliver
them to me till the release of the things stopped at
Dieppe; begging me to devise some means of opening
the communications, otherwise they could not deliver my
letters.   I thought this very strange, and replied that I
should complain about it to your majesty; that, as they
withheld my packets, I could not tell whether the communications were closed, or for what reason.

On the following day, Saturday, they sent Mr. Ouley,
councillor of state, to repeat the same thing, and to beg
me to consult with him upon some expedient for opening
the communications, otherwise I could not have my
packets: he proposed that I should write to the Governor of Dieppe, to desire him to allow the packets of the

queen to pass. I observed to him that if the said governor had detained the said couriers by order of your majesty, as there was reason to believe, my letter would
answer no purpose;" he told me "that they would be satisfied if I would but say in my letter that, provided he
had not detained them by the express command of your
majesty, he should release them," and this I agreed to do
in the presence of Mr. Roger, and he appeared satisfied.
We complained to him that Mr. Roger was still here,
having been detained a fortnight, without being able to
obtain an audience of the queen; that we had been prevented from informing your majesty of the death of the
Queen of Scotland; that our packets were stopped both
in going to your majesty and in coming from your majesty to us; begging him to remonstrate with the queen
and the members of the council. He excused the delay
of Mr. Roger's audience, under plea of the many engagements of the queen. As for the death of the Queen
of Scotland, he said "that her majesty had been compelled to this step for the safety of her life and the peace
of her kingdom; and he was sure that I must be convinced of the necessity which had forced the queen to
take it;" whereupon he talked a great deal on the subject, to hear what I should say about it; for, in fact, they
had sent him to me merely to learn what I should say
concerning this execution.

After he had done, I replied "that, so long as the Queen
of Scotland lived, your majesty had always given her
your protection, and that I had, by your orders, done all
in my power to save her life; that the efforts which I
had made to this end had given such great displeasure
to certain persons, that they had invented a very stupid
calumny against me, but which I hoped would turn to
their shame, when the queen became acquainted with the
truth. Now that the said Queen of Scotland was dead,

I had nothing more to do than to apprize your majesty of it; while awaiting your commands, I could neither talk nor answer any questions about the matter; but that, being refused a passport to enable me to acquaint you with the event, I had not cared to give them any answer for a long time ; that I begged them to send me my packets, and to obtain an audience for Mr. Roger."

He went away apparently quite satisfied, and on Sunday the queen sent for the said Mr. Roger, but without sending our letters ; he went to the court, but upon his arrival, was informed, by Messrs. the Admiral and Chamberlain, that the queen was indisposed, and begged him to excuse her for that day; but that, if he would deliver to them his letters, and read his credentials, they had been ordered to hear to them. He gave them his letters, and read his credentials, although he had no need to do so ; but as he had already waited a fortnight, we had agreed that he should read them ; besides, there was a second packet in their hands, concerning which we thought it very likely that there would be something to say to the queen. After listening to him, the aforesaid gentlemen went in to the queen, and on their return conducted him to Mr. High Treasurer. When in presence of the council, they begged him to show his credentials, which he did ; he had no answer from them, but a complaint of the stoppage of their packets, and saying that nevertheless they would not give up ours, and, in fact, mine are still in their possession. This, sire, was what passed up to Sunday.

On Monday we were informed that the queen, on hearing of the execution, was highly exasperated ; that she had put on mourning; that she complained of those of her council, and especially of Davison, her secretary of state, who, on Tuesday evening, was sent prisoner to the Tower. On Wednesday she sent again for Mr. Roger (to whom the gentlemen of the council sent the day before the letters of your majesty, which were for him, retaining mine). There the queen said to him, "that she was deeply afflicted by the death of the Queen of Scotland; that it never was her intention to have her put to death, although she had refused the request of M. de Bellèvre;" she said "that Davison had taken her by surprise, but he was now in a place where he would have to answer for it;" charging him to say this to your majesty, with every demonstration of grief, and almost with tears in her eyes, as the said Sieur Roger will tell you, together with many other things of importance, which he is charged to communicate to you.

This, sire, is all that has occurred relative to the death of the Queen of Scotland, in the narration of which I wished to add nothing concerning myself, deferring that for some other opportunity. The queen makes a show of being highly displeased with those of her council about this execution, which she said they had hurried more than she intended, but in particular with Davison, who delivered the warrant to Mr. Bele; for the Queen says that, when signing it, she told him not to deliver it without first speaking to her. He excused himself by saying, "he did not hear this order; that he has done nothing but by the command of the council, and especially of the treasurer," with whom the queen is said to be very angry. Mr. de Walsingham, who has been absent from court for two months, for the benefit of his health, has been ordered to investigate and report upon this affair; he returned on Tuesday last, and on his arrival the queen peremptorily forbade him to mention Davison's name to her.

Such, sire, is the present state of this affair. It is said that parliament will open on Monday, and that it will take under its protection the said Davison, who has done nothing but execute the sentence of the said parliament; added to which, the said Davison, being a councillor of state and a member of parliament, cannot be tried by any but those of the parliament, who will readily acquit him. The queen has sent a gentleman to Scotland, to excuse the death of the queen, upon the plea of her having been taken unawares.

I now come, sire, to what concerns myself. Your majesty will have perceived by a despatch of the 17th, which I forwarded by my steward, that M. Roger had not been able to obtain an audience, though he had attended at court for six successive days. On Sunday, 22nd, as I before mentioned, he showed his credentials to the council, and particularly complained of the detention of Destrappes and what had occurred at the trea‧surer's, to which they made no reply. On Wednesday, 25th, the queen sent for him, when he presented his credentials, and told her besides what your majesty had written in your letter of the 14th, after the audience of Wade; begging that she would place Destrappes in my hands, to be sent to your majesty, that you may examine and punish him should he be found guilty; likewise, that the queen would be pleased to grant me audience, that I might justify myself towards her; she refused both one and the other, saying she should wait for intelligence from Wade, he told her Wade had been heard, as she would perceive by his letter; to this he could get no other answer than that she would write to your majesty, complaining bitterly that I had not revealed a conspiracy formed against her, but without saying that I had either planned or instigated it, nor yet did any of her council allege that I had instigated the conspiracy, so clearly do they see the imposture of Stafort [Stafford], who is known to be the most worthless man in this kingdom. The said Roger then applied for the depositions of the

said Destrappes, Stafort, and Moudé, that he might take
them to your majesty, representing that Wade had carried only very brief extracts, upon which no judgment
could possibly be formed ; at which she affected great
surprise, and said, that Wade had carried the depositions
in full, and which were signed by their own hand, and
that she had given orders to that effect.

   This, sire, is all the information I can give you on this
subject, excepting that when the said Roger, on retiring
from the audience, waited upon M. de Walsingham, to
whom he related all that had passed at his audience, and
complained of the refusal the queen had given him, he
begged him to have patience for two or three days longer,
saying, that the queen was at present much incensed on
account of the death of the Queen of Scotland; but
that he would speak to her, and endeavour to soften her.

   I cannot answer the letter which your majesty wrote to
me on the 14th, for it is still in their hands, with all the
others addressed to me ; such a thing as was never before seen or heard of. Lastly, sire, they complain of
the arrest of their merchants and of the ports being
closed, thinking that they are authorised to do both
themselves, and that nobody has a right to resent it. In
consequence of this delay, I have at length consented
to dispatch one of my people with one of theirs to
Calais, and have written to M. Gourdon to permit both
to pass; and, notwithstanding this, I cannot obtain my
packets. I most humbly beseech your majesty to be
pleased to believe that all that has been alleged against
me is pure calumny, invented by those who have had the
audacity to put the Queen of Scotland to death, without
the consent of the queen their mistress, as time will
show; and to take honour and innocence under your
protection.

   As, in consequence of the said queen's death, her

estates, which she held in dower, revert to your majesty, with the casualties belonging to them, if you should be pleased to bestow on me any of these, I shall feel more encouraged to perform my very humble service. Praying God to grant your majesty a very long and very happy life. From London, this 27th February, 1587.

> Your very humble and very obedient
> subject and servant,
> DE L'AUBESPINE CHASTEAUNEUF.

M. de Courcelles to King Henry III.

Sire,—Having heretofore written to your majesty, what I had been able to learn respecting the intentions of your good nephew, the King of Scotland, on the death of the late queen, his mother, and what he had desired Mr. de Glasgow[1] to say in his name to your majesty, and to his relations and friends in France, I have since been informed that, to spare the expense of sending an ambassador into Spain, but more particularly to avoid the malicious interpretation which the ministers and Protestants of this kingdom might put upon such a step, he has ordered the said Sr. de Glasgow to wait upon the Spanish ambassador residing at your majesty's court, and to beg him to make his excuses to the king his sovereign, if he does not send expressly to condole with him on the death of the late queen his mother, desiring above all, that he will be pleased to assist him with his good counsel and the means of avenging the cruel execution which has been done upon her, and to treat with the said ambassador in such manner as he may deem proper for the good of his affairs, and for the reparation

---

[1] The Catholic Archbishop of Glasgow, long known in these letters as the Queen of Scots' agent and friend.

of the injury which has been done him; the which, sire, several persons have been of late endeavouring to make him forget by industrious artifices, either by occupying his mind with other matters, upon which they think to fix it, such as the maintenance of the Protestant church, persuading him to compel each of his subjects to make a profession of faith, and, upon this pretext, urging him to search out the Catholics, for fear they may bring upon him some descent of the Spaniards in this kingdom, or by the malicious reports which they have made to him respecting some noblemen, his subjects, who, as they say, neglect his orders and contravene the laws of the kingdom, by favouring and assisting the marauders on the borders.

And, in order to accomplish their intentions the more easily, they represented to him [King James], being in council three weeks ago, that in all kingdoms there have been in all ages certain established laws and customs, as well to hold the people in the obedience which they owe to their prince, as for the safety of the latter, with edicts threatening certain punishments for those who should infringe them; and upon such grounds the states of this kingdom, after due consideration, enacted for the common weal certain laws, as well for the encouragement, increase, and preservation of the true religion, and for the abolition of all papistical ceremonies (as they termed them), as also for the observance of the commandment of God, which is to love one's neighbour as one's self, and not to let him be oppressed and trodden under foot by thieves and robbers, who, they could assert, had never before met with such protection in that kingdom as they do at present from the justices and warders stationed on the borders of this country to keep order there, wherefore they cannot but be judged, deserving the punishment ordained by the said laws for the transgression of them:

moreover, that the nobles and people of this said kingdom, being ready to rise and take up arms on the first
bad impression they receive, and it being certain that
the King of Spain was endeavouring to subjugate and
bring under his yoke the Low Countries, to deprive the
inhabitants of their privileges, and to constrain them in
their consciences, that, after having thus reduced them,
he may turn his forces against this kingdom, and establish himself here with the aid and assistance of the
principal lords who profess popery, and who have for
this purpose conspired with the said King of Spain,
without, however, giving any intimation to the other
Catholics here, who are of lower condition, and who, one
may be sure, in case any commotion on account of religion should take place, would be ready to assist with all
their might, and to join themselves to the forces of the
said King of Spain, if they were to land, and with them
to overrun the country, to the great prejudice of King
James and his kingdom, and to the subversion of all
the laws, both ecclesiastical and civil, of this country,
which by such means would be brought under the unjust
tyranny and usurpation of the Pope of Rome, it was
necessary by all possible means to prevent such an
enterprise, which might be done, in the first place, by
the union of the Church of this kingdom, each of its
subjects making a profession of his faith, and by the
obedience which each of the lords shall render to the king
their sovereign, and which they shall attest in writing,
signed by their hands, whereby they shall promise to
associate and unite themselves inviolably with him in all
his undertakings, and render him all obedience, without
infringing his orders and commands in any way or manner whatever; to defend and maintain his authority in
deed and word, in opposition to all those who may dispute it, but especially to the tyranny of foreigners, pro-

fessing a different religion from that established in this said kingdom, who, in case they should attempt to enter or undertake any thing against it, and in case they transgress against this directly or indirectly, shall be held guilty of high treason, and punished as such, according to the laws and customs of the country.

And as they judged that these propositions which they put forth would not be well received by some of the lords of this kingdom, and especially the Catholics, who would not willingly assent to them, they concluded among themselves (as I have been informed), sire, that, to carry into effect the result of their deliberations, it was necessary to seize some of the said Catholics, and particularly the Earl of Morton. [1] Accordingly, the following day, the king mounted on horseback, and with those of his council took the road to Dumfries, where, without stopping day or night, he arrived, hoping, it is said, to surprise the aforesaid Earl of Morton, and compel him to answer to the unfavourable impressions produced in his mind against him — that he had mass said regularly; that he held communication with the Spaniards; that he had shut his eyes to the thefts and depredations committed daily by the marauders on the borders of his kingdom, which was contrary to the commission which he held; and, above all, that he would not obey any of his commands: but the said Sieur de Morton, having been apprized of this journey, and that the king was incensed against him by the persuasion of some who were his enemies, absented himself from the said Dunfris [Dumfries], so that the said king being unable to find him, after putting a stop to the malversations on the said borders, returned to this city, without further annoying the said Sieur de Morton about what had been

_____
[1] The heir of the notorious regent Morton, who it seems by this curious passage was a Catholic.

concluded, nor any of the others; having, however, issued orders for him to leave this said kingdom ; which he appears quite willingly to obey, and is preparing, they say, sire, to go over to France; but I have been informed that, should he be compelled to leave, he has determined to go to the King of Spain, with whom many suppose that he and the other Catholics of this kingdom are in communication. Nay, one of them informed me, a few days since, that, *in the month of August next, or at least in harvest time, there are to arrive here some Spanish troops, by means of which they hope to re-establish the Catholic religion in this kingdom, and then to proceed into England,*[1] of which the king has had some intelligence; but, whether considering it as uncertain, or that he has not the means of opposing it but by some secret enterprise, he affects ignorance of it ; and, although his council have remonstrated with him, he postponed the parliament, which was to have been held on the last day of the last month, until the xxth of the present, on which occasion it is thought there will be a great number of the noblemen of this kingdom, all the private quarrels between whom he manifests a desire to adjust, as the only means of strengthening himself against his enemies.

During his journey to Dunfris, I received by Le Couldray, who is with Monsieur d'Esnevals, the letter which your majesty was pleased to write me on the 14th of last March, and, agreeably to which, I waited on the King of Scotland on his return, and informed him that, from the knowledge you had of the great affection he bore to the late queen his mother, you were convinced that he must have been very indignant at the cruel execution which the Queen of England and her ministers

[1] The lines in italic are in cipher in the original, with a translation on the margin.

had since done upon her, the which execution was the
more lamentable, inasmuch, as it had been done upon a
sovereign princess, after being detained captive like a
malefactor, for the space of nineteen whole years, to be
sacrificed at last to men steeped in crime, if any ever
were, who, without her ever having given them offence,
had become her enemies, and without cause conceived
such hatred against her, that they could not be satisfied
but by shedding her pure and innocent blood ; that the
only thing wanting to complete their gratification, was to
see her heart fail her under all her afflictions and hardships, but that it had pleased God not to grant them the
power, notwithstanding the torments they had inflicted
on her, to shake her fortitude, for she had shown not
less constancy in her adversity than she had done
moderation and prudence in her prosperity , and that if,
for such a cruel execution, and several other injuries
which different princes and states had received from the
Queen of England and her ministers, she and they are
not visited with some punishment from God, it must be
believed that he has thought fit to grant them most
especial favour ; but that it is impossible to help thinking
that in his just judgment he will inflict on them some
condign punishment for this cruelty and for their demerits, and which may serve as an example to our
successors, that their utter reprobation had been the
cause of their too great prosperity, by which they have
been rendered insolent and incapable of controlling
themselves, full of arrogance, audacious in evil-doing,
eager to disturb their own peace and happiness by new
things, even by so cruel an execution, and thereby to
make themselves odious to all mankind, and to offend
all the kings and sovereign princes in the world, among
others your majesty, to whom she was so nearly allied,
but especially him, whose mother she was, who has

thereby received the greatest injury which could possibly be done him, and which was highly prejudicial to the safety of his life, for which he had now more cause to fear than during the lifetime of the late queen his mother, as they who put her to death had now but him alone, as a competitor for the crown of England. Whereupon, sire, he replied, that from his actions, one might judge with what affection he had exerted himself, to save the life of the queen his mother, but that he had been unable to obtain any thing from the Queen of England, who had proved cruel and unmerciful to her, and who wished, nevertheless, to persuade him, by the gentleman whom she had lately sent to him, as well as by letters written to him with her own hand, that *the murder* (as he told me she herself calls it) had taken place without her knowledge, with some lame excuses, and the grief which she declared that it caused her, as he circumstantially related to me, but with which I will not weary your majesty, sire, being the same as I informed you of in my preceding letters.

I shall only tell you that he observed to me that this being an injury which concerns generally all the princes his neighbours, he considered it advisable not to undertake any thing in the way of revenging it, but by advice and counsel, and especially that of your majesty, sire, who are included in this contempt and insult, as are also her relations in France: and to this end he had sent to Mons. de Glasgow, whom he has chosen, and whom, by letters which he is writing to you, he appoints hereditary ambassador, most express directions to beseech you very affectionately, to give him your good advice and counsel in what you may deem befitting his welfare and honour, for the reparation of an injury so ignominious, and a murder so cruel; which he hopes your said majesty will do, though he has been told that, since the death of the

queen his mother, you had entered into much closer
friendship with the Queen of England than before. I
replied, sire, that it was my opinion your majesty would
be highly satisfied as to the choice which he had made
of M^r. de Glasgow as his ambassador at your court, and
that he could not have applied to any king or prince,
from whom he might expect more salutary advice and
counsel, or who would feel more solicitude for the prosperity and advancement of his affairs, without any private
interest, than your majesty, who consider him not only
as your old friend, neighbour, and ally, but as your own
nephew; your majesty trusting on your part that he will
reciprocally show how much he values the friendship of
your majesty, and how desirous he is of retaining it after
the example of his predecessors. He told me that he
had not the least doubt of your majesty's good-will
towards him, having had abundant proofs of it in numberless good offices, which he will always be ready to
return by his best efforts.

He then began to talk of his journey to Dunfris
[Dumfries], and the order which he had given to
prevent the robberies and pillage daily committed by
the marauders dwelling on the western borders of his
kingdom, whose mode of life he took the trouble to
describe to me. I told him that he deserved great
praise for such an enterprise, by which he had shewn
himself the protector of the oppressed, as also for the
diligence he had used in putting down the said marauders,
who might be kept for the future in greater obedience,
and restrained from doing harm, since he himself had
thus taken the trouble to visit them in person. And,
after some further conversation on indifferent subjects,
he retired.

About three weeks since, sire, he received letters from
England, which, amongst other things, represented that

the Queen of England, as being innocent of the execution of the queen his mother, could not offer him any reparation for it, inasmuch as that would be acknowledging herself in fault towards him; but if he would mention any thing that he may desire of her, such as being declared the second person in England, or such conditions as he may consider advantageous to himself, the councillors of the Queen of England, who confess themselves guilty, but who, nevertheless, cannot make any offer of satisfaction for this injury because they are subjects of the Queen of England, will strive by all means in their power to act in such a manner as on every occasion to satisfy him, and to make him forget the grudge which he may bear them. And Archibald Duglas sends him word, that if he will intimate his wishes and what he desires of the Queen of England, he considers his affairs to be in such a train that he thinks he would be likely to obtain it; but, at the same time, he is not so sure of his success as to advise him to desist from applying to his old friends, kinsmen, and allies; but, in case he should not obtain any thing from them, it would be advisable not to reject or let slip this opportunity, which he considers the surest and most certain for his welfare and his advancement to the crown of England. The person who brought these letters has been sent back to-day, and is soon to be followed, as I have heard, by George Jong (Young), clerk of the council. I will endeavour to learn the object of his mission, and will not fail to give your majesty all the information I can obtain.

Three days ago, sire, Mr. Gray was committed prisoner to the castle of Edinburgh, upon a charge preferred against him by William Stuart, brother of him who was formerly Earl of Haran [Arran], that he had given him letters and instructions forged by the said Gray in the name of this king, as it is said, and addressed to Monsieur de Guise and M. de Glasgow, with some credentials to be shown to them on his behalf. It is, however, believed here, sire, that his life is not in danger, provided there is no other charge against him; but it is much to be feared that, at the next meeting of parliament, he will be accused of having advised and consented to the execution of the late Queen of Scotland, and many persons are of opinion that he will have the utmost difficulty to clear himself from the charge.

Sire, I pray God to give your majesty perfect health, and a very long and very happy life. At Edinburgh, the xiith day of May, 1587.

Your very humble and very obedient
servant and subject,
DE COURCELLES.

M. de Chateauneuf to King Henry III.

Sire,—Your majesty will have perceived by my last despatch that the Queen of England released Destrappes on the 29th of last month. Since then, I have had many conferences with the S^r. de Walsingham respecting your affairs ; the said lady sent me word to wait upon her at Croydon, at the house of the Archbishop of Canterbury, where she was going to take the air for four or five days. I did so on Saturday, the 6th of this month, the day fixed upon by her. On alighting at the inn where I intended to dine, the gentlemen of her council sent me an invitation to dine with them at the palace, where there were seven or eight of the principal of them, who paid me greater honour than they had ever done before; and, immediately after dinner, I went, accompanied by them all, to the said lady, who received me still more graciously; and, having spoken to her about urgent matters, such as the circumstance of the depredations, and the voyage of the S^r. de Crillon, which has caused much alarm here, she replied to me in the most courteous and polite manner possible, without my saying a word about Destrappes, a subject which I had resolved not to speak of at the first audience, but merely to treat of public affairs, as, in fact, she received me in presence of her whole court and my own suite, who were admitted into her private chamber. She told me that she was very glad to learn the object of Crillon's mission, but was astonished that he had not travelled by land, and she sent for a map to examine the route from Dieppe to Boulogne, not forgetting to tell me that, as he was going against those of the League, she was ready to afford him every assistance, and had given orders to that effect the day before, when informed of the matter by her ambassador, to whom Monsieur d'Espernon had spoken, adding that, if your majesty needed her forces, money, and munition, to be employed against those of the League, they should be at your service. I thanked her, sire, and said that your majesty had no need of the forces of your neighbours, as God had given you sufficient to chastise all those who would not obey you; that I had never understood the troops your majesty was sending to Boulogne had any other object than the reinforcement of the garrisons there and at Calais, and which were sent by sea on account of its being more convenient. She replied that she was aware that Monsieur d'Aumale had an army in Picardy, that he had taken a great many towns, and that your majesty had sent Monsieur de Nevers with more troops to command in the said province, and a world of other news which she had received from Paris: whereto I replied that I had not heard any of those particulars.

She then made some remarks on the English vessels

detained in France and on the closing of the ports. I
told her that she had been the first to order the ports to
be closed, as likewise my despatches to be withheld, and
the French vessels in this kingdom to be detained; that
your majesty was obliged to do the same in France, in
consequence of the great complaints made by your subjects of the depredations committed upon them by the
English and Dutch, and for which I could not obtain
any satisfaction. She told me that she had commissioned
four of the principal members of her council, to wit, the
high treasurer, the admiral, Lord Cobham, and S^r. de
Walsingham, to treat with me upon this matter, and in
future to do justice to your subjects, and all foreigners
who complained ; meanwhile, she begged me to write
and entreat you to release all her subjects, as she
would release all yours, assuring me those four would do
prompt and summary justice. On my taking leave, she
begged me to confer with them for the future, in order to
adjust the differences that may arise between your subjects
and hers relative to trade. I replied that I wished very
much to know what commission she had given to those
gentlemen, in order that I might send a copy to your majesty, as you had commanded me ; especially a year ago
she had given direction to three of them, with whom I had
a great many conferences, but which all ended in smoke,
and came to nothing. She said that it was not the custom in England to give a commission in writing, especially to members of her council, who, in such capacity,
exercise full power in this kingdom ; but that, when occasion required, the sovereign was accustomed to appoint,
by word of mouth, certain persons of his council to settle
particular affairs. I begged her to be pleased to give
them a special commission, as I did not wish to negotiate
with them unless in writing, to avoid a great many little
disputes which arise in the execution of things. She

5

told me that she would consider of it; and, nevertheless, begged me to go down with them to the council-chamber, which I did, we there agreed, subject to the approbation of your majesties, upon what you will see in the written memorandum, which I have kept separate that it may not interfere with this despatch.

I forgot to tell you, sire, that I complained of the English and Dutch having begun to stop the vessels laden with wheat, bound from Dantzic to France, contrary to that they had promised M^r. de Bellièvre and me and the passports which they had granted us; whereupon she said that our conference would remedy every thing. And, as she was very desirous of speaking to me about the death of the Queen of Scotland, and I, on the other hand, was anxious to get away without touching upon that subject or upon the affairs of Destrappes, she could not forbear calling the Sieur de Walsingham, and telling him to conduct me to the council-chamber, and, taking my arm, she said, laughing, " Here is the man who wanted to get me murdered ;" and, seeing me smile, she added, "that it was a thing she had never believed, as her letter to your majesty would bear witness, nor had she ever complained to the Sieur Roger, except of my having said I was not bound to reveal any thing to her, even though her life was in danger; that I had only spoken as an ambassador; but that she had always considered me to be a man of honour, who loved her, and to whom she could intrust her life; and it was in that quality she had complained of me, not as an ambassador; that she had been aware of the truth, and that it was a trick of two knaves, one of whom, Moudé [Moody],[1] was wicked enough to commit any bad action for money; and, as for the other, she would not name him, for the sake of those to

---

[1] The leader of one of the innumerable plots, real or fictitious, of that period.

whom he belonged; but that now she loved and esteemed
me more than ever; that allowances ought to be made
for the times and the anger of sovereigns; that, as she
had before written to your majesty against me, she would
now write in my favour, and assure your majesty that
she believed me to be perfectly innocent of such an act,
whereby she should show that she was willing to give
way first, that you might have reason to love her, and
grant an audience to her ambassador, and to give orders
for the release of the vessels of her subjects:" all that she
said being evidently prepared beforehand, to get herself
out of the scrape.

I replied: " Madam, I have come hither to treat of
the affairs of the king my master, and for no other
purpose; I have never considered that the duties of a
man of honour differ from those of an ambassador; nor
will I ever be guilty of an act derogatory to the dignity
of my office and my honour; I never said that I would
not reveal any conspiracy against your person, were I to
see it in danger, but that an ambassador was not compelled to reveal any thing, unless he chose to do so, and
neither for that nor for any other thing could he be
amenable to the laws of the country; that you consider
me innocent of the fact is a great satisfaction to me, and
even that you are pleased to bear testimony in my behalf
to the king; but still I entreat you to give me permission to send Destrappes to him, that from his lips the
matter may be cleared up for the satisfaction of his majesty and for my acquittal." She replied there was no
need of further acquittal; that Destrappes was at liberty
to go whenever he pleased, and she would order a passport to be given him, adding that he had fallen into
this trouble through an accident for which she felt much
grieved, knowing for certain that he was innocent. She
then used the following words:—" I have made inquiries

about him, and have learned, that he is of the profession
of the law, and intends to follow it in Paris. I am
sorry for the ill that I have brought upon him, for which
he will bear me a grudge as long as he lives; but tell
him I hope never to have a cause to plead in Paris,
where he might have an opportunity of revenging himself for the wrong I have done him." Such, sire, were
her very words, which I have repeated to your majesty,
to show that she acknowledges the truth of what I have
always written to you—that this calumny against me
was invented by these people here solely to serve their
own ends, and then to report the whole affair in France.

I thought to take leave of the said lady without
making any answer respecting Destrappes, or entering
upon the subject of the Queen of Scotland; but, as I
was standing, she took my hand, and led me into a
corner of the apartment, and said that, since she had
seen me, she had experienced one of the greatest mis-
fortunes and vexations that had ever befallen her, which
was the death of her cousin-germain, of which she vowed
to God, with many oaths, that she was innocent; that
she had indeed signed the warrant, but it was only to
satisfy her subjects, and that it was for the same reason
she had given a refusal to the ambassadors of France and
Scotland; yet it was never her intention to put her to
death, unless she had seen a foreign army invade England or a great insurrection of her subjects in favour
of the aforesaid Queen of Scotland; then she confessed
that perhaps she might have put her to death, otherwise
she would never have given her consent. That the
members of her council, and, among others, the four
who were present (but whose names she did not mention) had played her a trick which she could never forgive; and she swore, by God, that but for their long
services, and also because, what they had done had been

out of consideration for the welfare and safety of her person and of the state, they should have lost their heads. She begged me to believe that she was not so wicked as to throw the blame upon an humble secretary if it were not true; that this death will wring her heart as long as she lives on many accounts, but principally, sire, for her respect for the queen your mother, and for monseigneur your late brother, whom she so dearly loved, that she is ready to satisfy you upon this point; and she begged me particularly to do in this matter all the good offices which a minister, who desires to see peace between the two crowns, ought to do; that she should for ever feel obliged to me, adding that, if I approved it, she would consider about sending to your majesty a nobleman of importance for this purpose, and knit the bonds of friendship with you more firmly than ever, wishing me to be the instrument here of accomplishing this, repeating her protestations that she loved and honoured you, and desired your welfare, prosperity, and health, more than her own; that she offered you her men, money, and ships, against your enemies, and likewise the friendship of four German princes, who had written to her that they were ready to assist against those of the League with a goodly force, fully equipped, which would already have entered your kingdom, had she not kept them back; that if your majesty wished to avail yourself of these forces, she would engage to procure them for you: if, on the contrary, you were inclined to follow the counsels of those of the League, she protested that she would not meddle in any way with the affairs of your subjects, but that then she should consider her own security; that the Catholic king was daily making offers of peace and friendship, but she would not listen to them, knowing his ambition; on the contrary, she had sent Drake to ravage his coasts, and

was considering about sending the Earl of Leicester to
Holland to show that she was not afraid of war; with so
many other observations against those of the League,
that your majesty may easily conceive, from the length
of this despatch, that she had well prepared herself for
this audience, in which she detained me for three good
hours, as I let her say all she pleased.

Deeming it my duty to obtain some answer, I told
her that I was very glad that she desired the friendship
of your majesty, knowing how serviceable it had been
to her formerly; that I believed you entertained similar
sentiments on your part, as I was a witness that for two
years your majesty had never swerved from them; that
I should consider myself highly honoured in being the
instrument of so good a work, tending to the benefit of
all Christendom; and, as it was her pleasure, from my
having held this post in such troublesome times, that I
should be the instrument of bringing things into a better
train than they seemed to be, it was also my wish; but it
was necessary that I should tell her frankly that, if she
desired your friendship, she must desire it by deeds and
not by words: to assist with money and ammunition
those who are in arms against you, to instigate the German troops to enter France, to refuse to do justice to
any of your plundered subjects, to treat your ambassador
as she had treated me for the last four months, was not
courting your friendship in the way that it should be
sought. " Madam," said I, " there are three sovereigns
in Christendom: the king my master, the Catholic king,
and your majesty—under these three, Christianity is
stirring. You cannot quarrel with the other two, madam,
without great injury to yourself; you are at open war
with the one, and the other has every reason to believe
that the civil war in his kingdom is raised and fomented
by your means and counsels; now, opinion can only be

changed by deeds and not by words. We indeed believe that you can have peace with the Catholic king whenever you please; but this can only be done by restoring all that you hold in the Low Countries, in which case you will need the friendship of the king my master more than ever; and, therefore, madam, think of satisfying the king, if you please, since you are so desirous of his friendship."

Throughout this answer, sire, I purposely avoided any allusion to the death of the Queen of Scotland, because I had no commands on that point from you; I am certain, however, that they are extremely anxious to hear what your majesty will say to the Sieur de Staffort [Stafford] when he shall excuse this deed. The said lady told me in reply that she was not assisting the King of Navarre against your majesty, but against the Guises, who were striving to ruin him, intending then to fasten upon her at the instigation of the Catholic king; that, a fortnight ago, the Prince of Parma had boasted that he should go to France to join them, and then come and make war in her kingdom, but that she would take good care to prevent him; that she was not minded to give up what she held in the Low Countries, swearing an oath, that she would not let either the King of Spain or the Guises make game of a poor old creature, who had the body of a woman but the heart of a man; that, on this account, she wished for the friendship of your majesty, and entreated him to restore to the King of Navarre and those of his religion the edict of toleration, of which they had been deprived two years ago, if not for ever, at least for some time, during which, at a good council, which she offers to attend, all religious differences, which are not so great as people imagine, may be adjusted: for she is of opinion that two Christian sovereigns, acting in unison, may devise

an effectual expedient, and induce all others by their
authority to adopt it without caring for priests or ministers, giving me to understand that she considered
your majesty and herself as the heads of the two religions
which are now in Christendom. She then repeated her
desire of sending a person of high rank to your majesty,
asking what I thought of it.

Thereto I replied that all those whom she had in her
name sent to France had always been well received;
but, as at present all France was under arms, I could
not answer her, but that M. de Staffort was better able
to advise her on this point than I; with respect to the
other points, that to assist the King of Navarre, and to
say that it was against the Guises, was intermeddling in
your majesty's affairs more than she would like any one
to do in hers; she could certainly advise him to submit
for a time in matters of religion to your majesty's pleasure, till the meeting of the council which she had proposed, at which it might really be possible to adjust the
religious differences, not by means of two princes only
but by the general consent of all Christendom, which
otherwise might be broken up into parts, each prince,
even the most insignificant, establishing a different form
of religion in his own dominions, which in the end
would produce extreme confusion and the utter ruin of
the Christian religion. Therefore I begged her to reflect upon these four difficulties, which alone could prevent that close bond of amity with your majesty which
she desired.

She replied that, as to the assistance given to the King
of Navarre, she had said sufficient to satisfy me; with
respect to the German troops, she should not in any way
interfere; as for the depredations, she would for the future so arrange matters, that I should part from her better satisfied than any ambassador who had ever left this

kingdom ; and she commanded me again to assure you of her friendship, which she would express to you shortly by letters and an envoy sent for the purpose; and then she put me into the hands of MM. Leicester and Walsingham to conduct me to the council-chamber, where we treated upon what your majesty will find in a separate memorandum.

Now, sire, from the length of this despatch, which I most humbly beseech you to excuse, your majesty will perceive, in the first place, that, in regard to Destrappes, the queen now desires that the affair may be quashed ; nevertheless, I most humbly entreat you to be pleased to cause the said Destrappes to be examined ; and, after he has been heard by the members of your council as you may think fit, that you will be pleased to insist that Stafort be punished for his false accusations, though I have not much hope of this, he being in great favour with the queen and the principal persons of this court.

And, sire, the said Destrappes having fallen into this trouble through misfortune, I take the liberty of most humbly entreating your majesty, since this accusation has spread over all Christendom, to be pleased to declare him innocent, and to bestow on him the first appointment of counsellor of your court at a moderate price, he being truly worthy of that situation ; and it will also be of infinite service in exculpating me to know that, on his return, your majesty has bestowed favours upon him.

For the rest, sire, the Queen of England is greatly disappointed, having had unfavourable news respecting the King of Denmark, who appears desirous of having the King of Scotland for his son-in-law ; and also because the Duke of Parma interferes in this affair by the order of his master: so that the said lady is particularly desirous of your friendship, wishing at least to make it appear to the King of Scotland that she is upon the

best terms with you. For these few days past, she has
been doing all in her power to cause a report to be circulated in England and Scotland that she had settled
matters with the Catholic king, but, according to letters
from Antwerp, this has all gone off in smoke, and it is
believed that the Duke of Parma has refused all negotiation. As this has failed, they are spreading a similar
report respecting you, for I was received at court with
the greatest ceremony in the world, and, on leaving, the
Earl of Leicester went and waited for me in the presence-chamber, where he remarked to me in a loud tone
that the whole court rejoiced that I had been so well received by the queen ; that he, in particular, and all the
nobles had, for the last four months, felt extremely vexed
at what had occurred, being well aware that it was without cause or occasion, with many expressions in my
praise, which I should be ashamed to write to you ; and
he begged me to assure your majesty that he was your
servant, and should be as long as he lived.   After him,
all the other noblemen and gentlemen came, bowing and
complimenting me as if I were a new-comer, a circumstance no doubt contrived on purpose, and at the express
command of their mistress.

Your majesty will be pleased to inform me of your intentions in regard to the subjects of this despatch, and
on the enclosed memorandum, which I have agreed to
submit to the approbation of your majesty, for fear that
they should stop the corn which is on its way to France,
having heard that there are nearly two hundred vessels
laden, some of which I think they will not fail to seize ;
but I will get over as many as I can, which I think I
can do as far as regards the English ; but, as for the
people of Zealand, I am much afraid that they will take
some of them.   I wish there was some one at Flushing
to set this matter right ; indeed, I could send one of my

people with letters from the said lady, the Earl of Leicester, and this council, to prevent them from being seized.

The King of Navarre has sent the S^r. du Bartas to the aforesaid lady, of whom he had an audience on the 10th of this month; but, apparently, she gave him a very unfavourable reception, that I might hear of it, and that this, coupled with her extremely gracious behaviour to me the day before, might make me believe all she told me to be true. The said Du Bartas has assured her that the King of Navarre is in the field with good troops, and that he is going to join M. de Montmorency, that they may march together to meet the German troops, boasting much to her about the forces of the said king. The principal reason of the coming of the said Du Bartas is that he has been sent to Scotland to the king, who has several times before asked the King of Navarre for him, the said King of Scotland being so fond of the works of the said Du Bartas,[1] that he has turned the greatest part of them into Scottish verse, and has frequently said that if he had but the said Du Bartas about him, he should consider himself the happiest sovereign in the world. I have no doubt myself that this is some artifice of these people, who wish to have just now about the said king a man who is a stanch Huguenot and devoted to their interest.

I pray God, sire, to give your majesty perfect health, and a very long and very happy life.

Your very humble
and very obedient subject and servant,
De l'Aubespine Chateauneuf.

[1] Specimens of this noble poet's compositions may be found in Walton's Complete Angler. The admirers of that delightful book will not be sorry to trace Du Bartas in these letters, and note the personal affection young James of Scotland felt for this accomplished French Protestant.

1587. *July* 29 (*August* 8, N S.) The body of Mary Stuart is removed with great ceremony to Peterborough Cathedral

July 31. (*August* 10, N.S) It is interred on the right of the choir of the church, opposite to the tomb of Queen Catherine, first consort of Henry VIII.

August 3. The servants of the Queen of Scotland are sent to London. They are kept under guard there for fifteen days longer, during which time Nau goes before them to France.

Funeral and Interment of Mary, Queen of Scots.[1]

On Sunday, the 30th of July, reckoning according to the new reformation of the calendar, the 8th of August, 1587, about eight o'clock in the evening, there came to Fotheringhay Castle a carriage drawn by four horses, attired in mourning and covered with black velvet, with the arms of Scotland, the carriage or coach covered in like manner all round with small banneroles, exhibiting partly the arms of Scotland, partly those of the house of Anjou, from which the deceased husband of her majesty was descended. The king of the heralds[2] having arrived with about twenty men on horseback, both gentlemen and others, and some servitors and lacqueys, all dressed in mourning, went up to the chamber where the corpse was, directed it to be carried down and put into the said carriage, which was done with all possible reverence, all bare-headed and in silence; while this was doing, the servants, to whom no notice had been given, astonished at these preparations, were consulting among themselves whether they ought to offer to follow the body, to see what was going to be done with it, deeming that it was not their duty to let it be carried

[1] There cannot be a doubt that this paper, written in French, proceeds from one who had belonged to the household of the Queen of Scots.

[2] Mr. Dethick, Garter king at arms.

away, without being accompanied by some of them, the
said king of the heralds went and explained to them the
commission which he had received from his mistress,
touching the interment of the body and the funeral
which she had promised, for which he had been commanded to make arrangements, and to pay all the honours to the deceased that he could. Whereupon, wishing to comply with these directions, and having already
prepared many things necessary for this purpose, it was
thought more expedient to remove the corpse that night
than to wait till the day fixed for its interment, which
was the following Tuesday, the 1st of August, as well
on account of the distance, which was about three
French leagues from thence, and because the leaden
coffin would be too heavy to be carried in state, and it
could not take place on the 1st of August appointed
without collecting a great concourse of people, and pro-
ducing confusion or default of some kind; and as the
vault was already made, they purposed to deposit the
body in it this night, and on the Tuesday to perform the
funeral obsequies with due ceremony, for the greater convenience; and that it was advisable for some of them,
such as they should think proper, to accompany the corpse,
and to see what should be done with it, and that the
rest of the servants should go thither next day to attend
the funeral on the day appointed.

     All being thus prepared, the corpse was carried out
about ten o'clock at night, accompanied by the said
herald and other English, with seven servants of her
majesty, namely, Monsieur Melvin, Monsieur Burgoin,
Pierre Corion, Annibal Stonard, Jean Lander, and No-
colas de la Mare, preceded by men on foot bearing
lighted torches, to give light on the road, and arrived
about two in the morning at Peterbourg, which is a
small town, not walled any more than the other towns of

England, on the river ...., where has been built a
very handsome church, the work of an ancient king of
England named Peda. Here, in the times of the Catholic religion, there was an 'abbey of monks of St. Be-
nedict, now erected into a bishopric—for all the abbeys
have been suppressed—where canons officiate, according to their institution, in the same sort of dress and
vestments as ours.

In this church was interred that good Queen Catherine, wife of the late King Henry VIII., on the left side
within the choir, where there is still her monument,
adorned with a canopy, with her armorial bearings. On
the right side, exactly opposite, was made a grave, brick-
ed all round, and of sufficient depth, wherein was de-
posited the corpse of her majesty in the two coffins. In
the middle of the choir was erected a dome, resembling
the *chapelles ardentes* in France, excepting that it was
covered with black velvet, garnished all over with the
arms of Scotland, with bipartite banneroles, as it has
been said. Within it was placed the *representation*,
which was in the form of a bier covered with black velvet, and upon it a pillow of crimson velvet, on which was
laid a crown. The church was hung with black cloth,
from the door to the interior of the choir, sprinkled with
the said armorial bearings.

On the arrival of the body, the bishop of the said town
of Peterbourg, in his episcopal habit, but without mitre,
crosier, or cope, with the dean and some others in their
canonicals, came to receive the body at the entrance of
the church, and preceded it to the said grave, in which it
was put in the presence of all, without chanting or toll-
ing, or saying a word ; and then they deliberated about
saying some customary prayers, but agreed to defer them
till the day of the funeral. The workmen immediately
set about making an arch of brick over the grave, which

covered the whole, level with the ground, leaving only an aperture of about a foot and a half, through which might be seen what was within, and also for admitting the broken staves of the officers and the flags, which it is customary to put down at the funerals of sovereigns.

On Monday the preparations were completed; the rooms in which the banquet was to be held were hung, and the herald requested the servants, who had come thither to look at and consider the whole, explaining how he intended to proceed; that if they saw any thing wanting, any thing that needed amending or correcting, whatever it might be, that they thought not proper, and it should be made to their satisfaction; that such was the pleasure of his mistress, that nothing was to be spared, and that if he had failed to obey these directions it would be his fault, wishing the whole to be done in the most honourable manner possible. Whereto answer was very coldly made, that it was not for them to find fault; that his mistress and he were discreet enough to do what was right, as they had agreed, and that the whole was dependent on their pleasure.

The Queen of England had some days before sent cloth to make mourning for the servants of her majesty, as much as was necessary for the men to make a cloak a-piece for Monsieur Melvin, Monsieur Bourgoin, and a gown for each of the women, but some of them declined it, making shift with their own dresses, which they had got made for mourning, immediately after the death of the deceased; and as the head-dresses of the ladies and women were not according to the fashion of the country for mourning, a woman was sent on purpose to make others in their fashion, to be worn by them on the day of the funeral, and to be theirs afterwards; so anxious was that sweet Elizabeth to have it believed that she was sorry for the death of her majesty, that she furnished all the mourning dresses worn by those who walked in the procession, more than three hundred and fifty in number, paying the whole expense. The servants paid nothing for their subsistence till the third day of August, when they left Fotheringhay Castle to return all together with their baggage; on which day they began to be at their own cost, as well for their victuals as for their carriage, and afterwards they were not permitted to leave England, where they had to stay for nearly a month, at a very heavy expense.

A Remembrance of the Order and Manner of the Burial of Mary, Queen of Scots.[1]

On Sunday, being the 30th of July, 1587, in the 29th year of the reign of Elizabeth, the queen's majestie of England, there went from Peterborough, M—— Dethick, *alias* Garter principal king at arms, and five heralds, accompanied with forty horse and men, to conduct the body of Mary, late Queen of Scots, from Fotheringham Castle in Northamptonshire to Peterborough aforesaid, which queen had remained prisoner in England . . . . . . years; having for that purpose brought a royal coach, drawn by four horses, and covered with black velvet, richly set forth with escotcheons of the armes of Scotland, and little penons round about it ; the body being inclosed in lead, and the same coffined in wood, was brought down and reverently put into the coach, at which time the heralds put on their coats of armes, and bareheaded, with torches light, brought the same forth of the castle, about ten of the clock at night, and so conveyed it to Peterborough, ... miles dis-

---

[1] From Archæologia, vol i p. 355.

tant from Fotheringham Castle, whither being come
(about two of the clock on Monday morning), the body
was received most reverently at the minster door of
Peterborough, by the bishop, dean, and chapter, and
Clarenceux king of armes ; and, in the presence of the
Scots which came with the same, it was laid in a vault
prepared for the same, in the quire of the said church,
on the south side, opposite to the tomb of Queen Ka-
therine, dowager of Spain, the first wife of King Henry
the Eighth ; the occasion why the body was forthwith
laid into the vault, and not borne in the solemnity, was,
because it was so extreme heavy by reason of the lead,
that the gentlemen could not endure to have carried it
with leisure in the solemn proceeding; and, besides, it
was feared that the sowder might ripp, and, being very
hot weather, might be found some annoyance.

On Tuesday, being the first of August, in the morning, about eight of the clock, the chief mourner, being
the Countess of Bedford, was attended upon by all the
lords and ladies, and brought into the presence-chamber
within the bishop's palace, which all over was hanged
with black cloth; she was, by the queen's majesties gentlemen ushers, placed somewhat under a cloth of estate
of purple velvet, where, having given to the great officers their staves of office, viz. to the lord steward, lord
chamberlayne, the treasurer, and comptroller, she took
her way into the great hall, where the corpse stood; and
the heralds having marshalled the several companies,
they made their proceeding as followeth :

Two conductors in black, with black staves.

Poor women mourners, to the number of 100 two and
two.

Two yeomen harbingers.

The standard of Scotland borne by Sir George Savill,
knight.

Gentlemen in cloaks to the number of fifty, being attendants on the lords and ladies.

Six grooms of the chamber,[1] viz. Mr. . . . . . Eaton, Mr. . . . . Bykye, Mr. . . . . Ceavaval, Mr. . . . . . Flynt, Mr. . . . . Charlton. Mr. . . . . Lylle.

Three gentlemen servers to the queen's majesty, Mr. Horseman, Mr. Fynes, and Mr. Martin.

Gentlemen in gownes, Mr. Warme, Mr. Holland, Mr. Crewste, Mr. Watson, Mr. Allington, Mr. Darrel, and Mr. Fescue.

Scots in cloaks, 17 in number.

A Scottish priest.

Mr. Fortescue, master of the wardrobe to the queen's majestie.

The Bishop of Peterborough.

The Bishop of Lincoln.

The great banner, borne by Sir Andrew Nowel, knight.

The comptroller, Mr. Melvin (Sir Andrew Melville).

The treasurer, Sir Edward Montague.

The lord chamberlayne was Lord Dudley.

The lord steward was Lord St. John of Basing.

Two ushers.

Atchievements of honour borne by heralds,
{
The healme and creste borne by Portcullis.

Target, borne by York.

Sword, borne by the Rouge Dragon.

Coat, borne by Somerset.
}

Clarencieux king of arms, with a gentleman usher, Mr. Coningsbye.

---

[1] These were all officers of Queen Elizabeth's household.

The corpse borne by esquires in cloaks :

Mr. Francis Fortescue.
Mr. William Fortescue.
Mr. Thomas Stafford.
Mr. Nicholas Smith.
Mr. Nicholas Hyde.
Mr. . . . . Howlands, •
[the bishop's brother.

Eight bannerolles, borne by esquiers :

1. King Robert impaling Drummond.   By Mr. William Fitz Williams.

2. King James the 1st, impaling Beaufort.   Mr. Griffin, of Dingley.

3. Guelders.   {   By Mr. Robert Wingfield.

4. King James the 3rd impaling Denmark.   }   Mr. Bevill.

5. King James 4th impaling the arms of Henry 7th, of England.   }   Mr. Lynne.

6. King James 5th impaling Guise.   }   Mr. John Wingfield.

7. King of France impaling the arms of Mary of Scotland.   }   Mr. Spencer.

8. Lord Darnley impaling the arms of Mary, Queen of Scotland.   }   Mr. John Fortescue of Haywood.

The canopy, being of black velvet fringed with gold, borne by four knights, viz.

Sir Thomas Manners.
Sir George Hastings.
Sir James Harrington.
Sir Richard Knightley.

Assistants to the body. Four barons which bore up the corners of the pall of velvet.

The Lord Mordant.

The Lord Willoughby of Parham.

The Lord Compton.

Sir Thomas Cecill.

Mr. Garter, with the gentleman usher, Mr. Brakenbury.

The Countess of Bedford, supported by the Earls of Rutland and Lincolne, her train borne up by the Lady St. John of Basing, and assisted by Mr. John Manners, vice-chamberlain.

The Countess of Rutland, Countess of Lincoln.

The Lady Talbot, Lady Mary Savill.

The Lady Mordant, the Lady St. John of Bletshoe.

The Lady Manners, the Lady Cecill.

The Lady Montague, the Lady Nowel.

Mrs. Alington, Mrs. Curle.

Two ushers.

Eight Scottish gentlewomen.

The gentlewomen of Countesses and Baronesses, according to their degrees, all in black.

Servants in black coates.

The Countess of Bedford,	10.
Countess of Rutland,	8.
Countess of Lincoln,	8.
Lady St. John of Basing,	5.
All lords and ladyes,	5.
All knights and their wives,	4.
All esquires,	1.

The body being thus brought into the quire, was set down within the royal herse, which was twenty feet square, and twenty-seven feet in height, covered over with black velvet, and richly set with escotcheons of arms and fringe of gold; upon the body, which was covered with a pall of black velvet, lay a purple velvet cushion, fringed and tasseled with gold, and upon the same a close crown of gold set with stones; after the body was thus placed, and every mourner according to their degree, the sermon was begun by the Bishop of Lincoln, after which certain anthems were sung by the quire, and the offering began very solemnly, as followeth:

The Offering.

First, the chief mourner offered for the queen, attended upon by all ladies. The coat, sword, target, and helm, were severally carried up by the two Earls of Rutland and Lincoln, one after another, and received by the Bishop of Peterborough, and Mr. Garter king at arms.

The standard alone.

The great banner alone.

The lady chief mourner alone.

The train-bearer alone.

The two earls together.

The lord steward, }
The lord chamberlain. }

The Bishop of Lincoln alone.

The four lords assistants to the body.

The treasurer, comptroller, and vice-chamberlain.

The four knights that bore the canopy.

In which offering every course was led up by a herald, for the more order; after which, the two bishops and the Dean of Peterborough came to the vault, and over the body began to read the funeral service; which being said, every officer broke his staff over his head, and threw the same into the vault to the body; and so every one departed, as they came, after their degrees, to the bishop's palace, where was prepared a most royal feast, and a dole given unto the poor.

The following extract from Blackwood's History of Mary, Queen of Scots, furnishes particulars not given in the two preceding accounts of her funeral :—

The corpes was carryed into a chamber next adjoining, fearinge the saide maids should come to do any charitable good office. It did increase greatly their desire so to do after they did see their mistress corpes thorowe a little hole of the chamber wall, which [was] covered with cloath, but the wofull corpes was keepte a longe time in this chamber till it began to corrupt and smell strongly, so that in the end they were constrained to salt it, and to enbalm lightly to save charges, and after to wrap it up in a cake of leade, keeping it seven monthes there before it was put into prophane earth in the church of Peterborough. It is very true that this church is dedicated under the name of monsieur saint Peter, and Queen Catherine of Spain was interred therein after the Catholique fashion, but it is now prophaned like all the churches of Englande.

M. de Chasteauneuf to King Henry III.

Sire,—By order of the Queen of England, the funeral obsequies of the late Queen of Scotland were performed on the 11th of this month at Peterbourg, the episcopal town in the province in which the said lady died, and she was interred in the cathedral church, on the right side of the choir, and opposite to Queen Catherine, first wife of King Henry VIII. The obsequies were very solemn, and were attended by all the servants of the deceased;[1] and they are now returning, and among them her physician, who, having attended her from the first

[1] With the exception of Nau and Curle, her secretaries, who durst not appear.

day of her strict imprisonment to the hour of her death, was directed and commanded by her to kiss the hands of your majesty, the queen, and the queen your mother, and to present them with some remembrance from her.

The Queen of England is always hereabout, at the houses of noblemen, not having yet gone to Windsor, where her council is to assemble. Nothing further has occurred here, but what your majesty will see in a memorial which accompanies these presents, the bearer of which is young Pasquier, who was in the service of the said deceased. Her secretaries, Nau and Curlle, have been set at perfect liberty, and every thing which belonged to them before has been restored, after signing, in full council, a declaration that all the depositions which they had made aforetime were true, and that they had deposed without force, constraint, or bribery.

Sir, I beseech the Creator to give your majesty perfect health and prosperity, and a very long and very happy life.

London, this 26th day of August, 1587.

Your most humble and most obedient
servant and subject,
DE L'AUBESPINE CHASTEAUNEUF.

It is stated in Egerton, page 131, that the original of this letter is to be found in the King's Library, Desmême's Collection, No. 9513, intituled, " Original Letters of State, Vol. iii., fol. 443." The librarians, however, have no knowledge of it, and I have in vain examined the French manuscripts of the above-mentioned collection; none of them bears that title, or contains the preceding letter.—(Note by Prince Labonoff.'

1587. *December* 4. (*December* 14, N. S) Decree of the parliament at Paris, issued on the application of the Duke of Guise
and the Archbishop of Glasgow, relative to the execution of the
will of the late Queen of Scotland.

Decree of the Parliament of Paris, 14*th December,*
1587.—*N. S.*

Having seen the petition presented by Henry de Lorraine, peer and grand master of France, Duc de Guise;
James, Archbishop of Glasgow, ambassador of the late
Queen of Scotland in France ; John, Bishop of Ross, in
the kingdom of Scotland ; and Jehan de Champhuron,
keeper of the seals to the said lady :

By which it appears that, after the sentence of her
death was made known to her, she wrote and signed a
will with her own hand, containing several legacies and
directions, as well relative to the discharge of her debts
and the rewarding of her servants, as to the founding of
certain endowments, and for the execution of the same
chose and appointed the aforesaid petitioners, who felt
themselves highly honoured by such choice and appointment, made by so great and virtuous a queen :

The which are desirous of promoting the said execution, and with great cheerfulness and good-will to render
the said lady this last service, having not less affection
for her than during her lifetime, but doubt that there are
sufficient funds to satisfy the creditors, and to fulfil the
intentions of the said lady, who left no other property in
France but a house of small value, situate at Fontainebleau; several sums which she alleges to be due to her
from the king, but which, at present, it will be difficult
to recover, and some other claims contested by certain
gentlemen, and which have been in litigation for the last
twenty years :

The surplus, consisting in what may be in the hands of her treasurer, and rents due from her tenants, which they refuse to pay until some abatement be made, but which abatement the council of the said lady made a difficulty of directing, as it used to do, on account of her decease, without being authorised by the court; and, moreover, great'disputes having arisen between the creditors and legatees, as likewise with those who were in possession of the goods of the defunct, so that there was nothing but was disputed and involved in very long and intricate discussion, into which the petitioners cannot enter on account of the high and important affairs which they have in hand: and, further, that the said Archbishop of Glasgo and Ross, being liable to be sent for and recalled by the King of Scotland, who requested their places to be supplied; seeing the will of the said deceased queen, the conclusions and consent of the procureur-general of the king, and all things considered,

The said court, having regard to the said petition, and the consent of the said procureur-general,

· Has ordered, and orders, that by the advice of the relatives, friends, and council of the said deceased Queen of Scotland, and her legatees and creditors, there be elected one or two persons, who shall take upon themselves the execution of the will of the said lady, and the charge of management of her effects, in the capacity of executors in trust of the said will, and shall take all the necessary steps as well for commencing actions, as for defending any which may be brought against them in their said capacity by the creditors and legatees; and they shall also receive and pay all moneys, and engage to account for the proceedings of the execution, which they shall be expected to undertake by the advice of the petitioners, who shall continue to be honorary executors, but without being in any way bound for the said execution, or liable to be applied to by any one, or otherwise at all responsible; and, in order to proceed to the said election and execution of this present decree, it has appointed and appoints Jacques Brisard and Jean Chevallier counsellors in this matter.

1603. *April* 3 Death of Elizabeth, Queen of England. James VI , King of Scotland, succeeds her, and unites the two crowns.

1612. *October* 11. James I of England and VI. of Scotland removes the body of his mother, Mary Stuart, from Peterborough to Westminster.

It was probably about this time that James caused the castle of Fotheringay to be demolished.

Enquiry before the House of Lords, May 10th, 1839, *on the Destruction and Sale of Exchequer Documents.*

Frederick Devon, Esquire, called in, and examined as follows:

When you were last before the committee, you were asked whether you could find any evidence relative to Popham, as connected with the trial of Mary, Queen of Scots: have you discovered any thing?

I have.

"To John Popham, esquire, her Matie Attorney-General, by way of reward for his travaile out of the countrey (which means *into* the country), and for chardges and attendaunce from the middert of August 1586, unto the tenth day of October deo anno, at London and at the court, and for his pains in and about the examinacions, indictements, and trialls of Ballard, Babington, and the rest of the same conspiracy, and for his travaile, chardges and paines taken in the mattre of the Quene of Scottes at Fotheringay, and for his travail, paines and attendaunce taken in the draught of the commission and sentence, and other the proceedings against the said quene in the terme and vacacion time, and for his continual attendaunce from the begynning to the ende of this last parliament, by the Lord Treasurer and Under Treasurer's warr', dated the 2ᵈ Janˢ, 1586—100*l.*"

The next entry is a payment of 100*l.* to Thomas Egerton, Esquire, her Majesty's Solicitor-General, who was also at the trial of the Queen of Scots. In the same book (previously) is a payment of 270*l.* to the said Attorney and Solicitor-General, for services which are contained in a warrant dated 11th May, 1586.

" To George Pette, (who, I imagine, was Clerk of the the Crown, or employed by the Attorney and Solicitor-General,) for his great travail and paynes imployed in and aboute the engrossing and enrollinge of the judgem^ts of the late convicted traitors, the great commission and all the proceedings therein against the late Queen of Scottes and for giving his hoole attendance in and about the same, by the appointment and direction of Mʳ Attorney and Mʳ Solicitor-General, ever since Michaelmas terme and before—20*l.* And unto Thomas Wyndebanke, Clark of the Sygnet, for writing sundry commissions and lres in French in the great rolle conteyning the processe and sentence against the said Queen of Scottes—100ˢ; by like warr' dated the last of Dec. 1586—25*l.*"

" To . . . . . by the hands of Richard Cupe, clerk unto the said cofferer, towards the provision of achates and victuals against the funeralles of the Scottishe Quene, by a privy seal, dated the 11ᵗʰ of Julie, 1587— 207*l.* 19*s.*"

" To William Dethicke, Garter Principal King-at-Arms, for a hearse and other provisions of heraldrie, that he and the rest of the heraldes were to make for the

Scottish Quene's funerale, by privy seal 11th of July, 1587—406*l*."

" To Amias Poulett, knight, one of Hir Maj^{tie} privy counsaille, for the diettes and other his chardges susteyned in the custody of the late Quene of Scottes, until the tyme of hir decease and since, by a privy seal, dated 11th July, 1587—1300*l*."

There are several payments for the diet of the Queen of Scots in this book. There are payments to Davison of 500*l.*, and in the Book of Warrants (12 a.) William Davison has 1000*l.*, in October, 28 Eliz.; (*so that it would appear he was not in very great disgrace for the part he took*). 500*l.* is immediately after entered as being paid to the said William Davison, one of the queen's principal secretaries, also immediately afterwards is 1000*l.*; and I know, having seen it regularly entered on the Rolls, his pension was granted of 100*l.* a-year, which I have stated before in the preface to one of my books, even after James the First came to the throne, so that it would appear he either had great influence, or was not much disliked, although amerced 10,000*l.* in the Star Chamber, &c., and supposed to be under royal displeasure.

Where is this from ?—The issue and other books in the Pell Office ; but the chief of those are taken from books that were saved from the vault; and I find, on going through a book not saved from the vault, but in the Warrant Book, from the 12th of Elizabeth up to the 23rd of Elizabeth, an allowance was paid to the Earl of Shrewsbury of 52*l.* a-week, which appears to be paid about every six months, " for the maintenance and diet of the Queen of Scots;" it is paid from that date to the 23rd of Elizabeth, and then it is decreased to 30*l.* a-week. There is a payment in " 1584, 26th Eliz., to Bryan Cave, appointed for the removal of

the Scottish Queen to Tuttebury, of 500*l.* ;" and a payment, amongst others, " *to Monsieur Nau,*[1] *the Scottish
Queen's servant,* 73*l.* 10*s.* 2*d.* ; to Sir Amias Poulett,
1300*l.*, for the diet, &c. of the late Queen of Scots."

[1] This item deserves great attention, proving that Nau was,
long before the fatal catastrophe of his unfortunate royal mistress,
the paid agent of Queen Elizabeth. The Queen of Scots always
paid him his wages and expenses, and had even appointed payment of his arrears of salary in her will, if he was found to have
deserved it. See that document, previously quoted. It is desirable that the above item should be read in immediate conjunction with the following document, which proves that Nau
(called *de Naou* therein) was recommended and even forced into
the service of Mary Queen of Scots by Elizabeth herself:—

Queen Elizabeth to the Earl of Shrewsbury.
                                        March 29, 1575.
Right trusty and well-beloved cousin and councillor, we
greet you well.

Whereas the Queen of Scots hath been destitute of a French
secretary since the death of Rollet, and hath, by her own letters,
and by means out of France, desired us to suffer another to
come and supply that place about her, which we have hitherto
forborn to grant for divers good causes, and among other, for
the evil offices which her other secretary[1] did there, whereof you
are not ignorant. Now, forasmuch as the bearer hereof, called
De Naou, a Frenchman, hath been chosen and recommended to
us by our brother, the French king, with request he may go to
her and serve her as her secretary, and hath promised that he
shall carry himself in that even manner‛that becometh an honest
minister ; nor shall practise any hurtful or offensive thing, which
he himself hath also vowed and promised here, with offer that,
if at any time he shall be found faulty, he submitteth himself to
any punishment. Upon these respects, and at her earnest
request, we are pleased, that the said De Naou shall resort and
abide with her as her secretary. And so our pleasure is, you
should receive him into her company, and suffer him to serve

[1] By this sentence it would appear that Rollet was faithful to
his trust, and that Elizabeth would have permitted none but a
spy to take his place.

I was asked if I could find Beal's payment, who took the
warrant down ; I found the roll immediately before and
after, but I question whether it would be there ; I find
the payment of his salary ; he would be paid probably in

her in that place, admonishing him now at his entry, and also
hereafter, to have consideration of the caution, which our said
brother, the French king, hath given us for him, and also
of his own promise, as he will avoid the danger wherein he hath
condemned himself, if he be found faulty. Given under our
signet, at our Manor of St. James's, the 29th of March, 1575, in
the seventeenth year of our reign

To our trusty and well-beloved cousin and councillor, the
Earl of Shrewsbury, Earl Marshal of England.

This document is in Ellis's Original Letters, vol. ii., p 270,
where it may be seen in its original orthography. MS.
Lansdowne, 1236, fol. 47.—The question naturally arises, who
was Nau, the false secretary of the Queen of Scots, and by what
fatal error did she admit him into her service ? The answer
may well be rendered by this despatch from Queen Elizabeth to
the Earl of Shrewsbury, whereby it appears that she recommended him into the service of her unfortunate prisoner, after
the death of the faithful Rollet, so much regretted by Mary. It
seems that Nau had previously been proposed as the successor
of secretary Rollet by the King of France, but the earnestness
with which Queen Elizabeth seconded the appointment of this
man, (whose treachery ultimately furnished the pretence for the
execution of Mary,) can be only appreciated by the perusal of
the document above.

And when the above Exchequer documents relative to Mary
Queen of Scots (rescued from destruction by Frederic Devon,
Esq., and here printed) are perused, and it is found that among
the other secret-service money paid by Queen Elizabeth to the
agents surrounding her victim, the large sum of £73 was dis-
bursed to this Nau in 1584, what can be the inference ? It is
that a simple money item, in combination with other documents,
proves a lamp to lighten the dark places of history and to discover iniquity. How carefully, then, should the documents, by
which alone historical truth can be tested, be guarded by a great
country !

one of the larger sums by the Lord High Treasurer, or by Walsingham. "In the 28th Eliz., 3600*l.* yearly is granted to Sir Amyas Paulet, for the custody and diet of the said Queen, out of the lands of Lord Paget." In the 29th Eliz., money is ordered "for the repairs of Fotheringay Castle, because the divers meetings and consultations of great importance had been held there." I believe that is the result of my search. Almost the whole of those I have named, except the payments to Lord Shrewsbury, are from the books saved from the vaults.

Which would have been destroyed but for your inspection?—I do not say that; they were put by, by Mr. Bulley, as not to be destroyed; they would have been destroyed if they had remained in the vault.

APPENDIX.

APPENDIX.

THROUGHOUT the whole of the preceding collection of documents, allusions are made to the irreconcilable offence which the unfortunate Mary had given to Queen Elizabeth by the adoption of the arms and style of Queen of England, Scotland, and Ireland. The Scottish confederate lords and their ally John Knox were the agents who excited in the bosom of Elizabeth the inextinguishable hatred for this supposed aggression, which never was allayèd but by the blood of Mary. It is not difficult to perceive, by the tone of the following papers, that the sole foundation for the accusation which weighed so fatally against Mary in after life, was merely the quartering of the arms by way of augmentation at a tournament.

Just before the death of Mary's mother, Scotland, involved as it was in religious disputes, had been invaded by Queen Elizabeth under plea of affording support to the Reformers. Elizabeth was at that time a young woman, just settled on the throne of England. The Scottish lords, confederated against the queen-regent, worked on the jealousy which Elizabeth felt on account of her doubtful legitimacy, by inserting in their manifesto to that queen the following irritating information.[1]

[1] Sadler Papers, vol. i. p. 606.

7

1560.

Manifesto of the Scottish Lords.

"We know most certainly that the French have spread abroad (though most falsely), that our Queen Mary is right heir to England and Ireland; and to notify the same to the world, have, in paintings at public jousts in France and other places, this year, caused the arms of England, contrary to all right, to be borne publicly with the arms of Scotland, meaning nothing less than *any augmentation to Scotland*, to annex them both to the crown of France. And they have in *writings in wax*, in public seals, written, and engraven, adjoined the style of England and Ireland to the style of France, naming the French king, Francis II., husband to our queen and sovereign Mary, King of France, Scotland, England, and Ireland. Also they have further proceeded, and secretly sent into this realm of Scotland a seal to be used for the queen with the same style, and in manner of despite to the crown of England, they have sent to the dowager of Scotland, her mother, a staff for her to rest upon, having engraven on the top the said usurped arms."

True or false, this information never ceased to rankle in Elizabeth's mind while the troublous existence of her rival lasted. No person, however, saw this redoubted seal and staff, excepting Master Knox, whose most curious letter on a subject, which brought such fatal results to his unfortunate queen, here follows. Its leading spirit is assuredly that of the church *militant*.

John Knox to Mr. Railton.[1]

October, 1560.

Your letters, long looked for, received I in Edinburgh this 23rd of October. It is most assured that such a jewel [*the*

[1] In the Sadler Papers, vol. i. pp. 680, 681, 682, may be seen this do-

great seal just described] as your writings do specify is lately
comed to our realm, but it is kept marvellously secret,[1] and
the rather because these cold blasts of winter be able to cause
the beauty of such May-flowers to fade.

Thus much my eyes saw and my hands touched, a trim
staff for the queen, then regent [Mary of Guise], sent from
the persons whom before ye did specify, in which were all
things which ye express, gorgeously engraved on silver and
double gilt.   This staff was sent in the month of May, in the
same ship in which I came to Scotland, and was shown to me
in great secrecy.

The numbers and names of my needy brethren I did
signify to such as be in your company, and to the man
above, [*supposed to be Cecil*].   The number is now augmented, and their poverty also in such sort, that if relief be
not speedily provided, I fear that more than I will mourn
when we may not so well amend it.   God comfort them, for
their battle is strong !

The alteration that be here is this : the queen-regent, with
public consent of the lords and barons assembled, is deprived
of all authority and *regiment* [regimen] among us.   She, her
Frenchmen, and assistants, are, by open proclamation, declared and denounced enemies and traitors to this common-
wealth, for that, being thrice required and charged to desist
from fortifying Leith, she and they do obstinately proceed
in their wicked enterprise.   This was done Monday, before

cument, in the orthography used by Master John himself, who wrote fair
English for the era, with very few north country words or idioms.

[1] That is, it never existed, excepting in the brains of the polemics who
invented the description of it, to excite the fury of Queen Elizabeth.   For
the great seal of a kingdom to be kept "marvellous secret," which is used
for the purpose of authenticating public documents, would be a strange
anomaly.   The political polemics of that day, on both sides of the question, would have been wonderfully improved in their morals by the casti-
gation of our present periodical press, for their conduct looks ugly
enough in documentary history.

noon. There shall be appointed to occupy the authority a great council, the president and head whereof shall be my lord *Duck*.

[Which *Duck* was Thomas Howard, Duke of Norfolk, the general of Queen Elizabeth's invading force, who was afterwards beheaded for endeavouring to espouse Mary Queen of Scots. Master John resumes.]

The authority of the French king and queen [Mary] is *yet* received, and will be in *word*, till they deny our most just requests, which ye shall, God willing, shortly hereafter understand, together with our whole proceedings in the beginning of this matter, which we are to set forth in manner of history. The battle is begun sharp enow, God give the issue to his glory and to our comfort!

She [the queen-regent] hath yet small advantage, for the death of two of our soldiers, and for the hurting of three gentlemen, she hath lost two captains, and hath sore wounded many of her chief soldiers, to the number of twenty upon one day. They brag, and the queen especially, that ye [the English] will leave us in the midst of this trouble; and this [news] she hath by her last post, which came by you. My battle hath to this day been very bitter; but if ye frustrate my expectation, and the promises that I have made in your name, I heed not how few my dolorous days may be. What God hath wrought by me in this matter I will not now recite, but this I may say, that such offers are refused that *mo* [more] do judge us fools than praise our constancy.

We are determined to essay [try] the uttermost, but first we must have five thousand soldiers; for if we assault and be repulsed, then shall our enterprise be in great hazard, and our commons not able to abide together. Give advertisement, therefore, to such as favour us, that without delay our support be sent, as well by money as by men. If your eyes be single, ye may not *let* [hinder] succour to our present necessity. I must further require you to be a suitor to all such as ye know to be unfeigned favourers, and especially to our brethren in London, to have respect to our necessity.

The French ships keep the waters here, which is to us a great annoyance, and unto them a great relief. Provision would be had at times, which we cannot watch, by reason that all our ships are absent, and, as we fear, *staid* [detained] as many as be in France. I cannot write to any especial for lack of opportunity, for in twenty-four hours I have not four free, to natural rest and ease of this wicked carcase.

Remember my last request for my mother [Mrs. Bowes], and say to Mr George, [probably George Bowes], that I have need of a good and assured horse, for great watch is laid for my apprehension, and large money promised to any that shall kill me; and yet would I hazard to come to you, if I were assured that I might be permitted to open my mouth to call *agin* to Christ Jesus those unthankful children who *allate* [lately] have appeared utterly to have forgotten his loving mercies, which sometimes I supposed they had embraced. And this part of my care now poured into your bosom, I cease further to trouble you, being troubled myself, in body and spirit, for the troubles that be present and appear to grow. God give end to his glory, and to our comfort. This 23rd of October, at midnight.

P. S. Many things I have to write which now time suffereth not; but after, if ye make haste with this messenger, ye shall understand more . . . . . [*then some illegible words.*] I write with—sleeping eyes.

Advertise me if all things come to your hands close, [viz., sealed up.]

Such, as the writer himself says, "set forth in manner of history," is a lively picture of the proceedings in Scotland a few months before the return of Queen Mary, who was called on by adverse circumstances to govern a country,

thus convulsed, while yet in her teens ; the author of the
foregoing epistle being the spiritual guide, with undefined
authority in the land.

1561.

The queen, soon after her arrival from France, began to
think of making a progress through some of the principal
towns of her kingdom.   Her horses and mules having been
detained in England, she was obliged to purchase ten horses
at Stirling for the use of her household, preparatory to her
progress.   As the queen had no wheel-carriage, she set out
on her journey on horseback on the 11th of September,
1561.

In a note on the above passage, Chalmers says : On the
6th of September, 1561, the treasurer charged £211, given
to John Livingston, her master stabler, to buy ten horses for
her grace's household, and £1 13s. 4d. for incidental expences.   Ten *haikneys* were brought to Holyrood House,
perhaps as presents, for the persons who brought them were
paid "drink silver" or "bridle silver" of two crowns of the
sum for each, or £26 13s. 4d.   The queen and her ladies
probably rode on hackneys, as there is a charge in the same
accounts of "ane mollat bit to the queen's haikney."   Before
her progress there are also charges for saddles and bridles to
twelve of the queen's ladies, and for black riding cloaks to
fifteen of the queen's ladies.

During this journey, on the 24th of September, Randolph,
the ambassador to Queen Elizabeth, at the court of Mary,
wrote to Cecil that " at Stirling, the queen, lying in her bed,
having a candle burning by her, being asleep, the curtains
and tester took fire, and so was like to have smothered her
as she lay."   The ambassador sarcastically adds : " Such as
speak much of prophecies say that this is now fulfilled that
of old hath been spoken, ' that a queen should be burnt at
Stirling.' "

Randolph related another circumstance which occurred during his visit to Stirling, on Sunday, the 14th of September, in the chapel royal : " Her grace's devout chaplains would, by the good advice of Arthur Erskine, have sung a high mass: the Earl of Argyle [Justice General] and the Lord James [prime minister and afterwards Earl of Murray] so disturbed the quiet that some, both priests and clerks, left their places with broken heads and bloody ears.   It was a sport alone for some that were there to behold it ; others there were," and probably among them the queen, " that shed a tear or two, and then made no more of the matter."

1561.

The "Tragical History of the Stuarts," attached to "The Secret History of Whitehall, from the Restoration of King Charles II. to the year 1696," by D. Jones, gent., printed in 1696 and 1697, in two duodecimo volumes, contains a long, apparently faithful, and extremely interesting report of the interview which took place between the English queen and Secretary Maitland, commonly called the Lord of Lethington, whom Mary had sent as her envoy to the court of London.

" Soon after her arrival" [from France], says the author, " she despatched William Maitland ambassador to Queen Elizabeth, to confirm the peace lately made; but the chief of his errand appeared to be to press Elizabeth to declare her to be the next heir to the crown of England; which motion, because Queen Elizabeth did not a little stomach, and I do verily believe had some influence upon Queen Mary's future calamity, we shall a little more particularly insist upon, together with the queen's reply to the ambassador upon it.

" He began first to acquaint her how highly the queen his mistress was affected towards her, and how much she desired to maintain peace and amity with her; he also

carried to her letters from the nobility, in which was mentioned a friendly commemoration of former obligations and
courtesies. But one thing they earnestly desired of her,
that both publicly and privately she would show herself
friendly and courteous towards their queen ; and, being incited by good offices, she would not only preserve them in
her ancient friendship, but superadd daily stronger obligations, if possible, hereunto. As for their part, it should be
their earnest desire and study, to pretermit no occasion of
perpetuating the peace betwixt the two neighbour nations,
and that there was but one sure way to induce an amnesty
of all past differences, and to stifle the spring of them for
ever, by the Queen of England's declaring, by an act of parliament confirmed by the royal assent, that their queen was
heiress to the kingdom of England, next after herself and her
children, if ever she had any. And when the ambassador
had urged the equity and reasonableness of such a law, and
how beneficial it would be to all Britain, by many arguments,
he added, in the close, that she, being her nearest kinswoman, ought to be more intent and diligent than others in
having such an act made, and that the queen his mistress
did expect that testimony of good-will and respect from
her.

"To which the Queen of England made answer to this
purpose : 'I wonder she had forgot how that, before her departure out of France, that, after much urging, she promised
that the league made at Leith should be confirmed, she having faithfully engaged it should be so, as soon as e'er she returned to her own country. I have,' continued she, 'been
put off with words long enough, now it is time, if she had
any regard to her honour, that her actions should answer her
words.' To which the ambassador replied, that he was sent
on that embassy but a very few days after the queen's arrival, before she had entered upon the administration of any
public affairs; that she had been hitherto taken up in treat-

ing of the nobility, many of whom she had never seen before, who came from divers parts to perform their dutiful
salutations to her; but that she was chiefly employed
about settling the state of religion, ' which, how troublesome
and difficult a thing it is,' said he, ' yourself well know.'
Hence he proceeded to show that his mistress had had no
vacant time at all before his departure, neither had she yet
called fit men for her council to consult about various
affairs; especially since the nobility, who lived in the re-
motest parts of the north, had not been yet able to attend
her before his coming away, with whose advice matters of
such public moment could and ought to be transacted.

" Which words somewhat incensed Queen Elizabeth, and
she said, ' What need hath the queen to make any consulta-
tion about that which she hath obliged herself to under hand
and seal?' He replied, ' I can give no other answer at present, for I received no command about it, neither did our
queen expect that an account thereof would now be required
of me, and you may easily consider with yourself what just
causes of delay she at present lies under;' and, after some
other words, the queen returned to the main point, and
said, ' I observe what you most insist upon in behalf of the
queen; and, in seconding the requests of the nobles, you
put me in mind that your queen is descended from the
blood of the kings of England, and that I am bound to love
her by a natural obligation as being my near kinswoman,
which I neither can nor will deny. I have also made it evident to the whole world that in all my actions I never
attempted any thing against the good and tranquillity of
herself and her kingdom. Those who are acquainted with
my inward thoughts and inclinations are conscious that,
though I had just cause of offence given, by her using my
arms and claiming a title to my kingdom, yet I could hardly
be persuaded that these seeds of hatred came from others
and not from herself. However the case stands, I hope she

does not pretend to take away my crown whilst I am alive, nor hinder my children, if I have any, to succeed me in the kingdom. But if any calamity should happen to me before, as she shall never find that I have done any thing to prejudice the right she pretends to have to the kingdom of England, so I never thought myself obliged to make a disquisition into what that right is, and I am of the same mind still, and so shall leave it to those who are skilful in the law to determine. As for your queen, she may expect this confidently of me, that if her cause be just I shall not prejudice it in the least. I call God to witness that, next to myself, I know none that I would prefer before her, or, if the matter come to a dispute, that can exclude her. Thou knowest,' said she, ' who are the competitors; by what assistance, or in hopes of what force can such poor creatures attempt such a mighty thing ?'

"After some further discourse, the conclusion was short. ' That it was a business of great weight and moment, and that this was the first time she had entertained serious thoughts about it, and therefore she had need of longer time to dispatch it.' Some days after she sent for the ambassador again, and told him that she extremely wondered why the nobility should demand such a thing of her upon the first arrival of the queen, especially knowing that the causes of former offences were not yet taken away. But continued she, ' What, pray, do they require ? that I, having been so much wronged, should, before any satisfaction received, gratify her in so large a manner ; this demand is not far from a threat. If they proceed on in this way, let them know that I have force at home, and friends abroad, as well as they, who will defend my just right.' To which he answered, that he had shown clearly, at first ' how that the nobility had insisted on this hopeful medium of concord, partly out of duty to their own queen, in a prospect to maintain her weal and increase her dignity, and partly out of a desire to contribute and settle public peace and amity, and that they dealt more plainly with her than with any other prince. In this cause proceeds,' said he, ' your known and experimented goodwill towards them, and also upon the account of their own safety; for they knew they must venture life and fortune, if any body did oppose the right of the queen, or if any war did arise betwixt the nations on that account; and therefore their desires did not seem unwarrantable or unjust, as tending to the eradicating the seeds of all discords and the settling of a firm and solid peace.'

" She rejoined, ' If I had acted any thing that might diminish your queen's right, then your demand might have been just, that what was amiss might be amended; but this postulation is without an example, that I should wrap myself up in my winding sheet while I am alive, neither was the like asked before by any prince; however, I take not the good intention of your nobility amiss, and the rather because it is an evidence to me that they have a desire to promote the interest and honour of their queen; and I do put as great a value upon their prudence in providing for their own security, and of being tender of shedding Christian blood, which could not be avoided if any faction should arise to challenge the kingdom; but what such party can there be, or where should they have force? But, to let these considerations pass, suppose I were inclinable to assent to their demands, do you think I would do it rather at the request of the nobles than of the queen herself? But there are many other things that avert me from such a transaction. First, I am not ignorant how dangerous a thing it is to venture upon the dispute; the disceptation concerning the right of the kingdom I always mightily avoided, for the controversy has been already so much canvassed in the mouths of many concerning a just and lawful marriage, and what children were bastards and what legitimate, according as every one is addicted to this or that party, that, by reason of these disputes, I have been hitherto more backward in marrying. Once, when I took the crown publicly upon me, I married myself to the kingdom, and I wear the ring I then put on my finger as a badge thereof; however my resolution stands, I will be Queen of England as long as I live, and when I am dead let that person succeed in my place which hath most right to it; and if that chance to be your queen, I will put no obstacle to it. But, if another hath a better title, it were an unjust request to me to make a public edict to his prejudice ; if there be any law against your queen, 'tis unknown to me, and I have no great delight to sift into it; but if there should be any such law, I was sworn at my coronation that I would not change my subjects' laws.'

" ' As for the second allegation, that the declaration of my successor will knit a stricter bond of amity betwixt us, I am afraid rather it will be a seminary of hatred and discontent. What ! do you think I am willing to have some of my grave-clothes always before my eyes ? Kings have this peculiarity, that they have some kind of sentiments against their own children, who are born lawful heirs to succeed them. Thus Charles VII. of France somewhat disgusted Louis XI., and Louis XII. Charles VIII., and, of late, Francis ill re-sented Henry, and how likely it is I should stand affected towards my kinswoman, if she be once declared my heir, just as Charles VII. was towards Louis XI.; besides, and that which weighs most with me, I know the inconstancy of this people; I know how they loathe the present state of things ; I know how intent their eyes are upon a successor. 'Tis natural for all men, as the proverb is, to worship rather the rising than setting sun. I have learned that from my own times; to omit other examples, when my sister Mary was sat at the helm, how eager did some men desire to see me placed on the throne, how solicitous were they in advancing me thereto. I am not ignorant what danger they would have undergone to bring their design to an issue, if

my will had concurred with their designs ; now, perhaps,
the same men are otherwise minded, just like children, when
they dream of apples in their sleep, they are very joyful,
but, waking in the morning, and finding themselves frustrate
of their hopes, their mirth is turned into mourning. Thus
I am dealt with by those who, whilst I was yet a private
woman, wished me so well. If I looked upon any of them a
little more pleasant than ordinary, they thought presently
with themselves, that as soon as ever I came to the throne,
they should be rewarded rather at the rate of their own
desires than of the service they performed for me. But now,
seeing the event hath not answered expectation, some of
them do gape after a new change of things in hopes of a
better fortune, for the wealth of a prince, though never so
great, cannot satisfy the unsatiable desires of all men. But,
if the good-will of my subjects do flag towards me, or if their
minds are changed, because I am not profuse enough in my
largesses, or for some other cause, what will be the event
when the malevolent shall have a successor named, to whom
they may make their grievances known, and in their anger
and pet betake themselves ? What danger shall I then be
in, when so powerful a neighbour prince is my successor ?
the more strength I add to her in ascertaining her succession, the more I detract from my own security. This danger cannot be avoided by any precautions or by any bands
of law ; yet, those princes who have hope of a kingdom offered them will hardly contain themselves within the bounds
either of law or equity ; for my part, if any successor were
publicly declared to the world, I should think my affairs to
be far from settled and secured.'

"A few days after, the ambassador asked the queen
whether she would return any answer to the letter of the
Scottish nobility? 'I have nothing,' said she. 'at present, to
answer, only I commend their diligence and love to their
prince, but the matter is of such great weight that I cannot

so soon give a plain and express answer thereunto ; but when
the queen shall have done her duty in confirming the league
she obliged herself to ratify, then 'twill be reasonable to try my
affection towards her ; in the mean time, I cannot gratify her
in her request without diminution to my own dignity.' The
ambassador replied, he had no command about that affair, nor
ever had any discourse with his mistress concerning the same ;
neither did he then propound the queen's judgment concerning the right of succession but his own, and had brought
reasons to enforce it; but, as for the confirmation of the league
by her husband, 'twas enforced from the Queen of Scots
without the consent of those to whom the ratifying or dis-
annulling thereof did much concern ; neither was the thing
of such consequence as therefore to exclude her and her
posterity from the inheritance of England. ' I do not inquire,' said he, ' by whom, how, when, by what authority,
and for what reason that league was made, seeing I had no
command to speak about any such matter; but this I dare
affirm, that though it were confirmed by her in compliance
with her husband's desire, yet, so great a stress depending on
it, his queen in time would find out some reason or other why
it should and ought to be dissolved. I speak not this,' said he,
' in the name of the queen, but my intent is to show that our
nobility have cause for what they do, that so, all controversies being plucked up by the roots, a firm and sure peace
may be established amongst us.' As this aggravated the
spirits of Queen Elizabeth, so it was, no doubt, a great mor-
tification to Queen Mary ; but truckle she must, and so she
confirmed the league, resigning any pretensions to wear the
arms of England and Ireland during the other's life."

1562.

The following miscellaneous particulars, illustrative of the
tastes, habits, and manners of the Queen of Scots, relate
almost exclusively to that period of her life when she enjoyed

the power, as well as the state and title, of royalty. Of that
power she was deprived for ever upon her imprisonment in
the castle of Lochleven. This appears, therefore, to be a
proper place for the introduction of these gleanings.

Cotgrave tells us that Mary, after the decease of Francis II.,
was called by the people of France, " the white queen," because she wore that colour for mourning, a fashion which was
altered in 1559, at the funeral of Henry II., by the queen-
mother.

Mary always took great delight in dress, and this she
shows in several of the letters of this collection addressed to
her minister in Paris. " She had," says Chalmers, " a great
variety of dresses, as we learn from her wardrobe accounts.
They consisted of gownes, *vaskenis*,[1] skirts, sleeves, doublets,
veils, fardingales, cloikis.   She had ten pair of wolven
hois [woven hose] of gold, silver, and silk, three pair of woven
hose of worsted of Guernsey. She had thirty-six pair of
velvet shoes, passamented [laced] with gold and silver.   She
had six pair of gloves of worsted of Guernsey."

" Elizabeth," remarks the same writer, " is said to have received, as a present from France, a pair of black silk stockings,
which she had the honour to wear the first in England.   As
hose seems to be an elder word than stockings, it is not quite
certain whether Mary's *hois* may not have been silk stockings
woven with gold and silver, and of earlier importation and
use."

Mary's common wearing gowns appear to have been made
some of camlet, some of damask, and some of serge of
Florence, bordered with black velvet. Her riding cloaks and
skirts were of black serge of Florence, stiffened in the neck
and other parts with buckram, and mounted with passaments
[lace] and ribbons.

---

[1] Vasquine, we learn from Cotgrave, is a kirtle or petticoat, also a Spanish fardingale. We take it to be the *basquina* or loose robe which with
the mantilla-veil formed the national walking costume of Spanish ladies.

Her household-book, which is still preserved, furnishes a complete detail of the queen's establishment, but, says Chalmers, " some research and some skill are required to render it intelligible. Her cloth of gold, her tapestry, her Turkey carpets, her beds and coverlets, her *burd claithes,* her table cloathes of *dornick,* her vessels of glass, her chairs and stools covered with velvet, and garnished with fringes, her *doublettis, vaskenis,* and *skirtes,* though very gorgeous, may be allowed to have something of the tawdry appearance of a pawnbroker's warehouse."

For some time after her return to Scotland, the clothes and equipments for herself, her ladies, and attendants, were black, and some of the servants wore " black, and some of the servants wore " black grey." Randolph writes to Cecil respecting the intended interview between the two queens, that to avoid expence it was determined that all men should wear nothing but black cloth, as the queen had not cast off her mourning garments, and these she continued to wear till her marriage with Darnley in July, 1565.

As to the queen's amusements, we may see in the wardrobe-book that she was a chess player, but one of her great domestic amusements was shooting at the butts.

" The next day" [April 22, 1562] writes Randolph to Cecil, " after the council was risen, the queen's grace, as she doth oft, did in her privy garden shoot at the butts; where the duke and other noblemen were present, and I also admitted for one to behold the pastime." After some conference with the duke, he adds : " we ended our talk for that time, and gave ourselves again to behold the pastimes, which would have well contented your honour to have seen the queen and the master of Lindsay to shoot against the Earl of Marr and one of the ladies."

It was then the queen's ordinary practice to sit in the council-chamber sewing some work, when her ministers were assembled, to hear their discussions and conclusions.

Hawking was a favourite pastime with the great in the middle ages. Mary's father and grandfather were both passionately attached to this amusing as well as healthful sport; and a falconer and his assistants formed part of their establishments. James Lidsey, who was master falconer at the death of James V., with a salary of £66. 13s. 4d., had seven falconers under him; he continued to hold the office during Mary's minority, but his assistants were reduced to four. The queen herself was fond of hawking, and frequently partook of that diversion, with the lords and ladies of her court, in Lothian, and sometimes in Fife. In 1562, she sent a present of hawks to Queen Elizabeth, and her treasurer paid James Gray £80 for carrying them to London. After her second marriage, two additional falconers were added to her establishment on account of Darnley, who was passionately fond of the sport.

The queen had gardens at all her houses, though not perhaps of great extent, or much improved by bringing art to the aid of nature. In her gardens she delighted, (as was the practice of Elizabeth,) to receive and converse with ambassadors, and other public men on business. She was in the habit, not only of walking in gardens, but of taking long walks with her ladies and lords, and also with the foreign ambassadors, who, as we learn from Randolph's letters to Cecil, transacted much of their business in those walks. At Holyrood House there were two gardens, the southern and the northern, one of them probably the old garden of the abbey, the other formed by James IV. when he built the palace. The park to the same palace was enlarged by her father. At Linlithgow, at Stirling Castle, and at Falkland, she had gardens and parks. Lindsay, the poet, who flourished under James V., describes the hunting of the deer in the park at Falkland, with the other pastimes, of which he seems to have had his full share. At St. Andrew's, and at Perth, she had a house and garden, and she made use of those gardens, as we have seen, for the more private pastime of shooting at the butts.

It is related that the queen brought with her from France a young sycamore plant, which, nursed in the garden of Holyrood House, became the parent of all the beautiful groves of that tree so often celebrated in Scottish songs. Miss Benger says that it was in existence till about four years before her life of Mary was written (1823), when it was blown down, and its wood formed into trinkets, which were sold as precious relics.

The queen's musicians, as objects of amusement, and still more as essentials in her religious worship, engaged much of her attention. In her earliest age she had minstrels attached to her establishment. In 1561 and 2 she had five violars, or players on the viol. At the same time she had three players on the lute. Some of the valets of the chamber also played on the lute and sang. The queen herself played on the lute and the virginals, as we learn from Melvill. In 1564, when he was sent by Mary to Elizabeth, the latter asked "if his mistress played well," to which he answered, "reasonably, as a queen." Mary had also a schalmer, which was a sort of pipe or fluted instrument, but not a bagpipe; and pipers and schalmers were sometimes used synonymously in the trea·surer's books in the time of James IV. The queen had also a small establishment of singers. Melvill informs us that she had three valets of her chamber, who sung three parts, and wanted a bass to sing the fourth part; and Rizzio, being recommended to the queen as a person fit to make the fourth in concert, was drawn in sometimes to sing with the other valets.

Before the reformation, organs were the common instruments of music in churches, but in 1559 and 1560 they were generally destroyed as profane. That in the royal chapel in Stirling Castle was saved, because the mob could not reach it.

In December, 1562, Randolph informed Cecil that the queen's musicians, both Scotch and French, refused to play and sing at her mass and even-song on Christmas-day; "thus," he adds, "is her poor soul so troubled for the preservation of her silly mass, that she knoweth not where to turn herself for defence of it." In April, 1565, she had a band of music, concerning which Randolph writes : " Your honour shall know for certain that greater triumph there was never in any time of most popery than was this Easter at the resurrection and at her high mass; organs were wont to be the common music; she wanted now neither trumpets, drum, nor fife bagpipe nor tabor.

The queen's women formed a great object of her solicitude, though she had nothing like the female establishments of modern courts. The four Maries, Fleming, Beaton, Livingston, and Seaton, who had been her companions in infancy, and accompanied her to France, continued still about her, besides other " dames, damoisellis, and maidinnis."

To the service of the ladies were attached an embroiderer and a tapestry-maker; and each lady had a man and woman servant to attend her   At breakfast and collation, two dishes were allotted to each person of the higher class. Wine was served in profusion at every meal, and the daily consumption in the hall and the queen's chamber amounted to thirty gallons.

As Mary's mother was one of the largest of women, so was she " of higher stature" than Elizabeth, as we learn from Melvill. Elizabeth's hair was " more red than yellow," says the same writer, while Mary's was light auburn, with chesnut-coloured eyes. Mary had Grecian features, with a nose somewhat out of proportion long, as her father's was, the real hue of her hair was black, though she often wore light-coloured false hair. According to the general opinion, the Queen of Scots was handsomer than her rival.

When Elizabeth asked Melvill " whether she or his queen

danced best, the cautious Scot replied that his queen danced
not so high and disposedly as Elizabeth did :" he might have
added, that his queen danced the most gracefully, but he
had tact enough to keep in favour with the royal ques-
tioner.

In the summer of 1562, Mary, being entirely under the
influence of her illegitimate brother, who then bore the title
of the Earl of Marr (afterwards Murray), the Earl of Morton, and Maitland, set out on a progress to the northern
parts of the kingdom. It was during this progress that the
harsh and unjust proceedings against Gordon, Earl of
Huntley, impelled him to resort to arms, and brought ruin
upon that nobleman, though at this time the most powerful
in Scotland. These transactions occupied the whole of the
autumn.

During this progress, which more resembled a military
expedition, the queen came in September to Inverness.
The great object of Murray in bringing her to this place
seems to have been to wrest the castle from the keeping of
Lord Gordon, son of the Earl of Huntley, to whom it belonged hereditarily, as well as the sherifalty of that shire.
On the arrival of the queen and her train, possession was
demanded of Lord Gordon's deputy, who returned for answer
that he could not surrender it without the command of his
principal. Next day the country was raised for the assistance of the queen, and the keeper, whose force amounted
to only twelve or thirteen men, gave up the castle ; but he
was immediately hanged, and his head stuck up on the
building. Randolph, who accompanied the queen in this
progress, says : " In all those garboilles I never saw the
queen merrier, never dismayed, nor never thought I that
stomach to be in her that I find. She repented nothing
but, when the lords and other at Inverness came in the
morning from the watch, that she was not a man, to lie all

night in the fields, or to walk upon the causeway, with a
jack and knapsack, a Glasgow buckler, and a broadsword."

Randolph, in a letter to Cecil, dated "at Edenbourge,
the last of November, 1562," writes: "Immediately upon
the queen's arrival here [from her journey to the north],
she fell acquainted with a new disease, that is common in
this town, called here the ' new acquaintance,' which
passed also through her whole court, neither sparing lord,
lady, nor damoysell, not so much as either French or English. It is a pain in their heads that have it, and a soreness
in their stomachs, with a great cough, that remaineth with
some longer with other shorter time, as it findeth apt bodies
for the nature of the disease.

" The queen kept her bed six days. There was no appearance of danger, nor many that die of the disease except
some old folks."

From the symptoms mentioned by Randolph, this disorder, regarded as a new one three centuries ago, appears
to be the same that has been so prevalent during the last
fifty years, and has acquired the name of influenza.

1563.

When the queen returned from France, there came, in
the train of Mons. d'Ampville, one Chatelard, a gentleman
by birth, a scholar from education, a soldier by profession,
and a poet by choice. He went back to France with his
patron, after sharing in the amusements of Mary's court,
and not without being smitten with her charms. In November, 1562, he re-visited Scotland as the bearer of letters
from d'Ampville and others to the queen, by whom he was
favourably received. If we may believe Knox, Mary used
such personal freedoms with Chatelard as led him to use
similar freedoms in return.[1] At length, on the 12th of Fe-

[1] There is no evidence of this excepting in Knox's malignant words.

bruary, 1563, he ventured to conceal himself in the queen's bedchamber, when she was about to retire to it for the night, with his sword and dagger at his side. Her female attendants concealed this circumstance till the morning from their mistress, who immediately forbade Chatelard to come into her presence.

On the following day, Mary and part of her retinue left Edinburgh for Dunfermline, and next day proceeded to Burnt Island, where she was to sleep. Hither Chatelard also repaired in spite of her prohibition; and when she retired to her bedchamber, he entered it immediately after her, for the purpose, as he alleged, of clearing himself from the imputation against his conduct. Astonished at his audacity, "the queen was fain to cry for help." The Earl of Murray was sent for, and Mary ordered him " to put his dagger into the intruder." Murray, however, was content with causing him to be apprehended. The chancellor, the justice-clerk, and other councillors, were summoned from Edinburgh, the offender was brought to trial at St. Andrews, and executed on the 22nd of February, " reading over on the scaffold," as Brantome tells us, " Ronsard's hymn on death, as the only preparation for the fatal stroke."

As a safeguard against such intrusions, the queen took for her bedfellow Mary Fleming, a daughter of Lord Fleming's, one of the four Maries who had accompanied her to and from France, and continued to be one of her maids of honour till her marriage with Secretary Maitland.

1565.

A highly interesting letter of Randolph's to Queen Elizabeth describes the manner in which Mary received the proposal of a marriage with the Earl of Leicester. It is dated from Edinburgh, the 5th of February, 1564-5.

" May it please your majesty, immediately after the

receipt of your letter to this queen, I repaired to St. Andrews. So soon as time served, I did present the same,
which being read and, as appeared on her countenance, very
well liked, she said little to me for that time. The next
day she passed wholly in mirth, nor gave any appearance to
any of the contrary, ' nor would not,' as she said openly, ' but
be quiet and merry.'   Her grace lodged in a merchant's
house, her train was very few ; and there was small repair
from any part. Her will was, that for the time that I did
tarry I should dine and sup with her. Your majesty was
oftentimes dranken unto by her at dinners and suppers.
Having in this sort continued with her grace Sunday, Monday, and Tuesday, I thought it time to take occasion to
utter that which I received in command from your majesty
by Mr. Secretary's letter, which was to know her grace's
resolution touching those matters propounded at Berwick by
my Lord of Bedford and me to my Lord of Murray and
Lord of Liddington.   I had no sooner spoken these words
but she saith, ' I see now well that you are weary of this
company and treatment : I sent for you to be merry, and to
see how like a bourgeois wife I live with my little troop,
and you will interrupt our pastime with your great and
grave matters; I pray you, sir, if you be weary here, return
home to Edinburgh, and keep your gravity and great em-
bassade until the *queen* come thither ; for, I assure you,
you shall not get her here, nor I know not myself where she
is become ; you see neither cloth of estate nor such appearance that you may think there is a queen here ; nor I would
not that you should think that I am she at St. Andrews that
I was at Edinburgh.'
    " I said that I was very sorry for that, for that at Edin-
burgh she said that she did love my mistress, the queen's
majesty, better than any other, and now I marvelled how
her mind was altered.' It pleased her at this to be very
merry, and called me by more names than were given me in

my christendom.   At these merry conceits much good
sport were made.   'But well, sir,' saith she, 'that which I
then spoke in words shall be confirmed to my good sister,
your mistress, in writing; before you go out of this town
you shall have a letter unto her, and for yourself, go where
you will, I care no more for you.'   The next day I was
willed to be at my ordinary table, being placed the next
person (saving worthy Beton[1]) to the queen's self.

"Very merrily she passeth her time : after dinner she
rideth abroad.   It pleased her most part of the time to talk
with me ; she had occasion to speak much of France, for the
honor she received there, to be wife unto a great king, and
for friendship shewn unto her in particular by many, for
which occasions she is bound to love the nation, to shew
them pleasure, and to do them good.   Her acquaintance is
not so forgotten there, nor her friendship so little esteemed,
but yet it is divers ways sought to be continued.   She hath
of her people many well-affected that way, for the nourriture
that they have had there, and the commodity of service, as
those of the guard and men-at-arms; besides privileges
great for the merchants more than ever were granted to any
nation.   'What privately of long time hath been sought,
and yet is for myself to yield unto their desires in my marriage, her majesty cannot be ignorant, and you have heard.
To have such friends, and see such offers (without assurance
of as good), nobody will give me advice that loveth me.
Not to marry, you know it cannot be for me; to defer it
long many incommodities ensue.   How privy to my mind
your mistress hath been herein, how willing I am to follow
her advice, I have shewn many times, and yet I find in her
no resolution, no determination.   For nothing I cannot be
bound unto her ; and to place my will against hers, I have
of late given assurance to my brother of Murray and Lid-

---

[1] Mary Beaton, niece of the cardinal, who from her infancy had been
one of the queen's maids of honour.

dington that I am loath, and so do now shew unto yourself, which I will you to bear in mind, and to let it be known unto my sister, your mistress; and, therefore, this I say, and trust me I mean it, if your mistress will, as she hath said, use me as her natural born sister or daughter, I will take myself either as one or the other as she please, and will shew no less readiness to oblige her and honour her than my mother or eldest sister; but if she will repute me always as her neighbour Queen of Scots, how willing soever I be to live in amity and to maintain peace, yet must she not look for that, at my hands, that otherwise I would and she desireth. To forsake friendship offered, and present commodity for uncertainty, no friend will advise me, nor your mistress self approve my wisdom. Let her, therefore, measure my case as her own, and so will I be hers. For these causes, until my sister and I have further proceeded, I must apply my mind to the advice of those that seem to tender most my profit, that show their care over me, and wish me most good.'

" I requested her grace humbly, that forasmuch as I had moved her majesty by your highness's commandment to let her mind be known how well she liked of the suit of my Lord Robert Earl of Leicester, that I might be able somewhat to say or write touching that matter unto your majesty. ' My mind towards him is such as it ought to be of a very noble man, as I hear say by very many. And such one as the queen, your mistress my good sister, doth so well like to be her husband, if he were not her subject, ought not to mislike me to be mine. Marry, what I shall do lieth in your mistress's will, who shall guide me and rule me.'

" I made myself not well to understand those words, because I would have the better hold of them. She repeated the self-same words again, and I shewed myself fully contented with her speech, and desired that I might hastily return to your majesty whilst they were fresh in memory.

6

' My mind is not that you shall so hastily depart. At Edinburgh we may commune further; there shall be nothing forgotten or called back that hath been said. I have received,' said she, ' a very loving letter from my good sister, and this night or to-morrow will write another, which you must send away.' I offered all kind of service that lied in my power, reserving the duty to your majesty.

" I made a general rehearsal after of this whole conference to my Lord of Murray and Lord of Leddington; they were very glad that I had heard so much spoken of herself, whereby they might be encouraged to proceed further; but, without that principal point whereupon your majesty is to resolve, saith they, neither dare earnestly press her, nor yet of themselves are willing, for that in honour otherwise they see not how she can accord to your majesty's advice, nor so to bend herself unto you as they are sure she will, and therein offer their service to your majesty to the uttermost of their powers."

Of the queen's marriage with Darnley, and of the character of the latter, the English ambassador gives the following account in a letter to the Earl of Leicester, written on the last day of July, 1565.

" They were married with all the solemnities of the popish time, saving that he heard not the mass; his speech and talk argueth his mind, and yet would he fain seem to the world that he were of some religion. His words to all men against whom he conceiveth any displeasure, how unjust soever it be, so proud and spiteful, that rather he seemeth monarch of the world, than he that not long since we have seen and known the Lord Darnley.

" All honour that may be attributed unto any man by a wife he hath it wholly and fully, all praise that may be spoken of him he lacketh not from herself, all dignities that she can indue him with are already given and granted. No man pleaseth her that contenteth not him, and what may I say more, she hath given over unto him her whole will, to be ruled and guided as himself best liketh. She can as much prevail with him in any thing that is against his will as your lordship may with me to persuade that I should hang myself. This last dignity out of hand to have him proclaimed king, she would have had it differed until it were agreed by parliament, or had been himself twenty-one years of age, that things done in his name might have the better authority. He would in no case have it differed one day, and either then or never. Whereupon this doubt is risen amongst our men of law, whether she, being clad with a husband, and her husband not twenty-one years, anything without parliament can be of strength that is done between them. Upon Saturday at afternoon these matters were long in debating, and, before they were well resolved upon, at nine hours at night, by three heralds, at sound of the trumpet, he was proclaimed king. This day, Monday, at twelve of the clock, the lords, all that were in this town, were present at the proclaiming of him again, when no man said so much as ' amen,' saving his father, that cried out aloud, ' God save his Grace !'

" The manner of the marriage was in this sort. Upon Sunday, in the morning, between five and six, she was conveyed by divers of her nobles to the chappel. She had upon her back the great mourning gown of black, with the great wide mourning hood, not unlike unto that which she wore the doleful day of the burial of her husband. She was led unto the chappel by the Earls Lenox [1] and Athol, and there she was left until her husband came, who was also conveyed by the same lords. The ministers, two priests, did there receive them, the banns are asked the third time, and an in-' strument taken by a notary, that no man said against them or alledged any cause why the marriage might not proceed.

[1] Darnley's father.

The words were spoken, the rings, which were three, the middle a rich diamond, were put upon her finger, they kneel together and many prayers said over them. She carrieth out the . . . . . and he taketh a kiss, and leaveth her there, and went to her chamber, whither in a space she followeth, and there being required, according to the solemnities, to cast off her care, and lay aside those sorrowful garments and give herself to a pleasant life. After some pretty refusal, more I believe for manner sake than grief of heart, she suffereth them that stood by, every man that could approach, to take out a pin, and so being committed unto her ladies, changed her garments, but went not to bed, to signify unto the world that nought moved them to marry, but only the necessity of her country, not if she will to leave it destitute of an heir. To their dinner they were conveyed by the whole nobles. The trumpets sound, a largess cried, and money thrown about the house in great abundance to such as were happy to get any part. They dine both at one table upon the upper hand. There serve her these earls, Athol *shower* [sewer], Morton carver, Crawford cupbearer. These serve him in like offices, Earls Eglinton, Cassellis, and Glencairn. After dinner they dance awhile, and retire themselves till the hour of supper, and as they dine so do they sup. Some dancing there was, and so they go to bed."

1566.

Rizzio, a native of Piedmont, came over from France, in December 1561, in the suite of Monsieur Moret, the ambassador of Savoy, who was supposed to be commissioned to propose a marriage between the queen and the Duke of Nemours. Soon afterwards he was appointed a valet of the queen's chamber. Melvil informs us that the queen had three of these valets, who sung three parts, and wanted a bass for the fourth. Rizzio was recommended to the queen as a person capable of supplying this deficiency; and Birrel tells us that he was skilful in poetry as well as music. He continued in the queen's service as one of her valets and singers till December, 1564, when she appointed him 'her private secretary for the French language, instead of Roulet, whom she had brought from France, and whom she esteemed till he misbehaved. In this post Rizzio rendered himself extremely useful, and he was very active in promoting the marriage of his mistress with Darnley.

A joint letter from Randolph and the Earl of Bedford, who commanded the English forces on the borders, to the council of Queen Elizabeth, furnishes minute details of the circumstances attending the murder of Rizzio, a scene with which, as Raumer observes, there are few in the history of the world that can be compared.

" The queen's husband being entered into a vehement suspicion of David, that by him something was committed which was most against the queen's honour, and not to be borne of his part, first communicated his mind to George Douglas, who, finding his sorrows so great, sought all the means he could to put some remedy to his grief, and communicating the same unto my Lord Ruthven by the king's commandment, no other way could be found than that David should be taken out of the way. Wherein he was so earnest and daily pressed the same, that no rest could be had until it was put in execution. To this it was found good that the Lord Morton and Lord Lindsay should be made privy, to the intent that they might have their friends at hand, if need required, which caused them to assemble so many as they thought sufficient, against the time that this determination of theirs should be put in execution, which was determined the 9th of this instant, three days before the parliament should begin, at what time the said lords were assured that the Earls Argyle, Murray, Rothes, and their complices should have been forfeited, if the king could not be persuaded through this means to be their friends, who, for the desire he had that his intent should take effect the one way, was content to yield without all difficulty to the other, with this condition, that they would give their consents that he might have the crown matrimonial.

" He was so impatient to see these things he saw and were daily brought to his ears, that he daily pressed the said Lord Ruthven that there might be no longer delay ; and, to the intent it might be manifest to the world that he approved the act, was content to be at the doing of it himself. Upon the Saturday, at night, near unto eight of the clock, the king conveyeth himself, the Lord Ruthven, George Douglas' [1] and two other, through his own chamber, by the privy stairs up to the queen's chamber, joining to which there is a cabinet about twelve feet square, in the same a little low reposing bed, and a table, at the which there were sitting at the supper the queen, the Lady Argyle, [2] and David [Rizzio], with his cap upon his head. Into the cabinet there cometh in the king and Lord Ruthven, who willed David to come forth, saying ' that there was no place for him.' The queen said ' that it was her will.' Her husband answered ' that it was against her honour.' The Lord Ruthven said ' that he should learn better his duty,' and offering to have taken him by the arm, David took the queen by the *blightes* [plaits] of her gown, and put himself behind the queen, who would gladly have saved him, but the king having loosed his hands, and holding her in his arms, David was thrust out of the cabinet thorough the bed chamber, into the chamber of presence, where were the Lord Morton and Lord Lindsay, who intending that night to have reserved him, and the next

[1] This George Douglas was an illegitimate son of the Earl of Angus, and not George Douglas of Lochleven, who afterwards aided Mary's escape.

[2] Half-sister to Mary, being a natural daughter of James V., and wife of the Earl of Argyle. The queen's own account mentions her half-brother Lord Robert as likewise at table with her ; thus she was surrounded by her nearest relations.

day to hang him, so many being about them that bore him evil will, one thrust him into the body with a dagger, and after him a great many other, so that he had in his body above sixty wounds. It is told for certain that the king's own dagger was left sticking in him ; whether he struck him or not we cannot know for certain. He was not slain in the queen's presence, as was said, but going down the stairs out of the chamber of presence.

"There remained a long time with the queen her husband and the Lord Ruthven. She made, as we hear, great inter-cession that he should have no harm. She blamed greatly her husband that was the author of so foul an act. It is said that he did answer ' that David had more company of her than he, for the space of two months, and therefore, for her ho-nour and his own contentment, he gave his consent that he should be taken away.' ' It is not,' saith she, ' the woman's part to seek the husband, and therefore in that the fault was his own.' He said that when he came, she either would not or made herself sick. ' Well,' saith she, ' you have taken your last of me and your farewell.' ' That were pity,' saith the Lord Ruthven, ' he is your majesty's husband, and you must yield duty to each other.' ' Why may not I,' saith she, ' leave him, as well as your wife did her husband? Other have done the like.'

" The Lord Ruthven said that *she* was lawfully divorced from her husband, and for no such cause as the king found himself grieved. Besides, this man was mean, base, enemy to the nobility, shame to her, and destruction to her grace s country. ' Well,' saith she, ' it shall be dear blood to some of you if his be spilt.' ' God forbid !' saith the Lord Ruthven, ' for the more your grace shews yourself offended, the world will judge the worse.'

" Her husband this time speaketh little. Her grace con-tinually weepeth. The Lord Ruthven being evil at ease and weak, calleth for a drink, and saith, 'This I must do with your majesty's pardon,' and persuadeth her in the best sort he could that she would pacify herself.

" Before the king left talk with the queen, in the hearing of the Lord Ruthven, she was content that he should be with her that night.

" There were in this company two that came in with the king, the one Andrew Car of Fawsenside, who, the queen saith, would have stroken her with a dagger, and one Patrick Balentyne, brother to the Justice-clerk, who also, her grace saith, offered a dagge [a sort of pistol] against her body, with the cock down. We have been earnestly in hand with the Lord Ruthven to know the verity, but he assured us of the contrary. There were in the queen's chamber the Lord Robert,[1] Arthur Ersken, one or two other. These, at the first, offering to make some defence, the Lord Ruthven drew his dagger, and few *mo* weapons than that were not drawn nor seen in her grace's presence, as we are by the said lord assured."

Respecting the persons concerned in the murder of Rizzio, we are told, in the same letter, " the king hath utterly forsaken them, and protested before council that he was not consenting to the death of David Rizzio, and that it is sore against his will : he will neither maintain them nor defend them. Whereupon the next day public declaration was made at the market cross of Edinburgh, the 21st of this instant, against the lords, declaring the king's innocence in that matter.[2]

---

[1] This agrees with the queen's own statement.

[2] In no instance does Mary accuse her husband of Rizzio's murder. She was intimate enough with the springs of the leading factions to distinguish between the acts of her Catholic husband and his Calvinistic father, who was the leader of the conspiracy which destroyed Rizzio.

The simple truth was, Rizzio, for the want of a better, was her prime

" Of the great substance he [David] had there is much spoken. Some say in gold to the value of two thousand pounds sterling. His apparel was very good , as it is said, fourteen pair of velvet hose.   His chamber well furnished : armour, daggs, pistolets, harquebusses, twenty-two swords. Of all this nothing spoiled nor lacking, saving two or three daggs.   He had the custody of all the queen's letters, which all were delivered unlooked upon   We hear of a jewel that he had hanging about his neck of some price, that can not be heard of.   He had upon his back, when he was slain, a night-gown of damask furred, with a satin doublet, and hose of russet velvet."

On this description of Rizzio's dress, many calumnious reflections on Mary have been founded, by authors ridiculously ignorant of costume.   It is often asserted that Rizzio was supping with Mary dressed in his robe de chambre and stockings.   He was really in attendance on her as her secretary, dressed in the full evening dress of the European courts, as any portrait of that era will prove, in a robe of damask furred, worn over the doublet, and long pantaloons, called *hose* at that time—the word *night-gown*, till the beginning of the last century, being often used to designate a robe of full or evening dress, which is proved alike by Henry VIII.th's privy purse expenses and Richardson's novels.

This letter is dated March 27, 1566.   It must be received with caution.   It is well known that Randolph on his death-bed repented with the utmost horror of what he called his " *tricks as ambassador*," and called in vain on Walsingham to do the same.

---

minister and the main mover of the affairs of her government, as far as she was permitted to act as sovereign.   Hence the rage of the adverse party against him.   It is now known that Randolph, the author of this letter, was deep in the plot, therefore his version of it must not be trusted.

1567.

The letters of Sir Nicholas Throgmorton, who had been sent as Elizabeth's ambassador to Edinburgh, in place of Randolph, show how extremely unpopular was Mary's marriage with Bothwell.

On the 14th of July, 1567, he writes to Queen Elizabeth as follows:

" The Queen of Scotland remaineth in good health, in the castle of Lochleven, guarded by the Lord Lindsay and Lochleven, the owner of the house; for the Lord Ruthven is employed in another commission, because he began to show great favour to the queen, and to give her intelligence. She is waited on with five or six ladies, four or five gentlemen, and two chamberers, whereof one is a Frenchwoman. The Earl of Buchan, the Earl of Murray's brother, hath also liberty to come to her at his pleasure ; the lords aforesaid, which have her in guard, do keep her very straitly, and as far as I can perceive, their rigour proceedeth by their order from these men, because that the queen will not by any means be induced to lend her authority to prosecute the murder, nor will not consent by any persuasion to abandon the Lord Bothwell for her husband, but avoweth constantly that she will live and die with him, and saith that if it were put to her choice to relinquish her crown and kingdom or the Lord Bothwell, she would leave her kingdom and dignity to go as a simple damsel with him, and that she will never consent that he shall fare worse or have more harm than herself

" And, as far as I can perceive, the principal cause of her detention is, for that these lords do see the queen being of so fervent affection towards the Earl Bothwell as she is, and being put as they should be in continual arms, and to have occasion of many battles, he being with manifest evidence notoriously detected to be the principal murderer, and the lords meaning prosecution of justice against him according to his merits.

" The lords mean also a divorce betwixt the queen and him, as a marriage not to be suffered for many respects; which separation cannot take place, if the queen be at liberty and have power in her hands.

" Against the 20th day of this month there is a general assembly of all the churches, shires, and borough-towns of this realm, namely, of such as be contented to repair to these lords to this town, where it is thought the whole state of this matter will be handled, and, I fear me, much to the queen's disadvantage and danger; unless the Lord of Lethington, and some others which be best affected unto her, do provide some remedy; for I perceive the great number, and in manner all, but chiefly the common people, which have assisted in these doings, do greatly dishonour the queen, and mind seriously either her deprivation or her destruction. I use the best means I can, considering the fury of the world here, to prorogue this assembly, for that appeareth to me the best remedy; I may not speak of dissolution of it, for that may not be abiden, and I should thereby bring myself into great hatred and peril. The chiefest of the lords which be here present at this time dare not show so much lenity to the queen as I think they could be contented, for fear of the rage of the people. The women be most furious and impudent against the queen, and yet the men be mad enough; so as a stranger over busy may soon be made a sacrifice amongst them."

" It is a public speech," he writes again, July 18th, to the queen, " amongst all the people, and amongst all the estates (saving the councillors) that their queen hath no more liberty nor privilege to commit murder nor adultery than any other private person, neither by God's law nor by the laws of the realm."

Sir James Melvil relates the fate of Bothwell in the following terms:

"Now the Laird of Grange, his two ships being in readiness, he made sail towards Orkney, and no man was so frank to accompany him as the Laird of Tullybardenc and Adam Bothwell, bishop of Orkney. But the earl [Bothwell] was fled from Orkney to Shetland, whither also they followed him, and came in sight of Bothwell's ship, which moved the Laird of Grange to cause the skippers to hoist up all the sails, which they were loath to do, because they knew the shallow water thereabout. But Grange, fearing to miss him, compelled the mariners, so that for too great haste the ship wherein Grange was did break upon a bed of sand, without loss of a man, but Bothwell had leisure in the mean time to save himself in a little boat, leaving his ship behind him, which Grange took, and therein the Laird of Tallow, John Hepburn, of Banteun, Dalgleest,[1] and divers others of the earl's servants. Himself fled to Denmark, where he was taken and kept in strait prison, wherein he became mad and died miserably."

1568.

Of Mary's first abortive attempt to escape from Lochleven, Sir William Drury gives the following account, in a letter to Cecil. After mentioning the visit paid her there by the regent Murray, whom she upbraided for the rigour with which she was treated, he proceeds · "From that she entered into another purpose, being marriage ; praying she might have a husband, and named one to her liking, George Douglas, brother to the Lord of Lochleven. Unto the which the earl replied ' that he was over mean a marriage for her grace ;' and said further, ' that he, with the rest of the nobility, would take advice thereupon.' "

"This, in substance, was all that passed between the queen and the Earl of Murray, at that time. But after,

---

[1] These were soon afterwards put to death.

upon 25th of the last, she enterprised an escape, and was
the rather nearer effect, through her accustomed long being
abed all the morning. The manner of it was thus : There
cometh into her the landress early as other times before she
was wont, and the queen (according to such a secret practice) putteth on the weed of her landress, and so, with the
fardell of clothes and her muffler upon her face, passeth out
and entreth the boat to pass the Loughe [Lochleven], which,
after some space, one of them that rowed said merrily, 'Let
us see what manner of dame this is !' and therewith offered
to pull down her muffler, which, to defend, she put up her
hands, which they espied to be very fair and white, wherewith they entered into suspicion whom she was, beginning
to wonder at her enterprise. Whereat she was little dismayed, but charged them upon danger of their lives to row
her over to the shore, which they nothing regarded, but eft-
soons rowed her back again, promising her that it should be
secreted, and in especial from the lord of the house under
whose guard she lieth. It seemeth she knew her refuge,
and where to have found it if she had once landed, for there
did and yet do linger George Douglas, at a little village
called Kinross, hard at the Loughe side, and with the same
George Douglas one Semple and one Beaton, the which two
were sometime her trusty servants, and as yet appeareth they
mind her no less affection."

A second attempt, planned by George Douglas, was
equally unsuccessful. For his friendly offices he had been
previously expelled from the castle, but not till he had secured in her interest another Douglas, an orphan boy, who
had from infancy lived in the family, a poor dependant on
the Laird of Lochleven. Mary, however, discouraged by
former failures, wrote to the Queen Dowager of France,
that she was watched night and day, the girls of the castle

¹ In her letter, May 1st, 1568, to Catherine de Medicis, from the St.
Petersburgh Collection, vol. 1. pp. 64, 65.

sleeping in her chamber; and that, unless the French king interposed, she must be a prisoner for life. In the evening of the very next day, William Douglas had the dexterity to steal the keys from the hall where the laird and his mother were sitting at supper. At the appointed signal, the queen once more descended with her female attendant to the lake, where a little boat was waiting. Both hastily entered: the maiden assisted the youth in rowing, and, on approaching the shore, he flung the keys of the castle into the lake. Another coadjutor in this enterprise was John Beaton, who had held frequent communication with George Douglas, and with his assistance provided horses to facilitate the queen's deliverance. The keys of the castle were found on the 20th of October, 1805, and delivered to Mr. Taylor, of Kinross, by whom they were presented to the Earl of Morton, the lineal representative of the Douglas of Lochleven.

From letters of Mr. Lowther's, in the State Paper Office, we learn that when the Queen of Scots entered England, " her attire was very mean," and she had no other to change; that she had very little money, as he conceived; and he had himself defrayed the charge of her journey from Cockermouth to Carlisle, and provided horses for herself and attendants. Notwithstanding her apparel, however, Lord Scrope and Sir Francis Knollys could not but discover that she was as superior in person as in rank. The latter wrote to Cecil: " Surely she is a rare woman; for, as no flattery can abuse her, so no plain speech seems to offend her, if she thinks the speaker an honest man." On the 28th of June, Knollys again writes to Cecil : " So that now here are six waiting-women, although none of reputation but Mistress Mary Seaton, who is praised by this queen to be the finest busker, that is to say, the finest dresser of a woman's head of hair, that is to be seen in any country; whereof we have seen divers experiences since her coming hither : and among other pretty devices, yesterday and this day, she did set such a curled hair upon the queen, that was said to be a perewyke [perriwig], that showed very delicately ; and every other day she hath a new device of head-dressing without any cost, and yet setteth forth a woman gaily well."

Graham, the messenger sent by Scrope and Knollys to the Earl of Murray, for the queen's wardrobe at Lochleven Castle, returned with five small cart-loads and four horse-loads of apparel.

The letters of Sir Francis Knollys afford many interesting glimpses of Mary's character, and of the impatience manifested in this early period of her detention.

The day after his arrival at Carlisle, to take charge, jointly with Lord Scrope, of the royal fugitive, he writes to Queen Elizabeth :

" Repairing into the castle, we found the Queen of Scots in her chamber of presence ready to receive us ; where, after salutations made, and our declaration also of your highness' sorrowfulness for her lamentable misadventures and inconvenient arrival, although your highness was glad and joyful of her good escape from the peril of her prison, with many circumstances thereunto belonging, we found her in her answers to have an eloquent tongue, and a discreet head, and it seemeth by her doings she hath stout courage and liberal heart adjoining thereunto.   And after our delivery of your highness' letters, she fell into some passion with the water in her eyes, and therewith she drew us with her into her bed-chamber, where she complained unto us for that your highness did not answer her expectation for the admitting her into your presence forthwith, that, upon declaration of her innocency, your highness would either without delay give her aid yourself to the subduing of her enemies, or else being now come of good will and not of necessity into your highness' hands for a good and greatest part of her subjects, said she, do remain fast unto her still, your highness would at the least forthwith give her passage through your country into France, to seek aid at other princes' hands, not doubting but both the French king and the King of Spain would give her relief, in that behalf to her satisfaction.

"And now it behoveth your highness, in mine opinion, gravely to consider what answer is to be made herein, specially because that many gentlemen of diverse shires here near adjoining within your realm have heard her daily defence and excuses of her innocency, with her great accusations of her enemies very eloquently told, before our coming hither ; and therefore I, the vice-chamberlain, do refer to your highness' better consideration, whether it were not honourable for you in the sight of your subjects and of all foreign princes, to put her grace to the choice whether she will depart back into her country without your highness' impeachment, or whether she will remain at your highness' devotion within your realm here, with her necessary servants only to attend upon her, to see how honourably your highness can do for her. For by this means your highness, I think, shall stop the mouths of backbiters, that otherwise would blow out seditious rumours, as well in your own realm as elsewhere, of detaining of her ungratefully. And yet I think it is likely that, if she had her own choice, she would not go back into her own realm presently, nor until she might look for succour of men out of France to join with her there. Or, if she would go presently into her own country, the worse were, that peradventure with danger enough she might get into France, and that would hardly be done, if my Lord of Murray have a former inkling of her departure thither. And on the other side, she cannot be kept so rigorously as a prisoner with your highness' honour, in mine opinion, but with devices of towels or toys at her chamber-window or elsewhere, in the night, a body of her agility and spirit may escape soon, being so

near the border.   And surely to have her carried further
into the realm is the high way to a dangerous sedition, as I
suppose."

On the 11th of June he writes to Cecil ·

" This lady and princess is a notable woman. She seemeth
to regard no ceremonious honour beside the acknowledging of
her estate regal.   She sheweth a disposition to speak much,
to be bold, to be pleasant, and to be very familiar. ·She
sheweth a great desire to be avenged of her enemies · she
sheweth a readiness to expose herself to all perils, in hope of
victory ; she delighteth much to hear of hardiness and va-
liancie, commending by name all approved hardy men of her
country, although they be her enemies ; and she commendeth
no cowardice even in her friends   The thing that most
she thirsts after is victory, and it seemeth to be indifferent to
her to have her enemies diminish, either by the sword of
her friends, or by the liberal promises and rewards of her
purse, or by division and quarrels raised amongst themselves ,
so that, for victory's sake, pain and perils seemeth pleasant
unto her, and in respect of victory, wealth and all things
seemeth contemptuous and vile.   Now what is to be done
with such a lady and princess, or whether such a princess
and lady be to be nourished in one's bosom, or whether it be
good to halt and dissemble with such a lady, I refer to
your judgment."

Two days later he thus expresses himself to the same
minister :

" To be plain with you, there is no fair semblance of
speech that seemeth to win any credit with her ; and,
although she is content to take and allow of this message to
my Lord of Murray for abstinence from hostilities, because
it makes for her purpose to stay her party from falling presently from her, yet she seeth that this cold delaying will
not satisfy her fiery stomach, and surely it is a great vanity
(in mine opinion) to think that she will be staid by courtesy,

5

or bridled by straw, from bringing in of the French into Scotland, or from employing all her force of money, men of war, and of friendship, to satisfy her bloody appetite to shed the blood of her enemies. As for imprisonment, she makes none account thereof; and, unless she be removed as a prisoner, it seemeth that she will not be removed further into the realm, to be detained from her highness' presence. She plainly affirmeth that, howsoever she be detained, the Duke of Shattilleroe [Chatelherault], being heir apparent, shall prosecute her quarrel with the power of the French, and all the aid of her dowry and mass of money by any means to be levied and made for her.

" Now, she being thus desperately set, it is to be considered whether her highness defraying her here within her realm shall not thereby able her to employ £12,000 yearly, being her dowry in France, both against Scotland, and consequently against England, whereas, if she were at liberty, all her dowry would be spent upon her own finding, and the charges that her highness shall be at in defraying of her here would be well employed in Scotland, to the defending and expulsing of the French from thence. But I speak like a blind buzzard, and therefore will leave these matters to you that have judgment."

Again, on the 15th of June :

" Yesterday her grace went out at a postern to walk on a playing green towards Scotland ; and we, with twenty-four halberdiers of Master Read's band, with divers gentlemen and other servants, waited upon her, where about twenty of her retinue played at foot-ball before her the space of two hours, very strongly, nimbly, and skilfully, without any foul play offered, the smallness of their ball occasioning their fair play.

" And before yesterday, since our coming, she went but twice out of the town, once to the like play at foot-ball in the same place, and once she rode out a-hunting the hare, she galloping so fast upon every occasion, and her whole retinue being so well horsed, that we, upon experience thereof, doubting that upon a set course some of her friends out of Scotland might invade and assault us upon the sudden, for to rescue and take her from us, we mean hereafter, if any such riding pastimes be required that way, so much to fear the endangering of her person by some sudden invasion of her enemies, that she must hold us excused in that behalf."

On the 21st of the same month, Knollys represents Mary as declaring, " ' I will seek aide forthwith at other princes' hands that will help me, namely, the French king and the King of Spain, whatsoever come of me; because I have promised my people to give them aid by August.' And she said that she had found that true, which she had heard often of before her coming hither, which was that she should have fair words enow but no deeds And surely all deeds are no deeds with her, unless her violent appetite be satis-fied.[1] And saith she, ' I have made great wars in Scotland, and I pray God I make no troubles in other realms also:' and, parting from us, she said that, ' if we did detain her as a prisoner, we should have much ado with her.' "

" Yesterday," he writes on the 7th of July, " this queen, among other words, fell into this speech, that although she were holden here as a prisoner, yet she had friends that would prosecute her cause, and, saith she, ' I can sell my right, and there be those that will buy it, and peradventure it hath been in hand already.' Whereby she made me to think of your information touching the Cardinal of Lorraine's practice between her and the Duke of Anjou. But whether she spake this *bonâ fide*, or to set a good countenance of the matter as though she could do great things, I cannot tell.

" My Lord of Murray hath sent by our messenger to this

[1] For war and victory, according to Sir Francis Knollys' judgment of her character.

queen three coffers of apparel, but because her grace saith
that never a gown is sent her hereby, but one of taffeta,
and that the rest is but cloaks and coverings for saddles, and
sleeves, and partlets, and coifs, and such like trinkets, therefore we have sent to my Lord of Murray again for her
desired apparel, remaining in Lochleven ; but she doth offer
our messengers nothing at all for their pains and charges.
Wherefore her highness is like to bear the charge thereof
also.'

On the 12th of July, after acquainting Cecil with his
arrival at Bolton Castle with his charge, he proceeds :

"Since our departure from Carlisle with her, she hath
been very quiet, very tractable, and void of displeasant
countenance, although she saith she will not remove any
further into the realm without constraint."

" This house appeareth to be very strong, very fair, and
very stately, after the old manner of building, and is the
highest walled house that I have seen, and hath but one
entrance there into. And half the number of these soldiers
may better watch and ward the same, than the whole number thereof could do Carlisle Castle, where Mr. Read and
his soldiers, and Mr. Morton and Mr. Wilford took great
pains, and my Lord Scrope also was a late watcher. The
band was divided into five parts, so that the watch and
wards came about every fifth night and every fifth day, of
the which watch and wards we had five governors ; the first
was Mr. Read, and William Knollys, for his learning, accompanied him, the second was Mr. Morton, the third was Mr.
Wilford, the fourth was Barrett, Mr. Read's lieutenant, and
the fifth was West, his ensign-bearer, a very sufficient and
careful man also. This queen's chamber at Carlisle had a
window looking out towards Scotland, the bars whereof
being filed asunder, out of the same she might have been
let down, and then she had plain grounds before her to pass
into Scotland. But near unto the same window we found

an old postern door, that was dammed up with a rampire of earth of the inner side, of twenty foot broad and thirty foot deep, between two walls; for the commodity of which postern for our sally.to that window, with ready watch and ward, we did cut into that rampire in form of stair, with a turning about down to the said postern, and so opened the same, without the which device we could not have watched and warded this queen there so safely as we did Although there was another window of her chamber for passing into an orchard within the town wall, and so to have slipped over the town wall, that was very dangerous; but these matters I can better tell you at my return, upon a rude plat [plan] that I have made thereof.

In a postscript to this letter, Knollys adds

" The charges of removing of this queen hither was somewhat the larger because we were driven to hire four little cars, and twenty carriage horses, and twenty-three saddle horses for her women and men ; the which was well accomplished upon the sudden, to her commodity and satisfaction."

In one of his preceding communications, he had intimated that " this last week's charges came unto £56." In 1581, the allowance to the Earl of Shrewsbury was only £30 per week, and out of this he had to keep forty soldiers for a guard.

During the conferences opened at York in October, 1568, and transferred in the following month to Westminster, when the Duke of Norfolk, the Earl of Sussex, and Sir Ralph Sadler sat in judgment, to hear what the Earl of Murray, Morton, Lindsay, and the rest of the party confederated against her, had to allege ; and what Lord Herries, Lord Boyd, the Bishop of Ross, and others attached to Queen

Mary, could say in her behalf; Lord Herries made the following speech before the commissioners :[1]

My Lords,—We are heartily sorry to hear that these our countrymen should intend to colour their most unjust, ingrate, and shameful doings (as to the world is apparent) against their native liege lady and mistress that hath been so beneficial to them. Her grace [Queen Mary] hath made the greatest of them, from mean men in their own callings, earls and lords ; and now, without any evil deserving of her grace's part to any of them in deed or word, to be thus recompensed with calumnious and false-invented bruits [reports], whereof they themselves, that now pretend herewith to excuse their open treasons, were the first inventors, writers with their own hands of that devilish band [compact], the conspiracy of the slaughter of that innocent young gentleman, Henry Stuart [Lord Darnley], late spouse to our sovereign, and presented to their wicked confederate, James, Earl of Bothwell, as was made manifest before ten thousand people present at the execution of certain the principal offenders in Edinburgh.[2] But seeing they [i. e. Murray, Morton, &c.] can get no other cause to this their treasonable usurpation and manifest wrongs, — yea, such usurpation and wrongs, as never hath been seen the like, that subjects should do before, for the first and best of them hath not in parliament the first vote of eighteen of that realm. [*This seems to mean, that the lord of the highest rank of Mary's accusers was only the nineteenth in precedency among the Scottish nobility.*]

No, no, my lords, this is not the cause why they have put their hands on their sovereign, the anointed of God ; we will

---

[1] Sadler Papers, vol. ii. p. 334.

[2] This alludes to some dying confession of the wretched agents of the confederate lords who murdered Darnley, which does not of course appear among their confessions wholly edited by Mary's enemies.

plainly declare the very truth and cause of their usurpation
The queen's highness [Mary], our and their native sovereign, being of herself, as is well known, a liberal princess,
gave them in her youth, for their unshamefaced begging,
without their often deserving, two parts of the patrimony
pertaining to the crown of Scotland ;[1] and when her grace
came to further years and more perfect understanding,
(seeing that her successors, kings of that realm, might not
maintain their state upon the third part—albeit her grace
might, for the time, having so great dowry of France, and
other casualties not belonging to the Scottish crown)—and
for their evil deservings, procuring her slander, as far as in
them was, slaying her secretary, David Rizzio, an Italian,
in her grace's presence, caused her [to] use the privilege of
the laws always granted to the kings of that realm before
the full age of twenty-five years—they understanding this
to be a way, when it pleased her grace, and her successors
by the laws, to take from them the livings [estates] before
given them.

When they had herein advised with their Machiavelli's
doctrine, seeing her son an infant not a year old, they could
find no better way than to cut off their sovereign liege lady
(which, if it had not been for the queen's majesty of this
realm's great diligence, without doubt had been done), for
they understood they might long possess their [gains] ere
that infant had wit or power to displace them,[2] and, in the

[1] This speech of Lord Herries, whose manly character gives great
weight to whatever he said or wrote, deserves consideration on this point;
which is not difficult to be tested, he might have added that Morton
had a peculiar and selfish interest to destroy Lord Darnley, since he was
the claimant, by the female line, of the earldom of Angus, and much of
the patrimony of the house of Douglas ; his mother, Lady Margaret
Douglas (heiress of the last Earl of Angus, being his daughter by the
queen-dowager of Scotland, sister of Henry VIII.) had long claimed
possessions held by Morton, heir male of the house of Douglas.

[2] This speech of Lord Herries shows that each of the confederate lords

mean time, get great riches, under colour of a pretended authority. It was not the punishment of that slaughter [the death of Darnley] that moved them to this proud rebellion, but the usurping of their sovereign's supreme authority, to possess themselves of her riches and true subjects, we will boldly avow, and constantly do affirm the same, as by the sequel doth and shall plainly appear.

And as the queen's majesty [Elizabeth] hath written and said, she neither could nor would be judge in this case, considering the queen's grace, our mistress, and her progenitors have been free princes. Neither yet would her highness [Elizabeth] suffer them to come into her presence[1] that had thus used their native sovereign. So we cannot doubt but your right honourable lordships [the Duke of Norfolk, Earl of Sussex, and Sir Ralph Sadler], reporting this to her majesty, [Elizabeth], we shall find her of that good mind and disposition to our sovereign—her majesty's own blood—who, upon the affirmed promise of friendship and assistance between them, of her own free option and voluntary will is come into this realm, suing her highness's [Elizabeth's] help that her grace [Mary] may enjoy her own again, given her of God.

Howbeit, our sovereign had not time to advise with her states, but in a very simple manner put herself in her majesty's [Elizabeth's] hands upon these promises, trusting only in her majesty's honour ; and at her highness's [Elizabeth's] commandment and promises of assistance, hath left

had a selfish pecuniary interest to institute a long minority, instead of obeying an adult sovereign.

1 In this she did not keep her word, for when Murray and the rest of the accusers found that the commissioners of York were inclined to doubt the guilt of Mary, they went to Elizabeth at Hampton Court, where Murray had many private interviews with her, and shewed her the celebrated gilt casket and the forged love-letters of Mary to Bothwell.

the seeking of aid of other princes, having no other but her
majesty's [Elizabeth's] high honour to appeal her cause to.

And that ye, my lords, of the noble ancient blood of this
realm, are convened to hear and understand this cause, and
that your honours shall report the same to your sovereign,
is our great comfort, to expect good answer, which we
humbly require.

When the investigation at Westminster regarding Mary's
guilt or innocence broke up, challenges passed between her
defenders and her enemies, which La Mothe Fenelon, the
French ambassador, notices thus :

" The matter of the Queen of Scots seems to take another
course to what her adversaries thought, who have begun
just now to send cartels for combat, because they are themselves charged with rebellion, treason, and even with the
murder of the late King of Scots [Darnley], of which they
accused their queen. The Bishop of Ross has been coun-
termanded to Hampton Court on this business, he will inform me of all that will be proposed to him, for the purpose
of having my advice."

These combats were, most likely, prevented by this conference of the bishop and the queen [Elizabeth]. It must
be remembered, that it was the enemies of Mary, and not
her friends, who, after a congress in which their accusations
against her were heard with excessive partiality, made an
appeal to brute force. The intrepid firmness with which
Herries maintains his assertions in the face of this cartel,
though in a country incipiently hostile, does honour to himself and to his cause. Here are the cartels.

Challenge to Lord Herries by Lord Lindsay. [1]

Lord Herries,—I am informed that ye have spoken and

[1] From Pepysian Collection of State Papers, Magdalen College, Cam-

affirmed that my Lord Regent's Grace [Murray] and his company, here present, were guilty of the abominable murder of *umquhile* [the late] king, our sovereign lord's father. If ye have so spoken ye have said untruly, and therein have lied in your throat; which I will maintain, God willing, against you, as becomes me of honour and duty, and hereupon I desire your answer.

Subscrivit with my hand, at Kingston, the 22nd day of December, 1568.

Patrick Lindsay.

Lord Herries' answer to the above challenge, carried by John Hamilton, of Broomiehill.

Lord Lindsay,—I have seen *ane* writing of yours, the 22nd of December, and thereby understand—"Ye are informed that I have said and affirmed, that the Earl of Murray, whom ye call your regent, and his company, are guilty of the queen's husband's [Darnley's] slaughter, father to our prince; and if I have said it I have lied in my throat, which ye will maintain against me as becomes you of honour and duty."

In respect they have accused the queen's majesty, mine and your native sovereign, of that foul crime, for by the duty that good subjects owe, or ever has been seen to do to their native sovereign, I have said,—"There is of that

---

bridge, fol. 148. It is here given in English orthography, no original word, however, being altered. These cartels are mentioned in the despatches of La Mothe Fenelon, vol. i. p. 102. Lindsay, who was one of Rizzio's assassins, and the most brutal of Mary's enemies, was then at Kingston, close to Hampton Court, where Elizabeth gave frequent audience to the accusers of Mary, when the commissioners at York were found to be favourable to her. Lindsay was said to be ferocious but utterly ignorant, and it may be observed he does not write, but only signs, this cartel. He was one of the Scotch commissioners against Queen Mary in the course of the inquiry then pending.

company¹ present, with the Earl of Murray, guilty of that abominable treason, in the fore-knowledge and consent thereto."

That ye were privy to it, Lord Lindsay, I know not; and if ye will say I have specially spoken of you, ye have lied in your throat, and that I will defend as my honour and duty becomes me. But let aught of the principals that is of them, subscribe the like writing ye have sent to me, and I shall point them forth and fight with some of the traitors therein; for meetest it is that traitors should pay for their own treason.

Off London, this 22nd December, 1568.

HERYS.

1569.

Of Mary's condition, a month after her removal to Tut-bury, the following letter from Nicholas White (afterwards knighted, and made Master of the Rolls in Ireland) furnishes many interesting particulars.

" Sir, when I came to Colsell, a town in Chester way, I understood that Tutbury Castell was not above half a day's journey out of my way. Finding the wind contrary, and having somewhat to say to my Lord Shrewsbury touching the county of Wexford, I took post-horses and came thither about five of the clock in the evening, where I was very friendly received by the earl.

¹ Lord Herries points here at the Earl of Morton, and his words perfectly coincide with Bothwell's death-bed confession. Morton was one of the Scotch commissioners for accusing his queen of the crime of which he was convicted, and for which he was executed many years afterwards. Lord Herries, the same day, namely, December 22, when he received this challenge, sent copies of Lindsay's cartel and his answer to the Earl of Leicester, and declared his willingness to maintain all he had said in defence of his queen, at any hour or time. All Mary's accusers had their hands stained with Rizzio's blood; her defenders were men like Herries, of unblemished honour and character.

" The Queen of Scots, understanding by his lordship, that
a servant of the queen's majesty of some credit was come to
the house, seemed desirous to speak with me, and thereupon
came forth of her privy chamber into the presence chamber
where I was, and in very courteous manner bade me welcome,
and asked of me how her good sister did, I told her grace
that the queen's majesty (God be praised) did very well,
saving that all her felicities gave place to some natural passions of grief, which she conceived for the death of her kinswoman and good servant the Lady Knollys, and how by that
occasion her highness fell for a while, from a prince wanting
nothing in this world to private mourning, in which solitary
estate, being forgetful of her own health, she took cold,
wherewith she was much troubled, and whereof she was well
delivered.

" This much past, she heard the English service with a
book of the psalms in English in her hand, which she showed
me after. When service was done, her grace fell in talk with
me of sundry matters, from six to seven of the clock, beginning first to excuse her ill English, declaring herself more
willing than apt to learn that language ; how she used trans-
lations as a mean to attain it ; and that Mr. Vice-Chamberlain was her good school-master. From this she returned
back again to talk of my Lady Knollys.[1] And after many
speeches past to and fro of that gentlewoman, I, perceiving
her to harp much upon her departure, said, that the long
absence of her husband[2] (and specially in that article), together with the fervency of her fever, did greatly further her
end, wanting nothing else that either art or man's help could
devise for her recovery, lying in a prince's court, near her
person, where every hour her careful ear understood of her

[1] She was the daughter of Lord Hunsdon, the cousin-german of queen
Elizabeth ; it is said, she was more beloved by that queen than any of her
relatives. It appears by this passage that Lady Knollys died in the South,
at a distance from her husband.

[2] Sir Francis Knollys.

estate, and where also she was very often visited by her
majesty's own comfortable presence; and said merely that,
although her grace [Mary] were not culpable of this accident,
yet she was the cause without which their being asunder had
not happened. She said she was very sorry for her death, because she hoped well to have been acquainted with her. ' I
perceive by my Lord of Shrewsbury,' said she, ' that ye go
into Ireland, which is a troublesome country, to serve my
sister there.' ' I do so, madame; and the chiefest trouble
of Ireland proceeds from the north of Scotland, through the
Earl of Argyle's supportation.' Whereunto she little answered.

" I asked her how she liked her change of air. She said
if it might have pleased her good sister to let her remain
where she was, she would not have removed for change of
air this time of the year; but she was the better contented
therewith, because she was come so much the nearer to her
good sister, whom she desired to see above all things, if it
might please her to grant the same. I told her grace ' that
although she had not the actual, yet she had always the
effectual presence of the queen's majesty [Elizabeth] by
her great bounty and kindness, who, in the opinion of us
abroad in the world, did ever perform towards her the office
of a gracious prince, a natural kinswoman, a loving sister,
and a faithful friend; and how much she had to thank God
that, after the passing of so many perils, she was safely arrived into such a realm, as where all we of the common sort
deemed she had good cause, through the goodness of the
queen's majesty, to think herself rather princelike entertained, than hardly restrained of any thing that was fit for
her grace's estate; and for my own part did wish her grace
meekly to bow her mind to God, who hath put her into this
school to learn to know him to be above kings and princes of
this world; with such other like speeches as time and occasion then served, which she very gently accepted, and con-

fessed that indeed she had great cause to thank God for
sparing of her, and great cause likewise to thank her good
sister for this kindly using of her. As for contentation in this
her present estate, she would not require it at God's hands,
but only patience, which she humbly prayed him to give
her.

"I asked her grace, since the weather did cut off all ex-
ercises abroad, how she passed the time within. She said
that all the day she wrought with her needle, and that the
diversity of the colours made the work seem less tedious,
and continued so long at it till very pain did make her to
give it over; and with that laid her hand upon her left side
and complained of an old grief newly increased there. Upon
this occasion she entered into a pretty disputable comparison
between carving, painting, and working with the needle,
affirming painting in her own opinion for the most commend-
able quality. I answered her grace, I could skill of neither
of them, but that I have read *Pictura* to be *veritas falsa*.
With this she closed up her talk, and bidding me farewell,
retired into her privy chamber.

"She said nothing directly of yourself to me. Nevertheless, I have found that, which at my first entrance into her
presence chamber I imagined, which was, that her servant
Bethun [Beaton] had given her some privy note of me ; for,
as soon as he espied me, he forsook our acquaintance at
court, and repaired straight into her privy chamber, and from
that forth we could never see him. But after supper, Mr.
Harry Knollys and I fell into close conference, and he, among
other things, told me how loth the queen was to leave Bolton
Castle, not sparing to give forth in speech that the secretary
[Cecil] was her enemy, and that she mistrusted by this removing he would cause her to be made away ; and that her
danger was so much the more because there was one, dwelling very near Tutbury, which pretended title in succession
to the crown of England, meaning the Earl of Huntingdon.

But when her passion was past, as he told me, she said that though the secretary were not her friend, yet she must say that he was an expert wise man, a maintainer of all good laws for the government of this realm, and a faithful servant to his mistress, wishing it might be her luck to get the friendship of so wise a man.

" Sir, I durst take upon my death to justify what manner of man Sir William Cecil is, but I know not whence this opinion proceeds. The living God preserve her life long, whom you serve in singleness of heart, and make all her desired successors to become her predecessors. [1]

" But if I, which in the sight of God bear the queen's majesty [Elizabeth] a natural love beside my bounden duty, might give advice, there should be very few subjects in this land have access to or conference with this lady. For, beside that she is a goodly personage, and yet in truth not comparable to our sovereign, she hath withal an alluring grace, a pretty Scottish accent, and a searching wit, clouded with mildness. Fame might move some to relieve her, and glory joined to gain might stir others to adventure much for her sake. Then joy is a lively infective sense, and carrieth many persuasions to the heart, which ruleth all the rest. Mine own affection by seeing the queen's majesty our sovereign is doubled, and thereby I guess what sight might work in others. Her hair of itself is black, and yet Mr. Knollys told me that she wears hair of sundry colours.

"In looking upon her cloth of estate[2] [canopy], I noted this sentence embroidered, *En ma fin est mon commencement*, which is a riddle I understand not. The greatest personage in house about her is the Lord of Levenston and the lady his

[1] Nicholas White's expression is somewhat obscure—he wishes that all who desire by Elizabeth's death to occupy her place may die before her.

[2] The cloth of estate represented by letters the names of the queen's father and mother, with the arms of Scotland in the middle, quartered with the arms of Lorraine.

wife, which is a fair gentlewoman, and it was told me *both Protestants*. She hath nine women more, fifty persons in household, with ten horses. The Bishop of Ross lay then three miles off in a town called Burton-upon-Trent, with another Scottish lord, [1] whose name I have forgotten. My Lord of Shrewsbury is very careful of his charge, but the queen over-watches them all, for it is one of the clock at least every night ere she go to bed.

" The next morning I was up timely, and, viewing the site of the house, which in mine opinion stands much like Windsor, I espied two halberd men without the castle wall searching underneath the queen's bed-chamber window.

"Thus have I troubled your honour with rehearsal of this long colloquy which happened between the queen of Scots and me, and yet had I rather, in my own fancy, adventure thus to en-cumber you, than leave it unreported, as near as my memory could serve me, though the greatest part of our communica-tion was in the presence of my Lord of Shrewsbury and Mr. Harry Knollys ; praying you to bear with me therein, among the number of those that load you with long frivolous letters. And so I humbly take my leave, awaiting an easterly wind. From West Chester, the 26th of February.

" Your honour's assuredly to command,

" N. WHITE."

During the northern rebellion of 1569,[2] the regent Murray, endeavoured to bargain with Queen Elizabeth to put his un-fortunate sister, the Queen of Scots, into his hands in ex-change for the Earls of Westmorland and Northumberland.

---

[1] The Bishop of Ross is said to have chosen Burton for his residence that he might be less under the surveillance of the Earl of Shrewsbury's servants and retainers.

[2] Sadler Papers, vol. ii. p. 118, edited by Arthur Clifford, Esq.

An English spy, Robert Constable (too good a name for so
treacherous a man), was in treaty with Sir Ralph Sadler to
betray the Earl of Westmorland to the mercy of Elizabeth.
This man, who was, without knowing it, a narrator and author
of no little power, describes, in one of his most interesting
letters, a scene at a common hostelry, where (when he was
creeping about his dirty errand) he stole in, among the outlaws of Tynedale, and heard, in their company, an expression
of public feeling respecting the Queen of Scots, which might
have shamed the regent Murray, and his ally, Queen Elizabeth.

"So I left Farnihurst, and went to mine host's house,
where I found many guests of divers fashions, some outlaws
of England, some of Scotland, and some neighbours thereabouts, at cards, some [playing] for ale, some for plack [1] and
hardheads. So, after I had diligently inquired that here was
none of any surname, that had me on deadly feud, nor none
that knew me, I sat down and played for *hardheads* amongst
them, where I heard, *vox populi*, that the lord regent
[Murray] would not, for his own honour, nor for the honour
of his country, deliver the Earls of Northumberland and
Westmorland, if he had them both, unless it were to have
their queen [Mary of Scots] delivered to him. And if he
would agree to make that change, the borderers would start
up in his own country, and *reive* [take] both the earls and
the queen from him; and that he had better cut his own
luggs, than come again to seek Farnihurst; if he did, he
should be fought with ere he came over Sowtray Edge.
Hector of the Harlowe's head was wished to be eaten
amongst them at supper. This was a moss-trooper, who
had betrayed the Earl of Northumberland into the power of
the regent Murray.

[1] Small coins used in Scotland ; a *plack* and a *baubee* were, in the last
century, named as the price of a certain quantity of hot grey pease sold in
the streets of Edinburgh.

1571.

In May, the Earl of Shrewsbury informed Cecil that he had, with great difficulty, reduced the queen's attendants to thirty, but that she had entreated him, with tears in her eyes, to allow nine more to remain. Lord and Lady Livingston appear to have been the principal persons about her. She seems to have had five bed-chamber women and dressers. Castel was her physician, and Roulet her secretary. Above all, she had with her William Douglas, who had so essentially contributed to her escape from Lochleven Castle. The others were chiefly menials.

This establishment, on the discovery of the Duke of Norfolk's conspiracy, fomented by the Queen of Scots, was reduced in September to ten persons. When the order for this reduction was communicated to Mary by Lord Shrewsbury, he wrote to Elizabeth that " she was exceedingly troubled, weeping and sorrowing, and said that now she looked shortly that her life should end, ' for thus doth the queen use me,' saith she, ' to that purpose ; yet I desire,' saith she, ' that some good and learned man may be with me before my death, to comfort and stay my conscience, being a Christian woman, and the world shall know,' said she, ' that I died a true prince, and in the Catholic faith that I profess.' "

On her refusal to select the servants whom she wished to retain, the earl was obliged himself to name those who were to stay. He further mentioned, that neither she nor any of her attendants should depart out of the gates, till her majesty should otherwise command.

In December, the same year, the earl acquainted Cecil, now created Lord Burghley, that " this queen make eftesoons great complaint unto me of her sickly estate, and that she looked verily to perish thereby, and used divers melancholy words, that it is meant it should so come to pass without help of medicine, and all because I was not ready to send up her physician's letters unto you Which indeed I refused, for that I perceived her principal drift was, and is, to have some liberty out of these gates, which in no wise I will consent unto, because I see no small peril therein.

" Notwithstanding, lest she should think that the queen's majesty had commanded me to deny her such reasonable means as might save her life, by order of physic, I thought it not amiss, upon her said complaint and instance, to send up the said letters here inclosed, to be considered on as shall stand with the queen's majesty's pleasure. But truly I would be very loath that any liberty or exercise should be granted unto her, or any of hers, out of these gates, for fear of many dangers needless to be remembered unto you. I do suffer her to walk upon the leads here in open air, in my large dining chamber, and also in this court-yard, so as both I myself or my wife be always in her company, for avoiding all others' talk either to herself or any of hers. And sure watch is kept within and without the walls both night and day, and shall so continue, God willing, so long as I shall have the charge."

1572.

Catherine de Medicis to President De Thou.

Blois, March 22, N.S.—1572.

Monsieur le President,—I pray, according to what the king, my son, has written to you, that you will quietly inquire out the printer who has printed a book, translated from the Latin into French, (made or) written in London, against madame my daughter, the Queen of Scots. Meantime, get hold of and burn, secretly and without any notoriety, all you can find of the said book; serving also, under your hand, warnings to the said printers, how they print any more, under such penalties as you may advise. And this, if it is possible, must not remain a mere formulary. And you will do that thing which will be to the king my son and me most agreeable.

We pray to God, M. le President, to have you in his holy
and worthy keeping. Written at Blois, the 22nd day of
March, 1572.

(Signed)   CATERINE.

(Beneath)   PINART.

[Endorsed to M. de Cely (de Thou), councillor of the
council of the king, Charles IX., my son, and first president
of the parliament of Paris.]

Theie is a letter among the Harleian Manuscripts, which
offers a specimen of the fury of party feeling against the captive queen. It is anonymous both as to the writer and receiver, yet it was of consequence sufficient to be preserved
among the documents of the era.   So early as 1572, a person
affecting religious impressions, shamed not to howl for the
slaughter of a helpless female, incarcerated at the mercy of
her enemies, and liable, at their pleasure, to be destroyed by
them, either by private assassination, or the judicial murder
which was the end of her dolorous imprisonment.   A reader
of the following letter, who knew not a word of the case,
would infallibly draw the inference that Elizabeth was the
imprisoned victim and Mary the powerful tyrant.   And yet
Æsop's fables were read and quoted by every one in that
day, and of course the fable of the lamb accused of troubling
the water for the wolf was familiar to the *Christian* (as *he*
calls himself) who wrote this envenomed missive.   Those,
however, familiar with the principles of that time-serving
age will doubt whether the writer would have so affectionately advocated Elizabeth, had she been in the lamb's place at
the foot of the stream.

LETTER.

There is here such common lamenting, such remembrance

---

[1] Perhaps the letter was written to Walsingham, ambassador to France
in 1572.

backward, such seeing forward, such ominous fear of our queen [Elizabeth], that for mine own part I can speak with no man—and yet I speak with many—but they all hold it for most certain that our princess's life is in peril, and that her only safety is, with speed to execute the dangerous traitress and pestilence to Christendom [Mary Queen of Scots]; and if that be not speedily done, loyalty is discouraged, and true faith put out of hope.

It cannot be but the Scottish queen is appointed to be the means to overthrow religion, and to advance all papistry. Our good queen's life is the only impediment; and what will not papists do to remove any impediment? When Elizabeth is dead, two kingdoms joined in Mary, what security is there for *Christians?*

Think you, besides the zeal of papistry, that these ambitious hopes of earthly kingdoms will not carry them to attempt the murder (oh sorrow!) of our princess, who so much despiseth her own life? Will it not stir them forward whom no virtue, no pity, no honesty, no dutiful, no gracious, no merciful respect, can hold back?

Mary is now free from known contracts, for herself reckoneth Bothwell but as her fornicator, else she could not have contracted with the Duke of Norfolk. It is likely then that some marriage, if not an adoption, like the example of Joan of Naples, shall, or is already perhaps, practised with some mighty one, as for example, monsieur [the Duke of Anjou], or Don John of Austria. So is there no remedy for our Queen Elizabeth, for our realm of Christendom, but the due execution of the Scottish queen.

God forbid that our Queen Elizabeth should lose the honour of her gracious government, that posterity should say that she had destroyed herself, had undone her realm, had overthrown all Christianity in Christendom, if she do not duly and speedily execute the Scottish queen. Let her majesty be prayed to remember *conscience* and *eternity* !! God forbid so grievous a thing, as for her to carry out of this world to God's judgment the guiltiness of so much noble and innocent blood as has and shall be spilt, and what worse is, of the damnation of so many seduced souls, both here and in the world of Christendom, by advancing of papistry, and the withdrawal of true religion, and all for piteous pity and miserable mercy in sparing one horrible woman, that carries God's wrath wherever she goes—the sparing of whom has been told us by God's messenger to be a failing of God's service, who hath not for nothing delivered her into His ministers' hands, and miraculously detected her treason, either to have his people preserved by her due execution, or to add more inexcusableness to them that preserve her to waste the church of God.

It is true mercy to deliver so many—to deliver the earth from a devouring, wasting, unfeeling, destroying monster of unthankfulness[1] is a far more glorious act than all the labours of her *rules,* or than any one victory of the noblest prince that ever served God. Will Elizabeth leave England, and us all subject to an adulterous traitoress, a seeker of the life of her own saviour, one irritated *tyrant*—and shall I say, all in one word—Scottish Queen! Shall we not trust that her majesty, our mother, will not stick to command to kill a toad, a snake, or a mad dog, whom she findeth poisoning or gnawing the throats of her infants, and presently threatening the same to her life?"

This invective is considered, in some degree, excusable, because it was issued about the same time as the Massacre of Bartholomew; and so it might have been, if the helpless captive had been at the head of a Catholic army: as it is, it merely proves that persecutors are the same in spirit, of whatever religion they may please to call themselves; and

---

[1] It would have been very difficult for the author to define for what his monster, Mary Queen of Scots, had to be thankful to Queen Elizabeth.

when the assassins who murdered the helpless Protestants on that black day are called to their great account, the author of this letter will probably find himself in closer vicinity to them than will be at all agreeable to his feelings.]

1575.

James, Duke of Châtelherault, head of the house of Hamilton, and, by Act of Parliament, presumptive heir, after Mary and her son, to the crown of Scotland, died in the year 1575. He was first known as the Earl of Arran, and was guardian of Mary in her infancy. When he resigned her for education in France, he was created Duke of Châtelherault. Mary, in her captivity, appointed him the chief of three governors she appointed for Scotland. On the whole, he seems to have defended her cause to the best of his intellect and ability ; "but he being a plain and well-meaning man, was vexed with all manner of politic and crafty devices." So says Udal in his Life of Mary Queen of Scots, p. 245.

1580.

After Mary, Queen of Scots, had found relief from Buxton Baths for the pain in her side, Burleigh and Sussex fancied that they would do their ailments good, to the indignation of Elizabeth, whose suspicions were excited lest they should have friendly communication with Mary.

The Earl of Shrewsbury wrote to court July 26, 1580, " This day I go with my charge to Buxton Wells ;" his next letter mentions his prisoner with more kindness and sympathy than ever occurred in his epistles. " I came hither to Buxton," he says, " with my charge, the 28th of July. She had a hard beginning of her journey, for when she should have

taken her horse, he started aside, and therewith she fell and
hurt her back, which she still complains of, notwithstanding
she applies to the bath once or twice a day.   I do strictly
observe her majesty's commandment in restraining all resort
to this place, neither does she see, or is seen, by any more
than her own people, and such as I appoint to attend.   She
has not yet come forth of the house since her coming, nor
shall not before her parting."   Notwithstanding this severity
of restraint, Burleigh, by Elizabeth's orders, wrote him a
rating, when he implored permission " to remove to his seat
at Chatsworth *to sweeten his house*, that the Scottish queen
had been seen by strangers at Buxton;" this accusation occasioned a general inquisition regarding comers and goers,
and the result gives curious information as to the customs of
the times.   " For at her first coming to Buxton, there was
a poor lame cripple laid near, unknown to all my people, who
guarded the place ; and when she heard there were gentlewomen come, she cried out for some charitable person to give
her some linen, whereupon they [either Mary or one of her
maids] put one of their linen garments out to her through a
hole in the wall.   As soon as it came to my knowledge, I
was offended with her, and took order that no poor people
came into the house during that time, neither at the second
time of her abode was there any stranger at Buxton, for I
gave such charge that none of the country people should
come in to behold her."

<hr />

1581.

Leicester wrote in the month of April a letter of remonstrance to Shrewsbury, intimating that the French
ambassador complained of the diet of his royal prisoner,
" insomuch that, on Easter-day, she had scarcely any
meat, and that so bad she could not eat it," and that
Mary, finding fault, " the Earl of Shrewsbury told her he
had been cut off in her allowance, and could yield her no

better." Leicester's letter evidently implied that this conduct must be amended.

***

1584.

In August 1584, Sir Ralph Sadler was appointed warden
of the queen, with Somer, his son-in-law, for his assistant ;
and on the 2nd of the following month she was removed, in
pursuance of Elizabeth's orders, from Sheffield to Wingfield,
though Sadler wrote to Walsingham that he would rather
have had the custody of the captive queen with sixty soldiers
at the former place, than with three hundred at the latter, on
account of its openness.

At Wingfield, the queen was guarded by forty stout
soldiers, with the aid of eight persons of Shrewsbury's household.

Sadler soon became so disgusted with his office that he
besought Burleigh and Walsingham, "in the bowels of Jesus
Christ," to relieve him from it, as " he would rather be a
prisoner for life in the Tower than continue in so disagreeable a service." The queen was continually urging him to
keep a vigilant eye over his prisoner, and desired that the
servants who attended her should be furnished with " daggers
and petronels." Sadler, in reply to Walsingham, intimated
the improbability of her attempting to escape, considering
the extraordinary precautions and " her tenderness of body,
subject to a violent rheum upon any cold, which causeth a
plentiful distillation from above down to her left foot, which
is much pained and sometimes a little swollen." He explained the strength of the place, and the extraordinary pains
taken to prevent the possibility of escape ; and mentioned
the gentlemen living around the castle who were ready to
render assistance. Besides the establishment of the castle,
he had forty-three of his own servants, every one armed with
sword and dagger, some with pistols, and some with long shot.

He concluded with recommending the queen's ministers to enter into a treaty and end the matter with the Queen of Scots by an honourable composition.

1585.

The failure of the treaty which had been for some time on foot for Mary's liberation was extremely mortifying to her; but when she learned that the place of her residence and her keeper were again to be changed, she was thrown into despair. The fact was that at Wingfield the great difficulty was to obtain a sufficient supply of provisions and other necessaries: and Sadler, while enlarging on his own age, infirmities, and disabilities to Elizabeth, gave the following account of the state of the Queen of Scots at the end of 1584. "I find her much altered from that she was when I was first acquainted with her. This restraint of liberty, with the grief of mind which she hath had by the same, hath wrought no good effect in her temperament. She is not yet able to strain her left foot to the ground, and, to her very great grief, not without tears, finding that, being wasted and shrunk of its natural measure and shorter than the other, she feareth it will hardly return to its natural state, without the benefit of hot baths."

Sir Ralph, nevertheless, received orders to remove his prisoner to Tutbury Castle, in Staffordshire, and appointed the 13th of January, 1585, for leaving Wingfield, intending to reach Tutbury on the following day; but "the ways being so foul and deep, and she so lame, though in good health of body; myself also," adds Sadler, "being more unable than she is to travel, as I have not been well this month or more," they could not go through in a day. Accordingly they halted for the night at Derby. Elizabeth expressed displeasure that Sir Ralph had lodged the queen in the town. His answer was, that "it could not possibly be avoided; as he ascertained before, by sending persons of judgment to sur-

vey the country and to see if any other road passable by
coach and carriage could be found, but they could find no
other that was passable, and besides there was no gentleman's
house to lodge her at during the night; even the road to
Derby was bad enough at that season of the year, and he
was obliged to cause bridges to be made to get over some
bad passages. As to the information of a great personage,
delivered to him by some officious officer, that this queen was
offered to salute and kiss a multitude of the townswomen of
Derby, and of the speeches she was said to have made to
them, I do assert, that Mr. Sommer will be sworn, if need be,
I going before the queen, and he next behind her, yea, before all the gentlemen, on purpose, saving one that carried
up her gown, that her entertainment was this: In the little
hall was the good wife, being an ancient widow, named Mrs.
Beaumont, with four other women, her neighbours; as soon
as Queen Mary knew who was her hostess, after she had
made her curtesy to the rest of the women standing next to
the door, the queen went to the hostess and kissed her and
none other, saying that she was come thither to trouble her,
and that she was also a widow, and therefore trusted that
they should agree well enough together, having no husbands
to trouble them; and so went into the parlour, upon the
same low floor, and no stranger with her but the good wife
and her sister."

It had been reported to Elizabeth that Sadler had allowed
Mary to go a-hawking, and the honest old knight deemed it
necessary to justify himself in a letter to Walsingham, to this
effect. When he came to Tutbury, finding the country suitable for the sport of hawking, which he had always delighted
in, he sent home for his hawks and falconers, "wherewith to
pass this miserable life which I lead here." When they
came he used them sometimes not far from the castle;
"whereupon this queen, having earnestly entreated me that
she might go abroad with me to see the hawks fly, a pastime

indeed which she had singular delight in, and I, thinking it
could not be ill taken, assented to her desire ; and so hath
she been abroad with me three or four times hawking upon
the river here [the Dove], sometimes a mile, sometimes
two miles, but not past three miles when she was farthest
from the castle. She was guarded, he added, by forty or
fifty of his own servants and others on horseback, some armed
with pistols, which he knew to be a sufficient guard against
any sudden attempt that could be made for her escape.
Herein, he concludes, he used his discretion, and he thought
he did well ; "but," he says, "since it is not well taken, I
would to God that some other had the charge who would
use it with more discretion than I can ; for I assure you I
am so weary of it, that if it were not more for that I would
do nothing that would offend her majesty than for fear of any
punishment, I would come home and yield myself to be a
prisoner in the Tower all the days of my life rather than I
would attend any longer here upon this charge. And if I
had known, when I came from home, I should have tarried
here so long, contrary to all the promises which were made
to me, I would have refused as others do, and have yielded
to any punishment, rather than I would have accepted of
this charge ; for a greater punishment cannot be ministered
unto me than to force me to remain here in this sort, as it
appears things well meant by me are not well taken."

Sommer confirmed Sir Ralph's statement, denying that he
allowed the Queen of Scots more liberty than Shrewsbury
had done. He testified that when she went a-hawking she
was always attended by a strong guard, well mounted and
armed, and she had only four men and two gentlewomen with
her ; and her majesty may be assured that, "if any danger
had been offered, or doubt suspected, this queen's body
should first have tasted of the gall,"—so that Elizabeth's
officers were invested with the power of life and death over
their royal prisoner.

10

In the spring of 1585, Sir Ralph Sadler was relieved from his disagreeable office by Sir Amias Paulet, formerly ambassador in France, and in the sequel he had his old friend, Sir Drue Drury, given him for an assistant.

Soon after the custody of Mary was committed to Paulet, her letters to France were ordered to be sent to Walsingham to be forwarded. This direction she received with indignation. She exclaimed, as Paulet wrote to Walsingham, "that she would not be separated from her union with the King of France, who was her ally; and she could see plainly that her destruction was sought, and that her life would be taken from her, and then it would be said that she had died of sickness; but when she was at the lowest her heart was at the greatest, and, being prepared for extremity, she would provoke her enemies to do the worst."

The letters of Mary Queen of Scots, in the present volume, about this era, occasionally allude to her certain knowledge, that a dominant faction in Queen Elizabeth's council were incessantly labouring to bring her to a violent death. This assertion, expressed in the bitterness of anguish, was founded on fact. Mr. Tytler, in his recently published History of Scotland, unveils more than one black plot for this purpose, particularly that which was frustrated by the sudden death of the Regent Marr, in 1573. The following letter, published among Mr. Tytler's Proofs and Illustrations, (History of Scotland, vol. vii. p. 383,) edited and discovered by John Bruce, Esq., is in complete unison with Mary's series of letters, March, 1585. It is from the Earl of Leicester to some unknown political coadjutor, and, like most of the private letters of poor Mary's enemies, looks hideous in the broad light into which it is brought by the printing-press.

" Oct. 10, 1585.

" I have written very earnestly, both to her majesty and lord-treasurer [Burleigh], and partly, also, to yourself and Mr. Vice-chamberlain, for the furtherance of justice on the Queen of Scots;[1] and believe me, if you shall defer it, either for a parliament or a great session, you will hazard her majesty [Elizabeth] more than ever, for time to be given is *that* [what] the traitors and enemies to her will desire.

" Remember—upon a less cause—how effectually all the council of England once dealt with her majesty [Elizabeth] *for justice to be done upon that person,* for being suspected and infamed to be consenting, with Northumberland and Westmorland, in the rebellion [1569]. You *know the Great Seal of England was sent then, and thought just and meet,* upon the sudden for her execution; shall now her consent and practice for the destruction of her majesty's person with more regard to her danger than a less found fault? Surely I tremble at it; for I do assure myself of a new, more desperate attempt, if you shall fall to such temporising solemnities, and her majesty [Elizabeth] cannot but mislike you all for it, for who can warrant these villains from her if *that person*[2] *live,* or shall *live any time !* God forbid ! and be you all stout and resolute in *this speedy execution,* or be condemned of all the world for ever![2]

" It is most certain, if you would have her majesty [Elizabeth] safe, it must be done, for justice doth crave it, besides *policy.* It is the cause I send this poor lame man, who will

[1] Leicester bore her deadly malice ever since she refused the offer of his hand. He wrote this letter from the Low Countries.

[2] In Mary's letter to Mauvissière the reader may note that this instigator to her murder had been trying to insinuate himself into her favour in the preceding year, no doubt with the basest intentions. It will be perceived that Mary repulsed him, perhaps, too decidedly, hence this malignant attack privily on her life.

needs be a messenger for this matter ; he hath bidden such pain and travail here, as you will not believe ; a faithful creature he is to her majesty [Queen Elizabeth] as ever lived. I pray you let her not retain him still now, even to save his life, for you know the time of the year is past for such a man to be in the field,[1] yet he will needs be so, and means to return [*i. e.* to the war in the Low Countries], and you must procure his stay, as without my knowledge, or else I lose him for ever; but if he come hither it is not like[ly] he can continue; he deserves as much as any *good heart*[2] can do. Be his good friend, I pray you; and so God bless you! Haste—written in my bed on a cushion, this 10th, early in the morning.

"P. S. I pray you let not Ceandish [Cavendish] know I wrote this for his stay, but yet procure it in anywise.

"Your assured, &c."

At this time the Queen of Scots was in a very weak state. In June, Paulet reports that she was sometimes carried in a chair into the garden, her legs being so weak that, when she did sometimes use them, she was obliged to be supported by two of her gentlemen. He was satisfied that, without great negligence on his part, she could not escape : and adds, "If I should be violently attacked, so I will be assured that she shall die before me."

On the 16th of August, Paulet gives the following account

[1] Mr. Bruce points out that there is some error of the pen here ; for the wish of Leicester is evidently that the lame man may be detained, to save his life, lest he should lose it in battle against the Spaniards ; he seems to be the same as *Ceandish* in the postscript.

[2] The errand of this lame man was not much to the credit of the *goodness* of his *heart*—that of undertaking a journey from Holland to England to urge the private assassination of a helpless female prisoner! The words good and evil were strangely used in those days.

of a long conversation with his prisoner. She said "that she had given herself wholly to her majesty in all humble-ness, in all faithfulness, in all sincerity, in all integrity (I use her own words), and had renounced all foreign help to please her highness, and thereby given her to know that she de-pended wholly of her. That her words had no credit; she was not believed; and her proffers refused, when they might have done good. That she had proffered her heart and body to her majesty; her body is taken, and great care had for the safe keeping of it, but her heart is refused. She said, if she were employed she might do good, and when she shall be required hereafter, it will be too late: then she is said to boast. When she offered herself and her services with all humbleness; then she is said to flatter; that she feeled the smart of every accident that happened to the danger of her majesty's person or estate, although she were guiltless in hand and tongue. That if she had desired great liberty, her majesty might have justly been jealous of her, but she desired only reasonable liberty for her health. That if the treaty had proceeded between her majesty and her, she knowed France had now been quiet. That, in considering the in-dispositions of her body, she had no hope of long life, and much less of a pleasant life, having lost the use of her limbs, and therefore is far from the humours of ambition, desiring only to be well accepted where she shall deserve well, and by that means during her short days to carry a contented and satisfied mind. That it was not her calling to win fame by victories, but would think herself happy if, by her medi-ation, peace might be entertained in all the countries gene-rally, and in this country especially. That if she had spoken with the King of Navarre his ambassador, at his being here this last winter, she thinketh there had been now good amity between her majesty and the house of Guise, and did not doubt to have done some good if she had been made acquainted with his last coming here. That her son

is a stranger unto her, but if he should be possessed with
ambition, he might play with both hands and do bad offices.
That he did express to her in his letters 'that she was shut
up in a desert,' so as he could not send to her or hear from
her, which was the reason that he did help himself by other
means the best he could, and was forced to do so.   Finally,
that although' she had been esteemed as nobody, and had
determined when her help was hereafter required to be indeed as nobody, and so to answer; yet, for the love she
beareth her majesty and this realm, she will not refuse to
employ her best means, if it shall please her highness to use
her service, which she will do, not so much for respect of
her own particular as for her majesty's security and benefit
of this realm.   I omit the protestations of her sincere and
upright dealing with her majesty, and her solemn oaths, that
she had not of long time given or received any intelligence
to or from any of her friends, because they are no new
things unto you.   It seemed she would not satisfy herself
with speaking, and therefore I said the lesser, advising her
to comfort herself with your majesty's favour, whereof some
good effect would come, if herself or her friends did not give
cause to the contrary.   I know this kind of matter is not
new unto you, and perchance I should have forborne in
some other time to have reported the same; but considering the scope of her majesty's letter unto this queen, I
thought it agreeable with my duties to acquaint you with
her speeches, and so do refer them to your better consideration."

During the summer of this year the queen's health did
not improve.   In September, Paulet writes: "The indisposition of the queen's body and the great infirmity of her
leg, which is so desperate that herself doth not hope of any
recovery, is no small advantage to the keeper, who shall not
need to stand in great fear of her running away, if he can
foresee that she be not taken away from him by force."

In another report he says: "The queen is very much grieved with ache in her limbs, so as she is not able to move in her bed without great help, and when she is moved endures great pain."

<hr />

1586.

On the third of June, Paulet informed Walsingham: "The Scottish queen is getting a little strength, and has been out in her coach, and is sometimes carried in a chair to one of the adjoining ponds to see the diversion of duck-hunting; but she is not able to go [walk] without support on each side."

The helpless state to which the Queen of Scots was reduced by ill-health, did not, however, save her from persecution on account of fresh plots, which it was alleged, were raised by her friends against Elizabeth. In the month of August, Babington's conspiracy against the life of Elizabeth was discovered by Walsingham. Mary had been by this time removed to Chartley, whither orders were sent to Paulet to take her for a short period to Tixall, a mansion of Sir Walter Aston's, about three miles distant. Paulet accordingly went out with her on horseback, accompanied by her attendants, upon the pretext of hunting. Being informed by the way of the orders which Paulet had received, and that her secretaries, Nau and Curle, were to be separated from her, Mary was so exasperated that she used violent language to the messenger and of his mistress, and even called upon her people to protect her. Regardless of her passion, Paulet led away the Queen of Scots; the messenger returned with her two secretaries, who were sent prisoners to London; while Wood and Alley, despatched for the purpose by Walsingham, secured the queen's papers during her absence at Tixall.

Before the end of August the queen was taken back to Chartley. "As she was coming out of Sir Walter Aston's gate," says Paulet, in a report of the 27th, "she said with a loud voice, weeping, to some folks which were there assembled, ' I have nothing for you; I am a beggar as well as you ; all is taken from me.' And when she came to the gentlemen she said, weeping, ' Good God! I am not witting or privy to any-thing against the queen.' "

" She visited Curl's wife, who was delivered of a child in her absence, 'before she went to her own chamber, willing her to be of good comfort, and that she would answer for her husband in all things that might be objected against him.   Curl's child re-maining unbaptized, and the priest being removed before the arrival of their lady, she desired that my minister might baptize the child, with such godfathers as I might procure, so as the child might bear her name, which being refused [probably be-cause the child was to have been baptized and brought up ac-cording to the Catholic faith] she came shortly after in Curl's wife's chamber, where, taking the child on her knees, she took water out of a basin, and casting it upon the face of the child, she said, ' I baptize thee in the name of the Father, and the Son, and the Holy Ghost,' calling the child by her own name, Mary.   This may not be found strange in her, who maketh no conscience to break the laws of God and man.

" On her coming hither, Mr. Darell delivered the keys as well of her chamber as of her coffers to Bastian, which he re-fused by direction of his mistress, who required Mr. Darell to open her chamber-door, which he did, and then the lady, find-ing that the papers were taken away, said in great choler, ' that two things could not be taken away from her, her English blood and her Catholic religion, which she would keep unto her death,' adding these words, ' Some of you will be sorry for it,' meaning the taking away of her papers."

Those who read the heavy maledictions which the captive Mary writes, in the bitterness of a wounded heart, against her son, ought, in justification of both mother and son, at the same time to read the letter that the prime author of mischief, the

Scotch ambassador, Patrick Gray, wrote to his confederate in treachery, Archibald Douglas. Men are bad, indeed, when their own autographs remain to convict them of all that is base and treacherous in human nature.

The Master of Gray to Archibald Douglas.

For that within a day or two, his majesty [James] is to write answer to her majesty's [Elizabeth's] last, and that you are to hear, God willing, then at length from me, these lines shall be only to let your lordship know the state of matter, here [in Scotland] since my last, which is in no worse case yet; *bruits* [reports] are more abundant, proceeding from a convention, which has been lately held, of a number of the late lords who were about the king, holden at Cairn, the Earl of Crawford's house. The Earl of Huntley was there, Crawford, Montrose, *Arran*, and Doune.[1] What they mean all the world knows; it is to cut all our throats, and seize themselves of the king's majesty, though he himself, assure you, remains constant in all points. It may be thought, how dare they presume anything, if they have not his majesty's consent thereto? and this is ever the argument his majesty himself uses; but they ground themselves *a simili;* they having his majesty's good favour, albeit they [ask] themselves, why may he not forgive them sooners *nor* such [2] whom he headed to the death, as they now about him? This kind of argument makes them over bold and deceive us; in a day or two I shall get at a certainty of these matters.

The king's majesty hath commanded me *to write to you very*

---

[1] These had lately formed his ministry and household ; their leader, the Earl of Arran, we have seen by the curious cipher-letter to Mary Queen of Scots, April 12, 1584, was as inimical to Queen Mary as Patrick Gray or the Ruthvens.

[2] Those who participated in the Raid of Ruthven, who, with the exception of their leader, Ruthven, Earl of Gowry, were merely banished, and were now back again ruling at court. It may be seen here how one succession of daring traitors after another presumed on James's want of power and personal good-nature.

*earnestly, to deal for his mother's life; and I see, if it cannot
be done by you, he means to take the matter very highly.* All ·
this I take, as God judge me, to proceed from his own good-
nature, and to have no other matter secret, and therefore do you
what we can to avoid wrong constructions. This is a hard matter,
to speak truly, to the king our sovereign, not [for us] to make
any mediation for his mother, and yet the matter is also hard
on the other side *for you and me*, although we might *do her
good to do it ;* for I know, as God liveth, it shall be a staff [to
break] *our own heads.* Yet *I write to you, as he hath commanded* me to deal very *instantly* [earnestly], for her; but if
matters might stand well between the queen's majesty [Eliza-
beth] and our sovereign, I care not although she [Mary] were
out of the way.

His majesty [James] hath written to me, " that if ye receive
not a good answer at this time touching his mother, he will
send me [to England];" but I will make no answer till he himself comes here, which will be on Thursday next. I *will* [shall]
be very loth to enterprise any such commission, but of this you
shall hear further shortly, at his majesty's being at my house.
Remember, I pray you, his horses, his bucks and his hounds.[1]
I marvel you send me no word of my letters written to my
Lord Hunsdon and my Lord Admiral. Till my next I commit
you to God.

From Dumfries, this 11th of October, 1586.

Your lordship's as his own,

MASTER OF GRAY.

" Patrick Gray was eldest son of Patrick, sixth Lord Gray
of Scotland, by Barbara, daughter to Patrick, Lord Ruthven.
Having undermined the Earl of Arran (the profligate mentioned as the corrupter of young King James, in the cipher
letter of April, 12, 1584, which see in this volume), the Mas-

[1] Large presents of this kind were at this time sent into Scotland by
Elizabeth, to divert James's attention as much as possible from his mother's
tragedy—it may be seen at whose suggestion.

ter of Gray rose at the court of King James to a degree of
favour and confidence greater than Arran ever enjoyed, and
repaid it with the most detestable treachery. When ambassador from James to Elizabeth, an office frequently confided to
him, he became a conspirator with her against his country, and
when at home he was busily employed in thwarting the measures of his king, though bearing the office of his prime minister." The general charge made against him by history is, that
he advised the execution of the Queen of Scots at the very
time he was sent by her son to prevent it. " And this," adds
Mr. Lodge, " the letters of Gray, given by him at length," "fully
prove, and it is almost certain that his intrigues on that occasion
determined Elizabeth to put her to death."

Another editor of contemporary letters (the Sadler Papers)
has come to a similar conclusion regarding this man. He says
of Patrick Gray, " This faithless ambassador was soon gained
by Elizabeth's bribes, and promised to act as a spy on the
Scottish queen, to sow division between her son and her, and
finally, to connive at her murder, against which he was sent by
his young sovereign to remonstrate." The manner in which
he prompted Elizabeth to murder was by whispering in her ear,
a Latin proverb which may be translated, " When dead she
bites not."

To add to the capabilities of Patrick Gray for doing mischief
to poor Mary, he affected to be a Roman Catholic,[1] therefore
when King James appointed him his ambassador to plead for
his mother's life—young as he was in years and judgment of
character—it was natural for him to think that he had appointed an agent, who was violently partial to his mother's cause,
instead of an enemy to her. His affected catholicism was evidently a mask to fit him better for a spy, in which office he
consulted no party but that of his own interest.

King James indicted him for high treason after the execution
of his mother. The king probably never knew the depth of his

[1] See Archbishop Spottiswoode's History of the Reformation in
Scotland.

vileness in the matter, for he was only banished ; in truth, he
was the secret agent of many of the Scotch nobles who tried
him. When banished, he found his way to Rome, where, under
the character of a Scotch Catholic exile, he pursued his trade as
a spy in a very thriving manner, and transmitted intelligence
constantly to Elizabeth, " who, to her eternal dishonour," says
Mr. Lodge, " countenanced him to the last." He sneaked
home when he succeeded to his barony, in 1609 (when James I.
was on the English throne), and died before three years—in what
religion it would be a curious point to ascertain.

Archibald Douglas, the correspondent of Patrick Gray, was
at this time ambassador-resident from Scotland to Elizabeth.
He was a cousin of the Earl of Morton, and perfectly worthy
of the relationship , he had fled into Scotland in 1582, on the
inquiry into Morton's ill deeds, and, by some means or other,
had insinuated himself into the confidence of Mary, Queen
of Scots, whom he regularly betrayed to Elizabeth. He
had (very probably by his interest with Mary,) been invited
back to Scotland by young King James, cleared of all stigma,
and sent back to Scotland with the honourable office of
ambassador. He is the man whom Mary, in the first and
second volumes of her letters in this collection, so often names
with complacency as *Archubal Duglas.* He was one of the
blackest of Mary's betrayers, excepting, perhaps, her trusted
secretary, Nau. Mary having experienced great fidelity from
the two cousins of this Archibald Douglas, young George of
Lochleven and William Douglas (the same whom she calls in
her letters *Little Volly),* trusted him with the more good-will.
It was about the autumn of 1584 that Mary first began to form
an idea of the real characters of Patrick Gray and Archibald
Douglas. (See Sadler Papers, vol. ii.)

When the young king found that his ambassador-extraordi-
nary, Gray, and his ambassador-resident, Archibald Douglas,
were making no exertions to save the life of his unfortunate
mother, he wrote the angry epistles quoted among the stream
of letters in this volume, and sent another ambassador, Keith,

to urge different measures; but, alas! Keith only fulfilled the
old proverb, which deprecates sending "fire after fuel," for
Mr. Lodge deems Keith as treacherous and corrupt as the two
former ambassadors. Thus, neither James VI., nor the great
body of the Scottish people, were in fault at this crisis, but the
utter impossibility of finding an honest man among the dominant party of the Scottish ministry. Sir Robert Melville was
sent at last by King James, but came too late to rectify the
villanies of the other ambassadors.

The conduct of Elizabeth after the signature of the warrant
for the execution of the Queen of Scots betrays a manifest
conviction of the unjustifiable rigour of such a proceeding, and
a desire to spare herself the odium of commanding it; and it
would lead us to infer that the indignation afterwards shown by
her against Burleigh and the other members of her council,
but more especially against secretary Davison, proceeded not
so much from the despatch of the warrant without her knowledge, as from a disappointed expectation that they would have
found obsequious tools willing, for her sake, to incur the guilt
of murder. Such a fact would appear incredible, were it not
proved by the strongest evidence. Though the queen hesitated
to order the public execution of her royal prisoner, she felt no
scruple to direct her secretaries, Walsingham and Davison, to
urge Paulet and Drury to take the life of Mary in private.
These two wardens, however, were too circumspect to follow a
suggestion the adoption of which must have devoted them to
everlasting infamy.

The apology addressed by Davison to Walsingham respecting the execution of the warrant for Mary's death, given by
Camden, places it beyond doubt that this instrument was sent
from Whitehall, without the knowledge of Elizabeth, by the
members of her council; and it furnishes equal proof of the
anxiety which she felt to get rid of her prisoner by assassination.

"The queen," says the secretary, "after the departme of the French and Scottish ambassadors, of her own motion, commanded me to deliver the warrant for executing the sentence against the Queen of Scots. When I had delivered it, she signed it readily with her own hand. When she had so done, she had commanded it to be sealed with the great seal of England, and in a jesting manner said, 'Go tell all this to Walsingham who is now sick, although I fear me, he will die for sorrow when he hears of it.' She added also the reasons for her deferring it so long; namely, lest she might seem to have been violently or maliciously drawn thereto, whereas, in the mean time, she was not ignorant how necessary it was. Moreover, she blamed Paulet and Drury that they had not eased her of this care, and wished that Walsingham would feel their pulses in this matter. The next day after it [the warrant] was passed under the great seal, she commanded me by Killigrew that it should not be done; and, when I informed her that it was done already, she found fault with such great haste, telling me 'that in the judgment of such wise men another course might be taken.' I answered, 'that course was always safest and best which was most just.' But, fearing lest she would lay the fault upon me, as she had laid the putting to death of the Duke of Norfolk upon the Lord Burghley, I acquainted Hatton with the whole matter, protesting that I would not plunge myself any deeper in so great a business. He presently imparted it to the Lord Burghley, and the Lord Burghley to the rest of the council, who all consented to have the execution hastened, and every one of them vowed to bear an equal share in the blame, and sent Beal away with the warrant and letters. The third day after, when, by a dream which she told of the Queen of Scots' death, I perceived that she wavered in her resolution, I asked her whether she had changed her mind? She answered, 'No, but another course might have been devised.' And withal, she asked me whether I had received any answer from Paulet; whose letter when I showed it to her, wherein he flatly refused to undertake that which stood not with honour and justice, she, waxing angry, accused him and others who had bound themselves by the association of perjury and breach of their vow, as those who had promised great matters for their prince's safety, but would perform, nothing. Yet there are,' said she, 'who will do it for my sake.' But I showed her how dishonourable and unjust a thing this would be, and withal, into how great danger she would bring Paulet and Drury by it; for, if she approved the fact, she would draw upon herself both danger and dishonour, not without the note of injustice ; and, if she disallowed it, she would utterly undo men of great desert and their whole posterity. And afterwards she gave me a light check, the same day that the Queen of Scots was executed, because she was not yet put to death."

The letter from the secretaries to Paulet and Drury, dated the first of February, was answered by them on the following day ; and on the 8th Paulet again wrote to Davison in allusion to the detestable commission. "If I should say I have burnt the papers you wot of, I cannot tell if any body would believe me ; and, therefore, I keep them to be delivered to your own hands at my coming to London." This letter is in the State Paper Office; but Paulet had entered this correspondence in his letter-book, from which it has been transmitted and published. Chalmers, in a note to his Life of Mary, informs us "in the Harley MSS. (6994, Art. 29 and 30) there are copies of these letters, partly in the handwriting of Lord Oxford himself, which were lent by him to the Duke of Chandos, who returned them in a letter dated at Cannons, August 23rd, 1725, expressing his opinion that ' they are a very valuable curiosity, and deserve well to be preserved.' But neither Lord Oxford nor the duke seems to have known that they had been already published in 1722, by Mackenzie, in his life of Mary (Lives, iii. 340-1). They were also published in 1725, in Jebb's History of the Life and Reign of Mary (App. viii). It was not sufficient," adds Chalmers, " to say that those letters were curiosities ; they will for ever remain indubitable proofs of the murderous spirit of Elizabeth." They are republished in the present collection in this volume, see pages 229—232.

Davison's fate was particularly hard. Elizabeth affected extreme anger with him on the ground that he had despatched the warrant without her order; and his case being carried into the Star Chamber, he was fined £10,000 and utterly ruined.

Raumer takes a different view of this matter. He not only insists that Elizabeth was kept in ignorance of the despatch of the warrant till after the fatal catastrophe, but doubts whether she gave directions for the suggestion made by Davison to Paulet before the execution of the Queen of Scots, and whether she had seen Paulet's answer.

The same writer has transcribed from the Harleian MSS. and printed two letters from Burghley, the old, able, and faithful servant of Elizabeth, in confirmation of his views. The first, addressed to the queen herself, when bowed down by the weight of her displeasure, is as follows :

" Most mighty and gracious queen !—I know not with what manner of words to direct my writing to your majesty ; to utter any thing like a counsellor, as I was wont to do, I find myself debarred by your majesty's displeasure, declared unto me many ways ; to utter any thing in my defence, being in your majesty's displeasure, I doubt, whilst the displeasure lasteth, how to be heard without the increase of the same ; and to rest also dumb must needs both increase and continue your heavy displeasure. And therein is my misfortune far beyond others in like case, who, coming to your person, may with boldness say that for themselves which I also might as truly allege for myself. Therefore, most gracious queen, in these perplexities, I am sometimes deeply drawn down near to the pit of despair but yet sometimes also drawn up to behold the beams of your accustomed graces ; and therefore stayed and supported with the pillar of my conscience before God, and of my loyalty towards your majesty ; and so I am, I thank my God, prepared to suffer patiently the discomfort of one, and to enjoy the comfort of the other, knowing both to be in your power.

" I hear with grief of mind and body also that your majesty doth utter more heavy, hard, bitter, and minatory speeches against me than almost against any other, and so much the more do they wound me in the strings of my true heart, as they are commonly and vulgarly reported, although by some, with compassion of me, knowing my long, painful, dangerous, unspotted service ; but by divers others, I think with applause, as maligning me for my true service against your sworn enemies. And if any reproach, yea, if any punishment for me may pleasure your majesty, and not hinder your majesty's reputation (which is hardly to be imagined), I do yield thereunto, and do offer me, your majesty, (a sacrifice to satisfy your majesty's displeasure, or to pleasure any other person,) to acquit myself freely of all places of public governments or concernments, whereof none of them can be used by me to your benefit, being in your displeasure. And yet, nevertheless, I shall continue in a private state as earnest in continual prayers for your majesty's safety and my country, as I was wont to be in public actions. And whatever worldly adversity your majesty shall lay upon me, I shall, by assistance of God's grace, constantly and resolutely affirm, prove, and protest to the world, during the few days of my life, that I never did, or thought to do, any thing with mind to offend your majesty. But, in the presence of God, who shall judge both quick and dead, I do avow that I never was in my under age more fearful to displease my masters and tutors than I have always been inwardly, both out of and in your presence, to discontent your sacred majesty. I thank God, out of due reverence, and not out of doubtfulness now, to do my duty.

" Thus, most gracious queen, being by my own mishaps deprived of your presence, I have confusedly uttered my great griefs, and have offered the sacrifice of a sorrowful wounded heart, ready to abide your majesty, and to wear out the few, short, and weak threads of my old, painful, and irksome days as your majesty shall limit them ; being glad that the night of my age is so near, by service and sickness, as I cannot long wake to the miseries that I fear others shall see to overtake us, from the which I shall and do pray the Almighty God to deliver your person, as he has hitherto done, rather by miracle than by ordinary means.

" I beseech your majesty, pardon me to remember, to let you understand my opinion of Mr. Davison. I never perceived by him that you would have misliked to have had an end of the late capital enemy, and what your majesty minded to him in your displeasure I hear to my grief; but, for a servant in that place, I think is hard to find a like qualified person, when to reign [remain ?] in your majesty's displeasure shall be more your loss than his."

Thus far the first letter of Burghley to Elizabeth. The second, addressed to a person whose name does not appear, dated the 10th of March, 1587, is as follows :

" Her majesty was altogether ignorant of the deed, and not privy thereto until a reasonable time after the same was done. Besides her royal solemnly given word that she is ignorant of this transaction, there are many proofs which testify her dislike to the measure. She paid no attention to the demands of the parliament, which departed in no small grief of mind. After the dissolution of the parliament, all her counsellors, both privately and publicly, continued their solicitations by many urgent reasons, that concerned the safety of her own person, against which, though she had no reason to maintain her refusal, yet she dismissed them always unsatisfied with the only repugnant disposition of her mind. Of these arguments before the fact, the times, places, persons, were so many as there is nothing more notorious in court or country. And thus she continued her mind constantly, to the great grief of all who loved her, and saying that she had this repugnancy in her own nature. She did know that to have assented thereto had been agreeable to God's law and man's, and most pleasing to all her faithful subjects.

" Now for the time and manner of the fact done she was also ignorant, and so all of her council that had any knowledge

thereof did afterwards confess, that though *they were abused*
by one of the council, being her secretary, *whose office was in
all affairs* to deliver unto their knowledge her majesty's liking
or misliking, yet, in very truth, no one of them was able to
show *any other* proof of knowledge of her liking but the report
colourably uttered by the said secretary. Yet such was the
universal desire of all people to have justice done, and the benefit so manifest for the safety of her person, *that no man had
any disposition to doubt of the report.* And so it appeared
manifestly afterwards of what was done. She fell into such
deep grief of mind, and that accompanied with vehement, unfeigned weeping, as her health was greatly impaired. And
then she charged all her councillors most bitterly that were
privy thereto; and though they did affirm that they thought
that she assented, as they were informed only by the secretary,
yet she furtherwise commanded the secretary to the Tower,
who confessed his abuse in the report, having no such declaration to him made of her majesty's assent; and commanded the
greater part of her principal counsellors to places of restraint,
banishing a great part of them from her, notwithstanding the
great need she had of their presence and service all the time;
a matter seen in her court, universally misliked to see her so
greatly grieved and offended for a matter that was in justice
and policy most necessary. In this manner she continued a
long time to sorrow for that which was done, and in offences
against her councillors, and the prosecution of the cause, with
intention of displeasure. She called to her five of her judges
and men learned in law, and directed them to use all means
possible to examine her secretary of the grounds of his actions,
and how many were privy of his abuse; and also the most part
of her privy councillors; and to that end gave a like commission to a number of noblemen of the realm, though not privy
councillors, and to the two archbishops, and to all the chief
judges of the realm, who did very exactly proceed against the
secretary, upon his own confession, in public place of judgment; and did likewise examine the rest of the council upon

sundry interrogations, tending to burden them as offenders; and finding no proof against them of any thing material, but of their credulity to the secretary, the judges of the commission only proceeded against the secretary for his imprisonment in the Tower, a fine of 1000 marks for his contempt against her majesty, the process of which sentence is to be publicly seen in the Court of Chancery."

"The queen," it is further stated, "is innocent, and Davison guilty, he affirming truly that her majesty was neither willing nor privy thereto; but yet he affirmed, that he at the same time saw so imminent danger to her majesty's person, by the sufferance of another to live that was justly condemned to death, and the whole realm in a murmur against the life of the said person, as he was provoked in his conscience to procure justice to be done without her majesty's consent or knowledge. And upon the said trial, and the said secretary's own confession, and upon other proofs, tending to show the said secretary fully culpable of the fact, notwithstanding the allegation of the motive of his conscience, the lords and judges very solemnly gave sentence against him."

In the last letter which Paulet wrote to Walsingham on the 25th of February, 1587, he informed him that he had brought all the Scottish people from Chartley to Fotheringay, and discharged all the soldiers, except four for the gate. All the jewels, plate, &c., belonging to the late Queen of Scots, were divided among her servants, previously to the receipt of Walsingham's letter. None of the servants or attendants, he says, except Mrs. Kennedy, have any thing to show in writing to prove that they were given to them by the late Scottish queen; for they all affirm that they were delivered to them with her own hands. They have been collected together, and an inventory taken of them, and they are now entrusted to the care of Mr. Melvin, the physician, and Mrs. Kennedy. "The care of embalming the body of the late queen was committed to the high sheriff of this county, who, no doubt, was very willing to have it well done, and used therein the advice of a physician dwelling at Stamford, with the help of two surgeons; and, upon order given, according to your direction, for the body to be covered with lead, the physician hath thought good to add somewhat to his former doings, and doth now take upon him that it may continue for some reasonable time.'

The expense of the queen's funeral, as certified by the lord treasurer, was £320 14s. 6d.

After her body had lain in Peterborough cathedral twenty-five years, her son, James I., caused it to be removed to Henry the Seventh's chapel, Westminster Abbey, in October, 1612, and had a stately monument erected for her. For this monument, for Queen Elizabeth's, and for those of his own two daughters, Mary and Sophia, James paid £3500. Of the monument of the ill fated queen Mr. Brayley gives (Londiniana, vol. iv. p. 6—8.) the following description:—

" This monument, which stands in the south aisle, is an elaborate and costly architectural pile; like that of queen Elizabeth, in the north aisle, it is principally a composition from the Corinthian order, and of similar design; but its dimensions and elevation are much greater, the armorial crests which surmount the upper entablature reaching almost to the vaulting. It is constructed of different coloured marbles. The basement is raised on a two-fold step or plinth, and has four projecting pedestals on each side near the ends: on these stand eight columns, supporting the entablatures and canopy, beneath which, upon a sarcophagus, ornamented with lions' heads, &c., is a recumbent statue of the queen, very finely executed. Her head reposes on two embroidered cushions; and her hands are raised in prayer, but several of the fingers have been broken off. She wears a close coif, with a narrow edging, and a laced ruff and a tucker, both plaited. Her features are small, but peculiarly sweet and delicate. Her mantle, which is lined with ermine and fastened over the breast with a jewelled brooch, is folded gracefully over her knees and legs. The borders of her stomacher are wrought with chain-work; and her vest has a row of small buttons down the middle, with knots on each side. Her shoes are high-heeled, and round at the toes; at her feet is the Scottish lion sitting, crowned, supporting the emblems of sovereignty.

" The columns which sustain the canopy are fancifully diversified as to materials; the shafts of four of them being of black marble, and their bases and capitals of white marble, and the shaft, bases, &c., of four others, directly the reverse. Beneath the lower entablatures are circles surrounded by small cherubs; and upon them, over the cornice, are shields of arms and small obelisks. The underpart of the semicircular canopy is divided into several ranges of small panelling thickly ornamented with roses and thistles, in complete relief. In the spandrils at the sides are angels, draped, holding chaplets: on the summit are large shields, with the royal arms and supporters of Scotland; and at the angles are four unicorns, now broken and somewhat displaced, supporting smaller shields charged with badges."

The inscriptions, which are in Latin, include four verses of ten lines each, and record the unfortunate queen's royal descent and relations, the extraordinary endowments both of her body and mind, the troubles of her life, her constancy in religion, and her resolution in death.

INDEX.

THE END.

LONDON
PRINTED BY G. J. PALMER, SAVOY STREET, STRAND

13 *Great Marlborough Street.*

INTERESTING

HISTORICAL AND BIOGRAPHICAL WORKS.

JUST PUBLISHED BY MR. COLBURN,

TO BE HAD OF ALL BOOKSELLERS.

LIVES OF THE QUEENS OF ENGLAND,

FROM THE NORMAN CONQUEST,

WITH ANECDOTES OF THEIR COURTS,

DEDICATED, BY PERMISSION, TO HER MAJESTY,

Now first published from Official Records and other Authentic Documents, private as well as public.

BY AGNES STRICKLAND.

Vols. I. to VI., embellished with Portraits, are now ready, price 10s. 6d. each, bound.

OPINIONS OF THE PRESS.

"These volumes have the fascination of a romance united to the integrity of history."—*Times.*

"A most valuable and entertaining work."—*Chronicle.*

"This interesting and well-written work, in which the severe truth of history takes almost the wildness of romance, will constitute a valuable addition to our biographical literature."—*Morning Herald.*

"A valuable contribution to historical knowledge. It contains a mass of every kind of historical, antiquarian, and gossiping matter of interest."—*Athenæum.*

"The execution of this work is equal to the conception. Great pains have been taken to make it both interesting and valuable."—*Literary Gazette.*

"This elegant work, in which we have everything connected with the biographies of our female sovereigns, is one of the highest merit, and of permanent interest, evincing great learning, research, judgment, and taste."—*Dispatch.*

"Authentic memoirs of our English Queens is a work which has been much wanted, and Miss Strickland has spared neither labour nor research to complete this attractive work in an efficient manner."—*Sun.*

"This important work will form one of the most useful, agreeable, and essential additions to our historical library that we have had for many years."—*Naval and Military Gazette*

LETTERS

OF

MARY, QUEEN OF SCOTS,

Illustrative of her Personal History, now first published from
the Originals,

EDITED, WITH AN HISTORICAL INTRODUCTION AND NOTES,

BY AGNES STRICKLAND

A NEW EDITION, WITH IMPORTANT ADDITIONS,

Uniform with MISS STRICKLAND'S "LIVES OF THE QUEENS OF
ENGLAND," in 2 vols., with Portrait, &c., 21s. bound.

OPINIONS OF THE PRESS.

" The best collection of authentic memorials relative to the Queen of Scots
that has ever appeared."—*Chronicle.*

" No public or private library can be considered complete without this
valuable work."—*Morning Post.*

" A publication of the deepest interest, not alone to the student of history,
but to the most ordinary class of readers."—*Herald.*

" Undoubtedly the most valuable, and by far the most interesting work, illus-
strative of the life and character of Mary Stuart ever given to the world."—
Edinburg Evening Post.

" A work deeply interesting, in every personal respect, and of high historical
value."—*Literary Gazette.*

" A valuable contribution to English historical literature. It enables the
reader to form a most correct estimate of the character and talents of Queen
Mary."—*Britannia.*

" A most valuable and instructive work, both in an historical and a national
point of view."—*Caledonian Mercury.*

" No historical library can be complete without these volumes."—*Court
Journal.*

" A publication of great historical interest and value."—*Sunday Times*

" These volumes are among the most curious, interesting, and highly valuable
historical documents ever put on record."—*Naval and Military Gazette*

NEW HISTORICAL AND BIOGRAPHICAL WORKS.

A COMPANION TO "THE PEERAGE AND BARONETAGE."

Now in course of publication, in Four Parts, price 10s 6d each, (Two of which
have appeared), forming a single Volume of upwards of 1600 pages,
beautifully printed in double Columns,

HISTORY OF THE LANDED GENTRY:

A GENEALOGICAL AND HERALDIC DICTIONARY

OF THE

WHOLE OF THE LANDED GENTRY, OR UNTITLED ARISTOCRACY,

OF ENGLAND, SCOTLAND, AND IRELAND

By JOHN BURKE, Esq., Author of "The Peerage and Baronetage," &c., and
JOHN BERNARD BURKE, Esq , of the Middle Temple, Barrister-at-Law.

This work relates to the Untitled Families of Rank, as the "Peerage and
Baronetage" does to the Titled, and forms, in fact, a Peerage of the Untitled
Aristocracy

"A work which contains curious information nowhere else to be
found, and to which even professional genealogists may refer with
advantage."—*Quarterly Review.*

MR. BURKE'S PEERAGE AND BARONETAGE.
SEVENTH EDITION.

CONTAINING ALL THE NEW CREATIONS AND CORRECTIONS TO THE PRESENT TIME,
FROM THE PERSONAL COMMUNICATIONS OF THE NOBILITY, AND THE
VARIOUS AND PECULIAR SOURCES OF INFORMATION POSSESSED
BY THE AUTHOR

In One Vol., comprising as much matter as twenty ordinary volumes, with
Fifteen Hundred Engravings of Arms, &c., price 38s. bound.

'Mr. Burke s Peerage and Baronetage is the most complete, the
most convenient, and the cheapest work of the kind, ever offered to
the public "—*Sun*

MR. BURKE'S EXTINCT, DORMANT, AND
SUSPENDED PEERAGES,

A COMPANION TO ALL OTHER PEERAGES

This work connects, in many instances, the new with the old nobility, and shows in
all cases the cause which has influenced the revival of an extinct dignity in a new
creation. It should be particularly noticed, that this new work appertains nearly
as much to extant as to extinct persons of distinction , for, though dignities pass
away, it rarely occurs that whole families do.

New and cheaper Edition, beautifully printed, in double columns, One Vol. 8vo
With Emblazoned Title-page. &c., price 28s. bound.

NEW HISTORICAL AND BIOGRAPHICAL WORKS.

QUEEN VICTORIA, FROM HER BIRTH T(
HER BRIDAL.

2 vols. post 8vo., with Portraits, 21s. bound.

" These attractive volumes furnish not merely an adequate and authentic record of the pure and happy life of our young Queen, but the only available one that has hitherto been given to the world. The charming letters of Miss Jane Porter, contained in the work, offer some of the most delightful reminiscences of the infancy and childhood of Queen Victoria that have ever been made public."— *Naval and Military Gazette*

PRINCE ALBERT; AND THE HOUSE OI
SAXONY.

BY FREDERIC SHOBERL, ESQ.

Second Edition, Revised, with Additions—By Authority.

In One Vol. post 8vo., with a Portrait of the Prince. 8s. 6d. bound.

" The best and most authentic work on the subject of the prince-consort and his family."—*John Bull.*

HISTORY OF GEORGE IV., HIS COURT
AND TIMES.

BY THE REV. GEORGE CROLY.

2 vols. post 8vo. 21s. bound.

" These volumes have a higher degree of interest than could possibly arise from merely tracing the career of George IV. They are a history of his age, introducing us to all the great statesmen and wits of that period ; abounding in rapid and masterly sketches of character, brilliant reflections, and pleasant episodes , and embodying all that information current in the best informed circles of the day, which is necessary to be known if we would thoroughly understand the transactions of the period."—*Britannia.*

THE DIARY AND LETTERS OF MADAME
D'ARBLAY,
AUTHORESS OF " EVELINA," " CECILIA," &c.

Including the period of her Residence at the Court of Queen Charlotte.

EDITED BY HER NIECE.

*** New and revised editions of the first Five Volumes are now ready, in posl 8vo. price 10s. 6d. each, bound.   The Sixth Volume is in the Press.

" Madame D'Arblay lived to be a classic. Time set on her fame before she went hence, that seal which is seldom set, except on the fame of the departed. All those whom we have been accustomed to revere as intellectual patriarchs, seemed children when compared with her; for Burke had sat up all night to read her writings, and Johnson had pronounced her superior to Fielding, when Rogers was still a schoolboy, and Southey still in petticoats. Her Diary is written in her earliest and best manner ; in true woman's English, clear, natural, and lively. It ought to be consulted by every person who wishes to be well acquainted with the history of our literature and our manners. The account which she gives of the king's illness, will, we think, be more valued by the historians of a future age than any equal portions of Pepys' or Evelyn's Diaries."—*Edinburgh Review, January,* 1843.

DUE DATE

BIBLIOLIFE

Old Books Deserve a New Life
www.bibliolife.com

Did you know that you can get most of our titles in our trademark **EasyScript**™ print format? **EasyScript**™ provides readers with a larger than average typeface, for a reading experience that's easier on the eyes.

Did you know that we have an ever-growing collection of books in many languages?

Order online:
www.bibliolife.com/store

Or to exclusively browse our **EasyScript**™ collection:
www.bibliogrande.com

At BiblioLife, we aim to make knowledge more accessible by making thousands of titles available to you – quickly and affordably.

Contact us:
BiblioLife
PO Box 21206
Charleston, SC 29413

Printed in Great Britain
by Amazon.co.uk, Ltd.,
Marston Gate.